Itsuwaribito 空

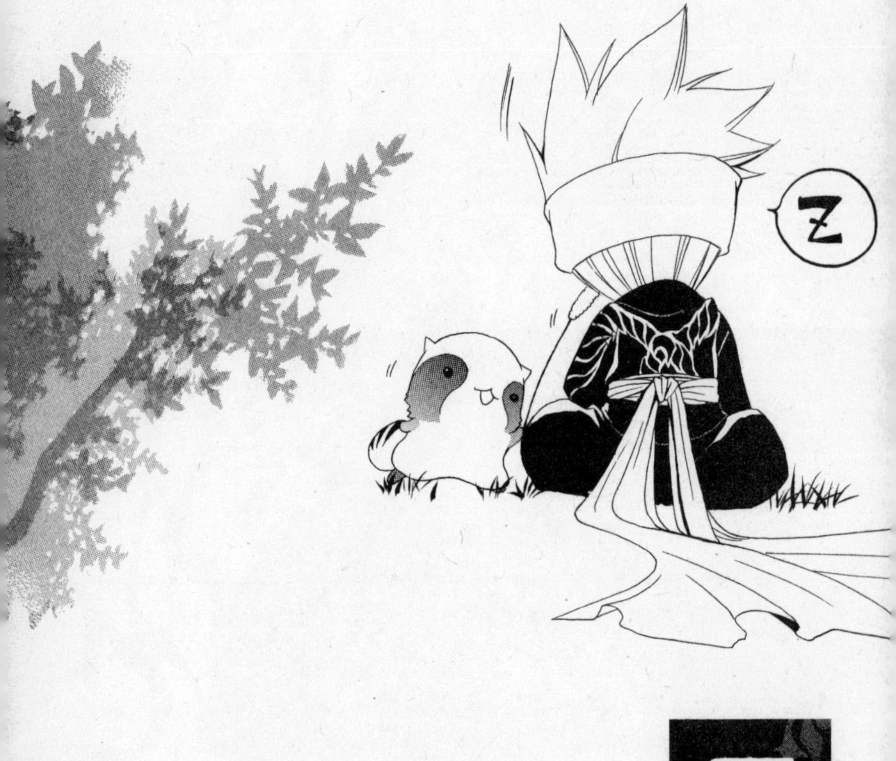
Z

5

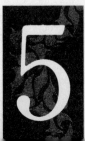

YUUKI IINUMA

Contents

Chapter 38 Forward!

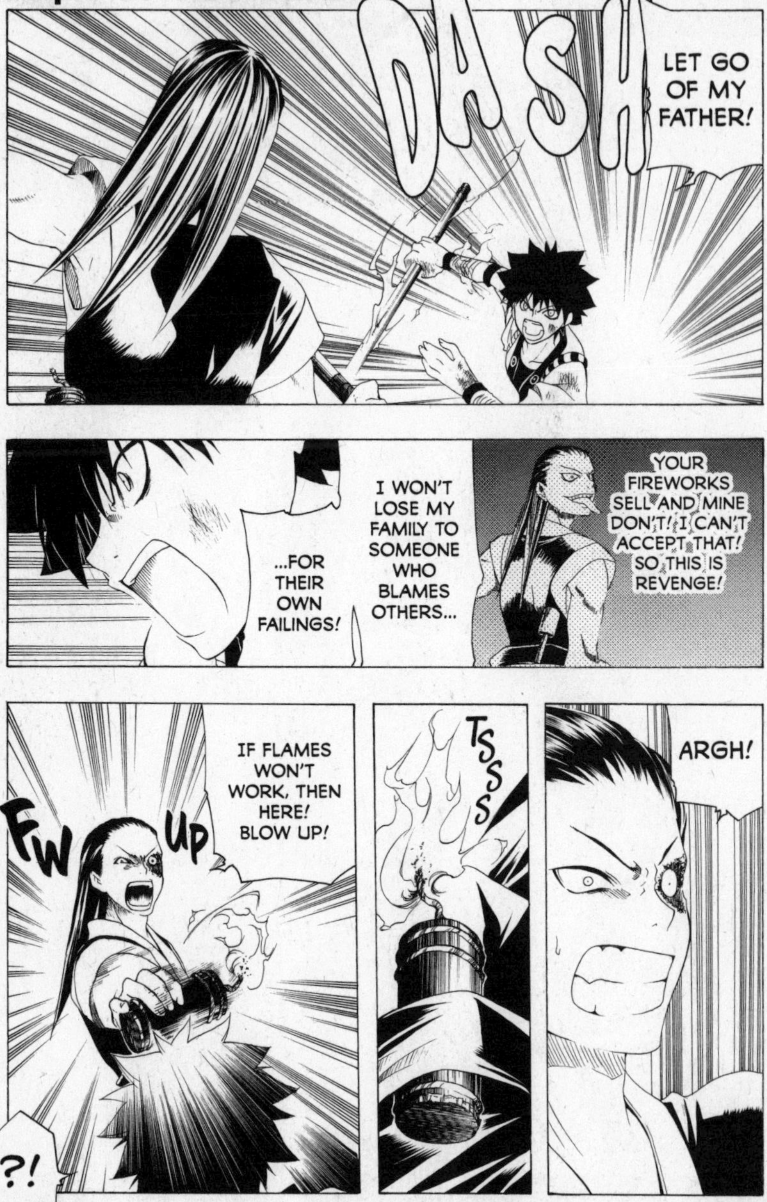

DASH
LET GO OF MY FATHER!
YOUR FIREWORKS SELL AND MINE DON'T! I CAN'T ACCEPT THAT! SO THIS IS REVENGE!
I WON'T LOSE MY FAMILY TO SOMEONE WHO BLAMES OTHERS...
...FOR THEIR OWN FAILINGS!
ARGH!
TSSSS
IF FLAMES WON'T WORK, THEN HERE! BLOW UP!
FWUP
?!

Chapter 38
Forward!

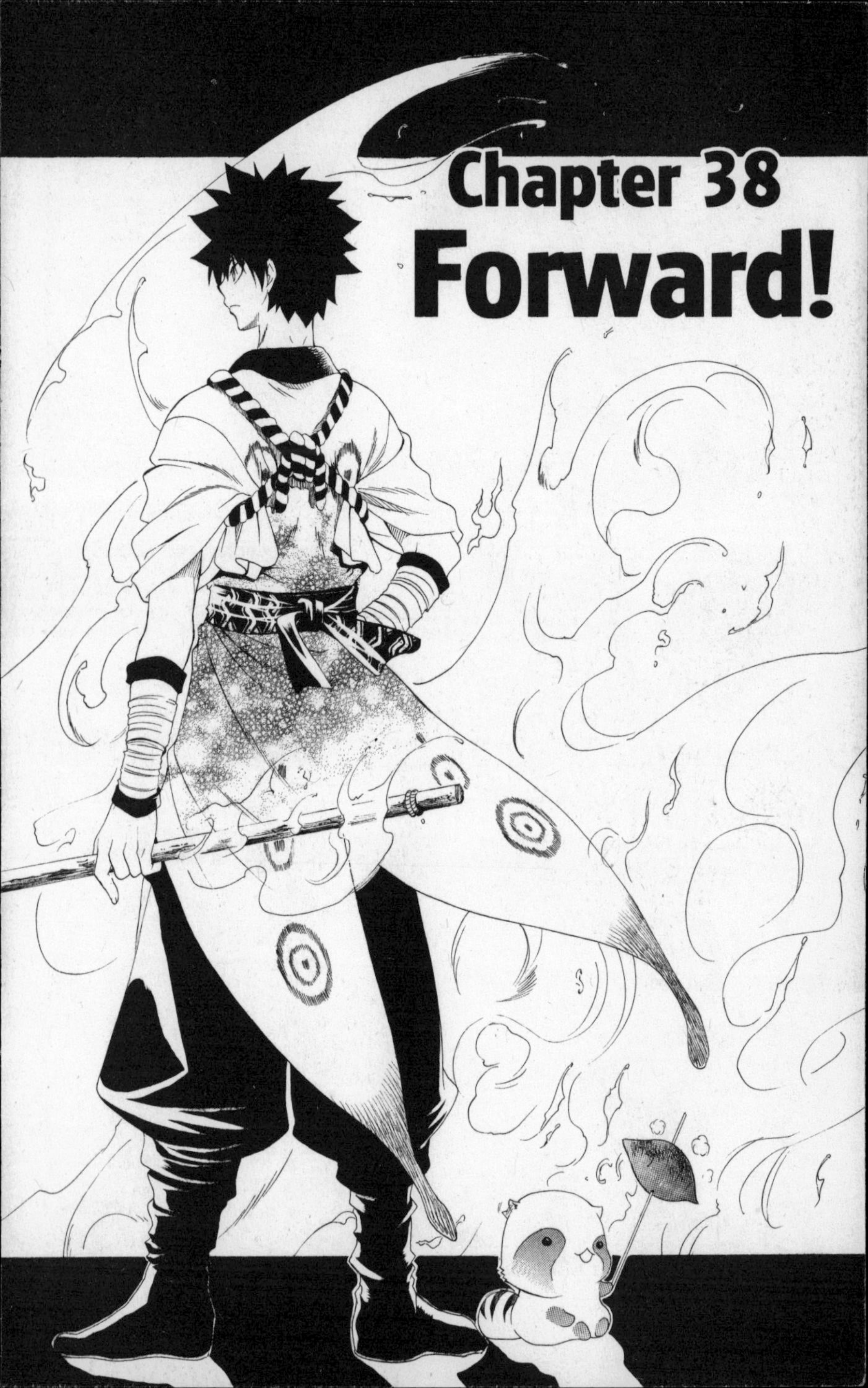

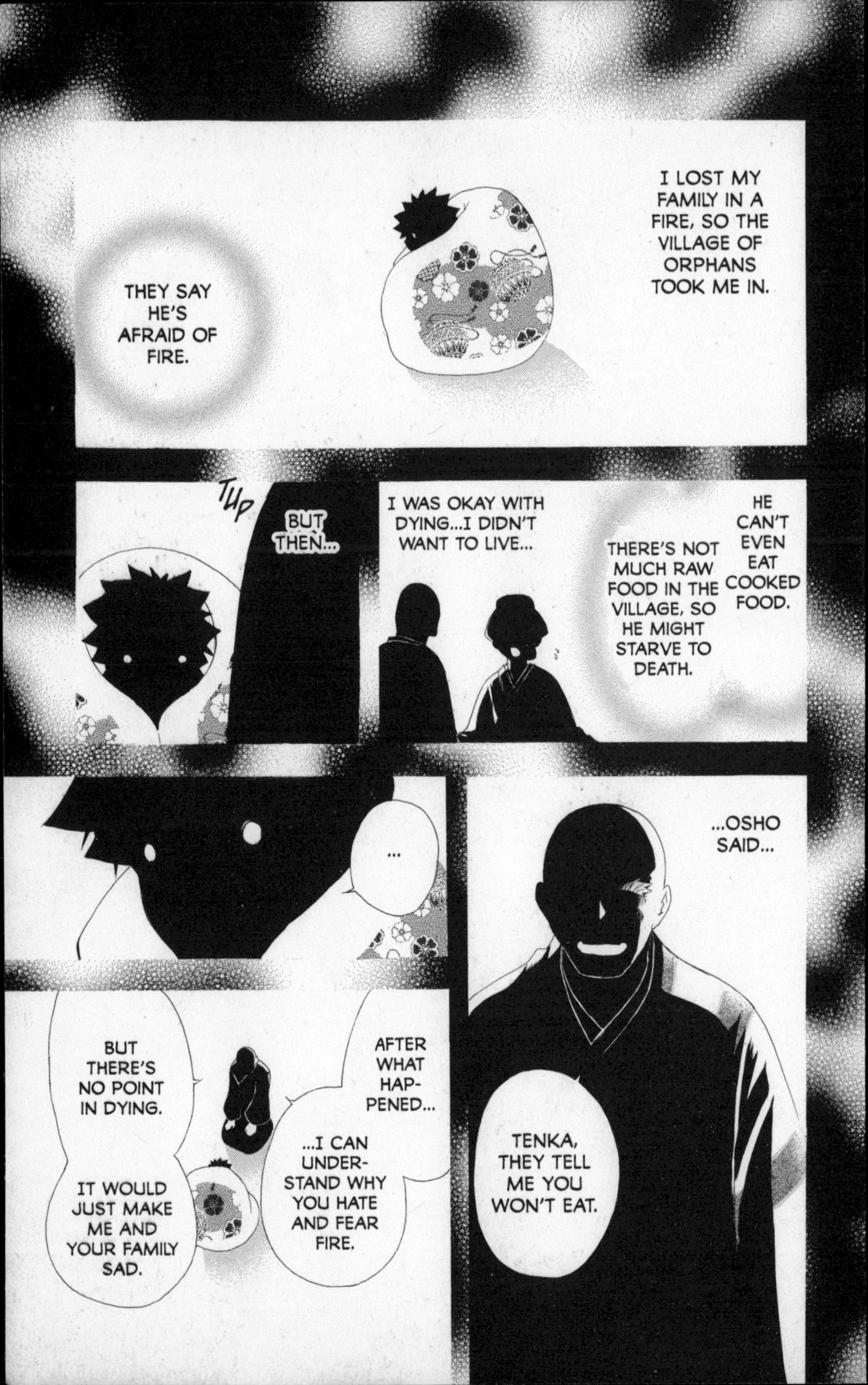

I LOST MY FAMILY IN A FIRE, SO THE VILLAGE OF ORPHANS TOOK ME IN.
THEY SAY HE'S AFRAID OF FIRE.
HE CAN'T EVEN EAT COOKED FOOD.
THERE'S NOT MUCH RAW FOOD IN THE VILLAGE, SO HE MIGHT STARVE TO DEATH.
I WAS OKAY WITH DYING...I DIDN'T WANT TO LIVE...
TUP
BUT THEN...
...OSHO SAID...
TENKA, THEY TELL ME YOU WON'T EAT.
...
AFTER WHAT HAP-PENED...
...I CAN UNDER-STAND WHY YOU HATE AND FEAR FIRE.
BUT THERE'S NO POINT IN DYING.
IT WOULD JUST MAKE ME AND YOUR FAMILY SAD.

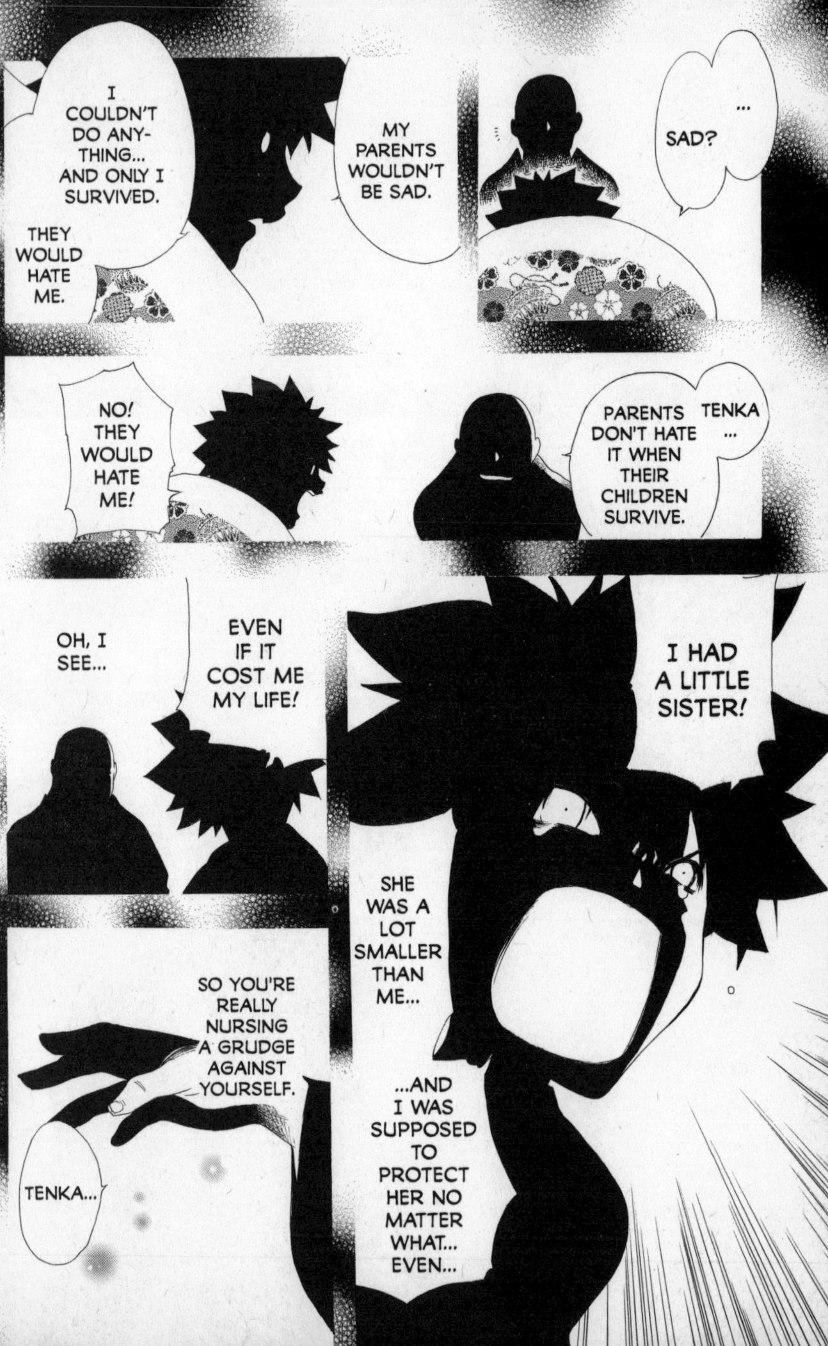
...
SAD?
MY PARENTS WOULDN'T BE SAD.
I COULDN'T DO ANY-THING... AND ONLY I SURVIVED.
THEY WOULD HATE ME.
TENKA...
PARENTS DON'T HATE IT WHEN THEIR CHILDREN SURVIVE.
NO! THEY WOULD HATE ME!
I HAD A LITTLE SISTER!
SHE WAS A LOT SMALLER THAN ME...
...AND I WAS SUPPOSED TO PROTECT HER NO MATTER WHAT... EVEN...
EVEN IF IT COST ME MY LIFE!
OH, I SEE...
SO YOU'RE REALLY NURSING A GRUDGE AGAINST YOURSELF.
TENKA...

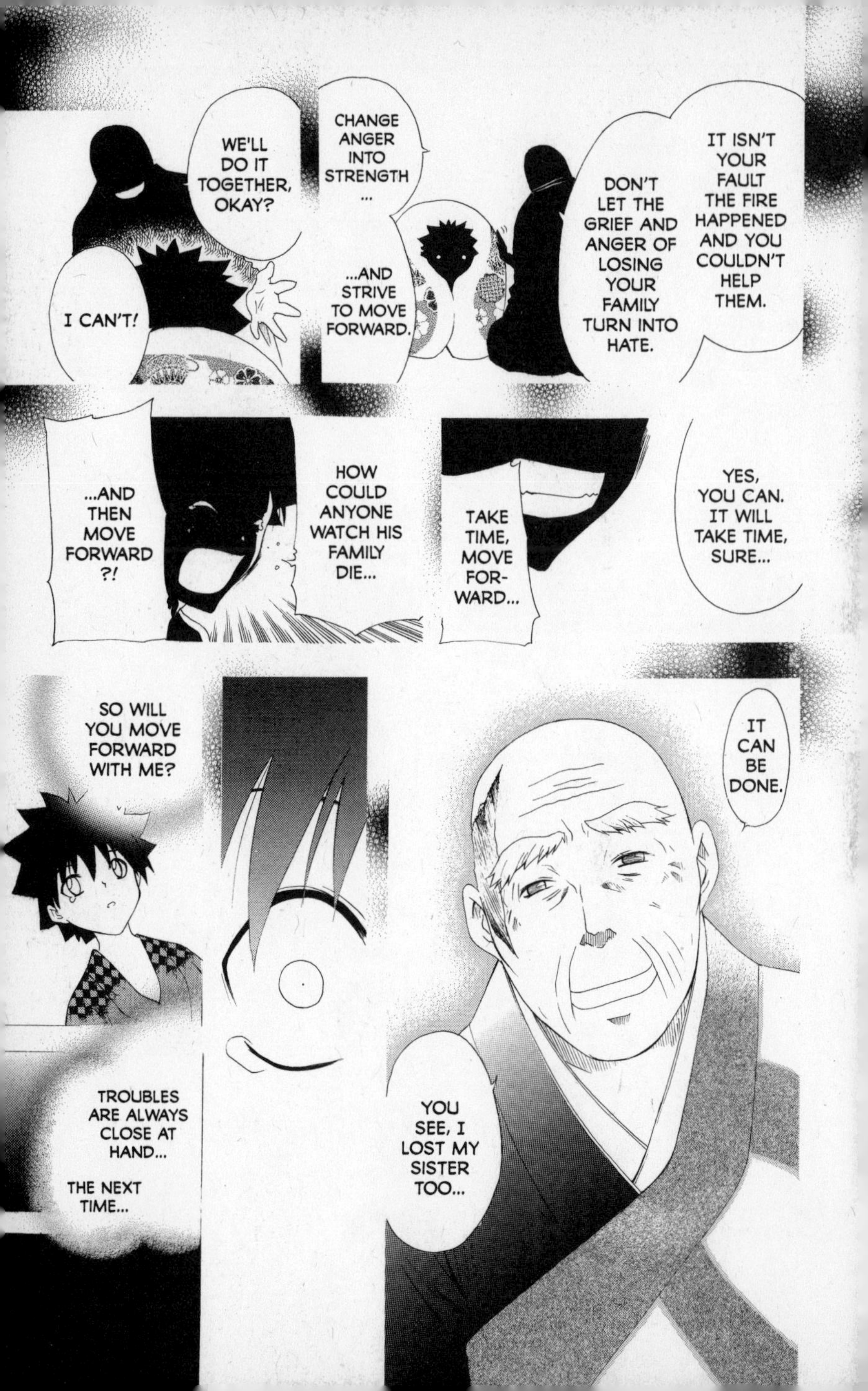
IT ISN'T YOUR FAULT THE FIRE HAPPENED AND YOU COULDN'T HELP THEM.
DON'T LET THE GRIEF AND ANGER OF LOSING YOUR FAMILY TURN INTO HATE.
CHANGE ANGER INTO STRENGTH...
...AND STRIVE TO MOVE FORWARD.
WE'LL DO IT TOGETHER, OKAY?
I CAN'T!
YES, YOU CAN. IT WILL TAKE TIME, SURE...
TAKE TIME, MOVE FOR-WARD...
HOW COULD ANYONE WATCH HIS FAMILY DIE...
...AND THEN MOVE FORWARD ?!
IT CAN BE DONE.
YOU SEE, I LOST MY SISTER TOO...
SO WILL YOU MOVE FORWARD WITH ME?
TROUBLES ARE ALWAYS CLOSE AT HAND...
THE NEXT TIME...

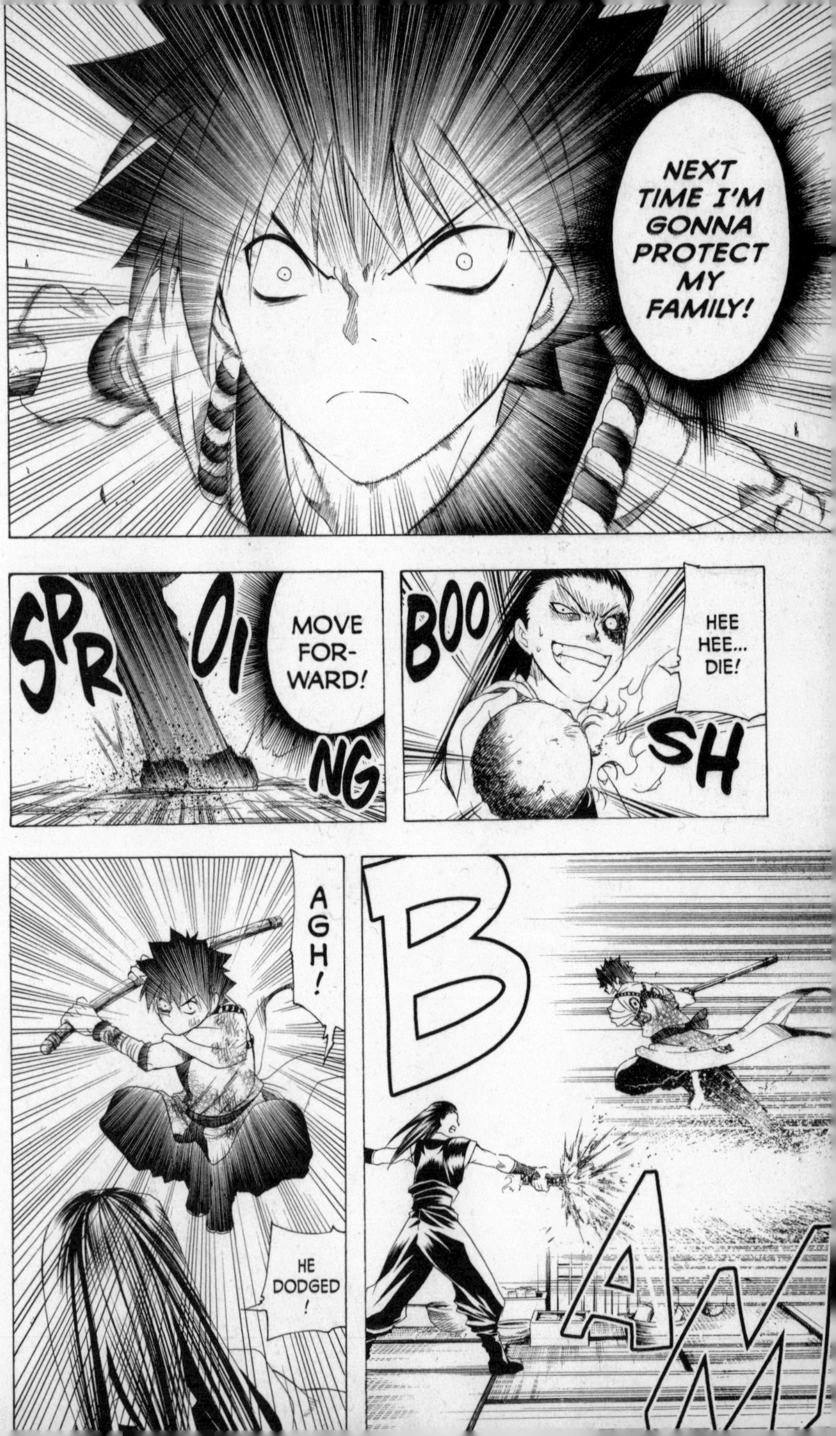
NEXT TIME I'M GONNA PROTECT MY FAMILY!
BOO
HEE HEE... DIE!
SH
SPROING
MOVE FOR-WARD!
B
AM
AGH!
HE DODGED!

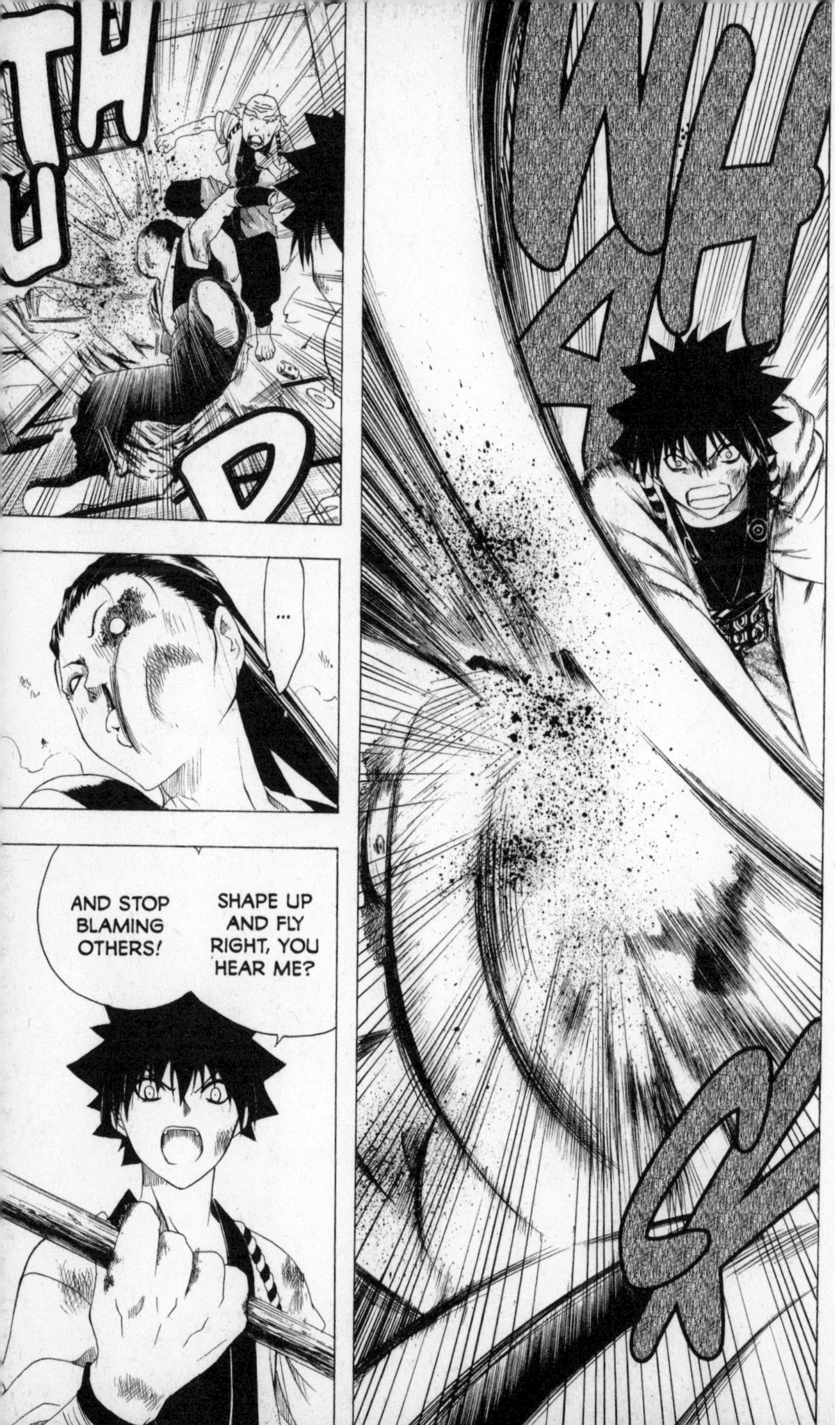
...
SHAPE UP AND FLY RIGHT, YOU HEAR ME?
AND STOP BLAMING OTHERS!

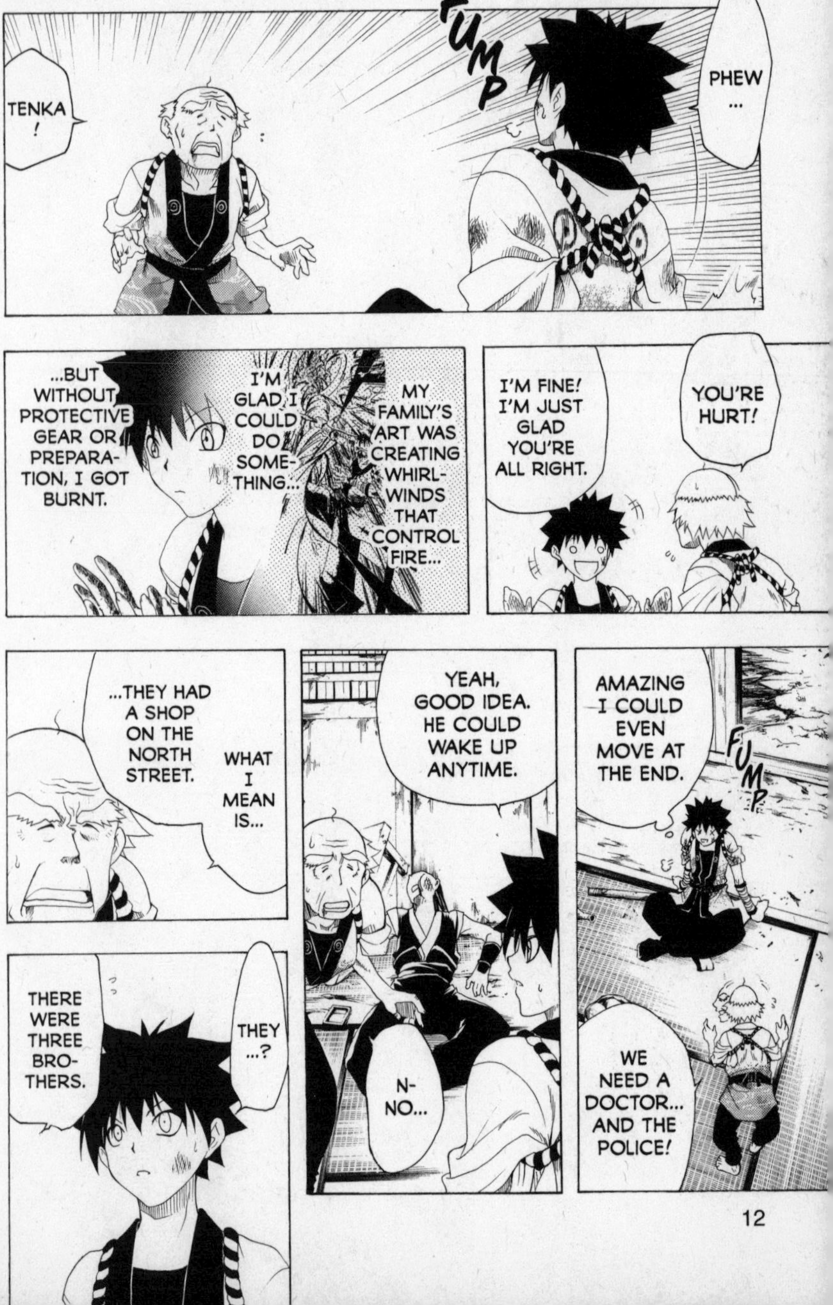
PHEW ...
FUMP
TENKA!
YOU'RE HURT!
I'M FINE! I'M JUST GLAD YOU'RE ALL RIGHT.
MY FAMILY'S ART WAS CREATING WHIRLWINDS THAT CONTROL FIRE...
I'M GLAD I COULD DO SOMETHING...
...BUT WITHOUT PROTECTIVE GEAR OR PREPARATION, I GOT BURNT.
AMAZING I COULD EVEN MOVE AT THE END.
FUMP
WE NEED A DOCTOR... AND THE POLICE!
YEAH, GOOD IDEA. HE COULD WAKE UP ANYTIME.
N-NO...
WHAT I MEAN IS...
...THEY HAD A SHOP ON THE NORTH STREET.
THEY ...?
THERE WERE THREE BROTHERS.

HIS BROTHERS MAY BE NEAR—

UNH!

WHOK

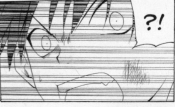

?!

THIS IS SAD, HOZO.

MY, MY...

CLOMP

THUD

FA-THER!

GRB

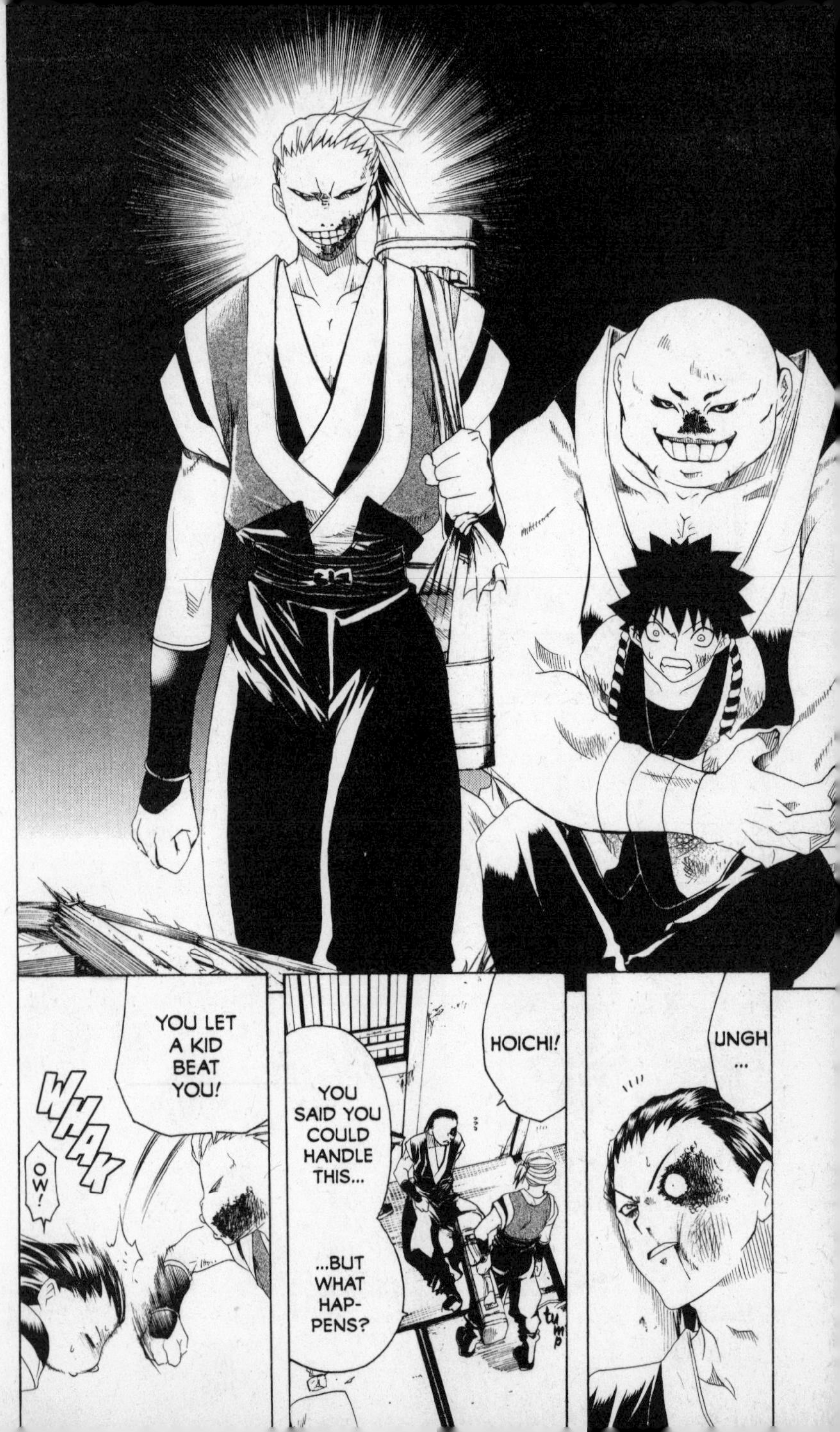
UNGH ...
HOICHI!
YOU SAID YOU COULD HANDLE THIS...
...BUT WHAT HAP-PENS?
tump
YOU LET A KID BEAT YOU!
WHAK
OW!

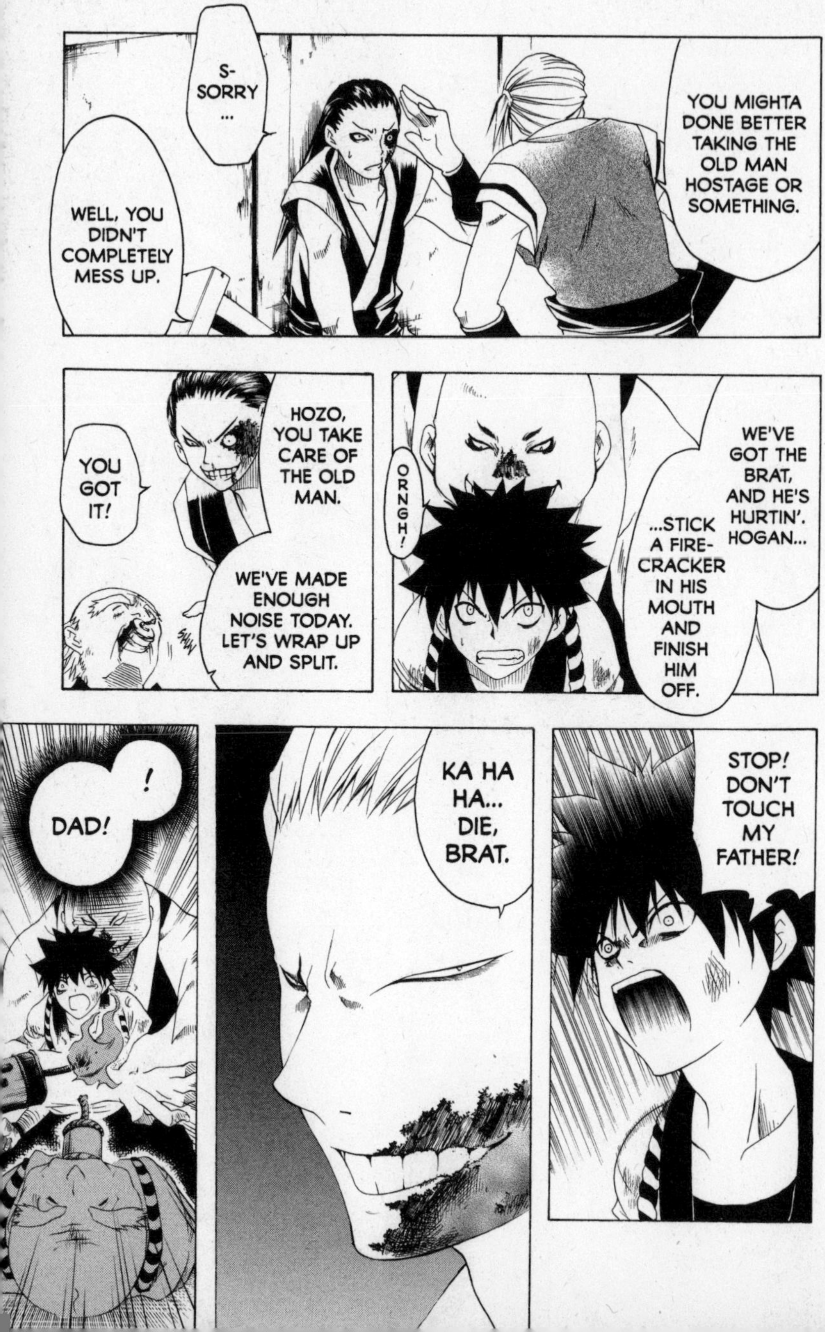
YOU MIGHTA DONE BETTER TAKING THE OLD MAN HOSTAGE OR SOMETHING.
S-SORRY...
WELL, YOU DIDN'T COMPLETELY MESS UP.
WE'VE GOT THE BRAT, AND HE'S HURTIN'. HOGAN...
...STICK A FIRE-CRACKER IN HIS MOUTH AND FINISH HIM OFF.
ORNGH!
HOZO, YOU TAKE CARE OF THE OLD MAN.
YOU GOT IT!
WE'VE MADE ENOUGH NOISE TODAY. LET'S WRAP UP AND SPLIT.
STOP! DON'T TOUCH MY FATHER!
KA HA HA... DIE, BRAT.
!
DAD!

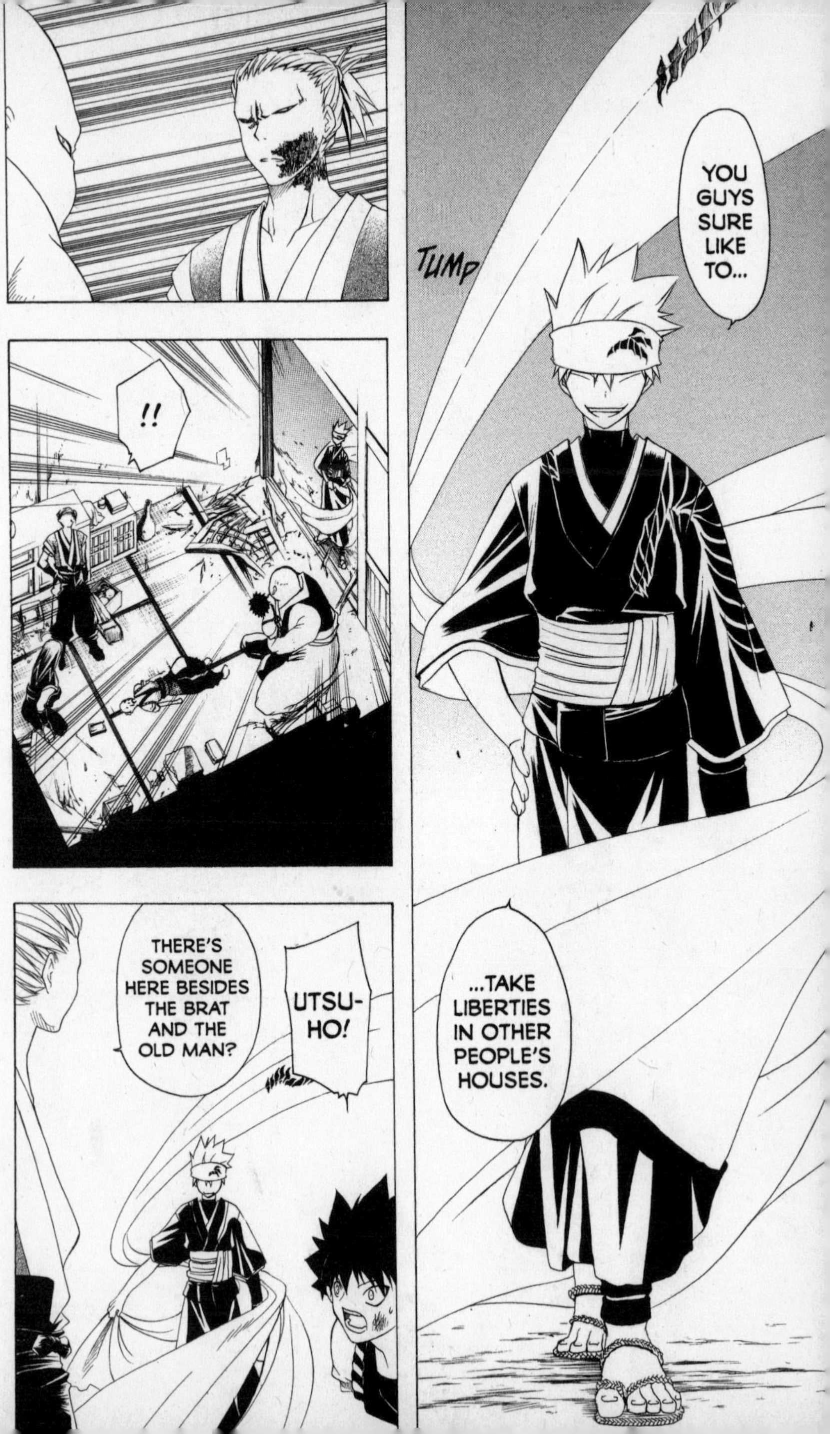
YOU GUYS SURE LIKE TO...
TUMP
...TAKE LIBERTIES IN OTHER PEOPLE'S HOUSES.
!!
UTSU-HO!
THERE'S SOMEONE HERE BESIDES THE BRAT AND THE OLD MAN?

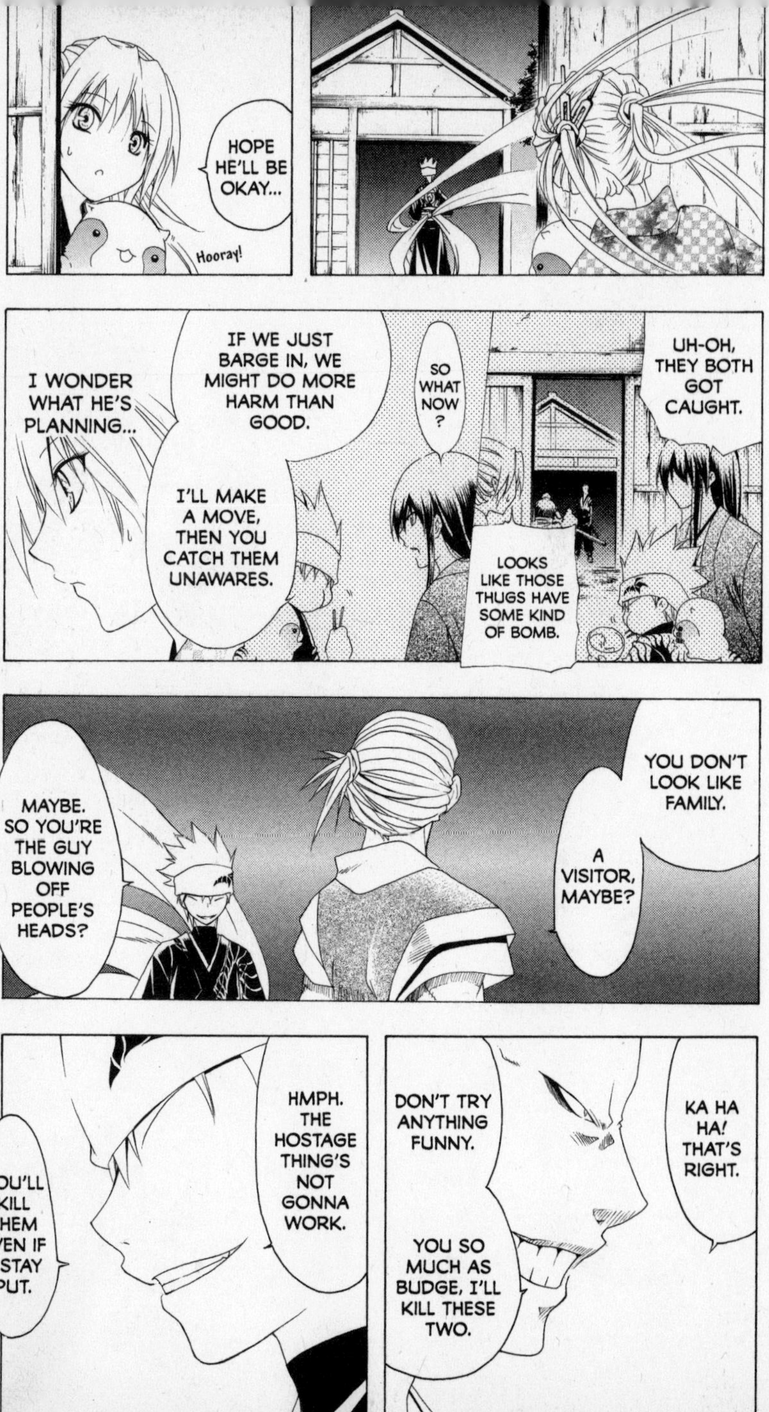
HOPE HE'LL BE OKAY...
Hooray!
UH-OH, THEY BOTH GOT CAUGHT.
SO WHAT NOW?
LOOKS LIKE THOSE THUGS HAVE SOME KIND OF BOMB.
IF WE JUST BARGE IN, WE MIGHT DO MORE HARM THAN GOOD.
I'LL MAKE A MOVE, THEN YOU CATCH THEM UNAWARES.
I WONDER WHAT HE'S PLANNING...
YOU DON'T LOOK LIKE FAMILY.
A VISITOR, MAYBE?
MAYBE. SO YOU'RE THE GUY BLOWING OFF PEOPLE'S HEADS?
KA HA HA! THAT'S RIGHT.
DON'T TRY ANYTHING FUNNY.
YOU SO MUCH AS BUDGE, I'LL KILL THESE TWO.
HMPH. THE HOSTAGE THING'S NOT GONNA WORK.
YOU'LL KILL THEM EVEN IF I STAY PUT.

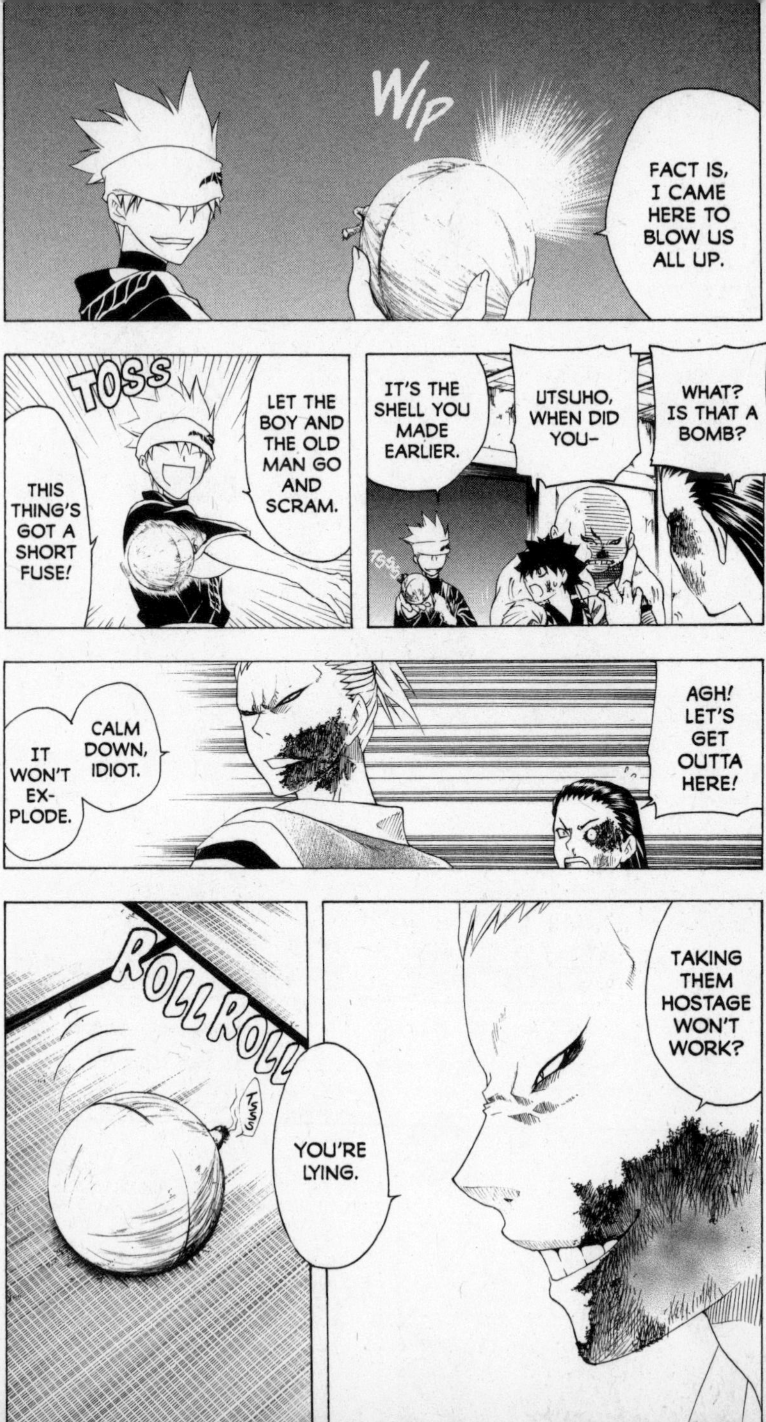
FACT IS, I CAME HERE TO BLOW US ALL UP.
WIP
WHAT? IS THAT A BOMB?
UTSUHO, WHEN DID YOU-
IT'S THE SHELL YOU MADE EARLIER.
LET THE BOY AND THE OLD MAN GO AND SCRAM.
TOSS
THIS THING'S GOT A SHORT FUSE!
AGH! LET'S GET OUTTA HERE!
CALM DOWN, IDIOT.
IT WON'T EX-PLODE.
TAKING THEM HOSTAGE WON'T WORK?
YOU'RE LYING.
ROLL ROLL
TSSS

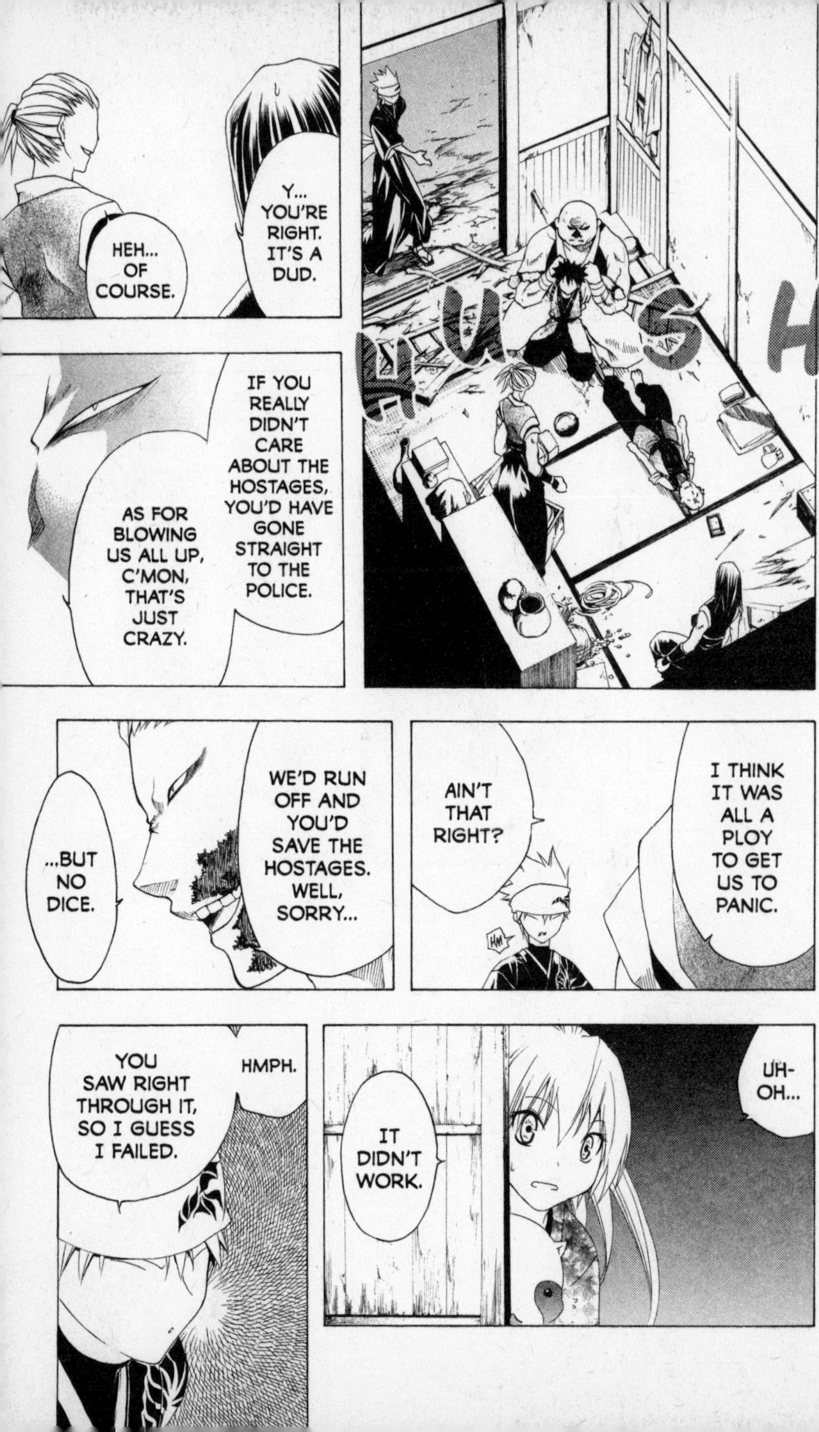
Y... YOU'RE RIGHT. IT'S A DUD.
HEH... OF COURSE.
IF YOU REALLY DIDN'T CARE ABOUT THE HOSTAGES, YOU'D HAVE GONE STRAIGHT TO THE POLICE.
AS FOR BLOWING US ALL UP, C'MON, THAT'S JUST CRAZY.
I THINK IT WAS ALL A PLOY TO GET US TO PANIC.
AIN'T THAT RIGHT?
HM
WE'D RUN OFF AND YOU'D SAVE THE HOSTAGES. WELL, SORRY...
...BUT NO DICE.
UH-OH...
IT DIDN'T WORK.
HMPH.
YOU SAW RIGHT THROUGH IT, SO I GUESS I FAILED.

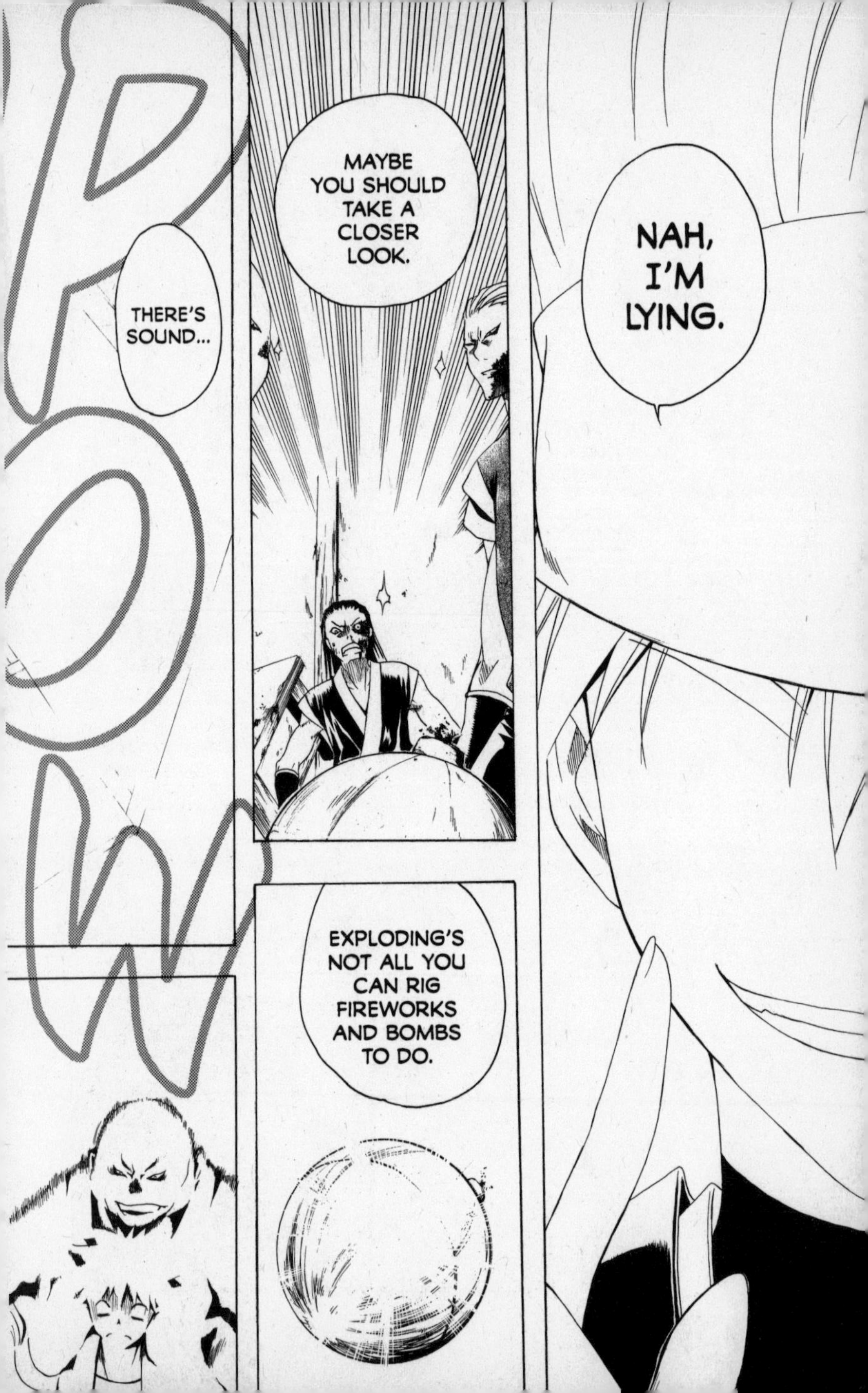
NAH, I'M LYING.
MAYBE YOU SHOULD TAKE A CLOSER LOOK.
EXPLODING'S NOT ALL YOU CAN RIG FIREWORKS AND BOMBS TO DO.
THERE'S SOUND...
POW

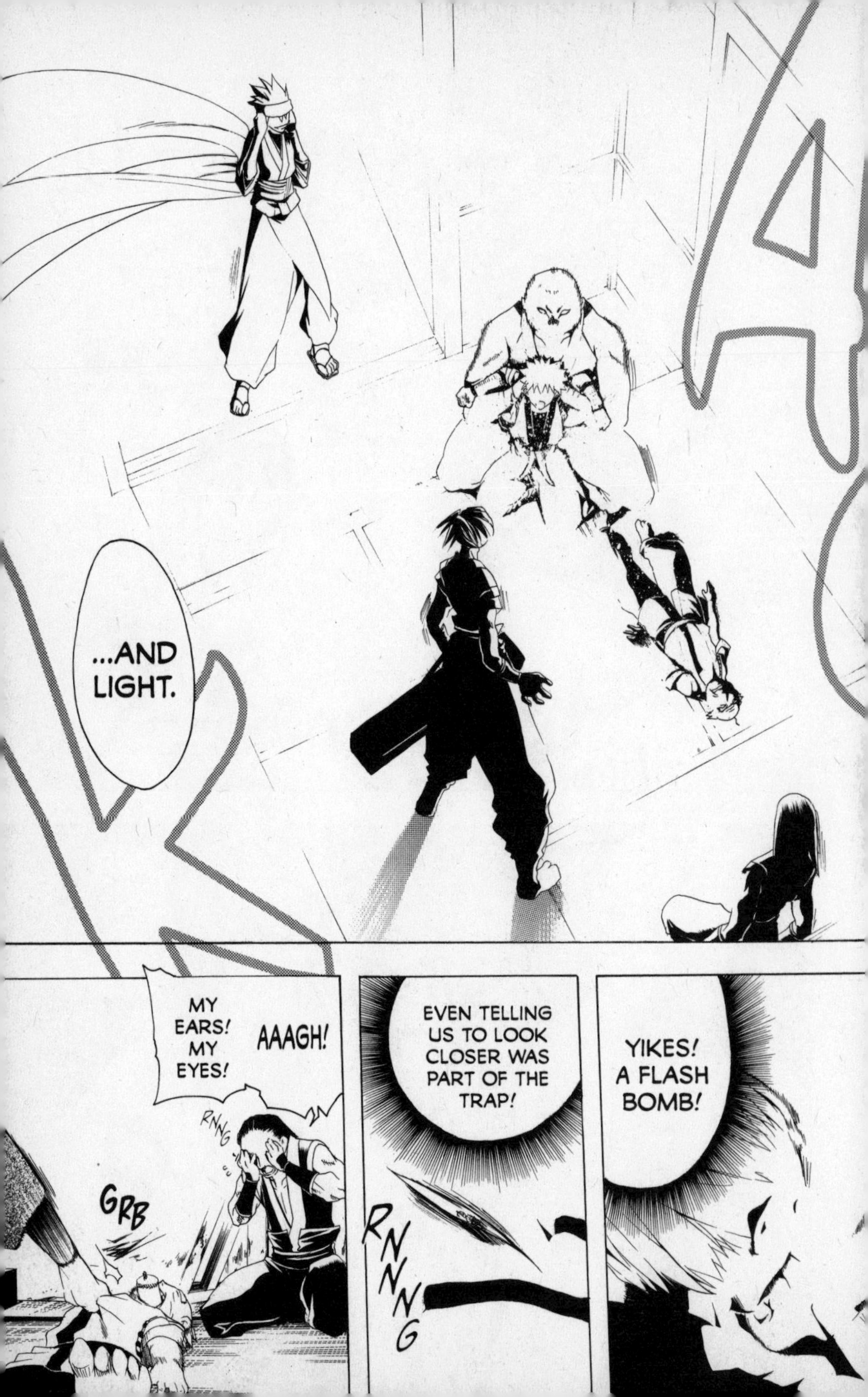
...AND LIGHT.
YIKES! A FLASH BOMB!
EVEN TELLING US TO LOOK CLOSER WAS PART OF THE TRAP!
RNNNG
AAAGH!
MY EARS! MY EYES!
RNNG
GRB

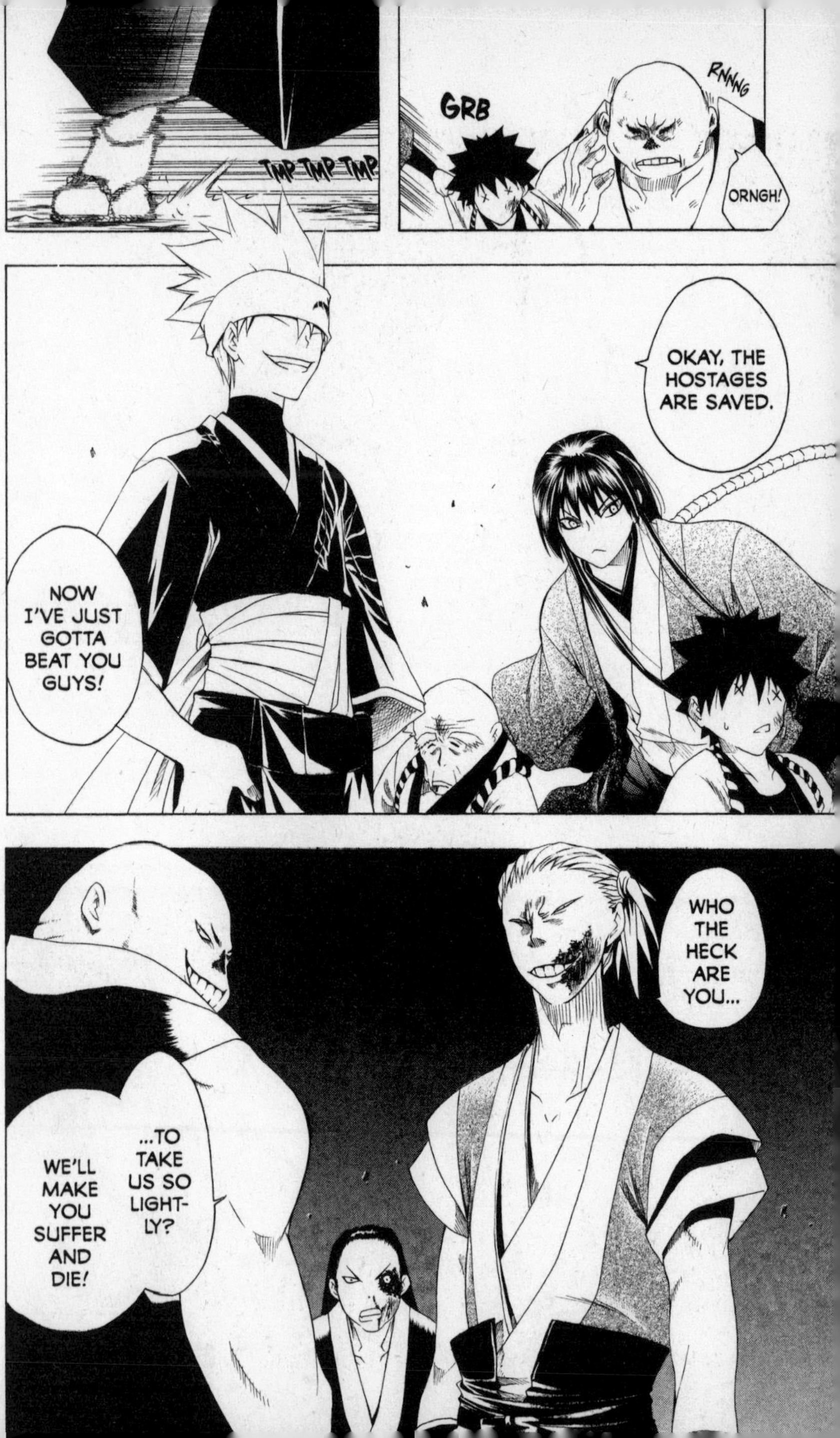

RNNNG
GRB
ORNGH!
TMP TMP TMP
OKAY, THE HOSTAGES ARE SAVED.
NOW I'VE JUST GOTTA BEAT YOU GUYS!
WHO THE HECK ARE YOU...
...TO TAKE US SO LIGHTLY?
WE'LL MAKE YOU SUFFER AND DIE!

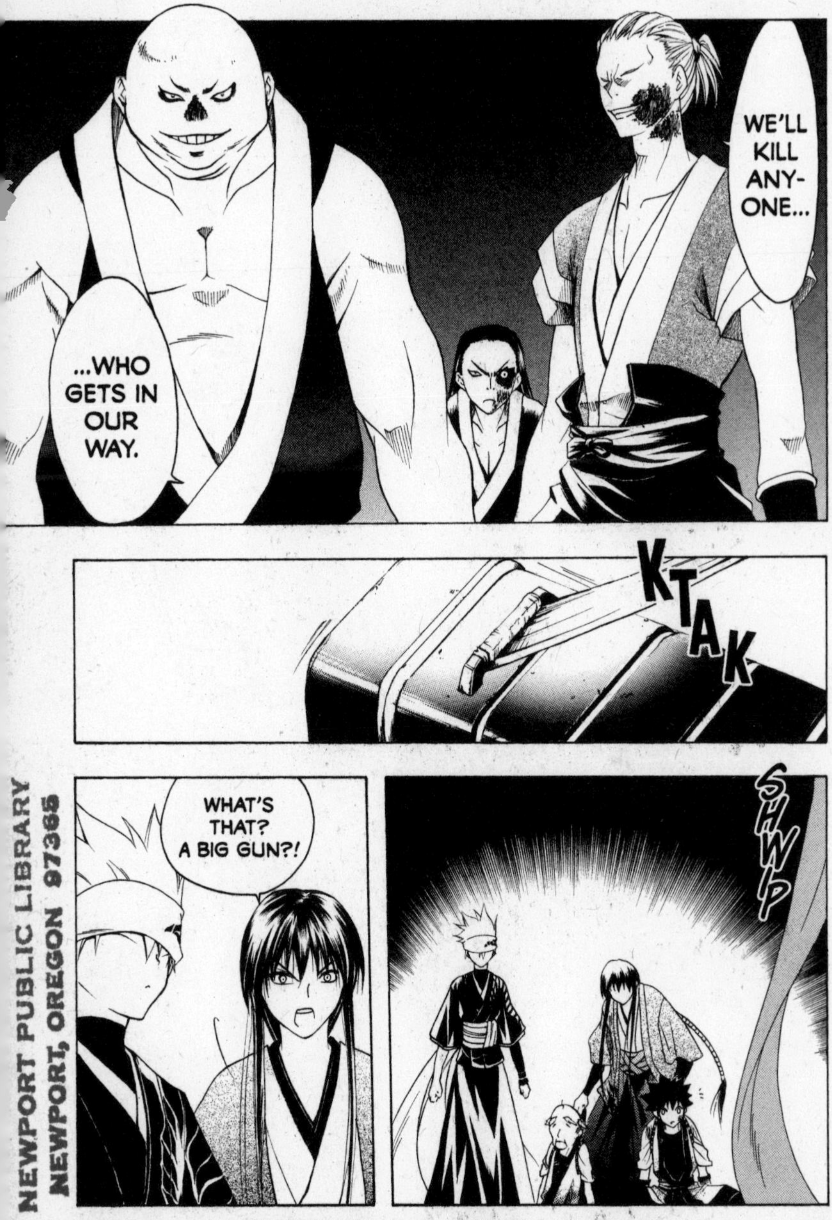
WE'LL KILL ANY-ONE...
...WHO GETS IN OUR WAY.
KTAK
SHWIP
WHAT'S THAT? A BIG GUN?!

Chapter 39 A Weapon Called Sen

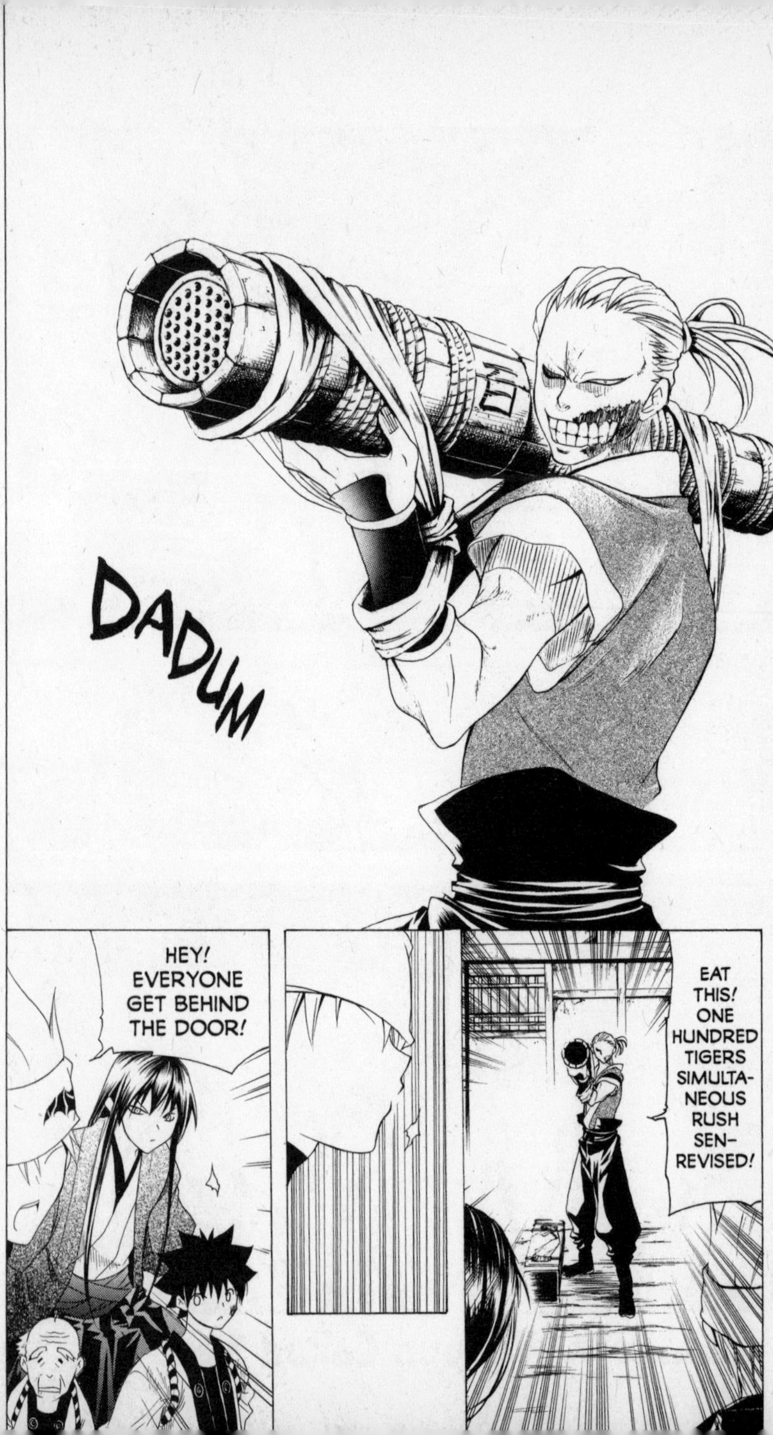
DADUM
EAT THIS! ONE HUNDRED TIGERS SIMULTANEOUS RUSH SEN—REVISED!
HEY! EVERYONE GET BEHIND THE DOOR!

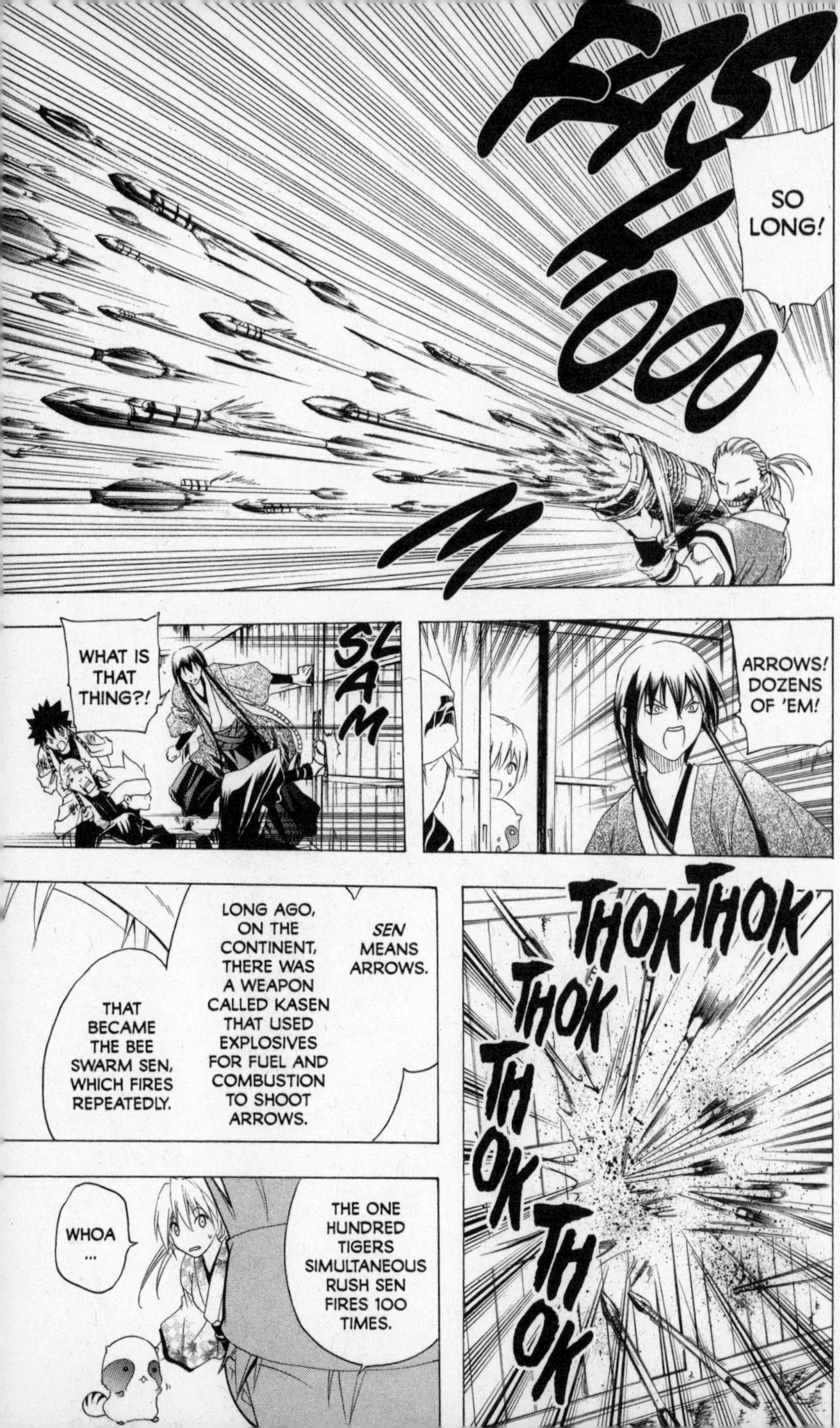

FASHOOOM
SO LONG!
ARROWS! DOZENS OF 'EM!
SLAM
WHAT IS THAT THING?!
THOKTHOK
THOK
THOK
THOK
SEN MEANS ARROWS.
LONG AGO, ON THE CONTINENT, THERE WAS A WEAPON CALLED KASEN THAT USED EXPLOSIVES FOR FUEL AND COMBUSTION TO SHOOT ARROWS.
THAT BECAME THE BEE SWARM SEN, WHICH FIRES REPEATEDLY.
THE ONE HUNDRED TIGERS SIMULTANEOUS RUSH SEN FIRES 100 TIMES.
WHOA ...

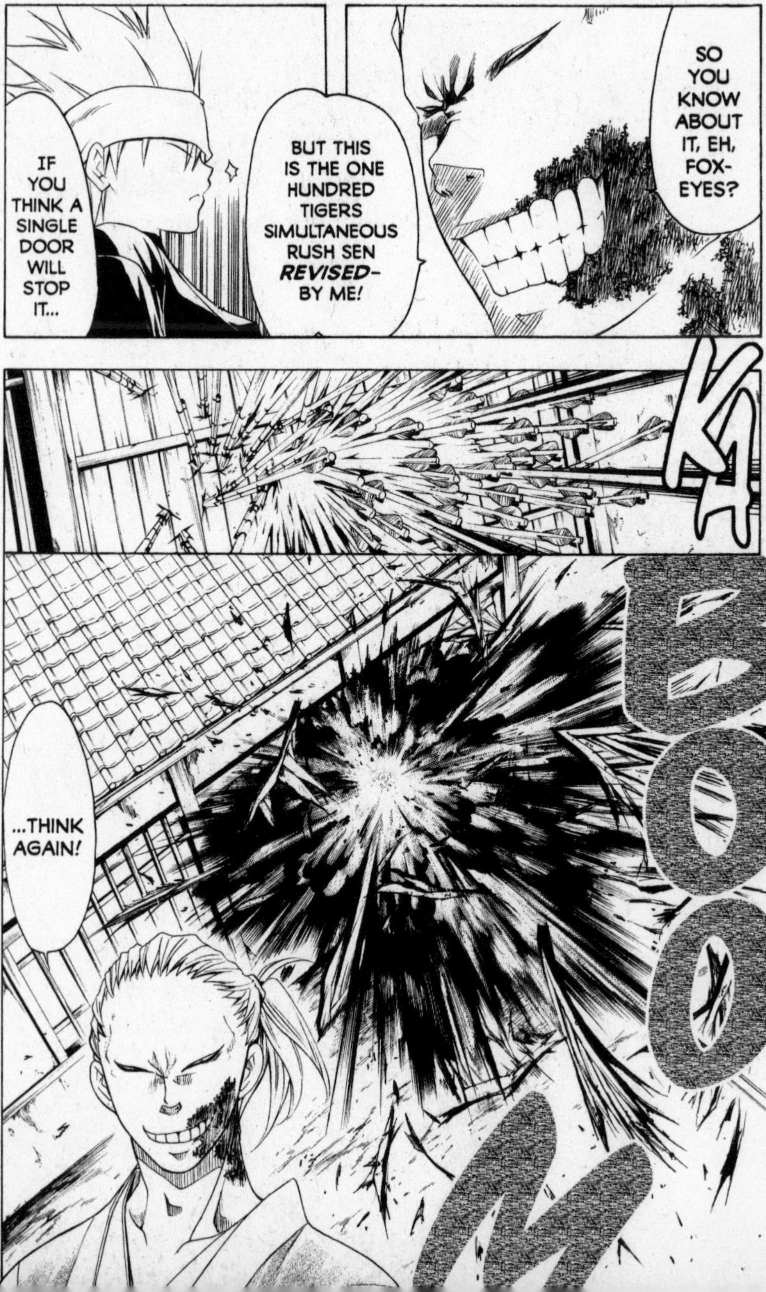
SO YOU KNOW ABOUT IT, EH, FOX-EYES?
BUT THIS IS THE ONE HUNDRED TIGERS SIMULTANEOUS RUSH SEN *REVISED*- BY ME!
IF YOU THINK A SINGLE DOOR WILL STOP IT...
KA
BOOM
...THINK AGAIN!

Chapter 39
A Weapon Called Sen

Itsuwari
Utsuho
Lie
Shaku
Shell
Thunder
Peony

Tanuki
Fox
Horse
Rabbit
Moth

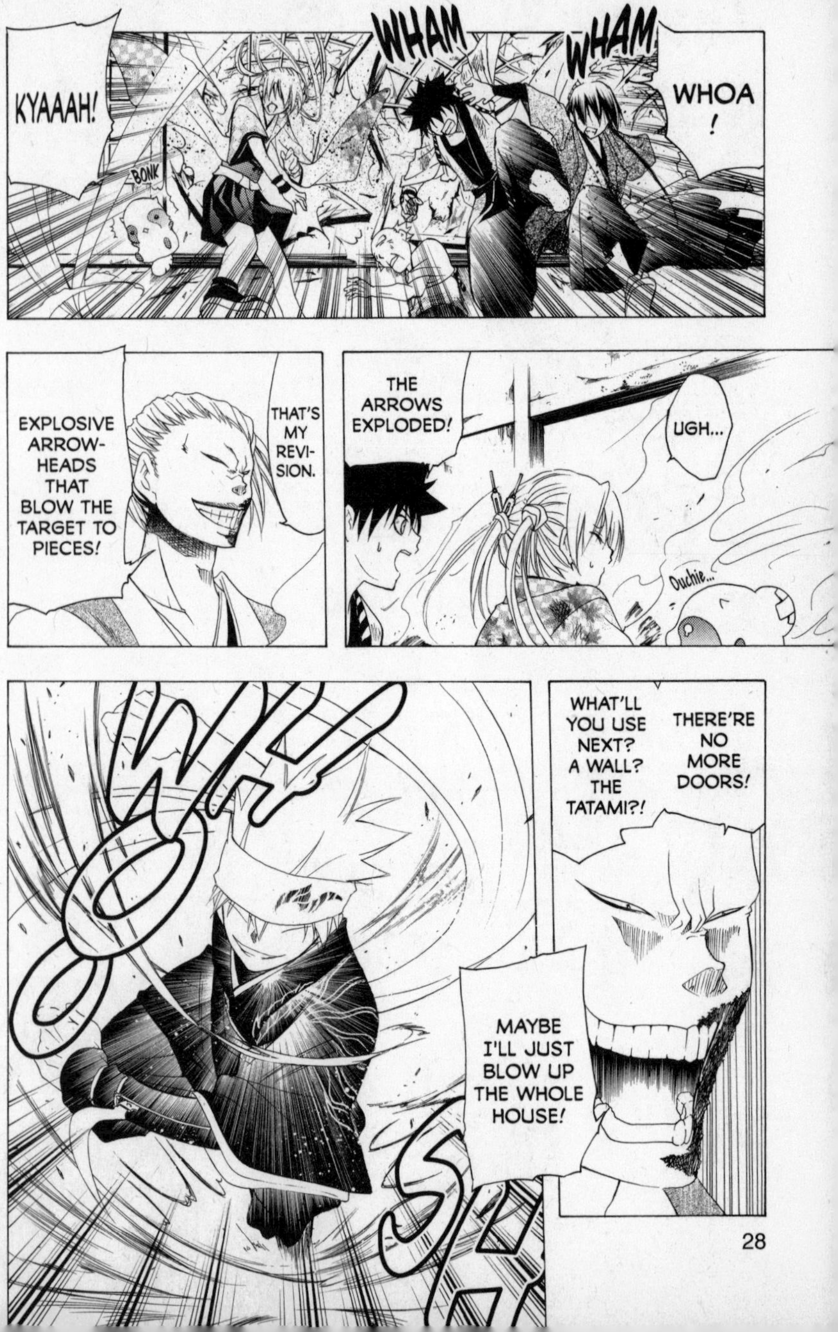
WHOA !
WHAM
WHAM
KYAAAH!
BONK
UGH...
THE ARROWS EXPLODED!
Ouchie...
THAT'S MY REVI- SION.
EXPLOSIVE ARROW- HEADS THAT BLOW THE TARGET TO PIECES!
THERE'RE NO MORE DOORS!
WHAT'LL YOU USE NEXT? A WALL? THE TATAMI?!
MAYBE I'LL JUST BLOW UP THE WHOLE HOUSE!

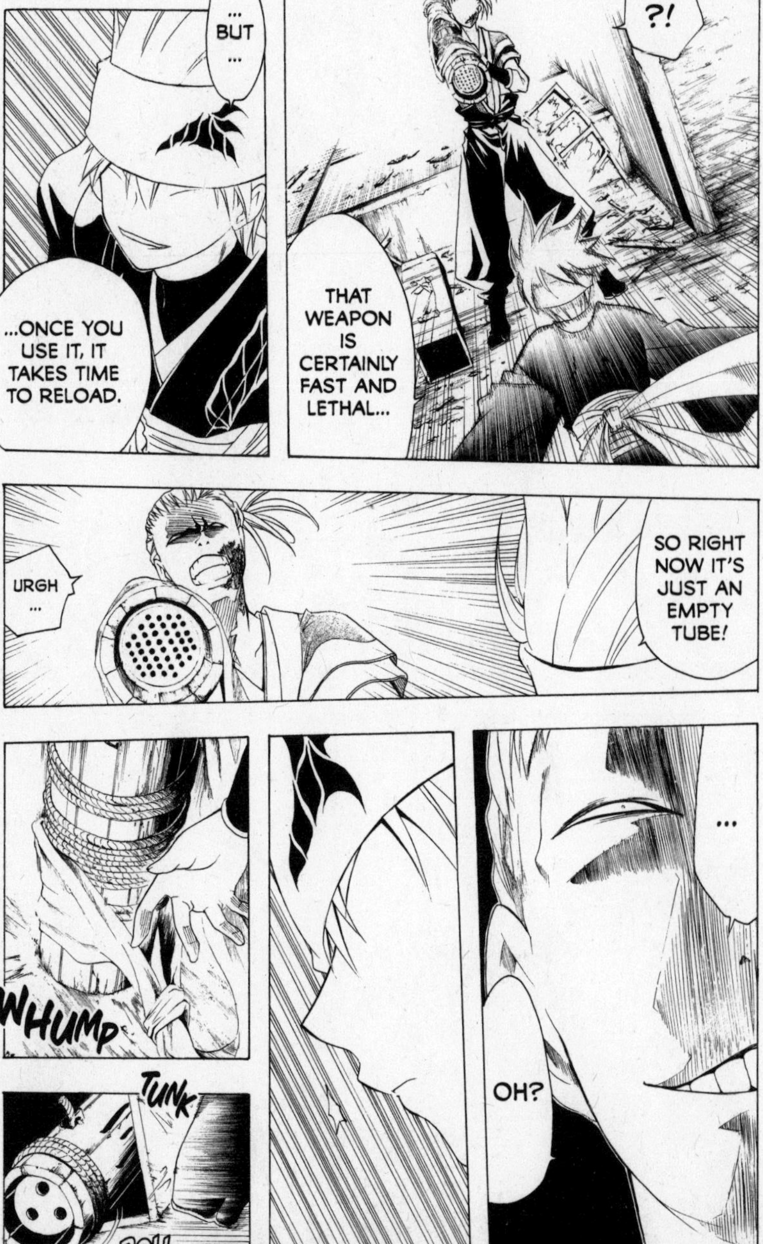
?!
THAT WEAPON IS CERTAINLY FAST AND LETHAL...
... BUT ...
...ONCE YOU USE IT, IT TAKES TIME TO RELOAD.
SO RIGHT NOW IT'S JUST AN EMPTY TUBE!
URGH ...
...
OH?
WHUMP
TUNK
ROLL

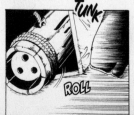

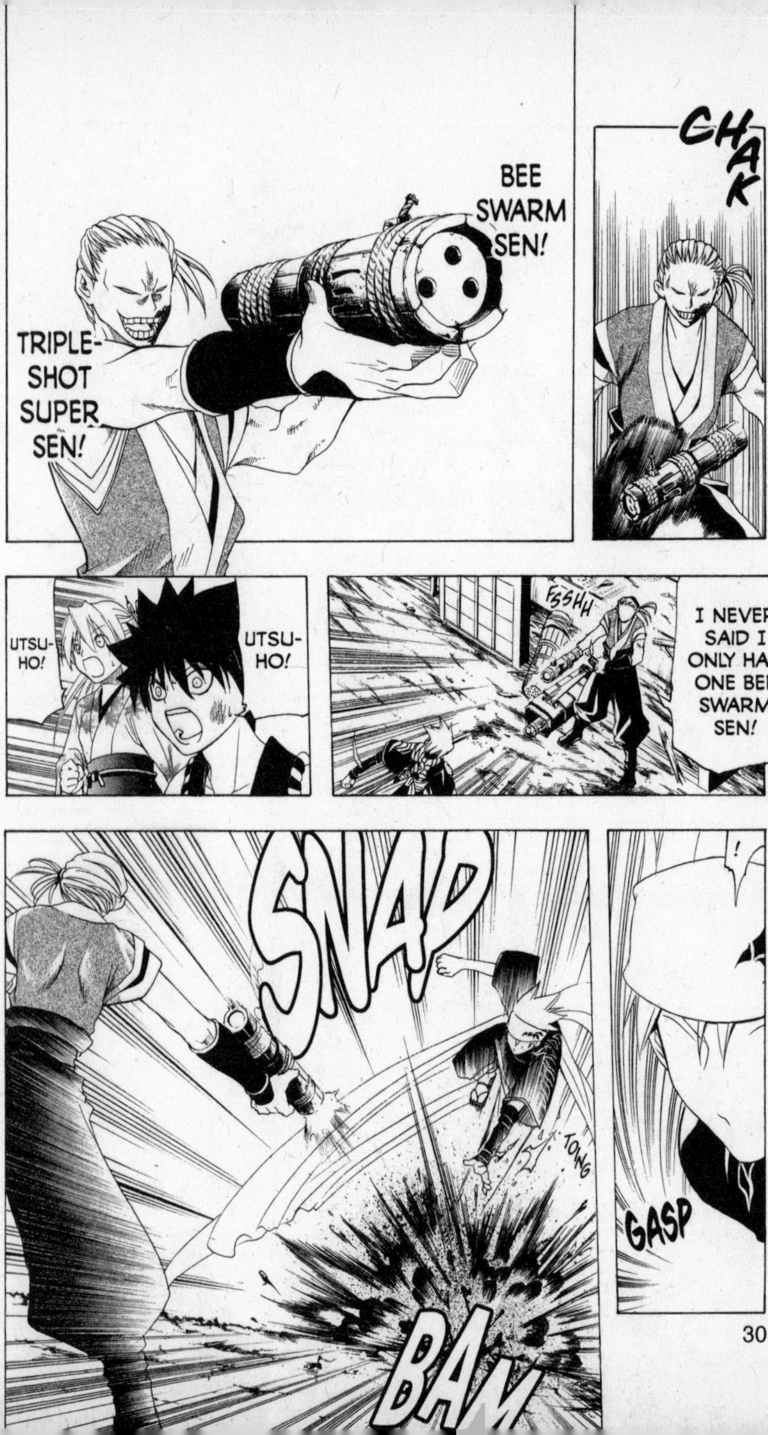
CHAK
BEE SWARM SEN!
TRIPLE-SHOT SUPER SEN!
FSSHH
I NEVER SAID I ONLY HAD ONE BEE SWARM SEN!
UTSU-HO!
UTSU-HO!
!
GASP
SNAP
TONG
BAM

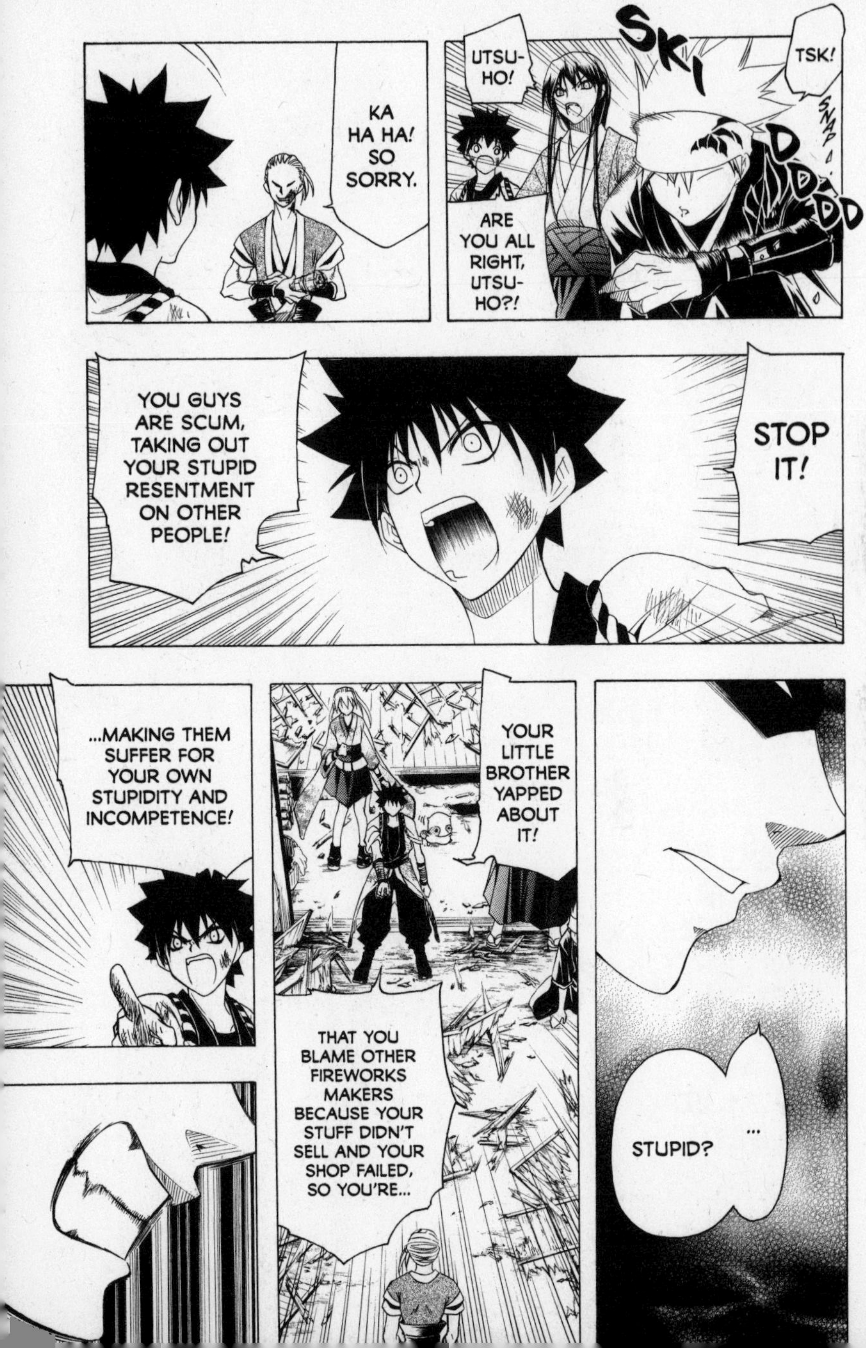
KA HA HA! SO SORRY.
UTSU-HO!
ARE YOU ALL RIGHT, UTSU-HO?!
SKI
TSK!
SNAP
DDDD
YOU GUYS ARE SCUM, TAKING OUT YOUR STUPID RESENTMENT ON OTHER PEOPLE!
STOP IT!
...MAKING THEM SUFFER FOR YOUR OWN STUPIDITY AND INCOMPETENCE!
YOUR LITTLE BROTHER YAPPED ABOUT IT!
THAT YOU BLAME OTHER FIREWORKS MAKERS BECAUSE YOUR STUFF DIDN'T SELL AND YOUR SHOP FAILED, SO YOU'RE...
...
STUPID?

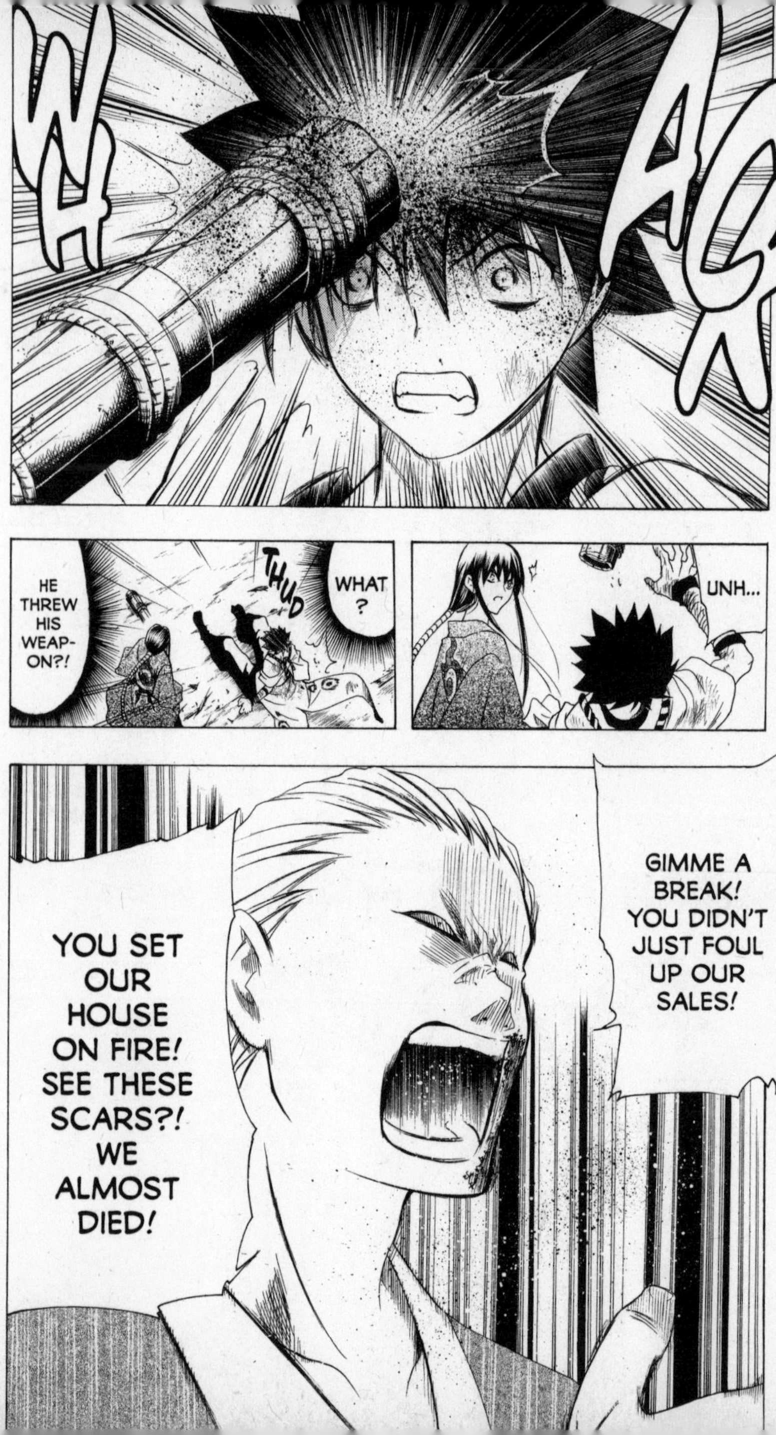
WHACK
UNH...
WHAT?
THUD
HE THREW HIS WEAPON?!
GIMME A BREAK! YOU DIDN'T JUST FOUL UP OUR SALES!
YOU SET OUR HOUSE ON FIRE! SEE THESE SCARS?! WE ALMOST DIED!

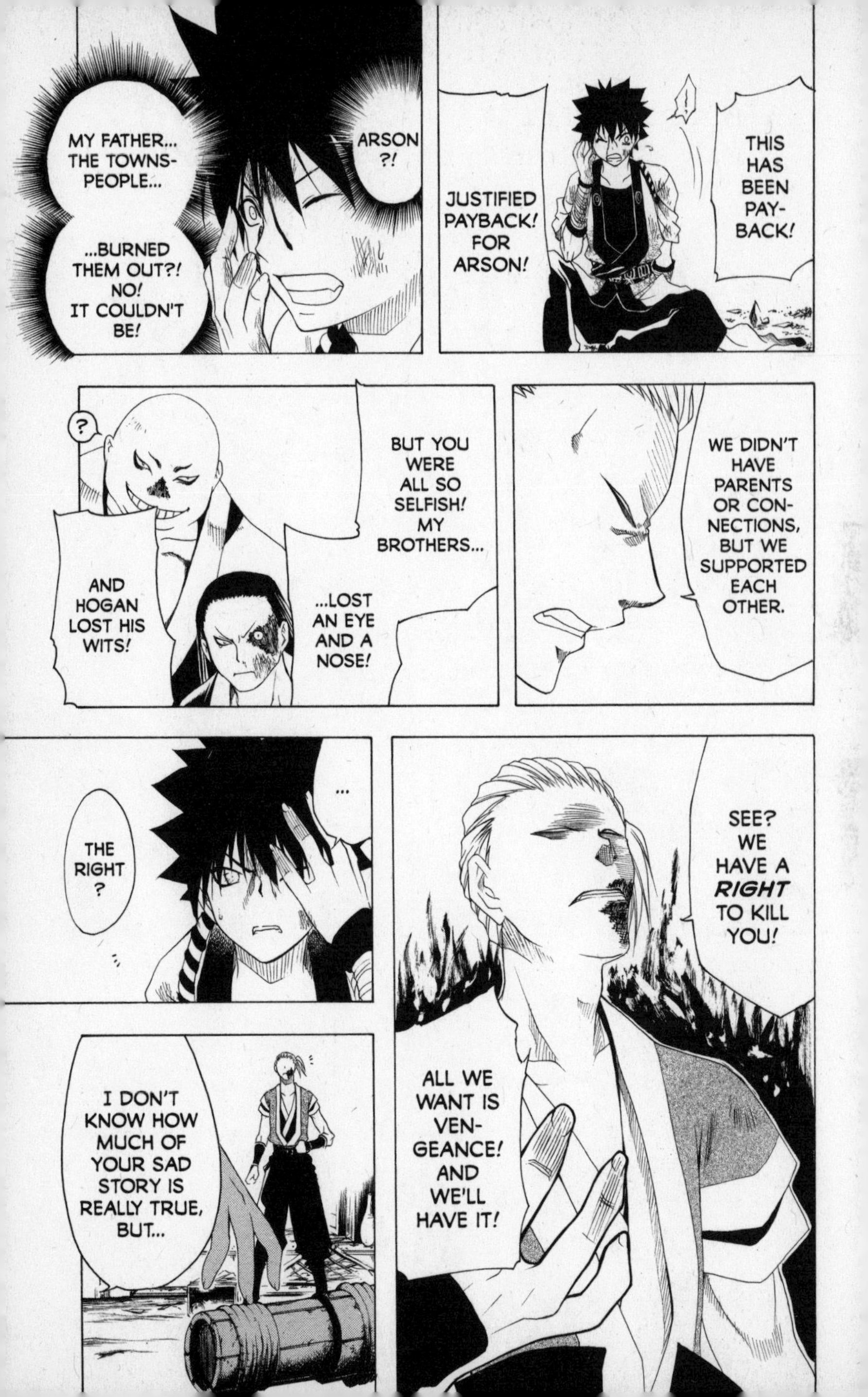
!
THIS HAS BEEN PAYBACK!
JUSTIFIED PAYBACK! FOR ARSON!
ARSON?!
MY FATHER... THE TOWNSPEOPLE...
...BURNED THEM OUT?! NO! IT COULDN'T BE!
WE DIDN'T HAVE PARENTS OR CONNECTIONS, BUT WE SUPPORTED EACH OTHER.
BUT YOU WERE ALL SO SELFISH! MY BROTHERS...
?
...LOST AN EYE AND A NOSE!
AND HOGAN LOST HIS WITS!
SEE? WE HAVE A *RIGHT* TO KILL YOU!
ALL WE WANT IS VENGEANCE! AND WE'LL HAVE IT!
...
THE RIGHT?
I DON'T KNOW HOW MUCH OF YOUR SAD STORY IS REALLY TRUE, BUT...

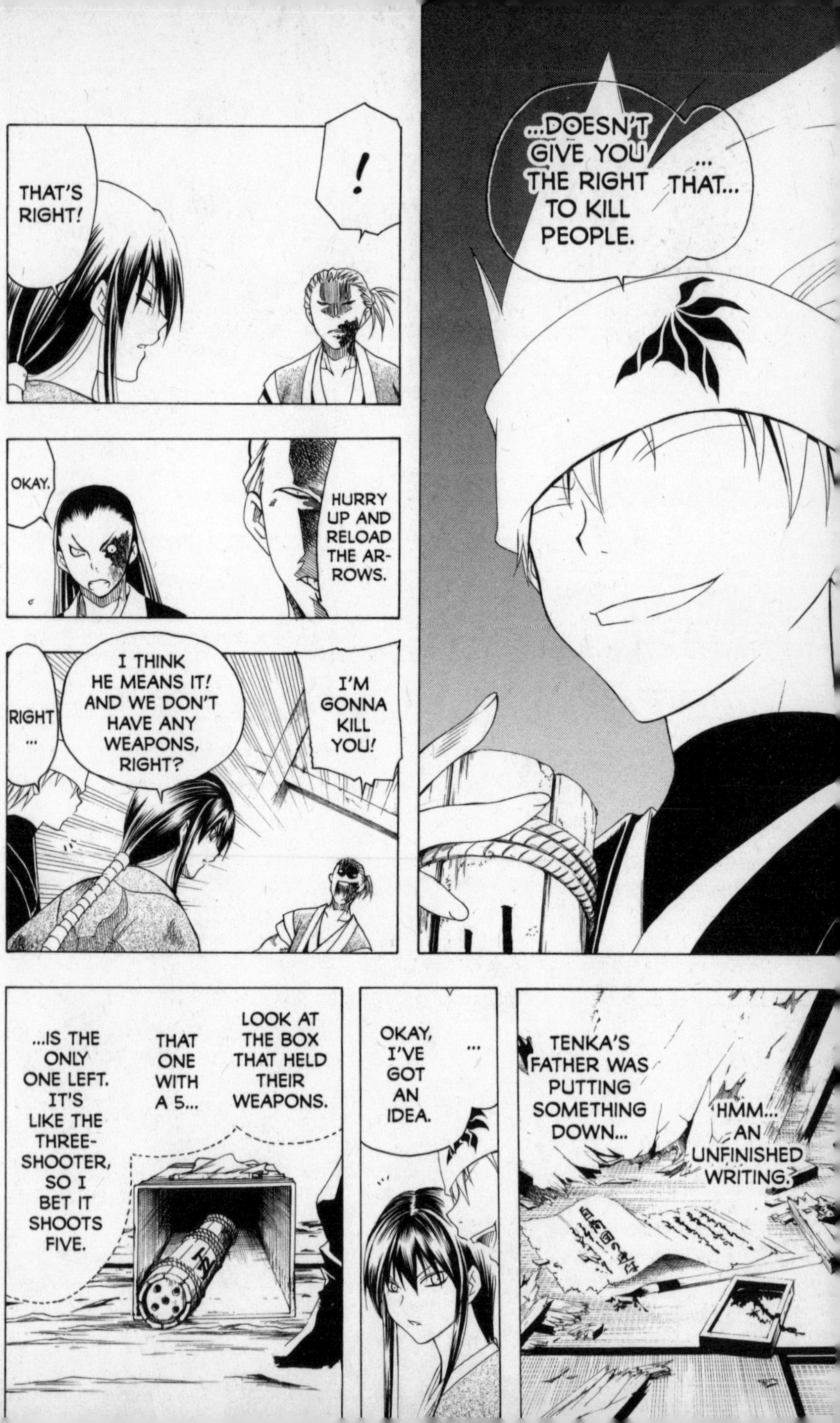
... THAT...
...DOESN'T GIVE YOU THE RIGHT TO KILL PEOPLE.
!
THAT'S RIGHT!
HURRY UP AND RELOAD THE AR-ROWS.
OKAY.
I'M GONNA KILL YOU!
I THINK HE MEANS IT! AND WE DON'T HAVE ANY WEAPONS, RIGHT?
RIGHT ...
TENKA'S FATHER WAS PUTTING SOMETHING DOWN...
HMM... AN UNFINISHED WRITING.
...
OKAY, I'VE GOT AN IDEA.
LOOK AT THE BOX THAT HELD THEIR WEAPONS.
THAT ONE WITH A 5...
...IS THE ONLY ONE LEFT. IT'S LIKE THE THREE-SHOOTER, SO I BET IT SHOOTS FIVE.

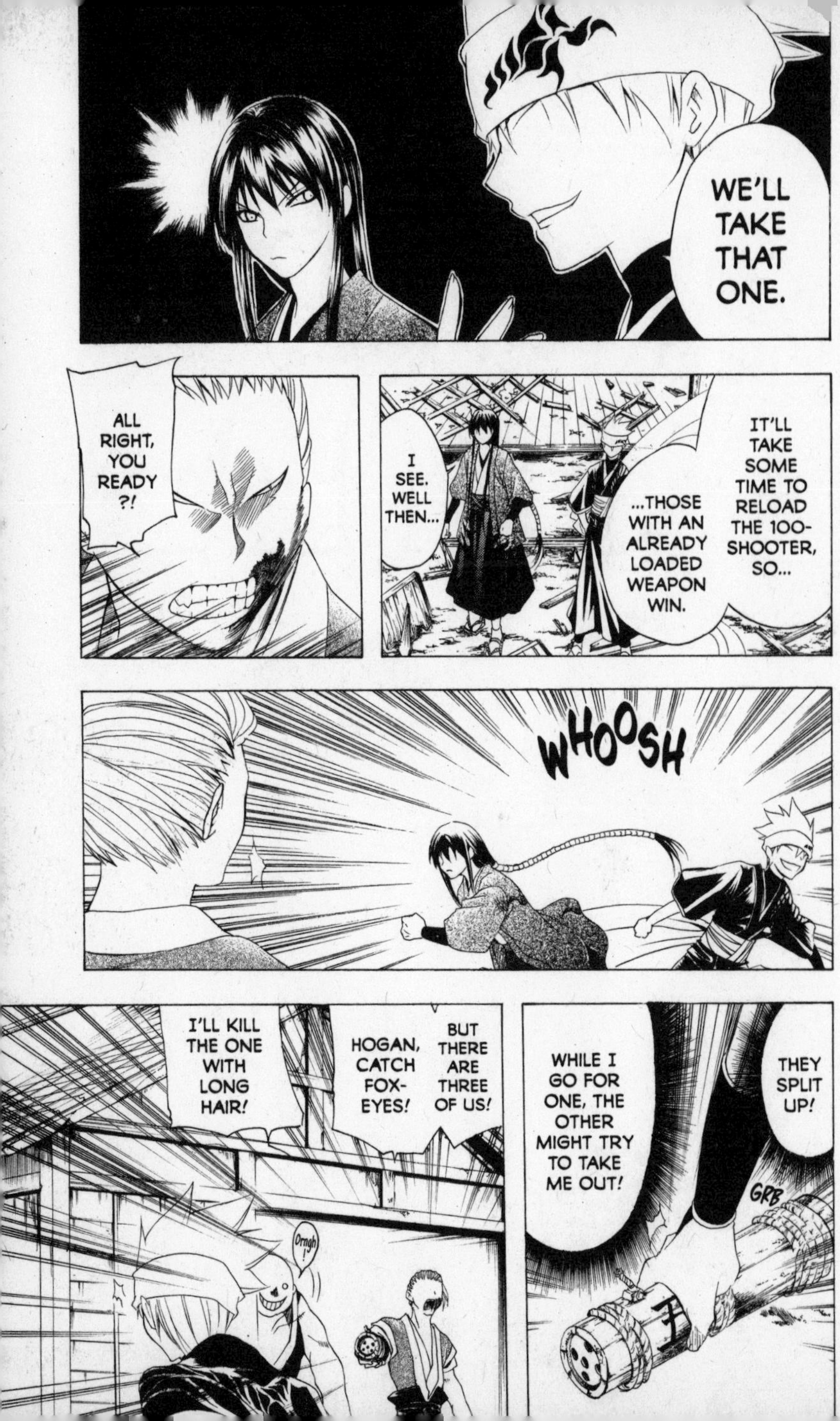
WE'LL TAKE THAT ONE.
IT'LL TAKE SOME TIME TO RELOAD THE 100-SHOOTER, SO...
...THOSE WITH AN ALREADY LOADED WEAPON WIN.
I SEE. WELL THEN...
ALL RIGHT, YOU READY ?!
WHOOSH
THEY SPLIT UP!
WHILE I GO FOR ONE, THE OTHER MIGHT TRY TO TAKE ME OUT!
GRB
BUT THERE ARE THREE OF US!
HOGAN, CATCH FOX-EYES!
I'LL KILL THE ONE WITH LONG HAIR!
Orngh!

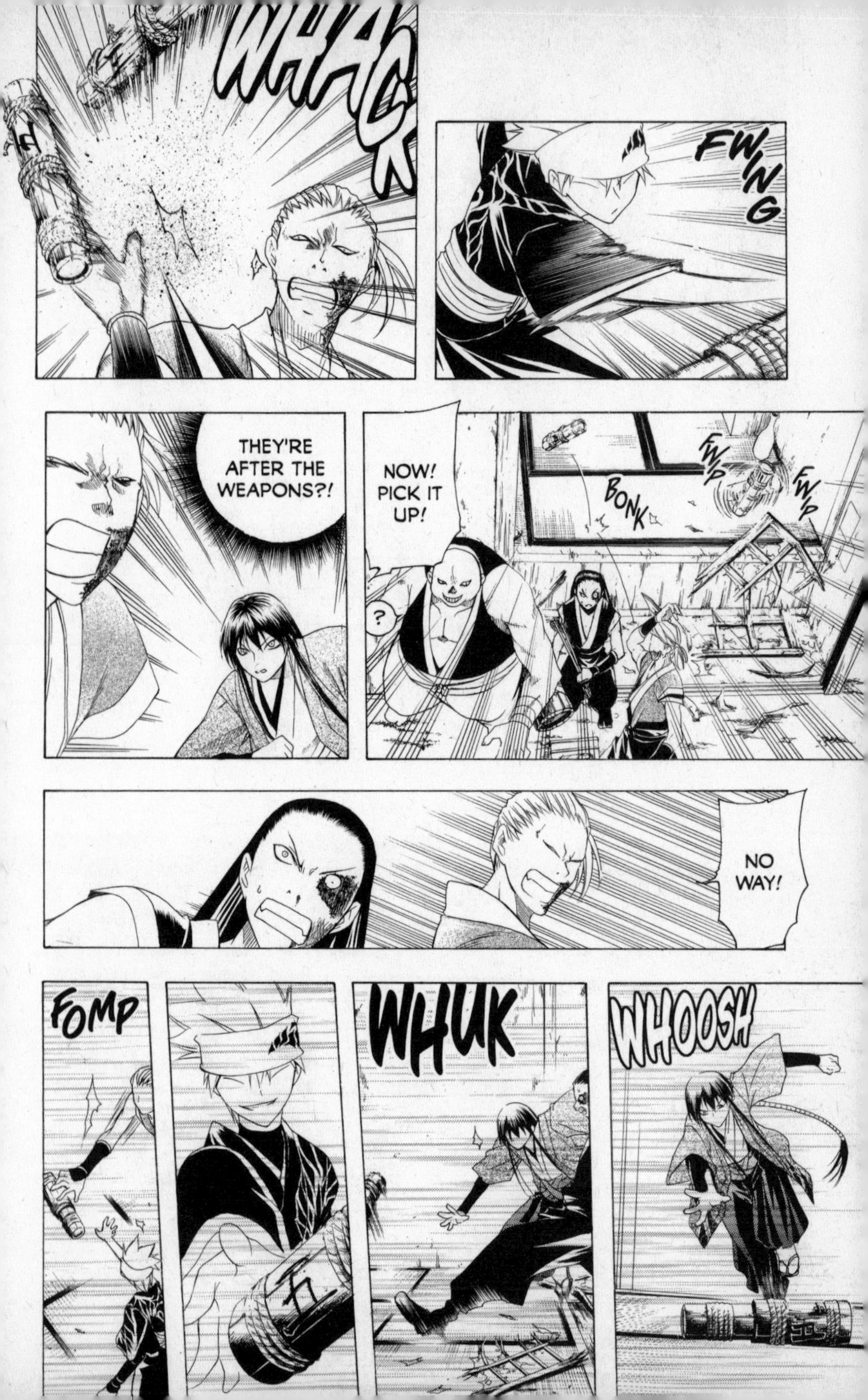
FWING
WHACK
FWIP
FWIP
BONK
NOW! PICK IT UP!
?
THEY'RE AFTER THE WEAPONS?!
NO WAY!
WHOOSH
WHUK
FOMP

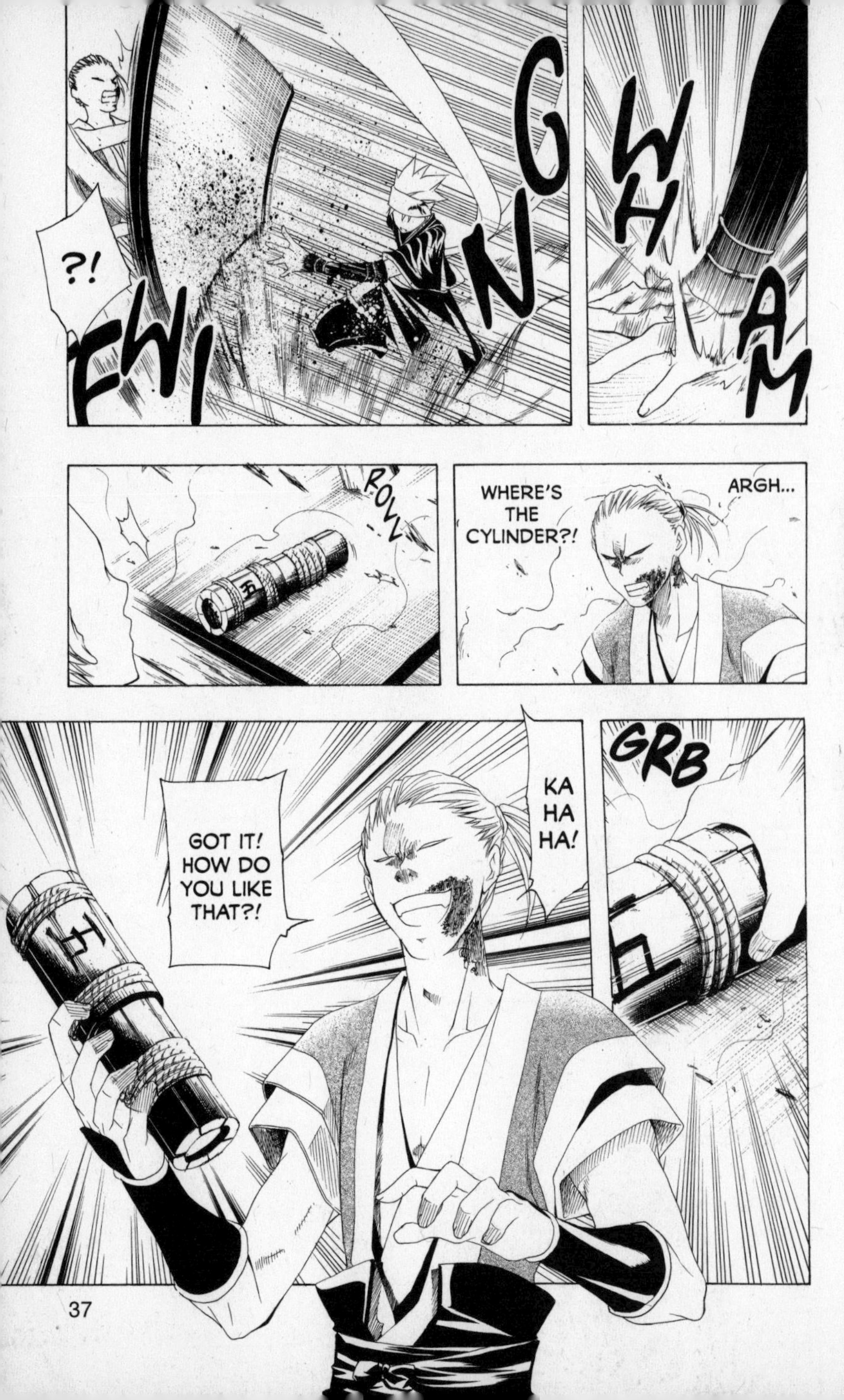
WHAM
?!
FWING
ARGH...
WHERE'S THE CYLINDER?!
ROLL
GRB
KA HA HA!
GOT IT! HOW DO YOU LIKE THAT?!

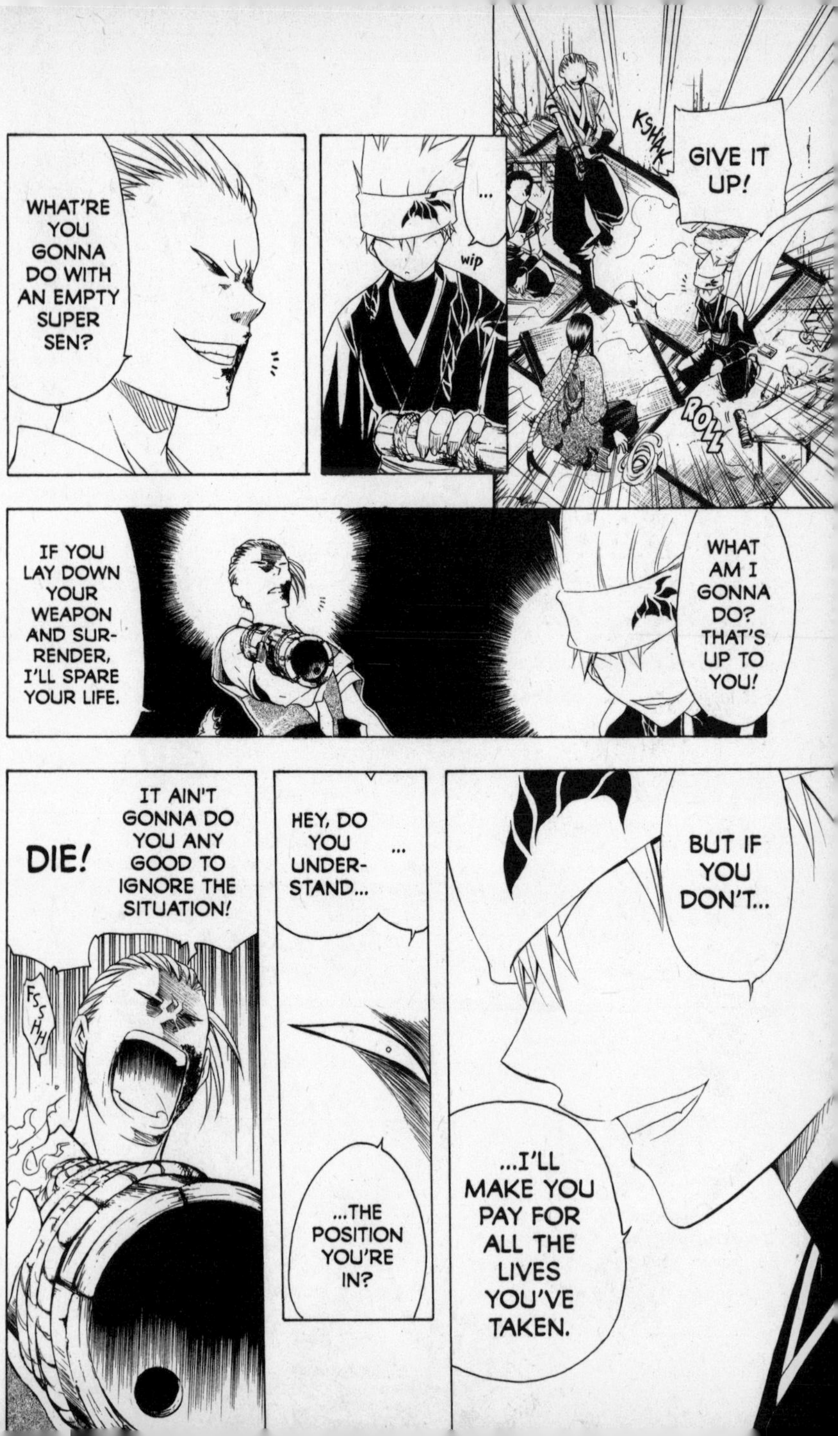
KSHAK
GIVE IT UP!
ROLL
...
wip
WHAT'RE YOU GONNA DO WITH AN EMPTY SUPER SEN?
WHAT AM I GONNA DO? THAT'S UP TO YOU!
IF YOU LAY DOWN YOUR WEAPON AND SUR-RENDER, I'LL SPARE YOUR LIFE.
BUT IF YOU DON'T...
...I'LL MAKE YOU PAY FOR ALL THE LIVES YOU'VE TAKEN.
HEY, DO YOU UNDER-STAND...
...
...THE POSITION YOU'RE IN?
IT AIN'T GONNA DO YOU ANY GOOD TO IGNORE THE SITUATION!
DIE!
FSSHH

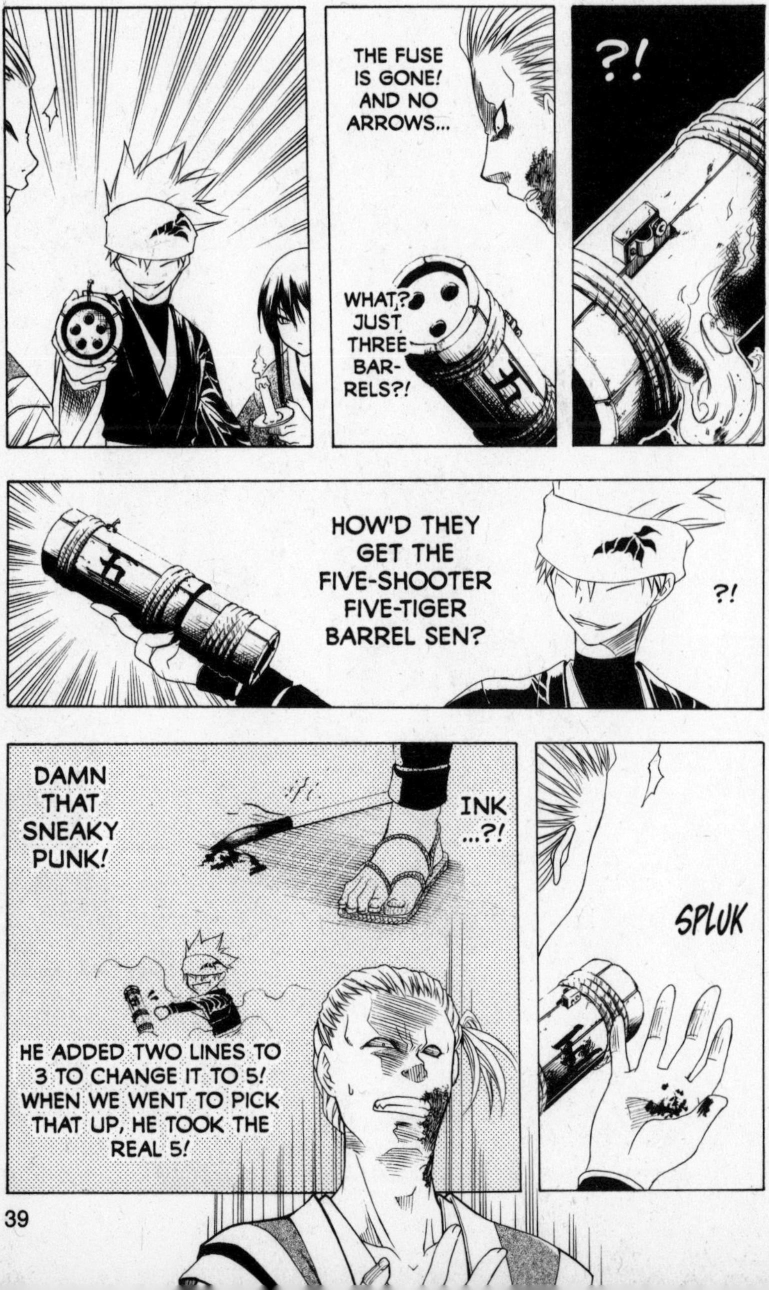
?!
THE FUSE IS GONE! AND NO ARROWS...
WHAT?! JUST THREE BARRELS?!
HOW'D THEY GET THE FIVE-SHOOTER FIVE-TIGER BARREL SEN?
?!
SPLUK
INK ...?!
DAMN THAT SNEAKY PUNK!
HE ADDED TWO LINES TO 3 TO CHANGE IT TO 5! WHEN WE WENT TO PICK THAT UP, HE TOOK THE REAL 5!

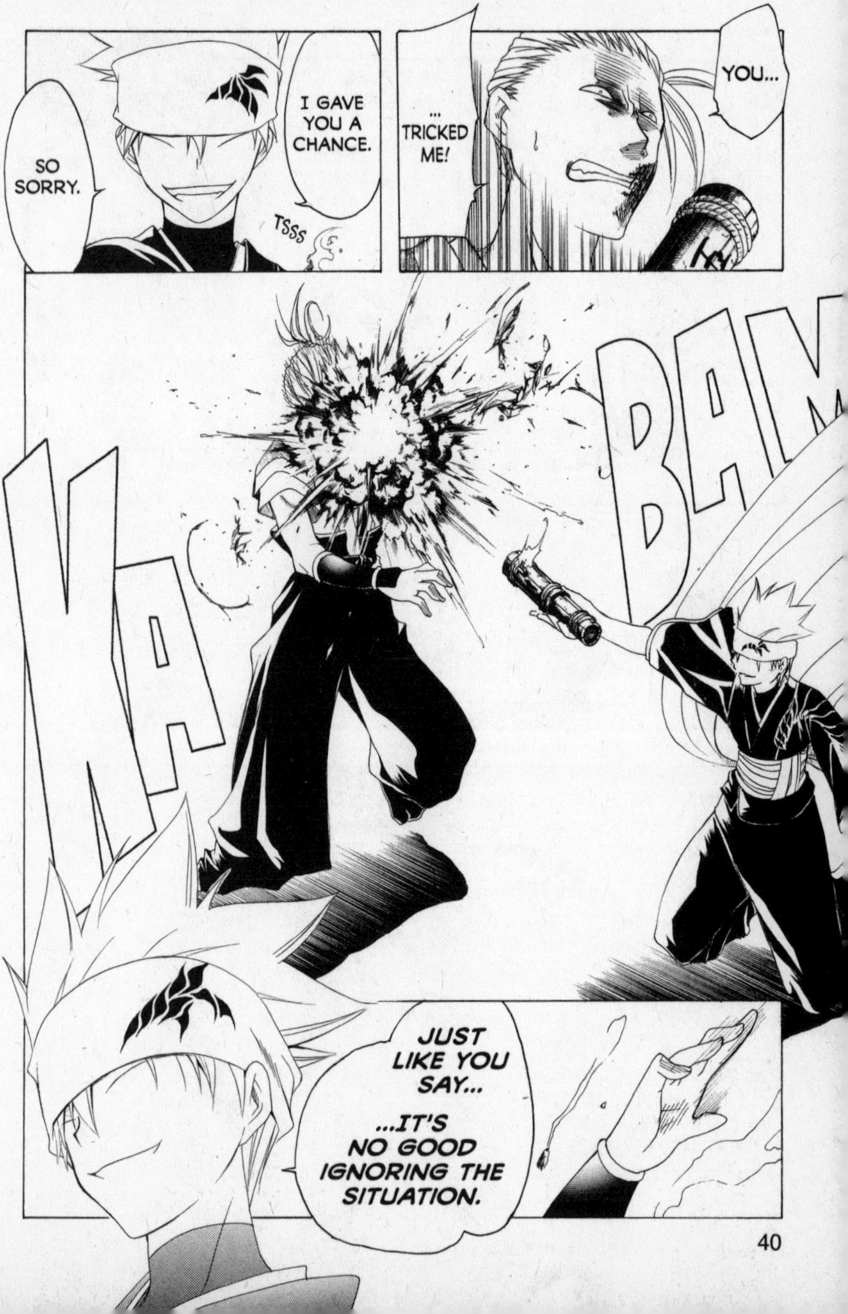
YOU...
...TRICKED ME!
I GAVE YOU A CHANCE.
SO SORRY.
TSSS
BAM
KA
JUST LIKE YOU SAY...
...IT'S NO GOOD IGNORING THE SITUATION.

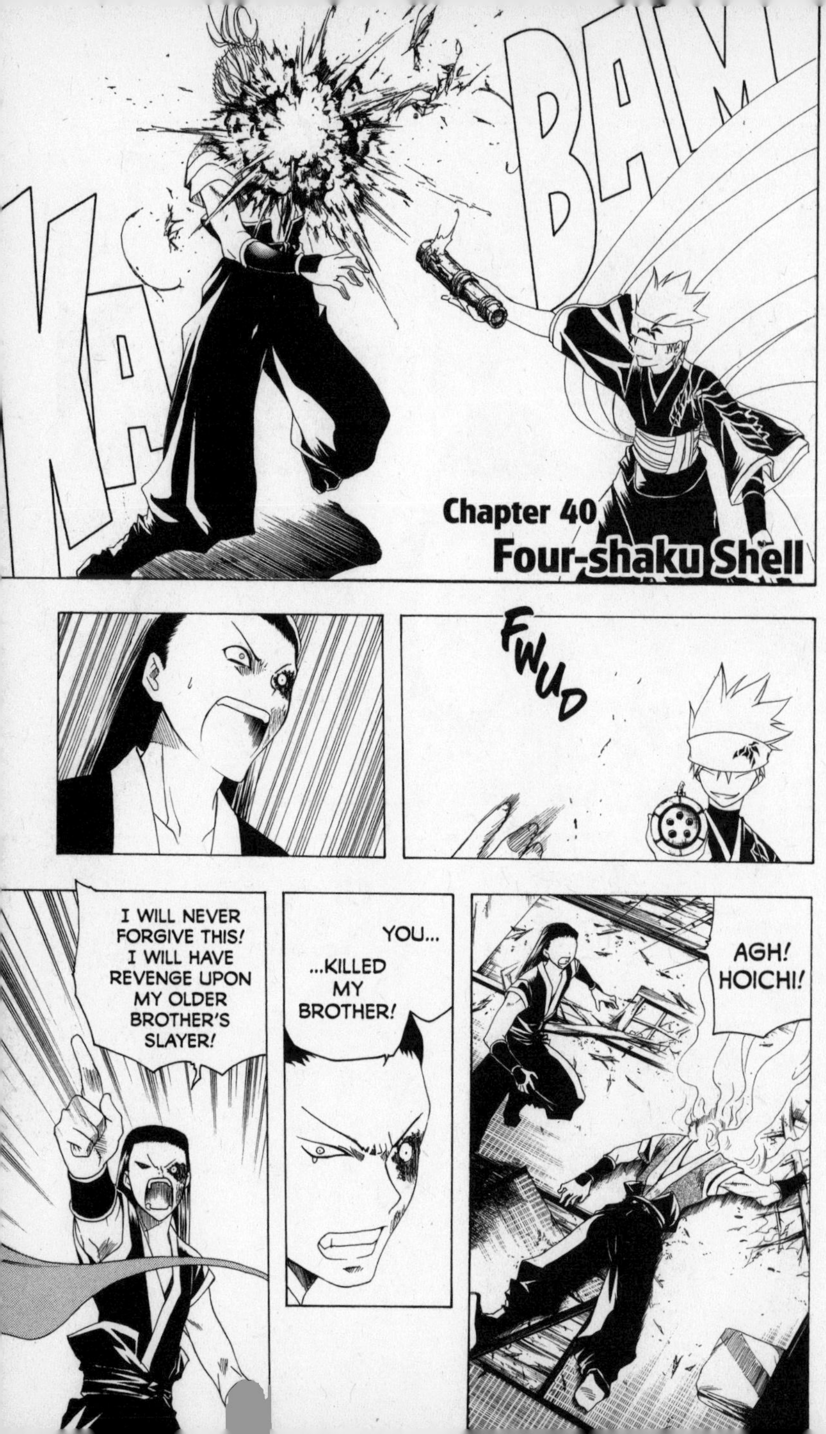
BAM
Chapter 40
Four-shaku Shell
FWUD
AGH! HOICHI!
YOU...
...KILLED MY BROTHER!
I WILL NEVER FORGIVE THIS! I WILL HAVE REVENGE UPON MY OLDER BROTHER'S SLAYER!

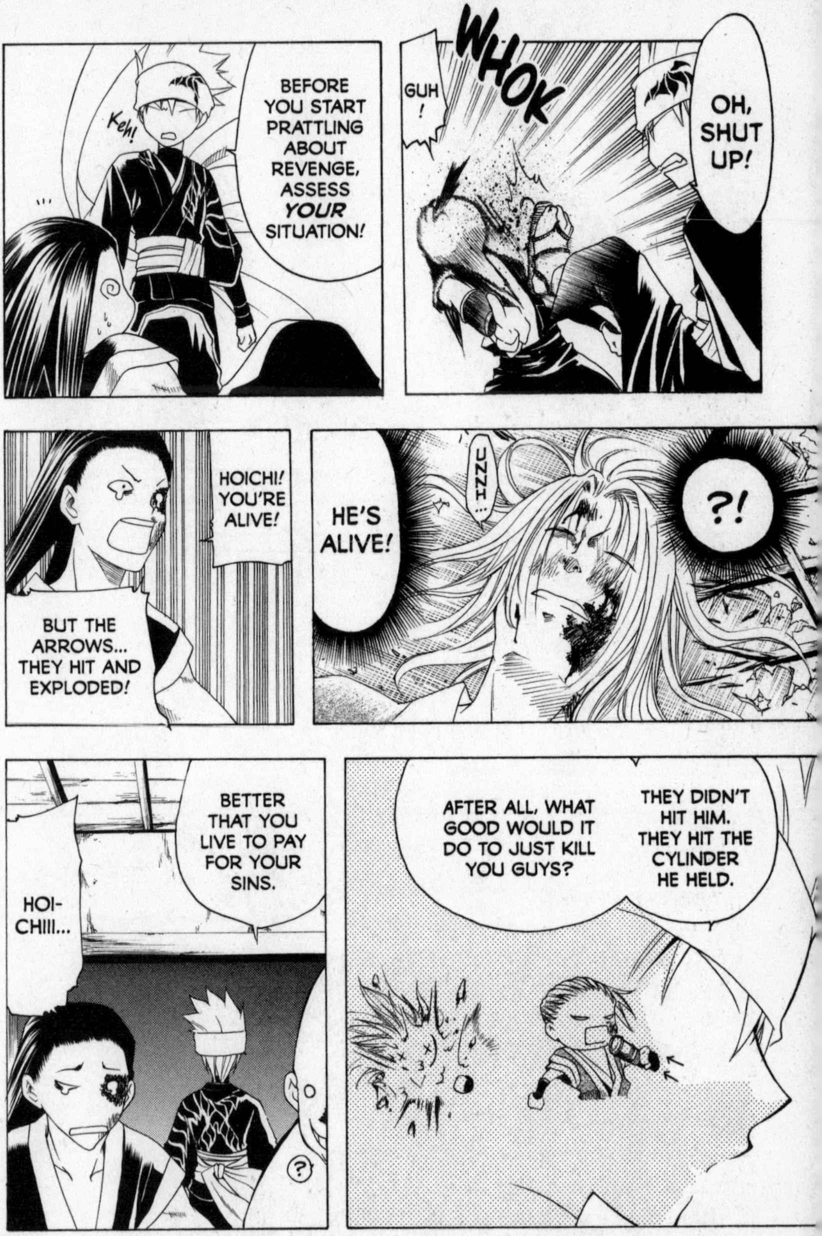
OH, SHUT UP!
WHOK
GUH!
Keh!
BEFORE YOU START PRATTLING ABOUT REVENGE, ASSESS *YOUR* SITUATION!
?!
UNNH...
HE'S ALIVE!
HOICHI! YOU'RE ALIVE!
BUT THE ARROWS... THEY HIT AND EXPLODED!
THEY DIDN'T HIT HIM. THEY HIT THE CYLINDER HE HELD.
AFTER ALL, WHAT GOOD WOULD IT DO TO JUST KILL YOU GUYS?
BETTER THAT YOU LIVE TO PAY FOR YOUR SINS.
HOI-CHIII...
?

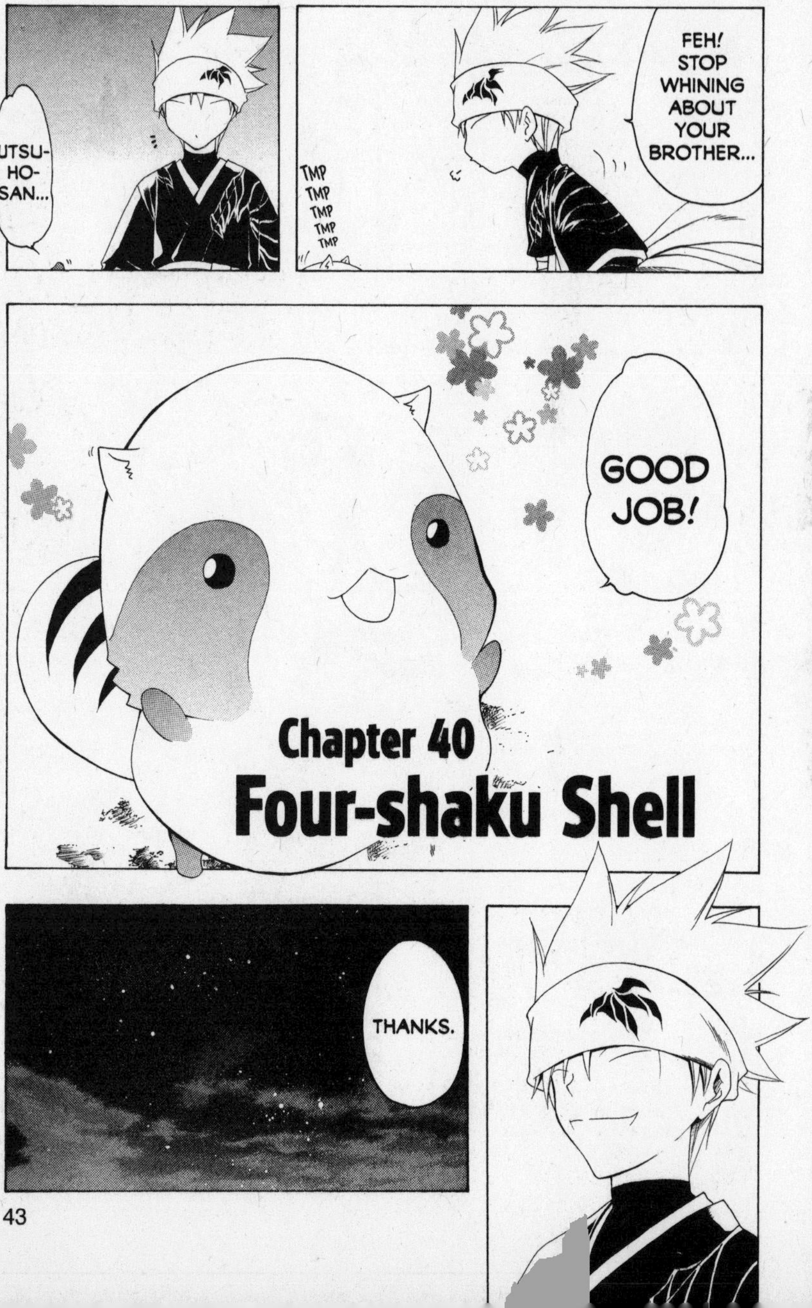
FEH! STOP WHINING ABOUT YOUR BROTHER...
TMP TMP TMP TMP TMP
UTSU-HO-SAN...
GOOD JOB!
Chapter 40
Four-shaku Shell
THANKS.

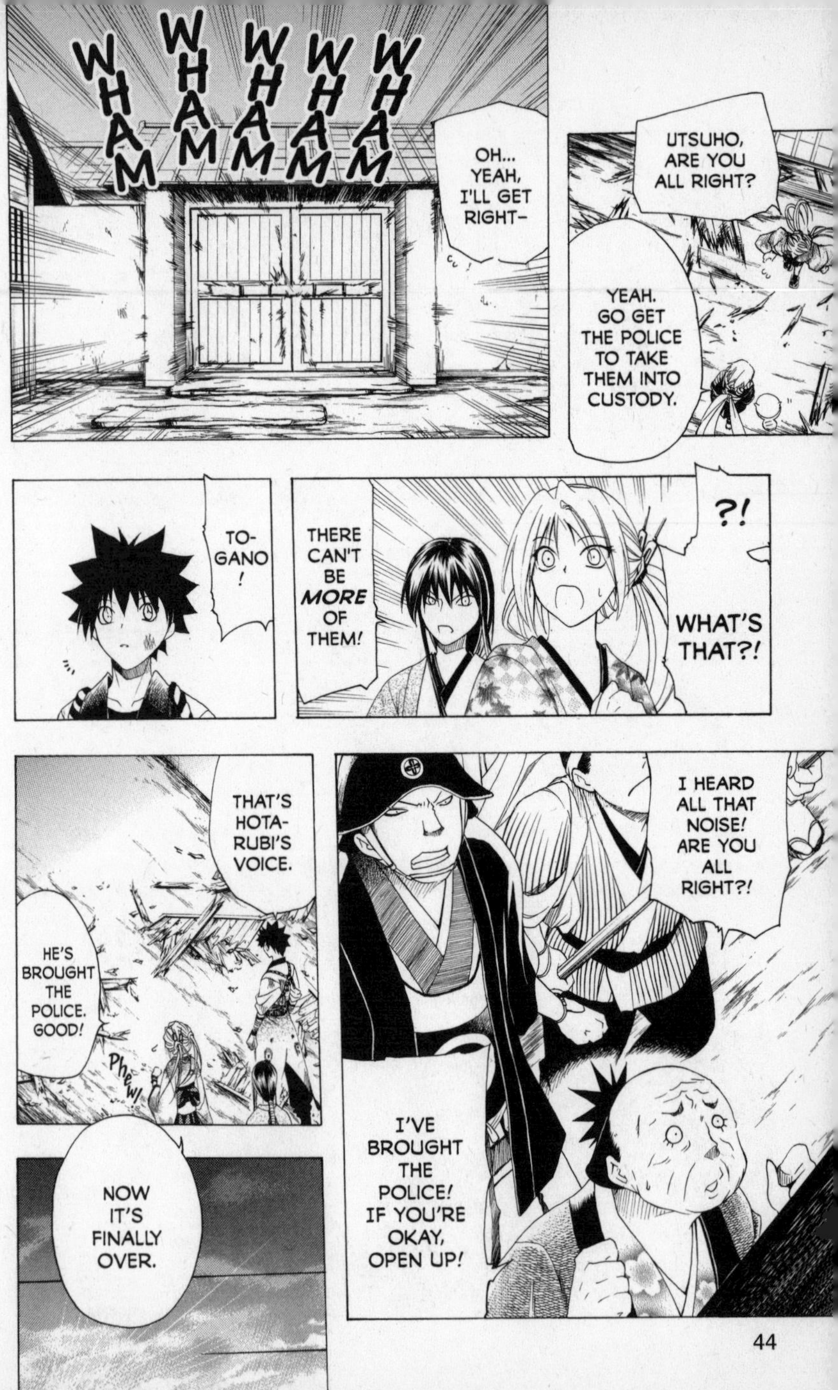
UTSUHO, ARE YOU ALL RIGHT?
YEAH. GO GET THE POLICE TO TAKE THEM INTO CUSTODY.
OH... YEAH, I'LL GET RIGHT–
WHAM
WHAM
WHAM
WHAM
WHAM
?!
WHAT'S THAT?!
THERE CAN'T BE *MORE* OF THEM!
TO-GANO!
I HEARD ALL THAT NOISE! ARE YOU ALL RIGHT?!
I'VE BROUGHT THE POLICE! IF YOU'RE OKAY, OPEN UP!
THAT'S HOTA-RUBI'S VOICE.
HE'S BROUGHT THE POLICE. GOOD!
Phew!
NOW IT'S FINALLY OVER.

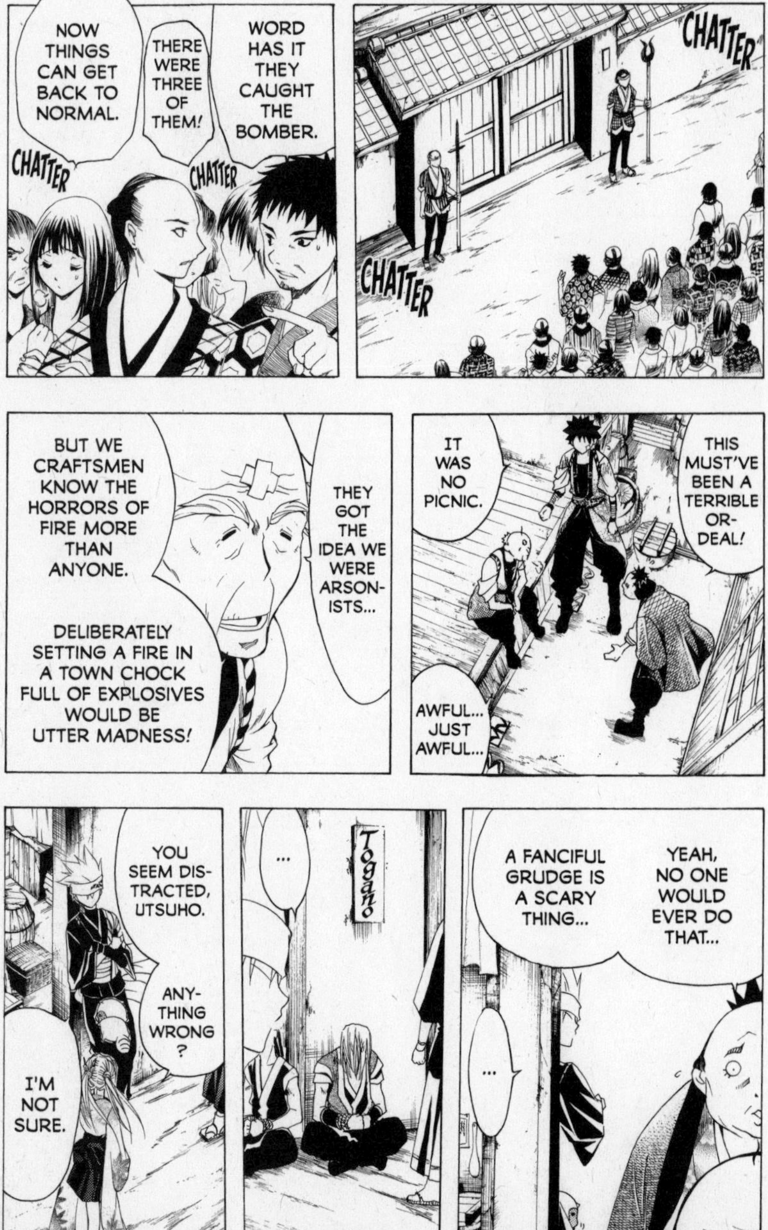
CHATTER
CHATTER
WORD HAS IT THEY CAUGHT THE BOMBER.
THERE WERE THREE OF THEM!
NOW THINGS CAN GET BACK TO NORMAL.
CHATTER
CHATTER
THIS MUST'VE BEEN A TERRIBLE OR-DEAL!
IT WAS NO PICNIC.
AWFUL... JUST AWFUL...
THEY GOT THE IDEA WE WERE ARSON-ISTS...
BUT WE CRAFTSMEN KNOW THE HORRORS OF FIRE MORE THAN ANYONE.
DELIBERATELY SETTING A FIRE IN A TOWN CHOCK FULL OF EXPLOSIVES WOULD BE UTTER MADNESS!
YEAH, NO ONE WOULD EVER DO THAT...
A FANCIFUL GRUDGE IS A SCARY THING...
...
Togano
...
YOU SEEM DIS-TRACTED, UTSUHO.
ANY-THING WRONG?
I'M NOT SURE.

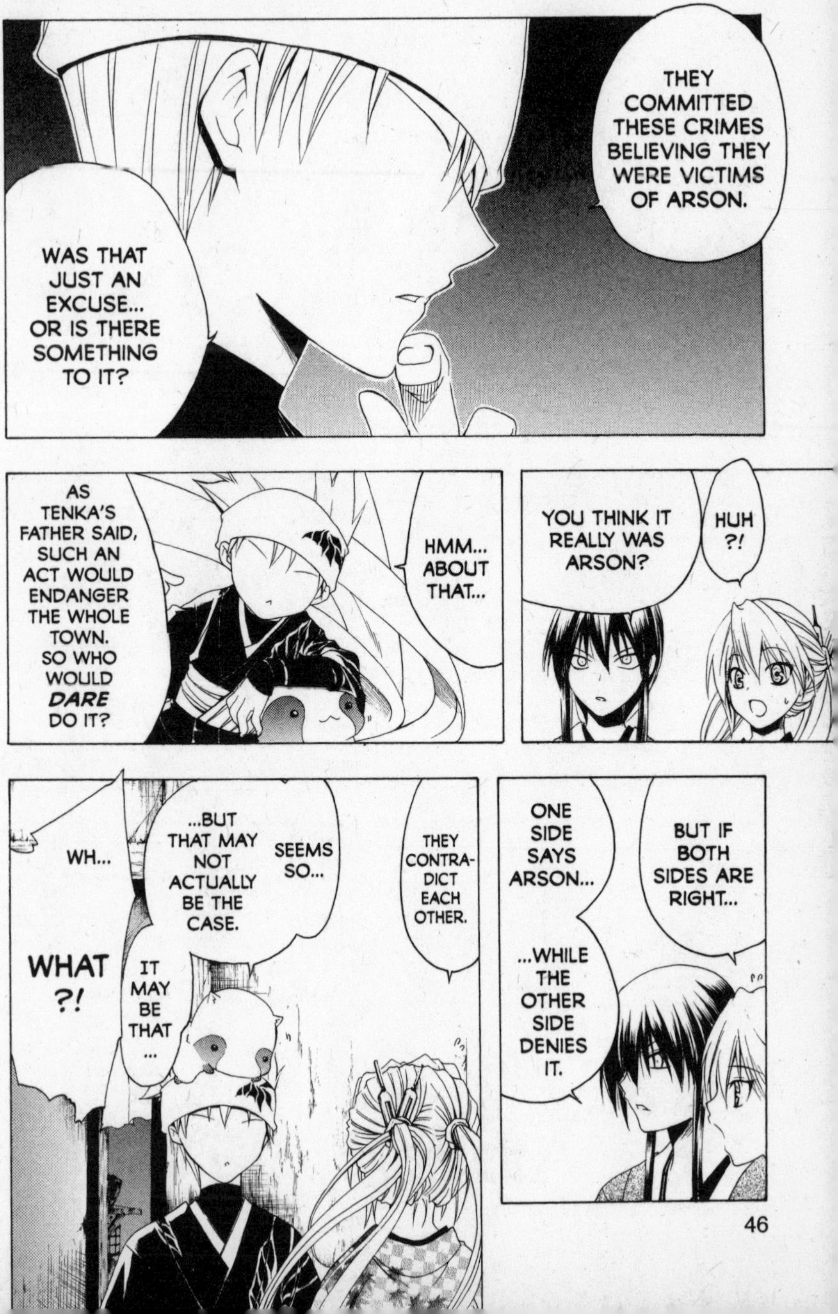
THEY COMMITTED THESE CRIMES BELIEVING THEY WERE VICTIMS OF ARSON.
WAS THAT JUST AN EXCUSE... OR IS THERE SOMETHING TO IT?
HUH?!
YOU THINK IT REALLY WAS ARSON?
HMM... ABOUT THAT...
AS TENKA'S FATHER SAID, SUCH AN ACT WOULD ENDANGER THE WHOLE TOWN. SO WHO WOULD *DARE* DO IT?
BUT IF BOTH SIDES ARE RIGHT...
ONE SIDE SAYS ARSON...
...WHILE THE OTHER SIDE DENIES IT.
THEY CONTRA-DICT EACH OTHER.
SEEMS SO...
...BUT THAT MAY NOT ACTUALLY BE THE CASE.
WH...
IT MAY BE THAT ...
WHAT?!

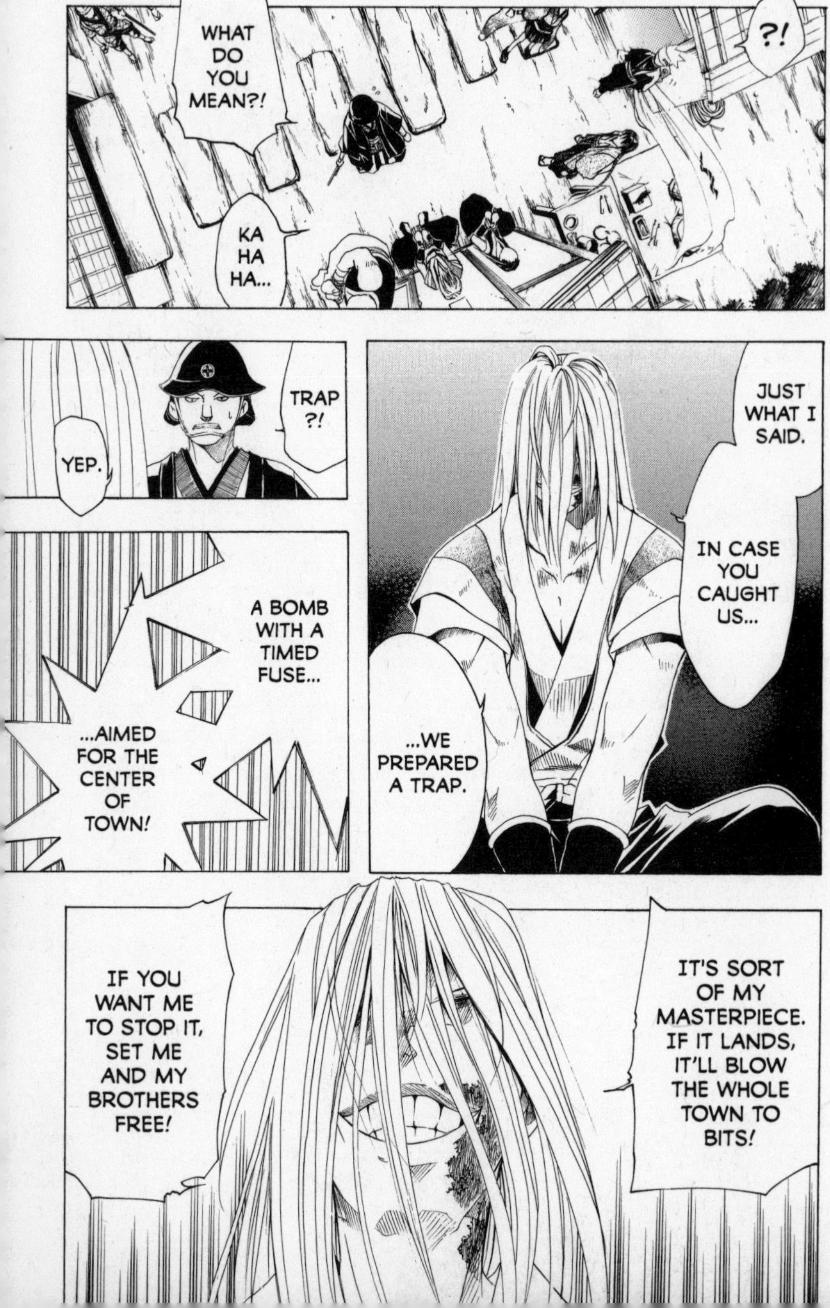
?!
WHAT DO YOU MEAN?!
KA HA HA...
JUST WHAT I SAID.
IN CASE YOU CAUGHT US...
...WE PREPARED A TRAP.
TRAP?!
YEP.
A BOMB WITH A TIMED FUSE...
...AIMED FOR THE CENTER OF TOWN!
IT'S SORT OF MY MASTERPIECE. IF IT LANDS, IT'LL BLOW THE WHOLE TOWN TO BITS!
IF YOU WANT ME TO STOP IT, SET ME AND MY BROTHERS FREE!

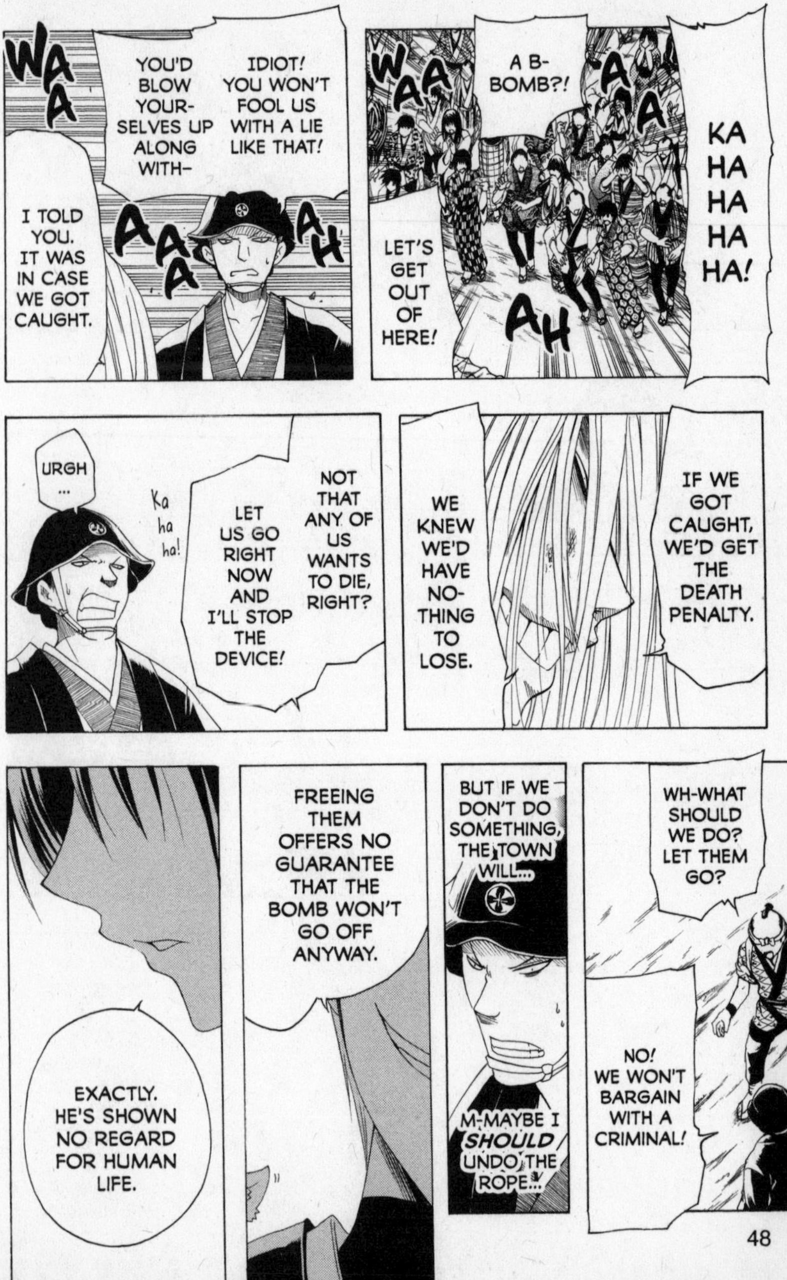
KA HA HA HA HA!
A B-BOMB?!
AAA
WAA
LET'S GET OUT OF HERE!
AH
IDIOT! YOU WON'T FOOL US WITH A LIE LIKE THAT!
YOU'D BLOW YOURSELVES UP ALONG WITH—
WAA
AH
AAA
I TOLD YOU. IT WAS IN CASE WE GOT CAUGHT.
IF WE GOT CAUGHT, WE'D GET THE DEATH PENALTY.
WE KNEW WE'D HAVE NOTHING TO LOSE.
NOT THAT ANY OF US WANTS TO DIE, RIGHT?
LET US GO RIGHT NOW AND I'LL STOP THE DEVICE!
Ka ha ha!
URGH ...
WH-WHAT SHOULD WE DO? LET THEM GO?
NO! WE WON'T BARGAIN WITH A CRIMINAL!
BUT IF WE DON'T DO SOMETHING, THE TOWN WILL...
M-MAYBE I *SHOULD* UNDO THE ROPE...
FREEING THEM OFFERS NO GUARANTEE THAT THE BOMB WON'T GO OFF ANYWAY.
EXACTLY. HE'S SHOWN NO REGARD FOR HUMAN LIFE.

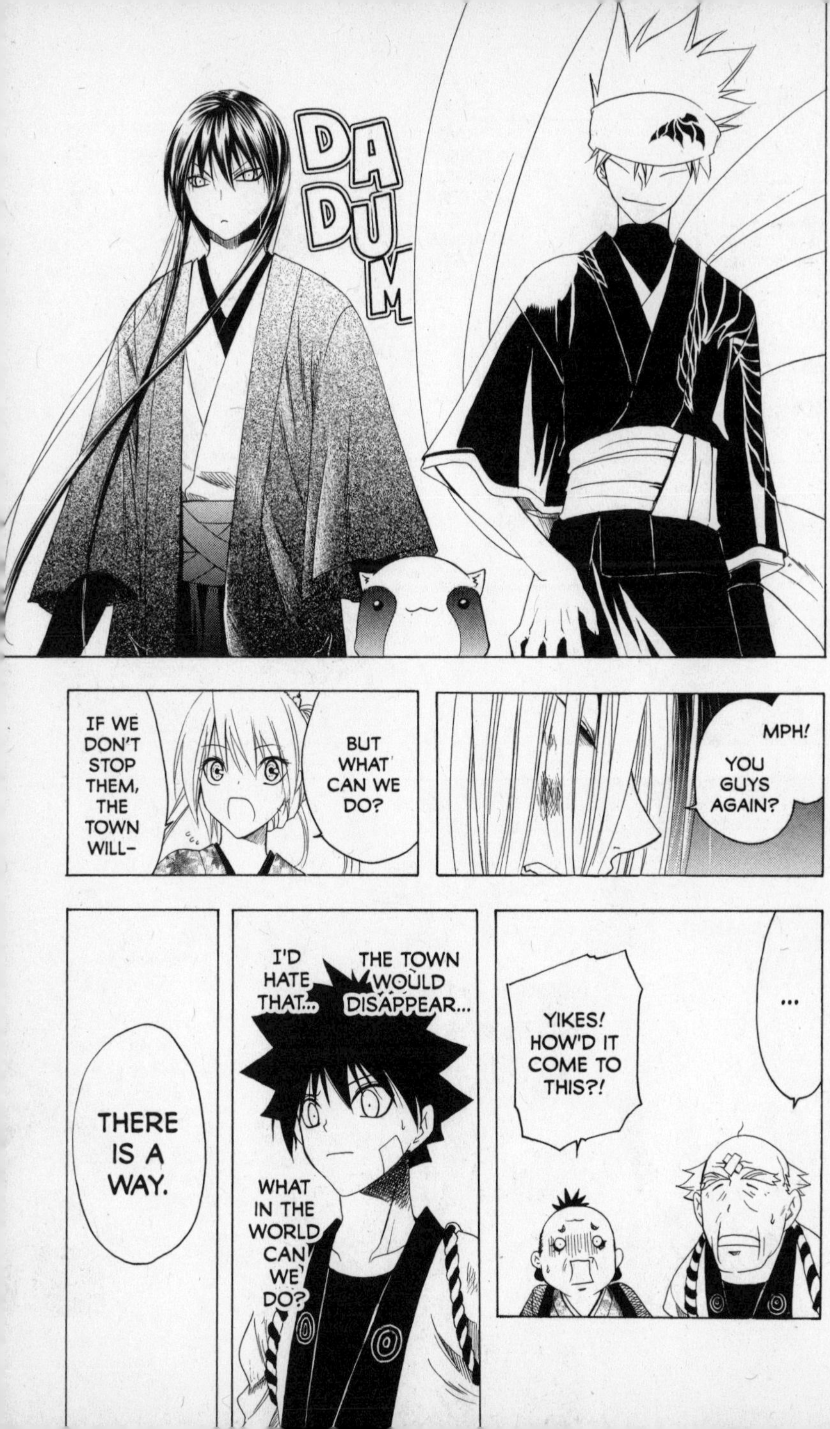
DA DUM
MPH! YOU GUYS AGAIN?
BUT WHAT CAN WE DO?
IF WE DON'T STOP THEM, THE TOWN WILL-
...
YIKES! HOW'D IT COME TO THIS?!
THE TOWN WOULD DISAPPEAR...
I'D HATE THAT...
WHAT IN THE WORLD CAN WE DO?
THERE IS A WAY.

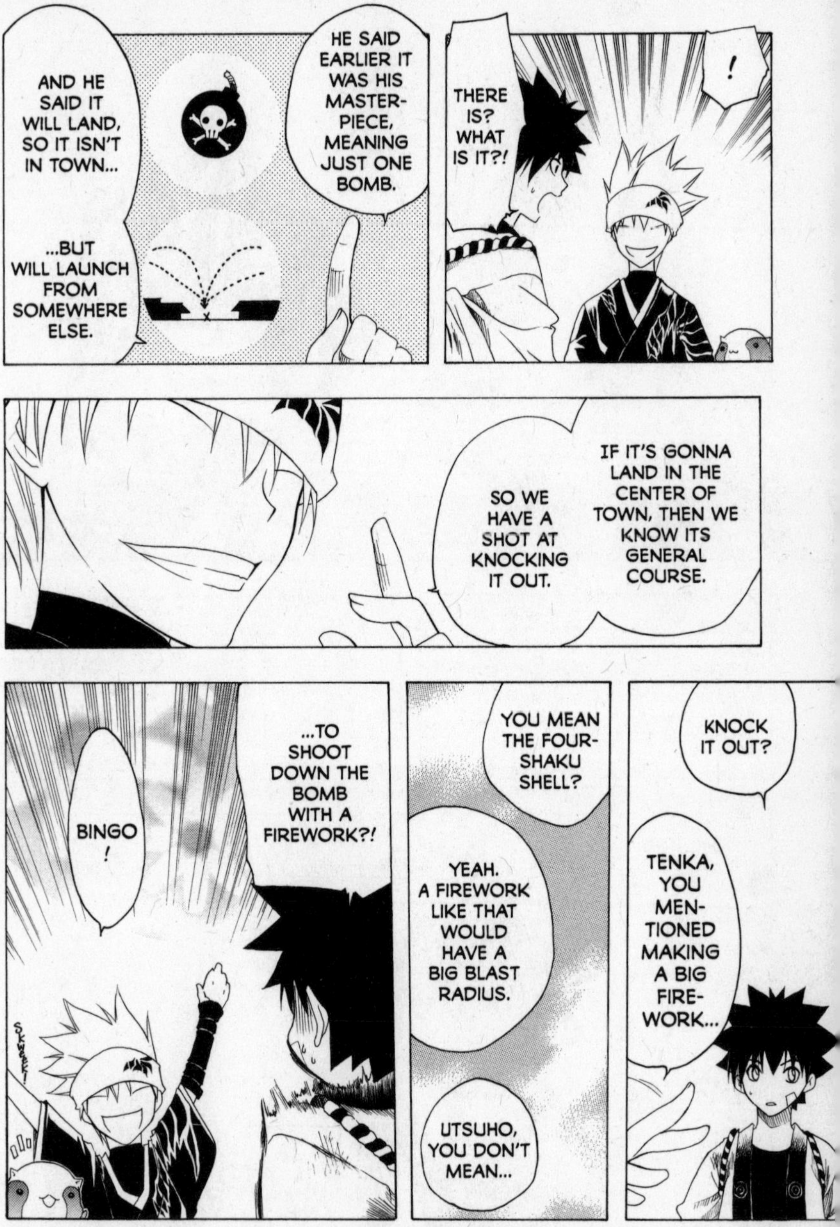
!
THERE IS? WHAT IS IT?!
HE SAID EARLIER IT WAS HIS MASTER-PIECE, MEANING JUST ONE BOMB.
AND HE SAID IT WILL LAND, SO IT ISN'T IN TOWN...
...BUT WILL LAUNCH FROM SOMEWHERE ELSE.
IF IT'S GONNA LAND IN THE CENTER OF TOWN, THEN WE KNOW ITS GENERAL COURSE.
SO WE HAVE A SHOT AT KNOCKING IT OUT.
KNOCK IT OUT?
TENKA, YOU MEN-TIONED MAKING A BIG FIRE-WORK...
YOU MEAN THE FOUR-SHAKU SHELL?
YEAH. A FIREWORK LIKE THAT WOULD HAVE A BIG BLAST RADIUS.
UTSUHO, YOU DON'T MEAN...
...TO SHOOT DOWN THE BOMB WITH A FIREWORK?!
BINGO!
SKWEEK!

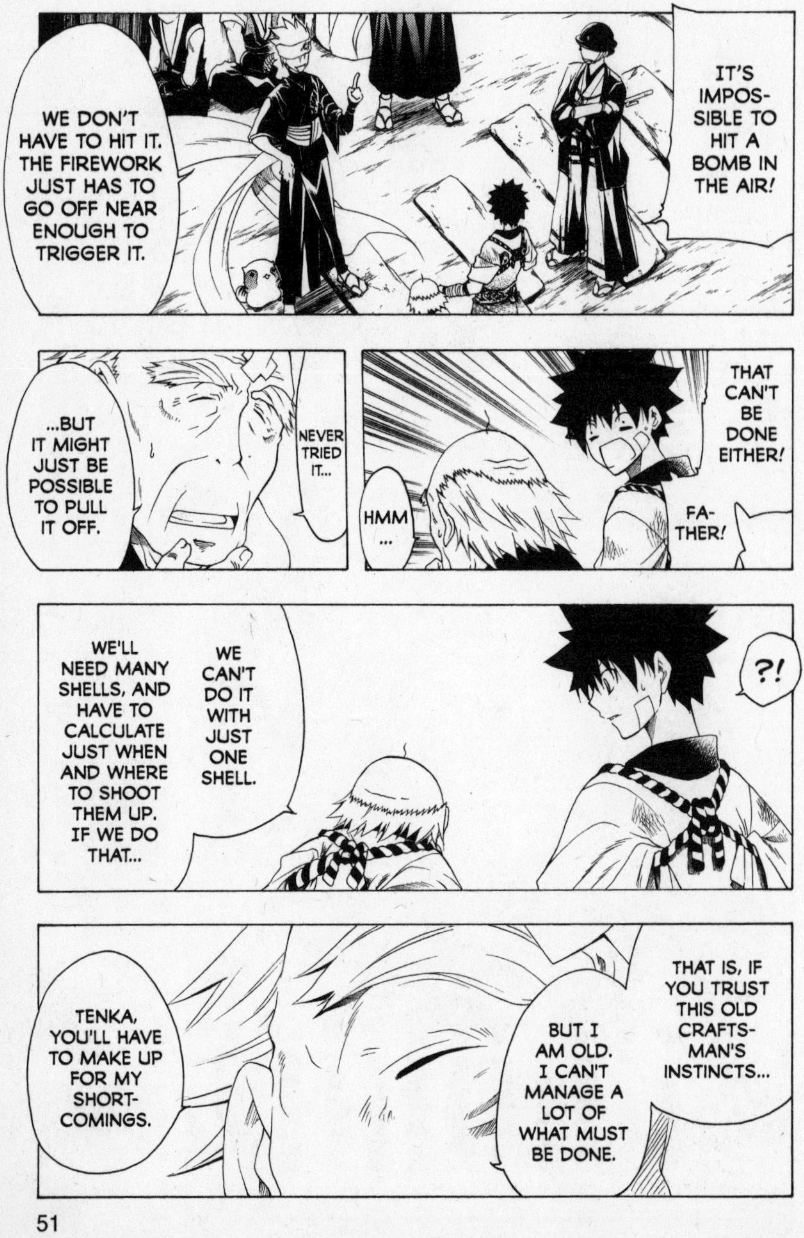
IT'S IMPOSSIBLE TO HIT A BOMB IN THE AIR!
WE DON'T HAVE TO HIT IT. THE FIREWORK JUST HAS TO GO OFF NEAR ENOUGH TO TRIGGER IT.
THAT CAN'T BE DONE EITHER!
FATHER!
HMM...
NEVER TRIED IT...
...BUT IT MIGHT JUST BE POSSIBLE TO PULL IT OFF.
?!
WE CAN'T DO IT WITH JUST ONE SHELL.
WE'LL NEED MANY SHELLS, AND HAVE TO CALCULATE JUST WHEN AND WHERE TO SHOOT THEM UP. IF WE DO THAT...
THAT IS, IF YOU TRUST THIS OLD CRAFTSMAN'S INSTINCTS...
BUT I AM OLD. I CAN'T MANAGE A LOT OF WHAT MUST BE DONE.
TENKA, YOU'LL HAVE TO MAKE UP FOR MY SHORTCOMINGS.

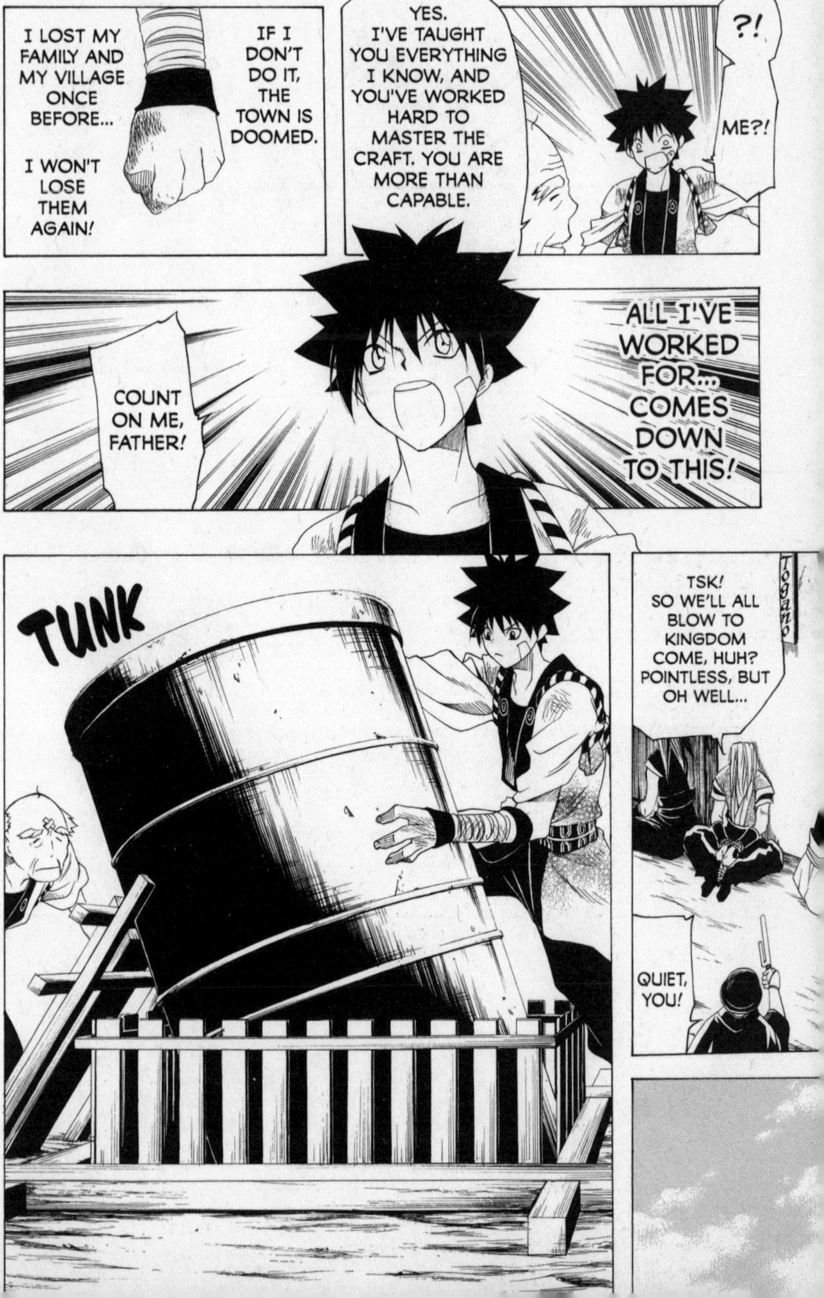
?!
ME?!
YES. I'VE TAUGHT YOU EVERYTHING I KNOW, AND YOU'VE WORKED HARD TO MASTER THE CRAFT. YOU ARE MORE THAN CAPABLE.
IF I DON'T DO IT, THE TOWN IS DOOMED.
I LOST MY FAMILY AND MY VILLAGE ONCE BEFORE...
I WON'T LOSE THEM AGAIN!
ALL I'VE WORKED FOR... COMES DOWN TO THIS!
COUNT ON ME, FATHER!
Togano
TSK! SO WE'LL ALL BLOW TO KINGDOM COME, HUH? POINTLESS, BUT OH WELL...
QUIET, YOU!
TUNK

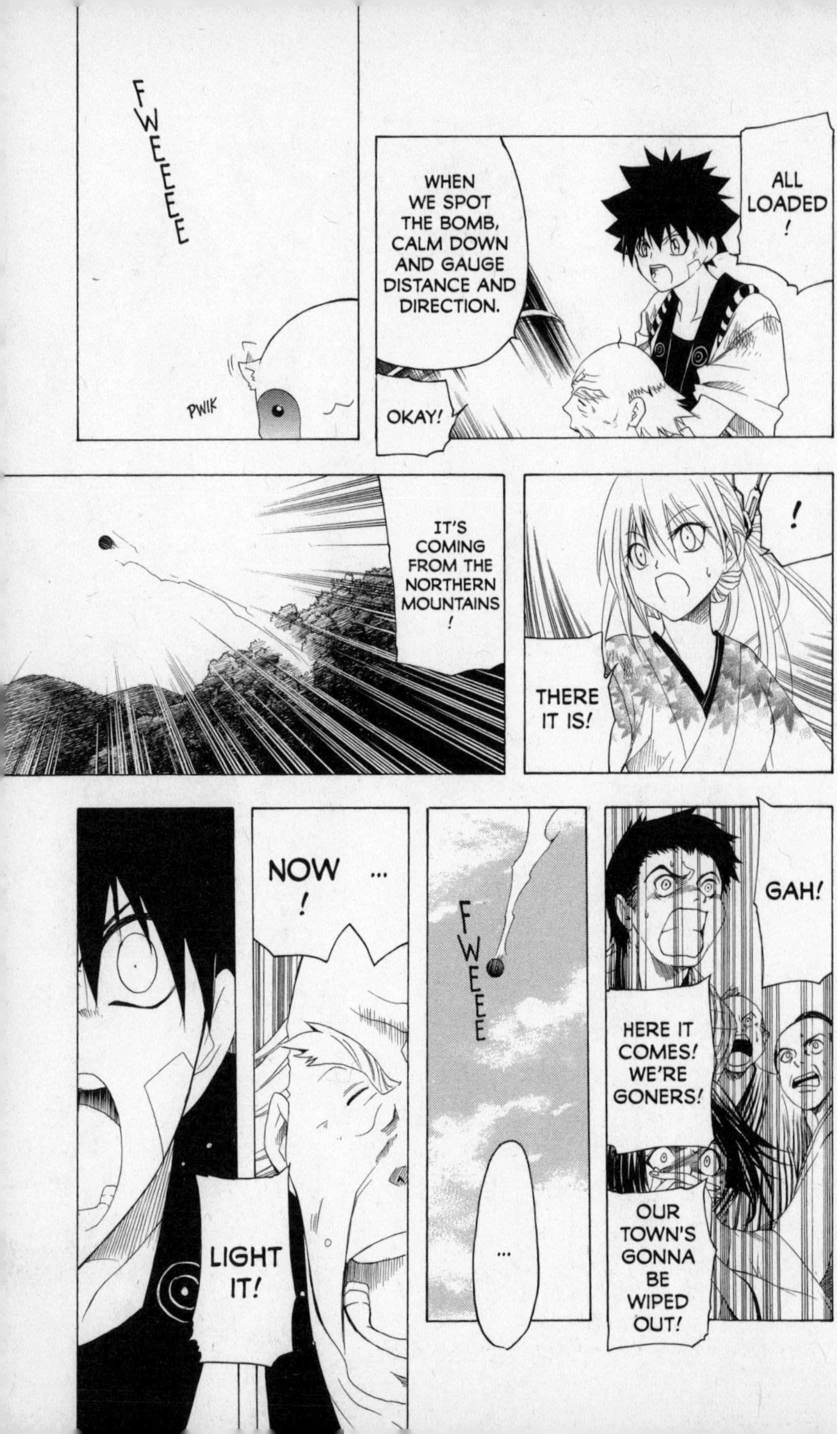
ALL LOADED!
WHEN WE SPOT THE BOMB, CALM DOWN AND GAUGE DISTANCE AND DIRECTION.
OKAY!
FWEEEEE
PWIK
!
THERE IT IS!
IT'S COMING FROM THE NORTHERN MOUNTAINS!
GAH!
HERE IT COMES! WE'RE GONERS!
OUR TOWN'S GONNA BE WIPED OUT!
FWEEE
...
NOW...!
LIGHT IT!

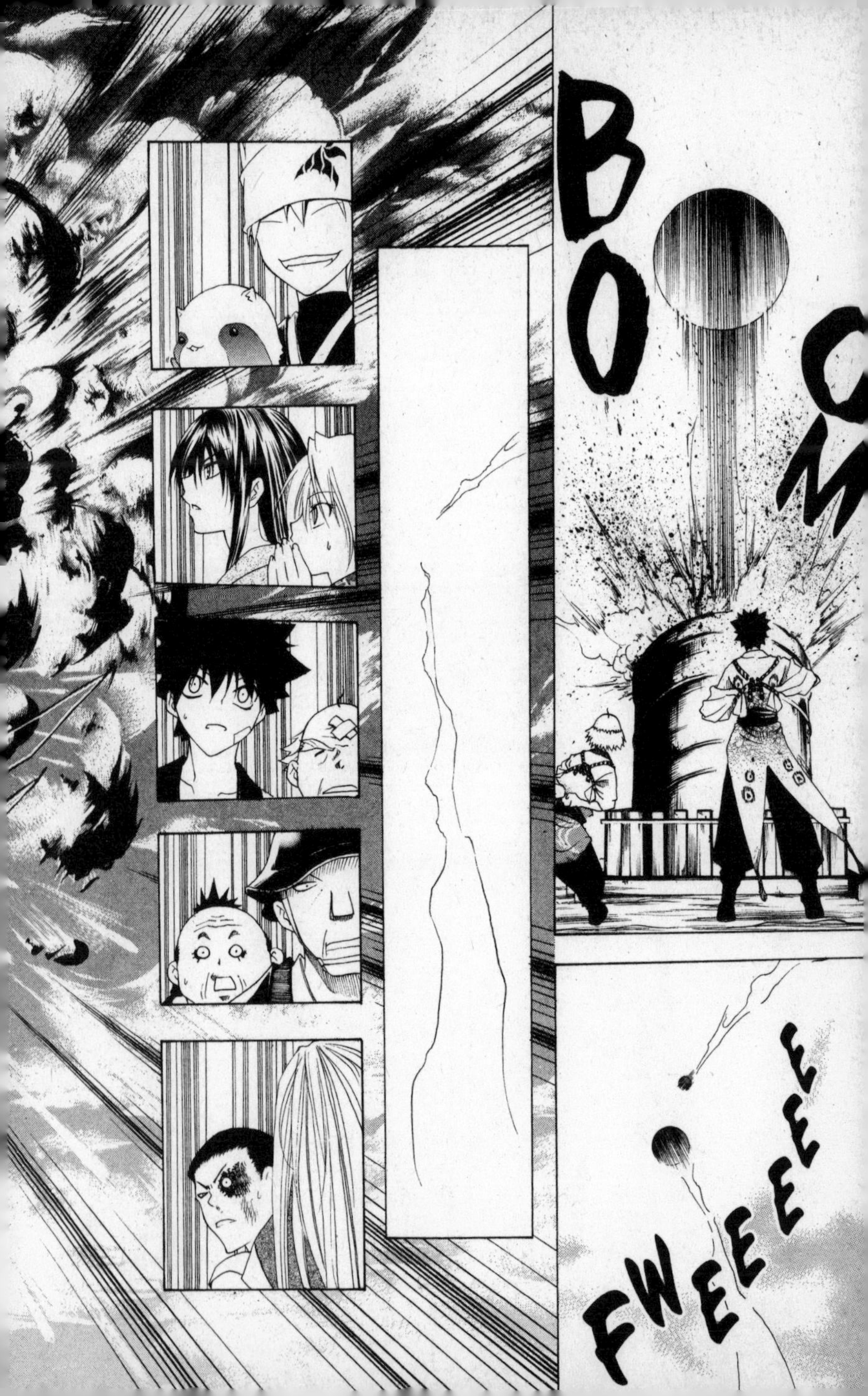
BOOM
FWEEEEEE

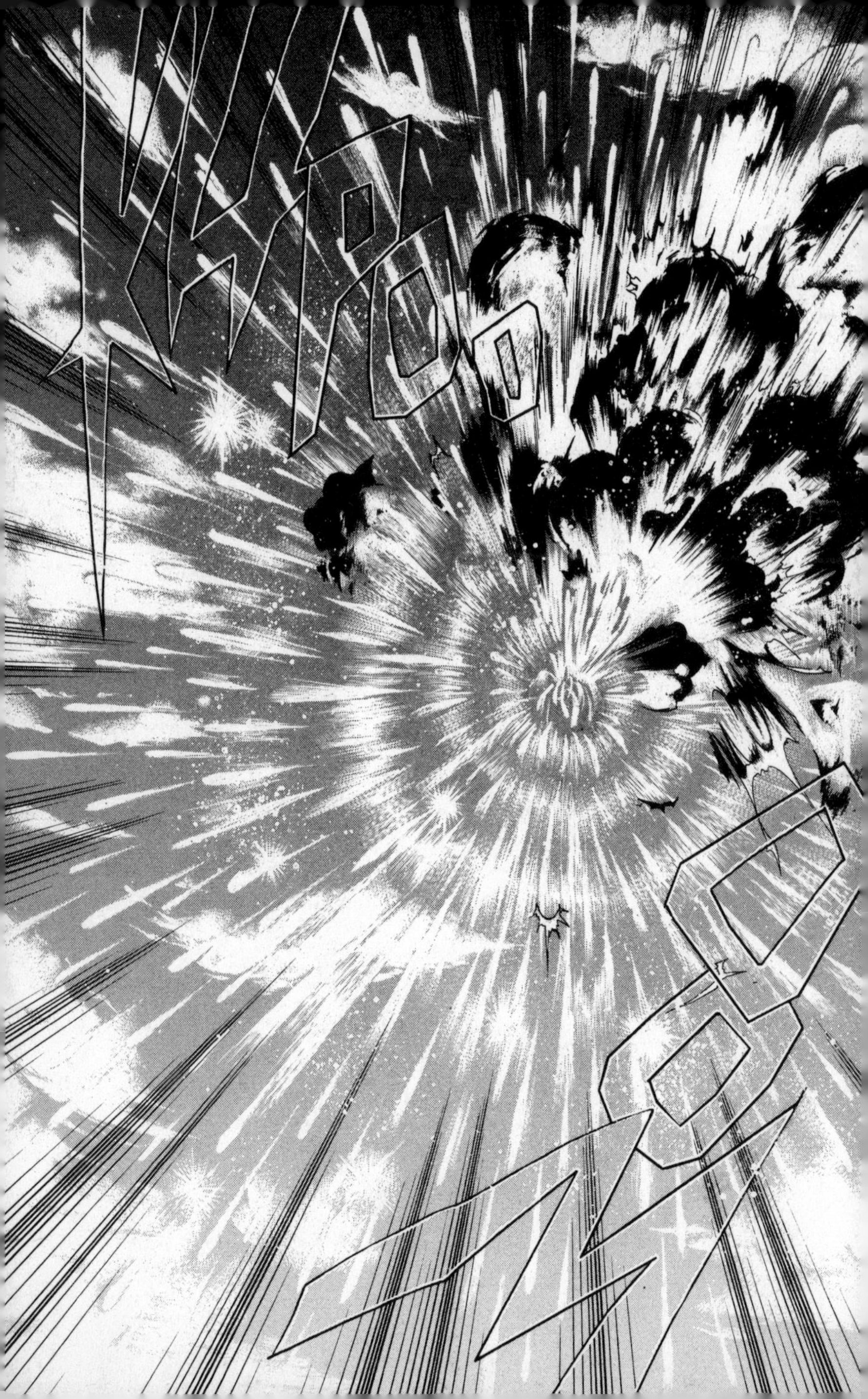

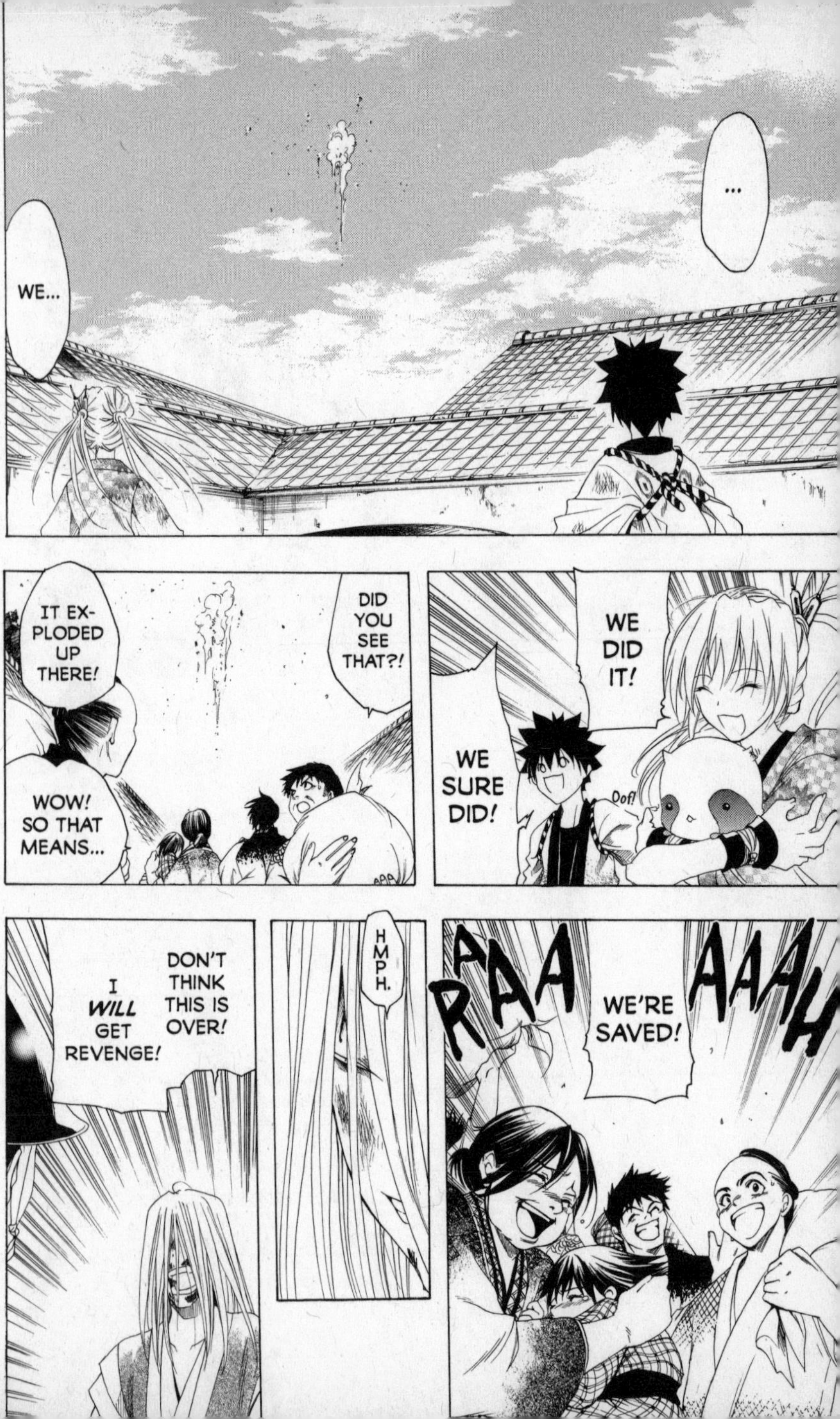
...
WE...
WE DID IT!
WE SURE DID!
Oof!
DID YOU SEE THAT?!
IT EXPLODED UP THERE!
WOW! SO THAT MEANS...
RAAAAAAH
WE'RE SAVED!
HMPH.
DON'T THINK THIS IS OVER!
I *WILL* GET REVENGE!

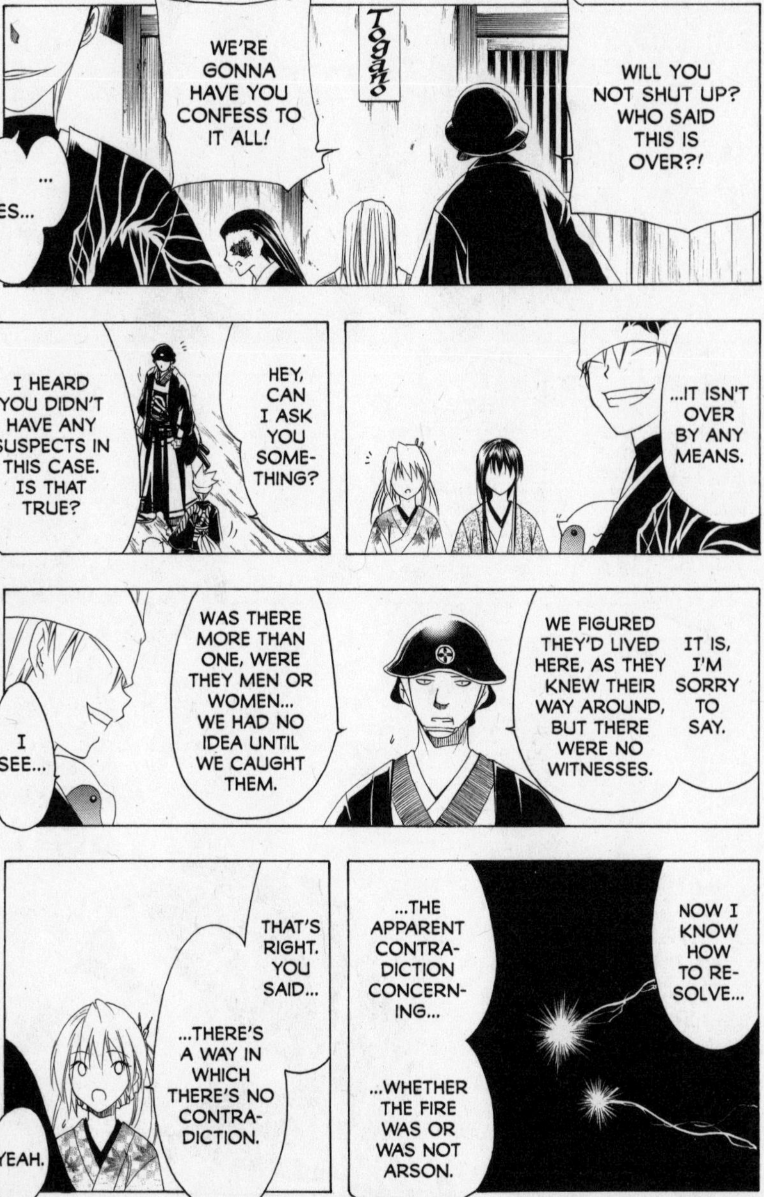
WILL YOU NOT SHUT UP? WHO SAID THIS IS OVER?!
Togano
WE'RE GONNA HAVE YOU CONFESS TO IT ALL!
... YES...
...IT ISN'T OVER BY ANY MEANS.
HEY, CAN I ASK YOU SOME-THING?
I HEARD YOU DIDN'T HAVE ANY SUSPECTS IN THIS CASE. IS THAT TRUE?
IT IS, I'M SORRY TO SAY.
WE FIGURED THEY'D LIVED HERE, AS THEY KNEW THEIR WAY AROUND, BUT THERE WERE NO WITNESSES.
WAS THERE MORE THAN ONE, WERE THEY MEN OR WOMEN... WE HAD NO IDEA UNTIL WE CAUGHT THEM.
I SEE...
NOW I KNOW HOW TO RE-SOLVE...
...THE APPARENT CONTRA-DICTION CONCERN-ING...
...WHETHER THE FIRE WAS OR WAS NOT ARSON.
THAT'S RIGHT. YOU SAID...
...THERE'S A WAY IN WHICH THERE'S NO CONTRA-DICTION.
YEAH.

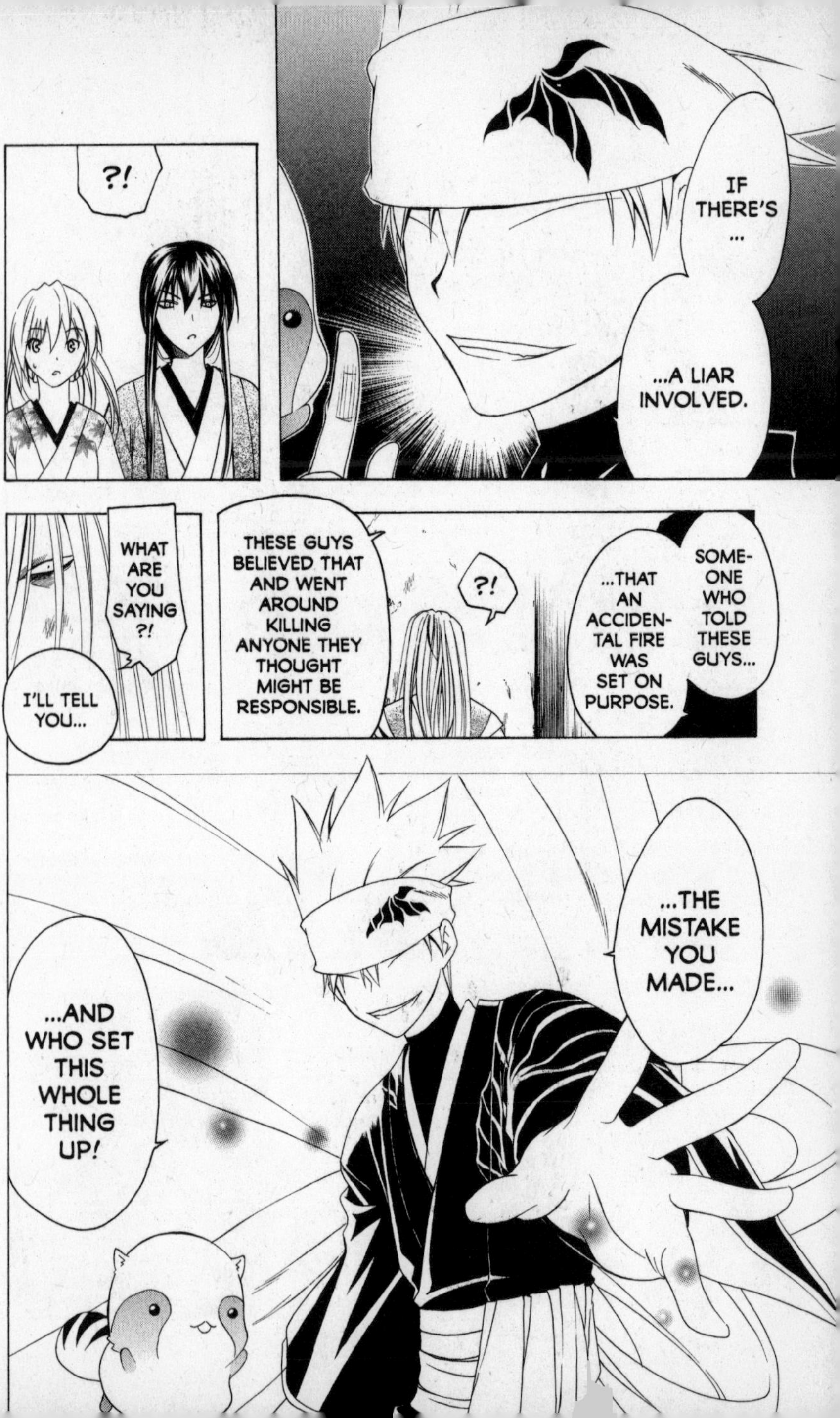
IF THERE'S ...
...A LIAR INVOLVED.
?!
SOME-ONE WHO TOLD THESE GUYS...
...THAT AN ACCIDEN-TAL FIRE WAS SET ON PURPOSE.
?!
THESE GUYS BELIEVED THAT AND WENT AROUND KILLING ANYONE THEY THOUGHT MIGHT BE RESPONSIBLE.
WHAT ARE YOU SAYING ?!
I'LL TELL YOU...
...THE MISTAKE YOU MADE...
...AND WHO SET THIS WHOLE THING UP!

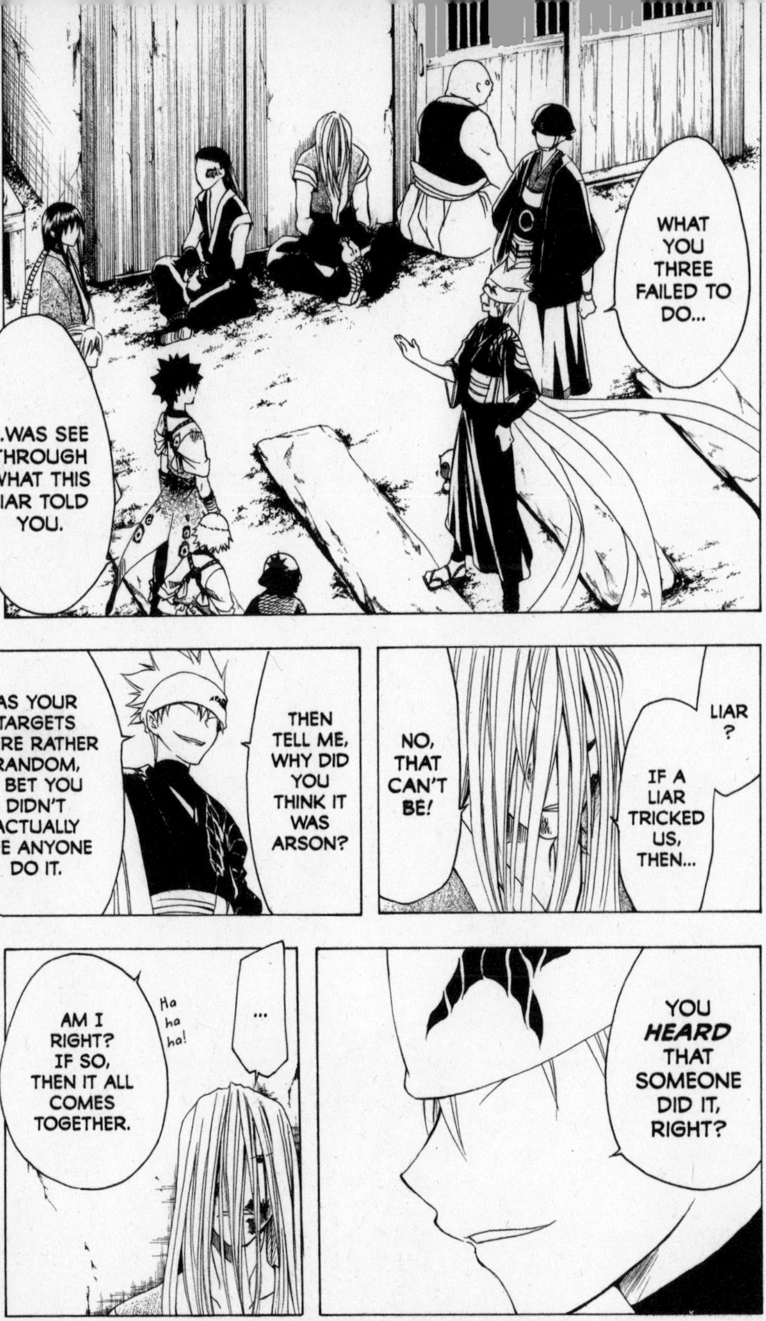
WHAT YOU THREE FAILED TO DO...
...WAS SEE THROUGH WHAT THIS LIAR TOLD YOU.
LIAR?
IF A LIAR TRICKED US, THEN...
NO, THAT CAN'T BE!
THEN TELL ME, WHY DID YOU THINK IT WAS ARSON?
AS YOUR TARGETS WERE RATHER RANDOM, I BET YOU DIDN'T ACTUALLY SEE ANYONE DO IT.
YOU *HEARD* THAT SOMEONE DID IT, RIGHT?
...
Ha ha ha!
AM I RIGHT? IF SO, THEN IT ALL COMES TOGETHER.

Chapter 41 The Liar's Identity

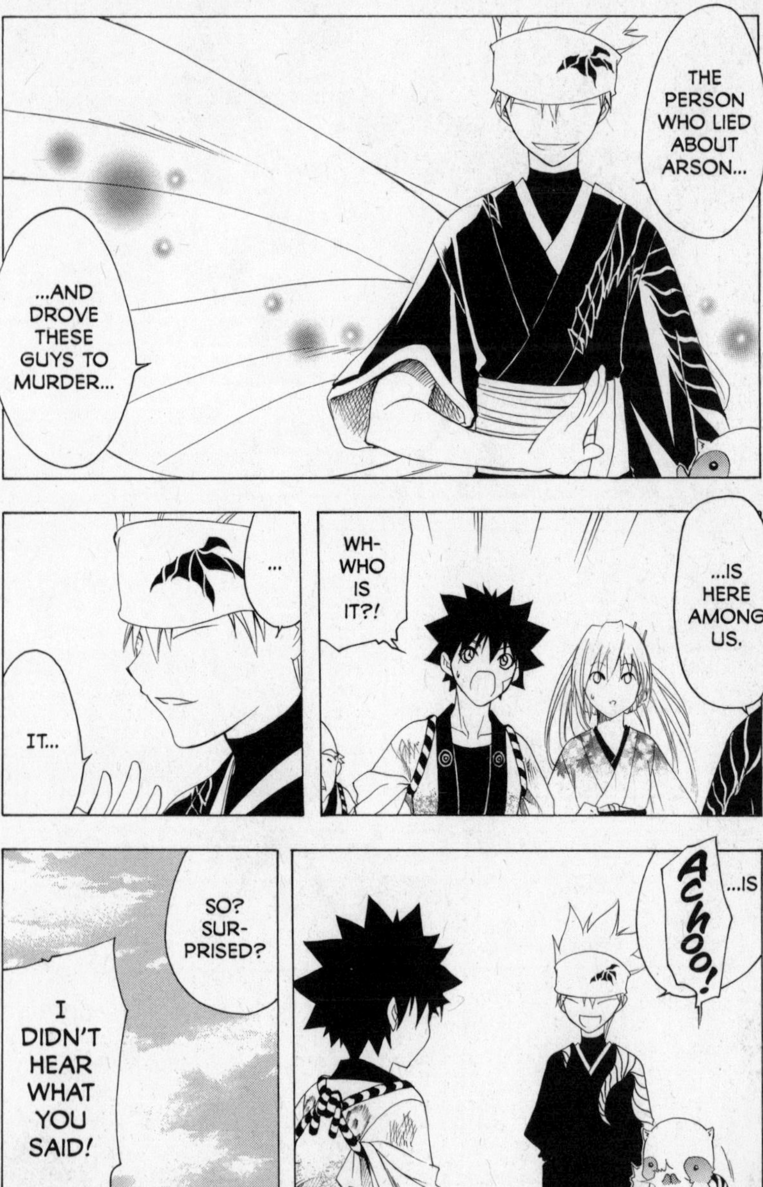
THE PERSON WHO LIED ABOUT ARSON...
...AND DROVE THESE GUYS TO MURDER...
...IS HERE AMONG US.
WH-WHO IS IT?!
...
IT...
...IS
ACHOO!
SO? SUR-PRISED?
I DIDN'T HEAR WHAT YOU SAID!

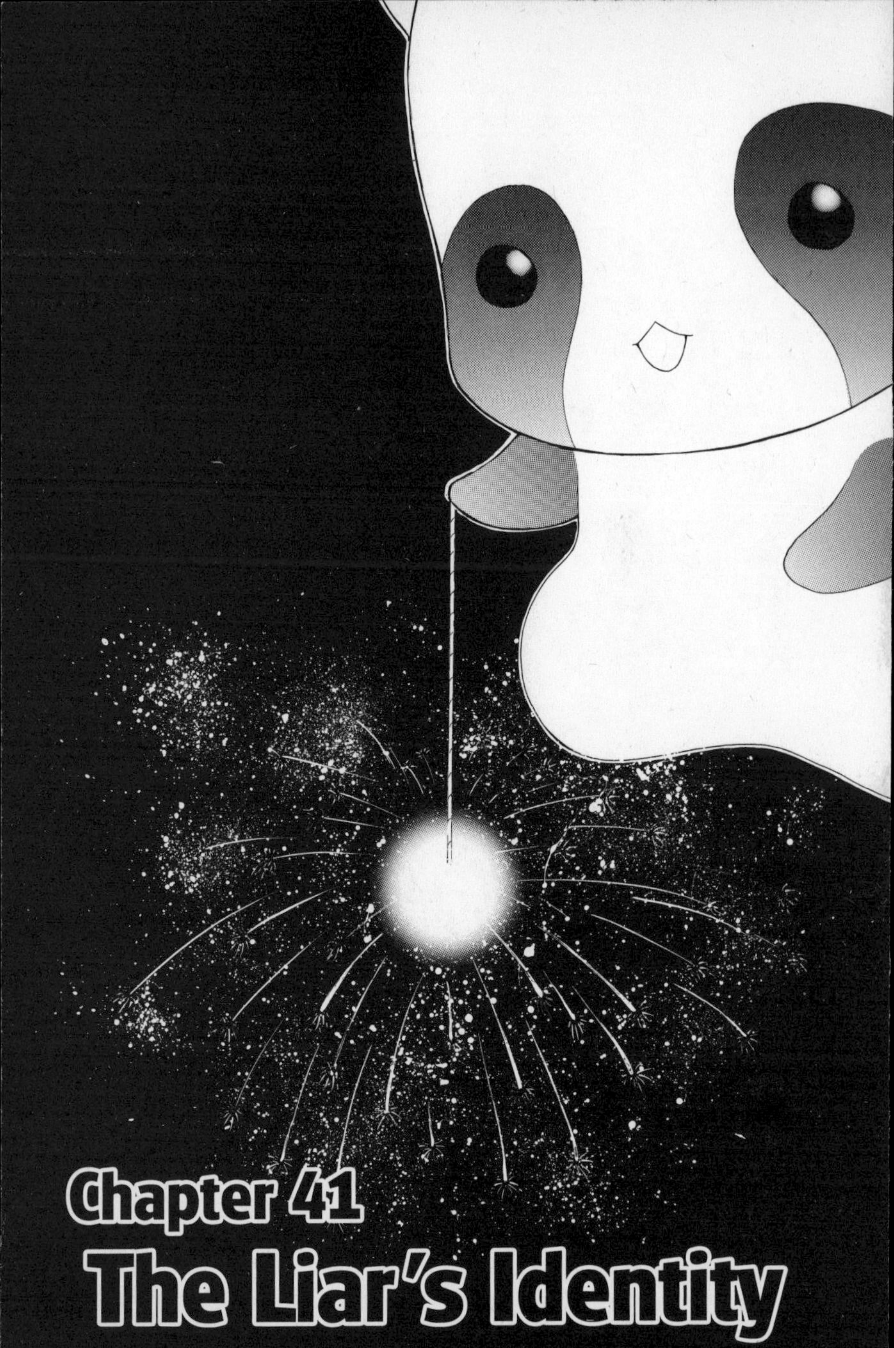

Chapter 41
The Liar's Identity

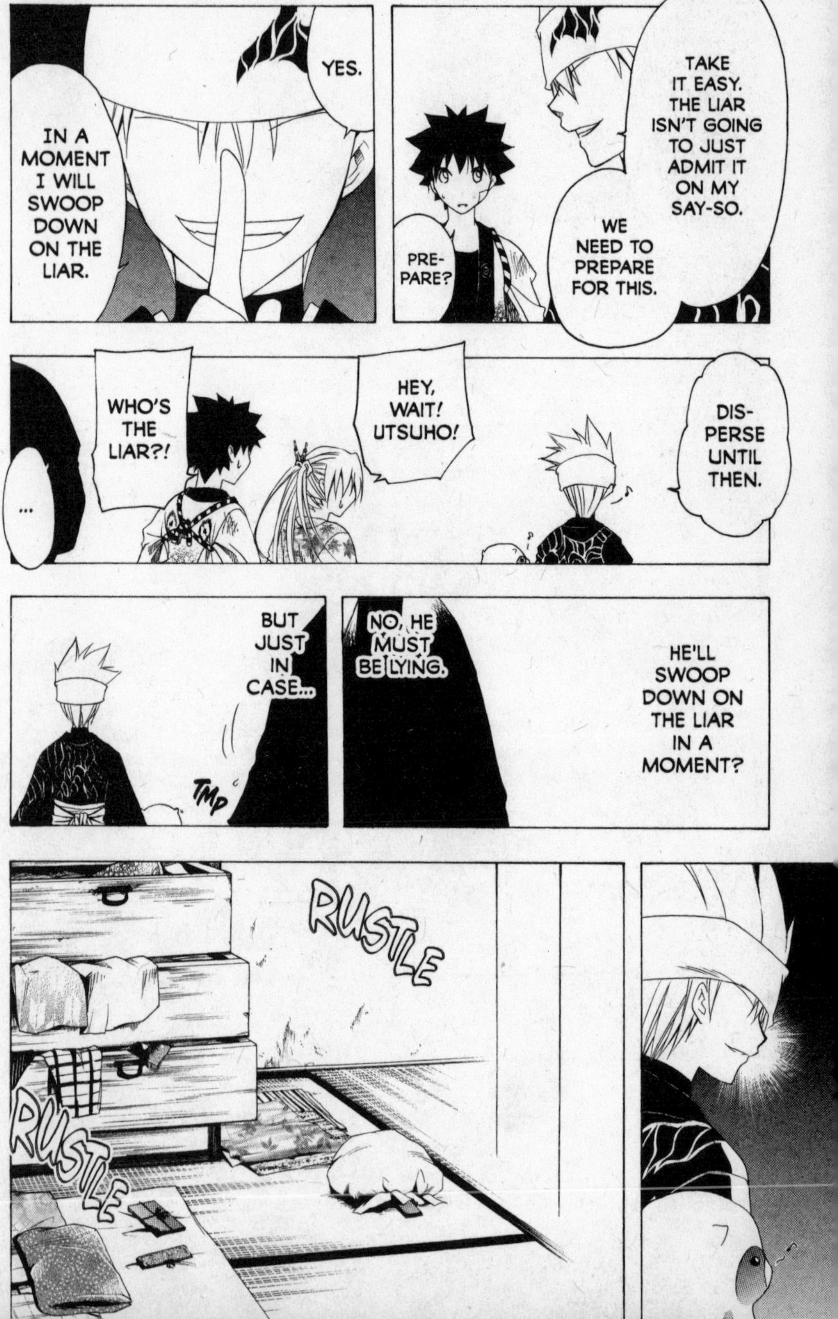
TAKE IT EASY. THE LIAR ISN'T GOING TO JUST ADMIT IT ON MY SAY-SO.
WE NEED TO PREPARE FOR THIS.
PRE-PARE?
YES.
IN A MOMENT I WILL SWOOP DOWN ON THE LIAR.
DIS-PERSE UNTIL THEN.
HEY, WAIT! UTSUHO!
WHO'S THE LIAR?!
...
HE'LL SWOOP DOWN ON THE LIAR IN A MOMENT?
NO, HE MUST BE LYING.
BUT JUST IN CASE...
TMP
RUSTLE
RUSTLE

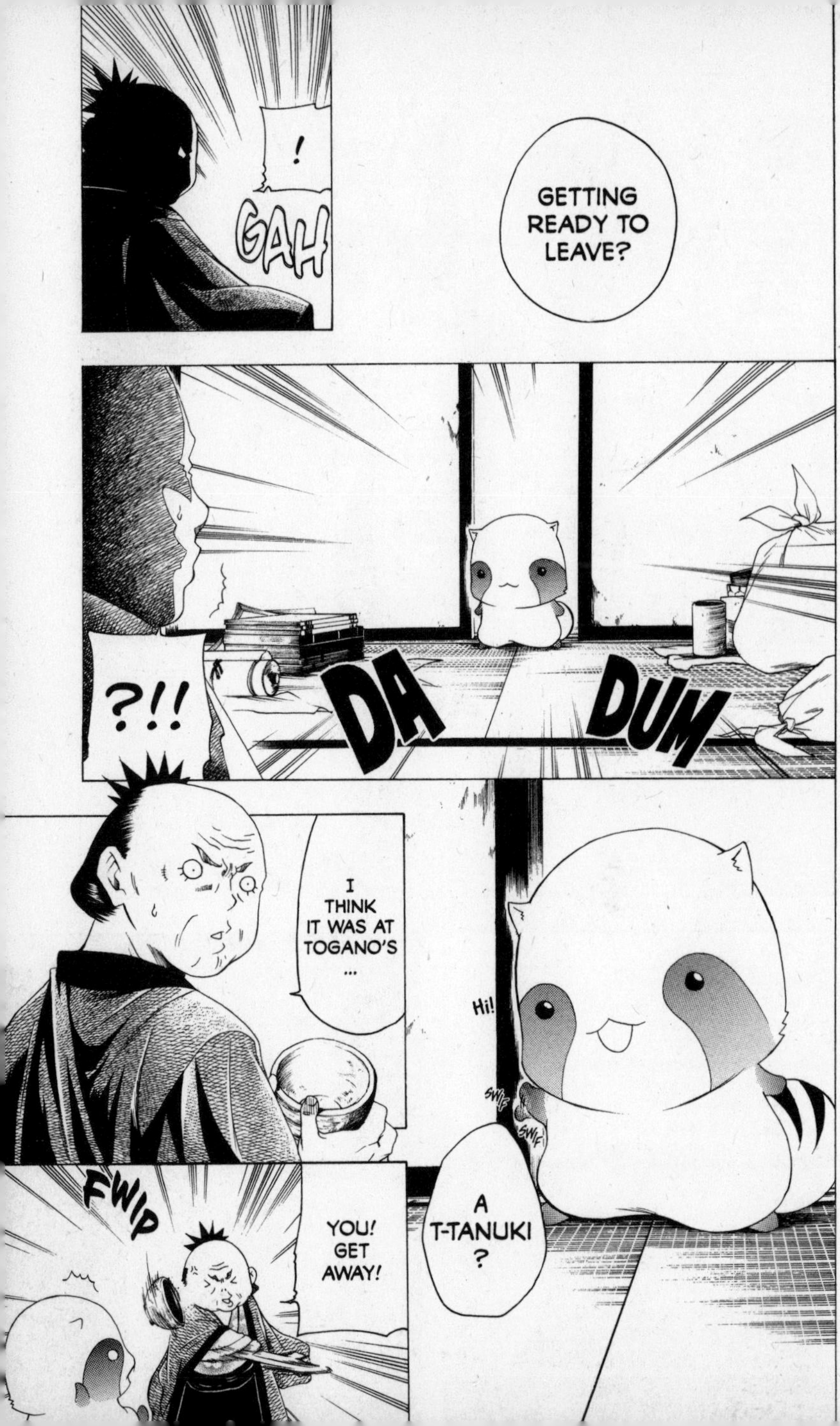

GETTING READY TO LEAVE?
!
GAH
DA DUM
?!!
Hi!
SWIF
SWIF
A T-TANUKI?
I THINK IT WAS AT TOGANO'S ...
FWIP
YOU! GET AWAY!

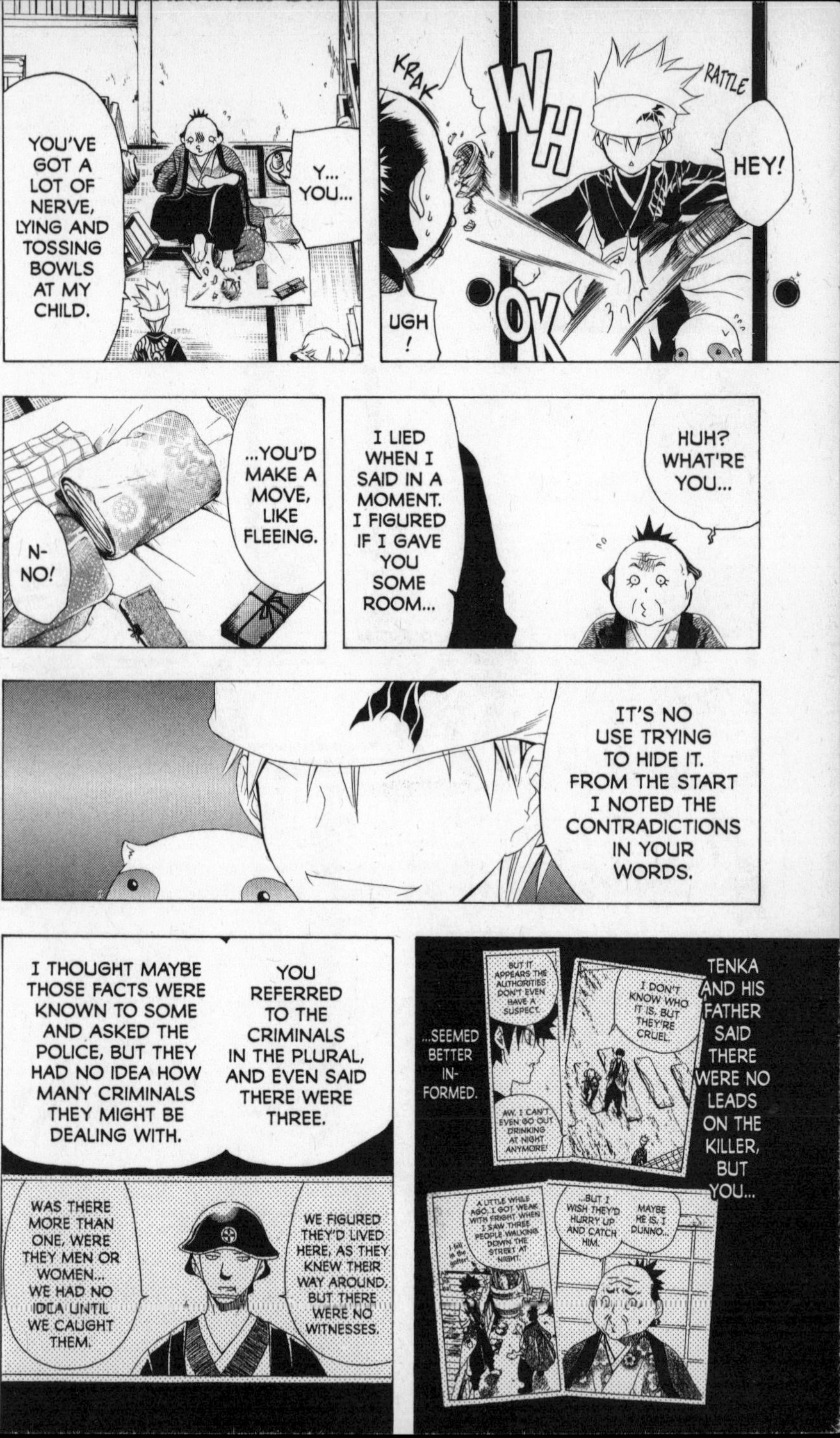
RATTLE
HEY!
WH
OK
KRAK
UGH!
Y... YOU...
YOU'VE GOT A LOT OF NERVE, LYING AND TOSSING BOWLS AT MY CHILD.
HUH? WHAT'RE YOU...
I LIED WHEN I SAID IN A MOMENT. I FIGURED IF I GAVE YOU SOME ROOM...
...YOU'D MAKE A MOVE, LIKE FLEEING.
N-NO!
IT'S NO USE TRYING TO HIDE IT. FROM THE START I NOTED THE CONTRADICTIONS IN YOUR WORDS.
TENKA AND HIS FATHER SAID THERE WERE NO LEADS ON THE KILLER, BUT YOU...
I DON'T KNOW WHO IT IS, BUT THEY'RE CRUEL.
BUT IT APPEARS THE AUTHORITIES DON'T EVEN HAVE A SUSPECT.
AW, I CAN'T EVEN GO OUT DRINKING AT NIGHT ANYMORE!
...SEEMED BETTER INFORMED.
MAYBE HE IS, I DUNNO...
...BUT I WISH THEY'D HURRY UP AND CATCH HIM.
A LITTLE WHILE AGO, I GOT WEAK WITH FRIGHT WHEN I SAW THREE PEOPLE WALKING DOWN THE STREET AT NIGHT.
I fell in the gutter!
YOU REFERRED TO THE CRIMINALS IN THE PLURAL, AND EVEN SAID THERE WERE THREE.
I THOUGHT MAYBE THOSE FACTS WERE KNOWN TO SOME AND ASKED THE POLICE, BUT THEY HAD NO IDEA HOW MANY CRIMINALS THEY MIGHT BE DEALING WITH.
WE FIGURED THEY'D LIVED HERE, AS THEY KNEW THEIR WAY AROUND, BUT THERE WERE NO WITNESSES.
WAS THERE MORE THAN ONE, WERE THEY MEN OR WOMEN... WE HAD NO IDEA UNTIL WE CAUGHT THEM.

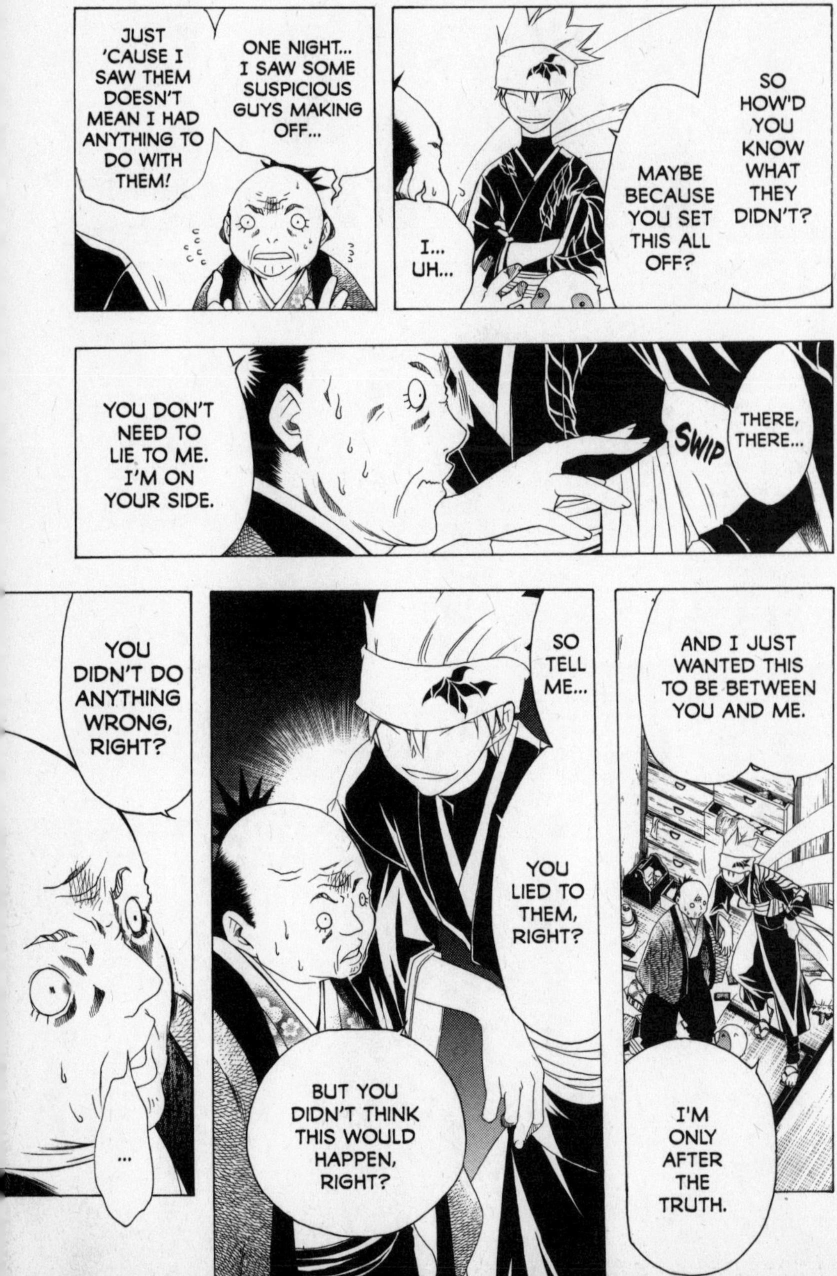
SO HOW'D YOU KNOW WHAT THEY DIDN'T?
MAYBE BECAUSE YOU SET THIS ALL OFF?
I... UH...
ONE NIGHT... I SAW SOME SUSPICIOUS GUYS MAKING OFF...
JUST 'CAUSE I SAW THEM DOESN'T MEAN I HAD ANYTHING TO DO WITH THEM!
THERE, THERE...
SWIP
YOU DON'T NEED TO LIE TO ME. I'M ON YOUR SIDE.
AND I JUST WANTED THIS TO BE BETWEEN YOU AND ME.
I'M ONLY AFTER THE TRUTH.
SO TELL ME...
YOU LIED TO THEM, RIGHT?
BUT YOU DIDN'T THINK THIS WOULD HAPPEN, RIGHT?
YOU DIDN'T DO ANYTHING WRONG, RIGHT?
...

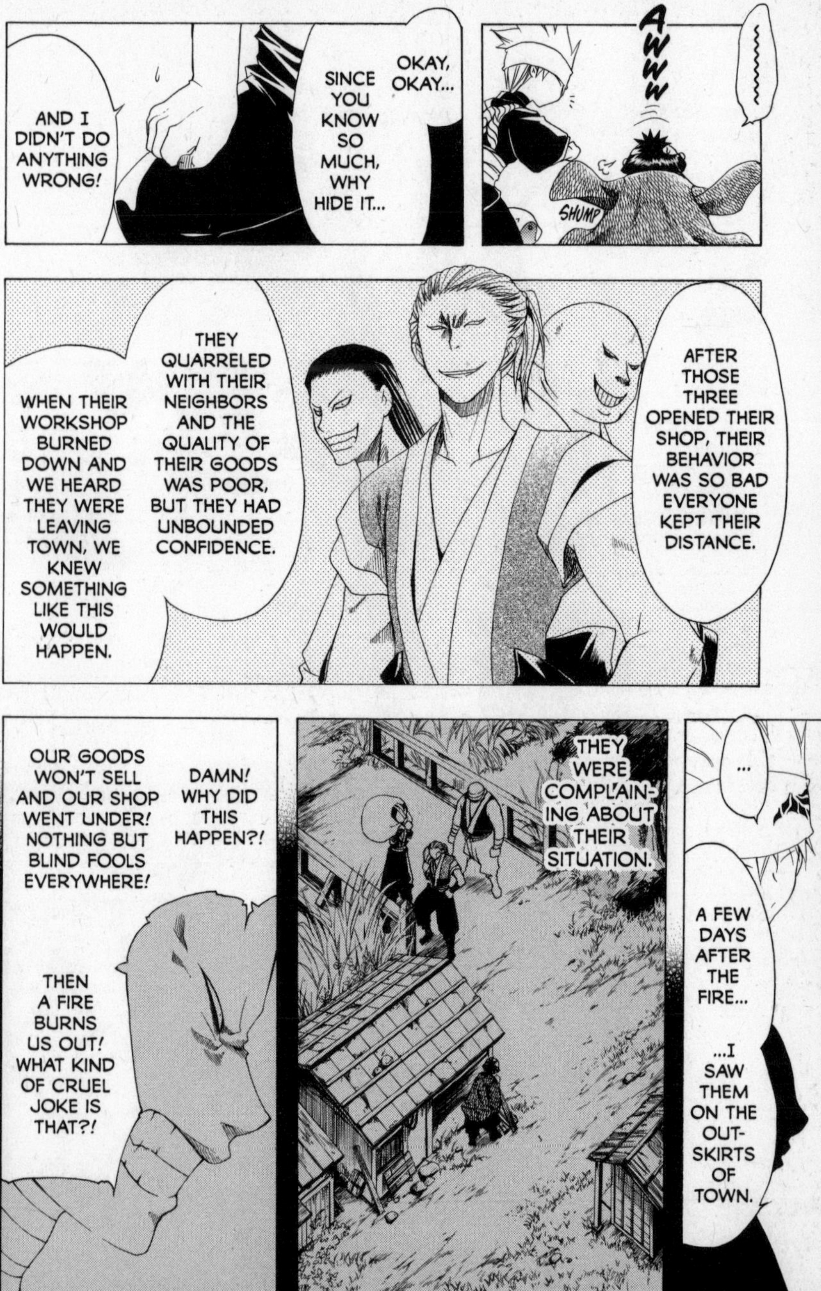
AWWW
....
SHUMP
OKAY, OKAY...
SINCE YOU KNOW SO MUCH, WHY HIDE IT...
AND I DIDN'T DO ANYTHING WRONG!
AFTER THOSE THREE OPENED THEIR SHOP, THEIR BEHAVIOR WAS SO BAD EVERYONE KEPT THEIR DISTANCE.
THEY QUARRELED WITH THEIR NEIGHBORS AND THE QUALITY OF THEIR GOODS WAS POOR, BUT THEY HAD UNBOUNDED CONFIDENCE.
WHEN THEIR WORKSHOP BURNED DOWN AND WE HEARD THEY WERE LEAVING TOWN, WE KNEW SOMETHING LIKE THIS WOULD HAPPEN.
...
A FEW DAYS AFTER THE FIRE...
...I SAW THEM ON THE OUT-SKIRTS OF TOWN.
THEY WERE COMPLAIN-ING ABOUT THEIR SITUATION.
DAMN! WHY DID THIS HAPPEN?!
OUR GOODS WON'T SELL AND OUR SHOP WENT UNDER! NOTHING BUT BLIND FOOLS EVERYWHERE!
THEN A FIRE BURNS US OUT! WHAT KIND OF CRUEL JOKE IS THAT?!

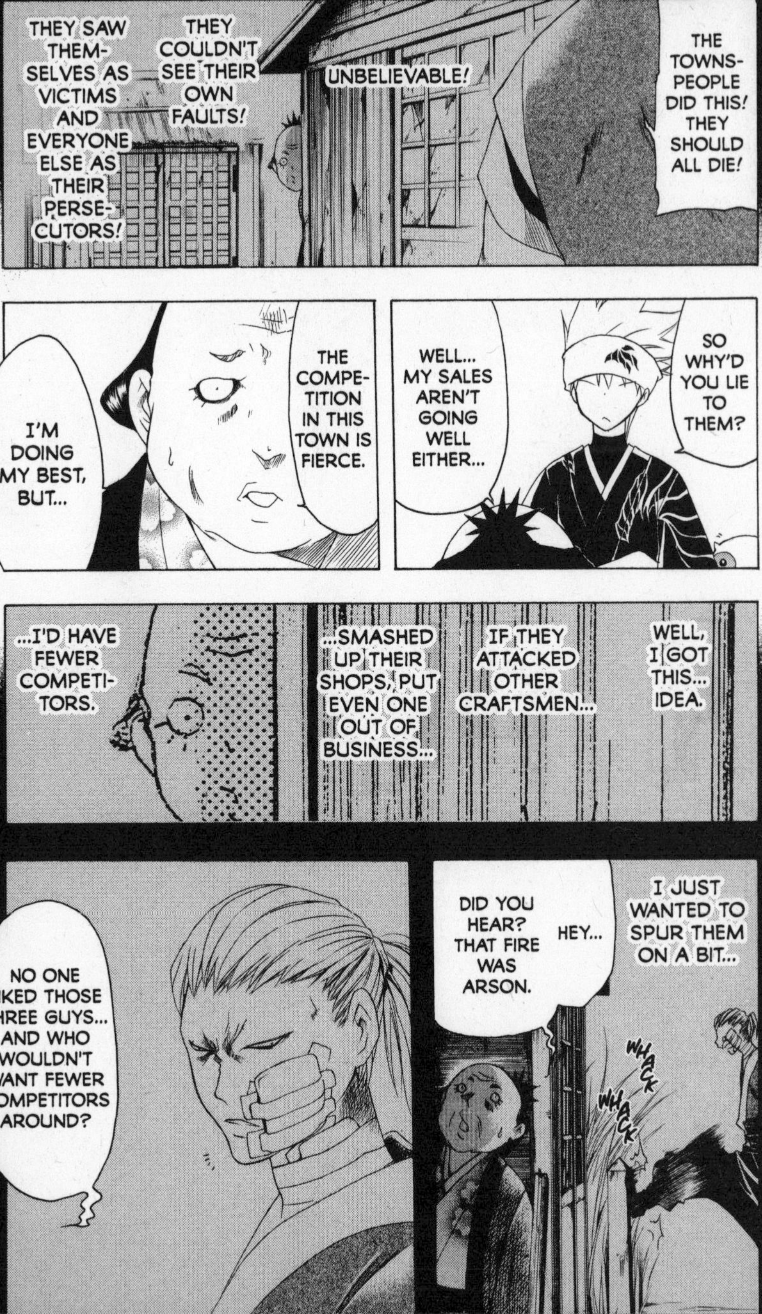
THE TOWNS-PEOPLE DID THIS! THEY SHOULD ALL DIE!
UNBELIEVABLE!
THEY COULDN'T SEE THEIR OWN FAULTS!
THEY SAW THEM-SELVES AS VICTIMS AND EVERYONE ELSE AS THEIR PERSE-CUTORS!
SO WHY'D YOU LIE TO THEM?
WELL... MY SALES AREN'T GOING WELL EITHER...
THE COMPE-TITION IN THIS TOWN IS FIERCE.
I'M DOING MY BEST, BUT...
WELL, I GOT THIS... IDEA.
IF THEY ATTACKED OTHER CRAFTSMEN...
...SMASHED UP THEIR SHOPS, PUT EVEN ONE OUT OF BUSINESS...
...I'D HAVE FEWER COMPETI-TORS.
I JUST WANTED TO SPUR THEM ON A BIT...
HEY...
DID YOU HEAR? THAT FIRE WAS ARSON.
WHACK
WHACK
NO ONE LIKED THOSE THREE GUYS... AND WHO WOULDN'T WANT FEWER COMPETITORS AROUND?

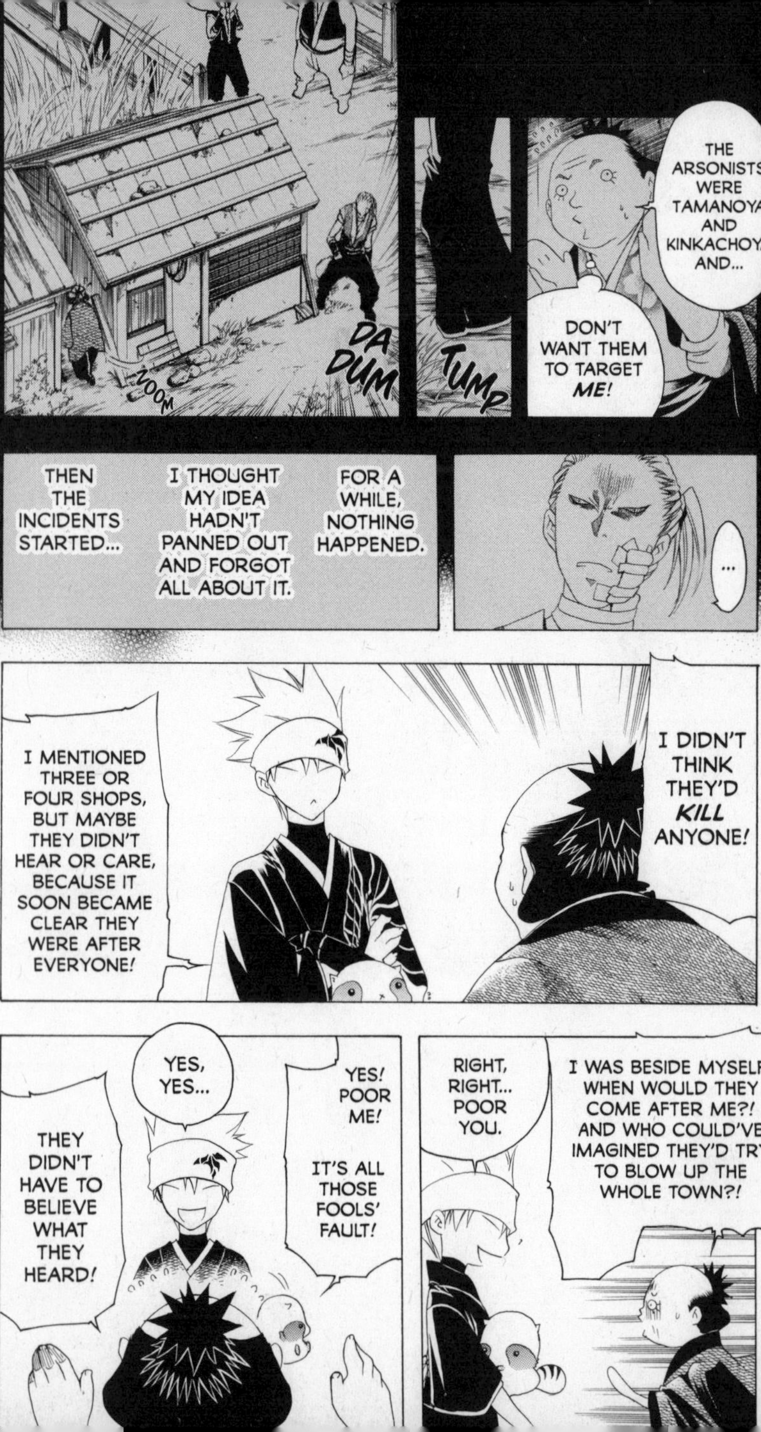
THE ARSONISTS WERE TAMANOYA AND KINKACHOYA AND...
DON'T WANT THEM TO TARGET *ME!*
TUMP
DA DUM
ZOOM
...
FOR A WHILE, NOTHING HAPPENED.
I THOUGHT MY IDEA HADN'T PANNED OUT AND FORGOT ALL ABOUT IT.
THEN THE INCIDENTS STARTED...
I DIDN'T THINK THEY'D *KILL* ANYONE!
I MENTIONED THREE OR FOUR SHOPS, BUT MAYBE THEY DIDN'T HEAR OR CARE, BECAUSE IT SOON BECAME CLEAR THEY WERE AFTER EVERYONE!
I WAS BESIDE MYSELF! WHEN WOULD THEY COME AFTER ME?! AND WHO COULD'VE IMAGINED THEY'D TRY TO BLOW UP THE WHOLE TOWN?!
RIGHT, RIGHT... POOR YOU.
YES! POOR ME!
IT'S ALL THOSE FOOLS' FAULT!
YES, YES...
THEY DIDN'T HAVE TO BELIEVE WHAT THEY HEARD!

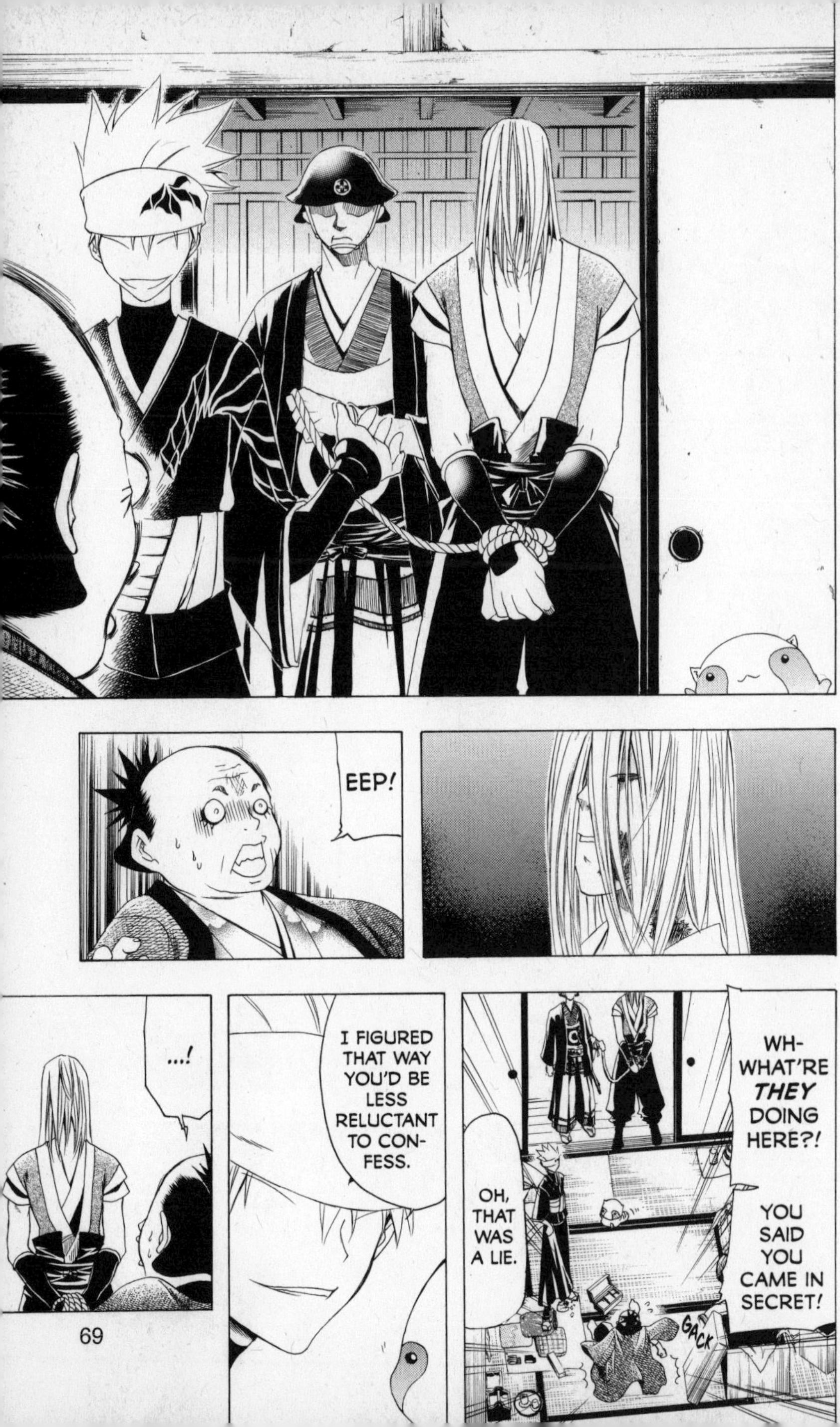
EEP!
WH- WHAT'RE *THEY* DOING HERE?!
YOU SAID YOU CAME IN SECRET!
OH, THAT WAS A LIE.
GACK
I FIGURED THAT WAY YOU'D BE LESS RELUCTANT TO CON- FESS.
...!

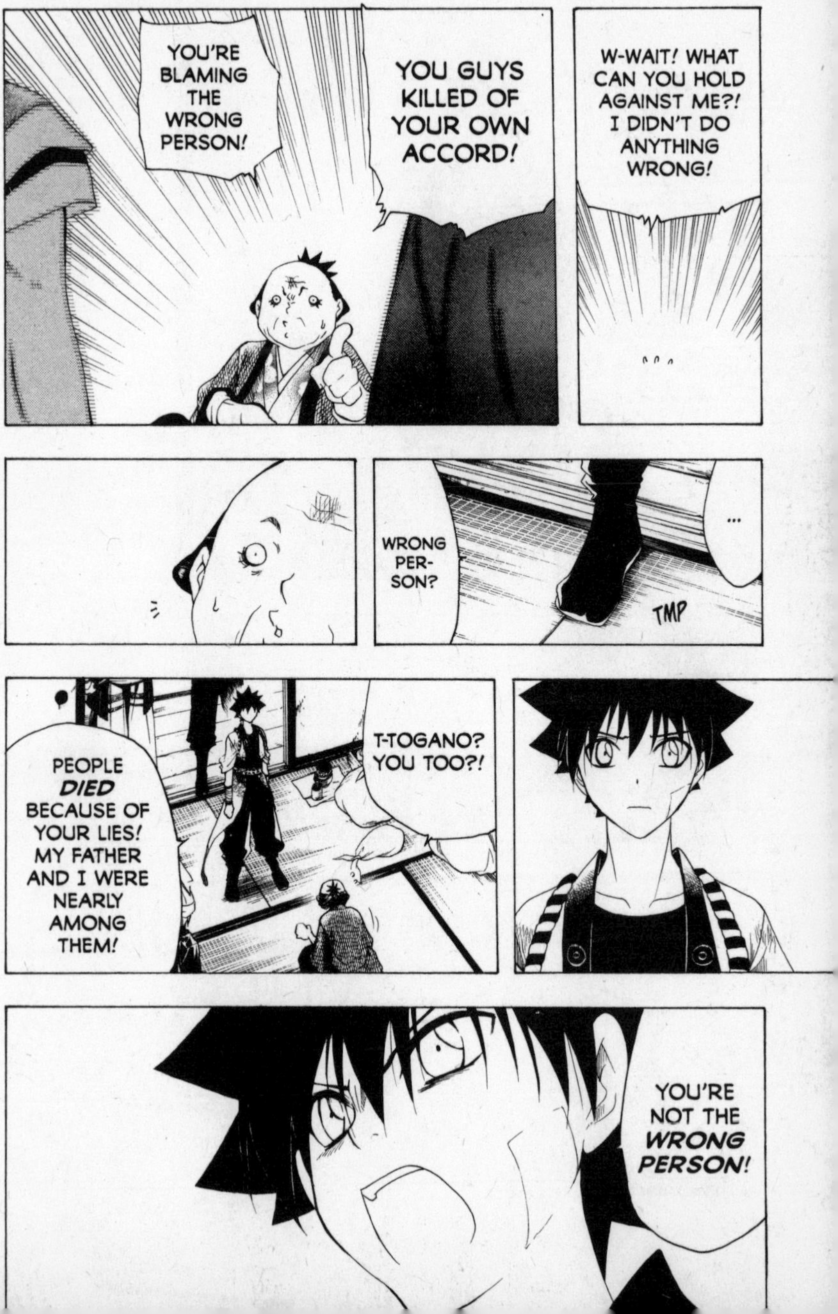
W-WAIT! WHAT CAN YOU HOLD AGAINST ME?! I DIDN'T DO ANYTHING WRONG!
YOU GUYS KILLED OF YOUR OWN ACCORD!
YOU'RE BLAMING THE WRONG PERSON!
...
WRONG PER-SON?
TMP
T-TOGANO? YOU TOO?!
PEOPLE *DIED* BECAUSE OF YOUR LIES! MY FATHER AND I WERE NEARLY AMONG THEM!
YOU'RE NOT THE *WRONG PERSON!*

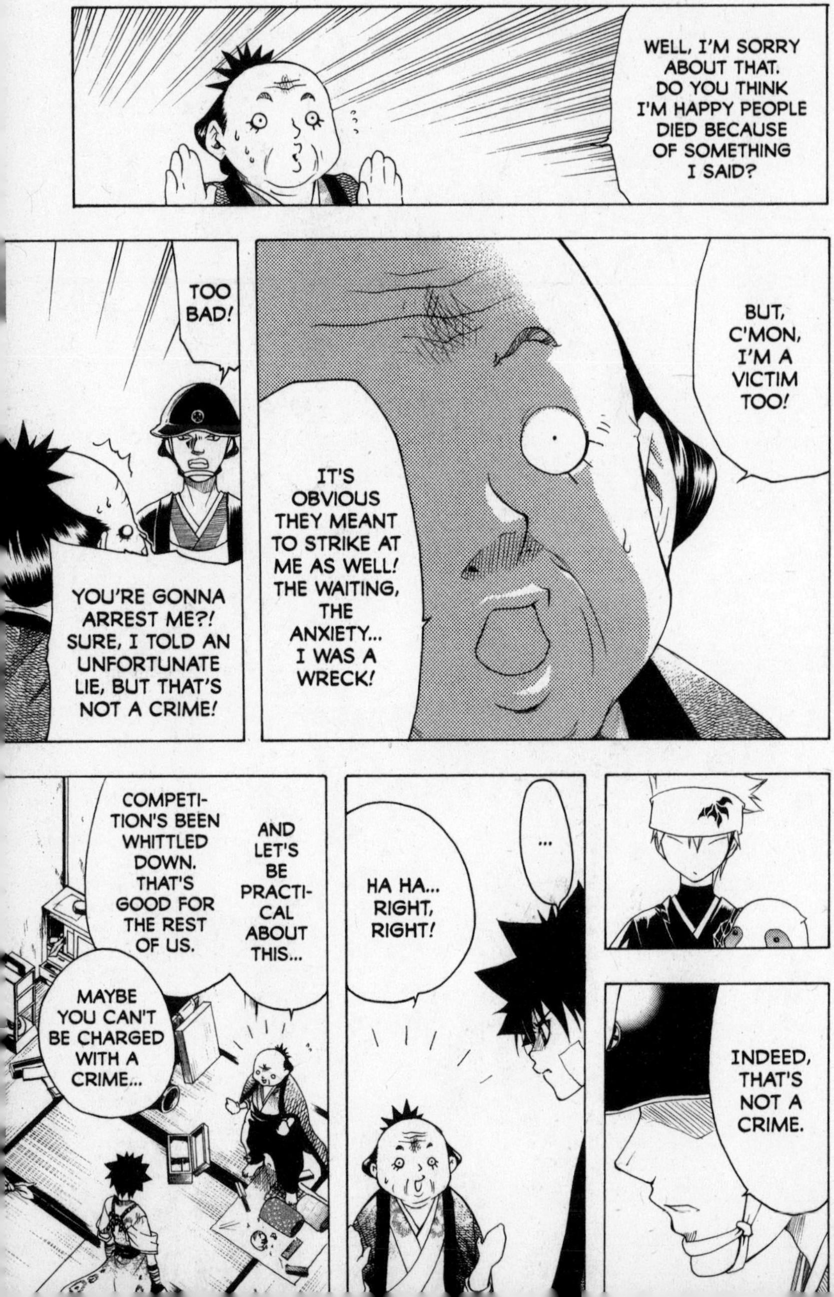
WELL, I'M SORRY ABOUT THAT. DO YOU THINK I'M HAPPY PEOPLE DIED BECAUSE OF SOMETHING I SAID?
BUT, C'MON, I'M A VICTIM TOO!
IT'S OBVIOUS THEY MEANT TO STRIKE AT ME AS WELL! THE WAITING, THE ANXIETY... I WAS A WRECK!
TOO BAD!
YOU'RE GONNA ARREST ME?! SURE, I TOLD AN UNFORTUNATE LIE, BUT THAT'S NOT A CRIME!
INDEED, THAT'S NOT A CRIME.
...
HA HA... RIGHT, RIGHT!
AND LET'S BE PRACTICAL ABOUT THIS...
COMPETITION'S BEEN WHITTLED DOWN. THAT'S GOOD FOR THE REST OF US.
MAYBE YOU CAN'T BE CHARGED WITH A CRIME...

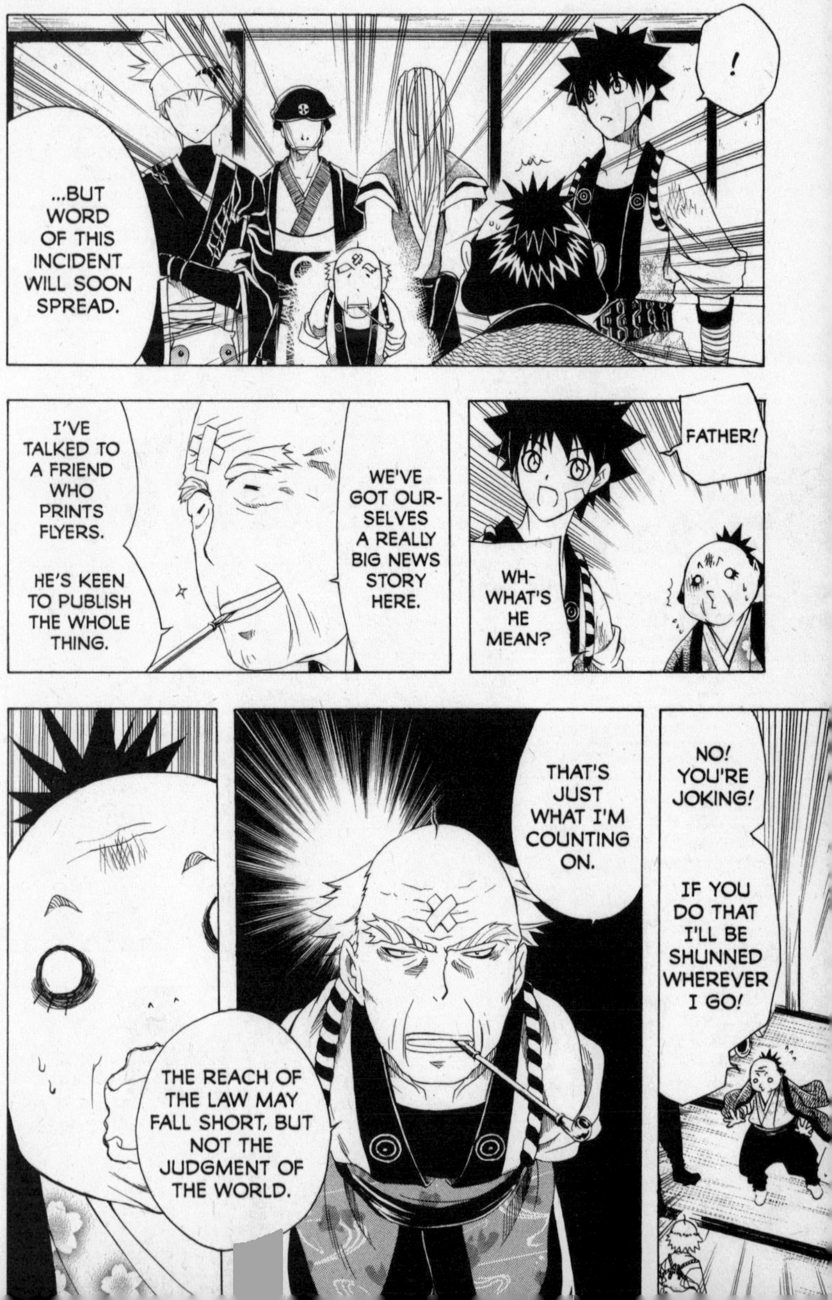
!
...BUT WORD OF THIS INCIDENT WILL SOON SPREAD.
FATHER!
WH- WHAT'S HE MEAN?
WE'VE GOT OUR-SELVES A REALLY BIG NEWS STORY HERE.
I'VE TALKED TO A FRIEND WHO PRINTS FLYERS.
HE'S KEEN TO PUBLISH THE WHOLE THING.
NO! YOU'RE JOKING!
IF YOU DO THAT I'LL BE SHUNNED WHEREVER I GO!
THAT'S JUST WHAT I'M COUNTING ON.
THE REACH OF THE LAW MAY FALL SHORT, BUT NOT THE JUDGMENT OF THE WORLD.

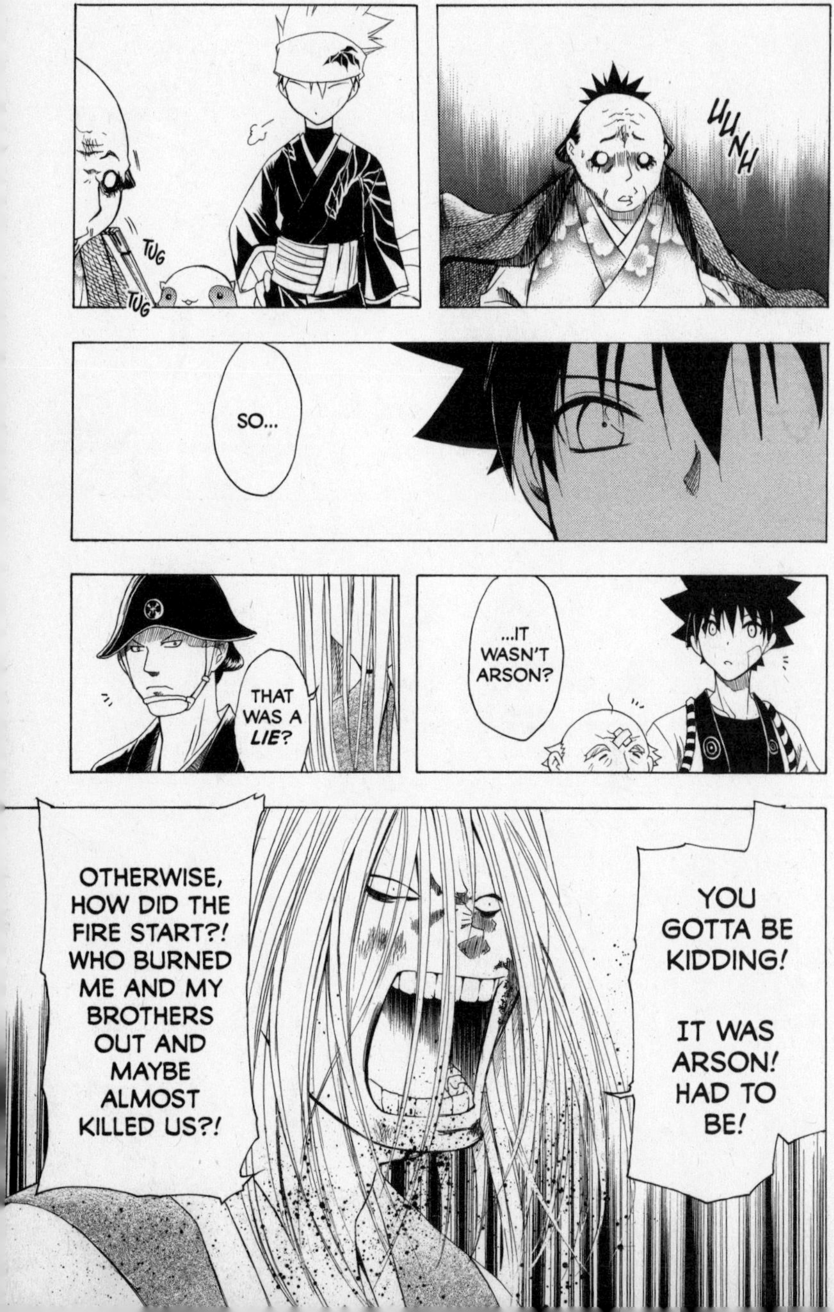

UUNH
TUG
TUG
SO...
...IT WASN'T ARSON?
THAT WAS A *LIE*?
YOU GOTTA BE KIDDING!
IT WAS ARSON! HAD TO BE!
OTHERWISE, HOW DID THE FIRE START?! WHO BURNED ME AND MY BROTHERS OUT AND MAYBE ALMOST KILLED US?!

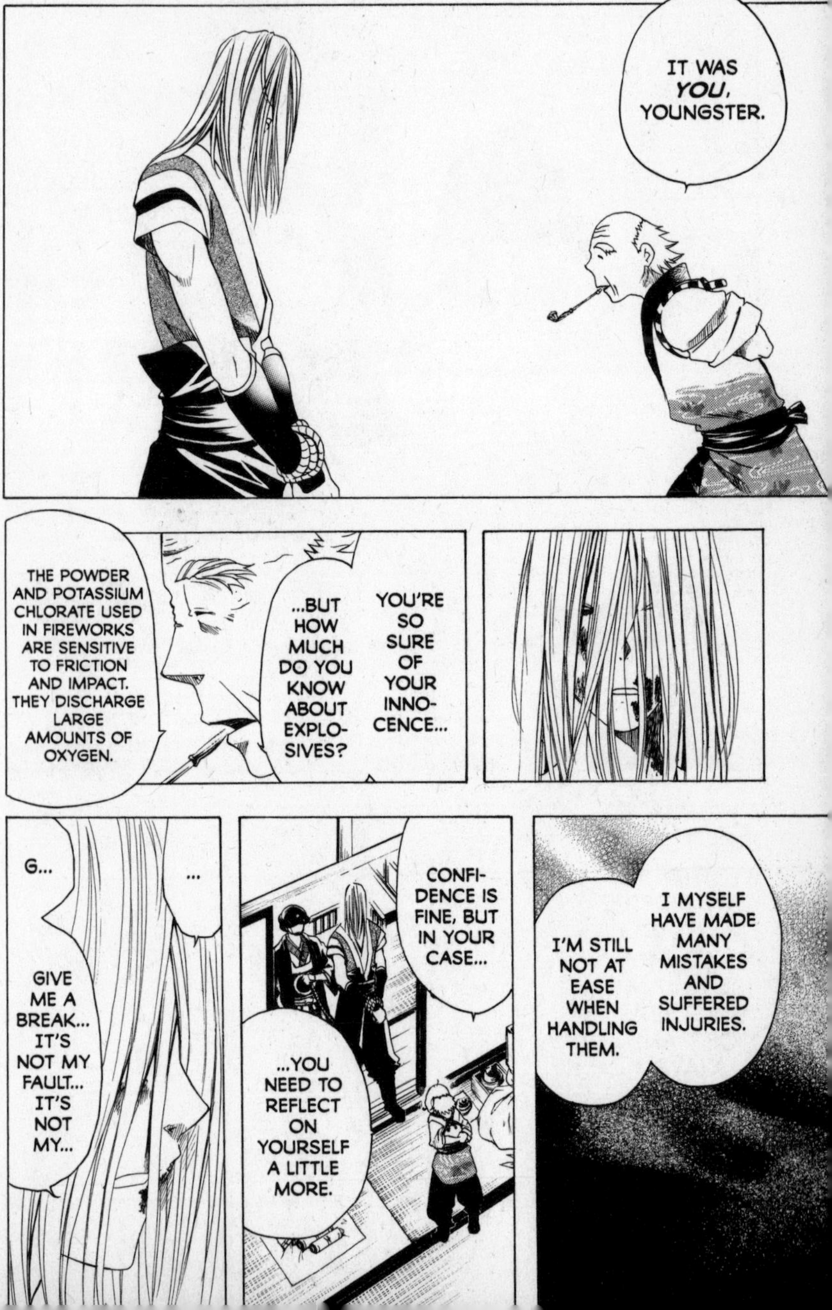
IT WAS *YOU*, YOUNGSTER.
YOU'RE SO SURE OF YOUR INNOCENCE...
...BUT HOW MUCH DO YOU KNOW ABOUT EXPLOSIVES?
THE POWDER AND POTASSIUM CHLORATE USED IN FIREWORKS ARE SENSITIVE TO FRICTION AND IMPACT. THEY DISCHARGE LARGE AMOUNTS OF OXYGEN.
I MYSELF HAVE MADE MANY MISTAKES AND SUFFERED INJURIES.
I'M STILL NOT AT EASE WHEN HANDLING THEM.
CONFIDENCE IS FINE, BUT IN YOUR CASE...
...YOU NEED TO REFLECT ON YOURSELF A LITTLE MORE.
...
G...
GIVE ME A BREAK... IT'S NOT MY FAULT... IT'S NOT MY...

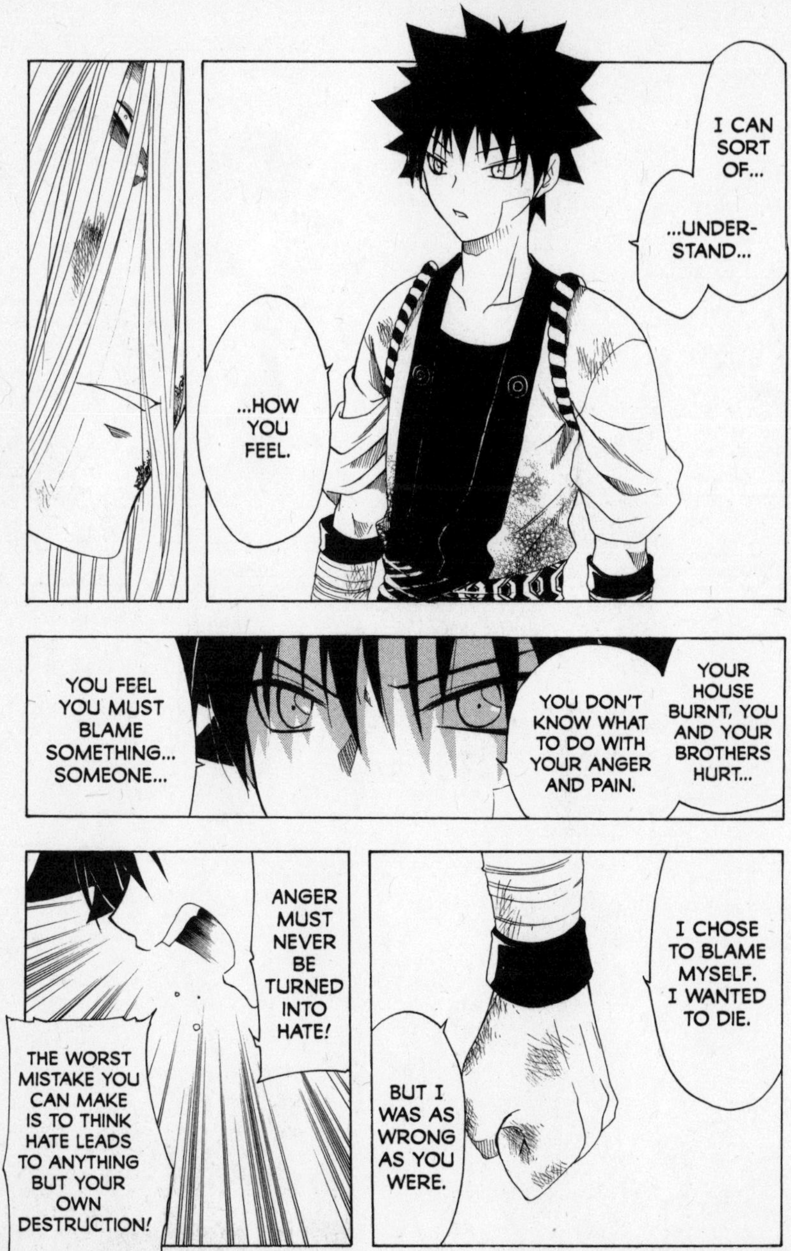
I CAN SORT OF...
...UNDER-STAND...
...HOW YOU FEEL.
YOUR HOUSE BURNT, YOU AND YOUR BROTHERS HURT...
YOU DON'T KNOW WHAT TO DO WITH YOUR ANGER AND PAIN.
YOU FEEL YOU MUST BLAME SOMETHING... SOMEONE...
I CHOSE TO BLAME MYSELF. I WANTED TO DIE.
BUT I WAS AS WRONG AS YOU WERE.
ANGER MUST NEVER BE TURNED INTO HATE!
THE WORST MISTAKE YOU CAN MAKE IS TO THINK HATE LEADS TO ANYTHING BUT YOUR OWN DESTRUCTION!

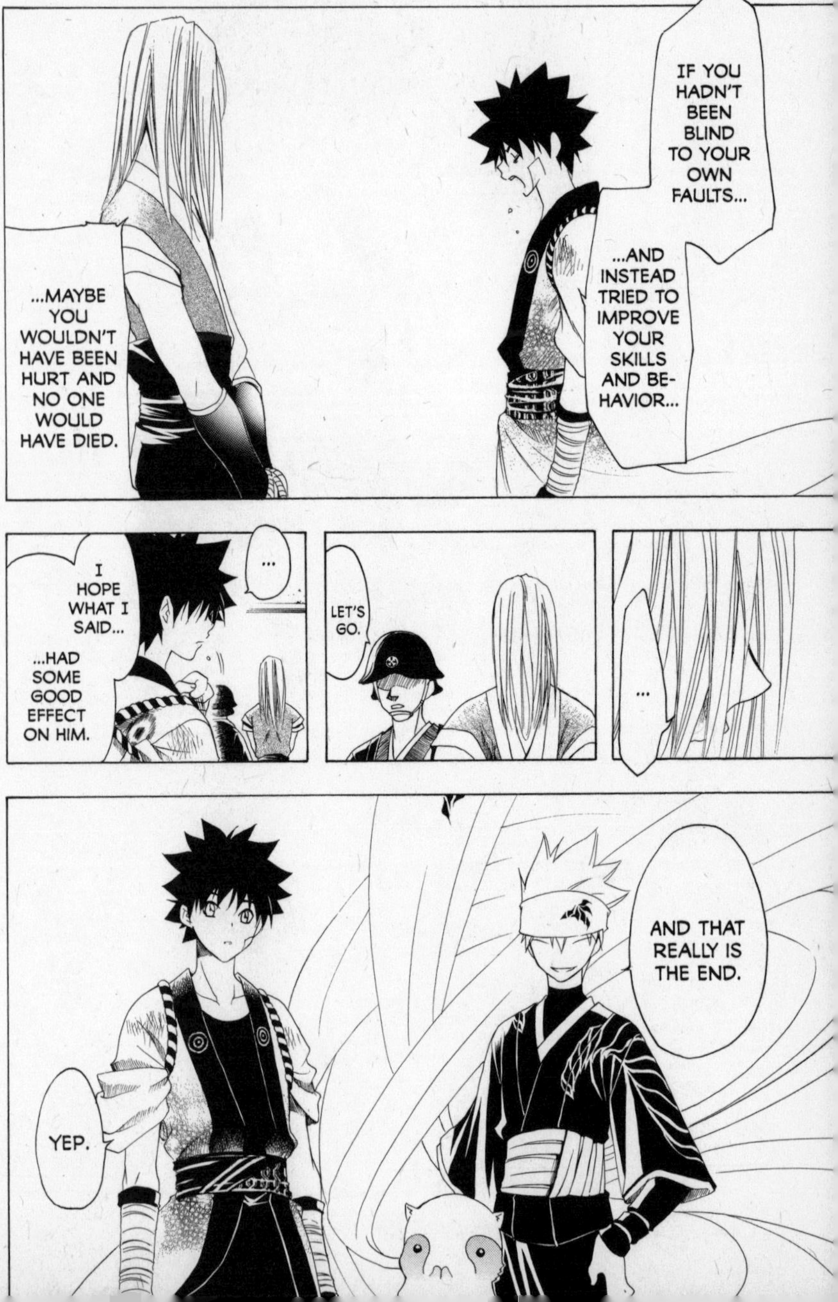
IF YOU HADN'T BEEN BLIND TO YOUR OWN FAULTS...
...AND INSTEAD TRIED TO IMPROVE YOUR SKILLS AND BE-HAVIOR...
...MAYBE YOU WOULDN'T HAVE BEEN HURT AND NO ONE WOULD HAVE DIED.
...
LET'S GO.
...
I HOPE WHAT I SAID...
...HAD SOME GOOD EFFECT ON HIM.
AND THAT REALLY IS THE END.
YEP.

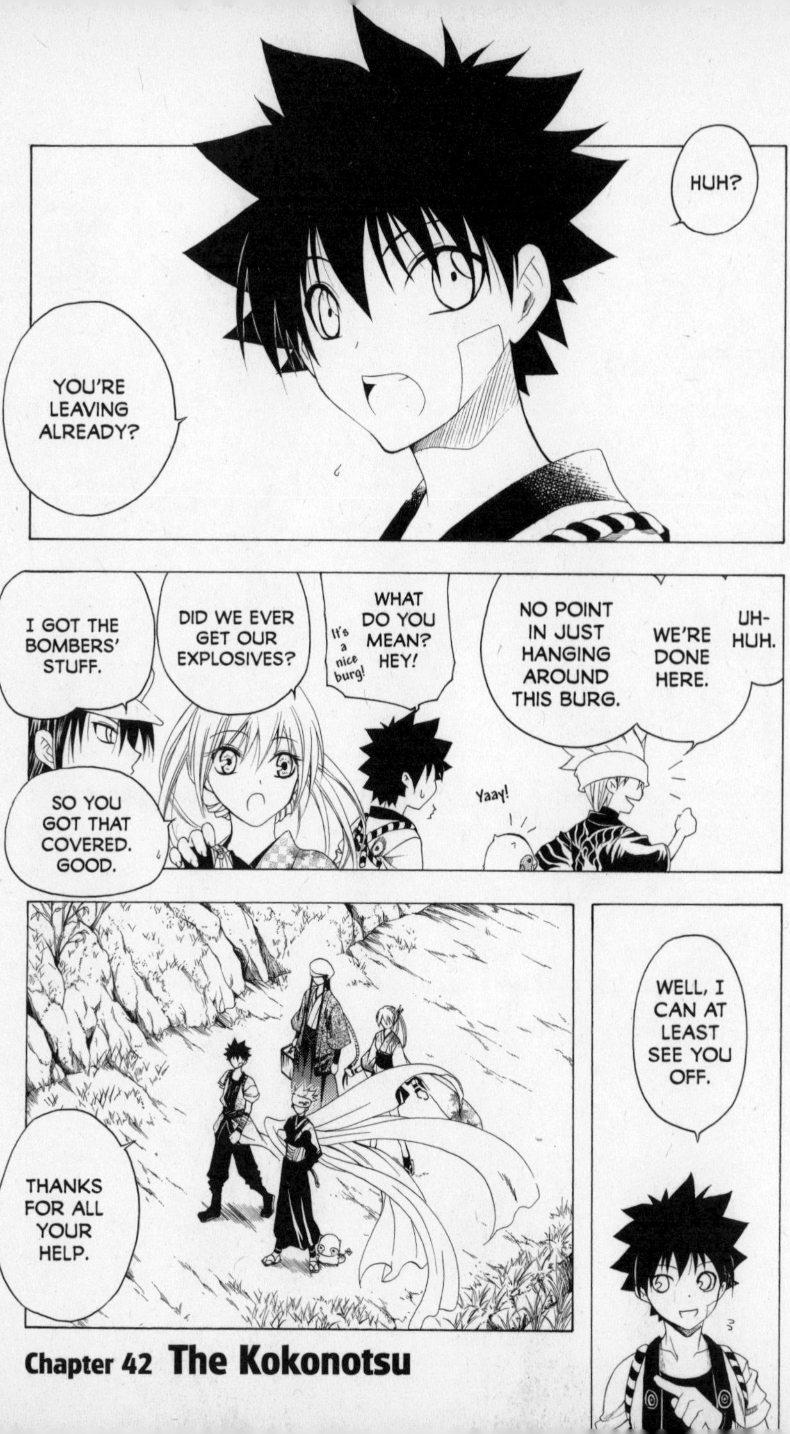
HUH?
YOU'RE LEAVING ALREADY?
UH-HUH.
WE'RE DONE HERE.
NO POINT IN JUST HANGING AROUND THIS BURG.
Yaay!
WHAT DO YOU MEAN? HEY!
It's a nice burg!
DID WE EVER GET OUR EXPLOSIVES?
I GOT THE BOMBERS' STUFF.
SO YOU GOT THAT COVERED. GOOD.
WELL, I CAN AT LEAST SEE YOU OFF.
THANKS FOR ALL YOUR HELP.

Chapter 42 The Kokonotsu

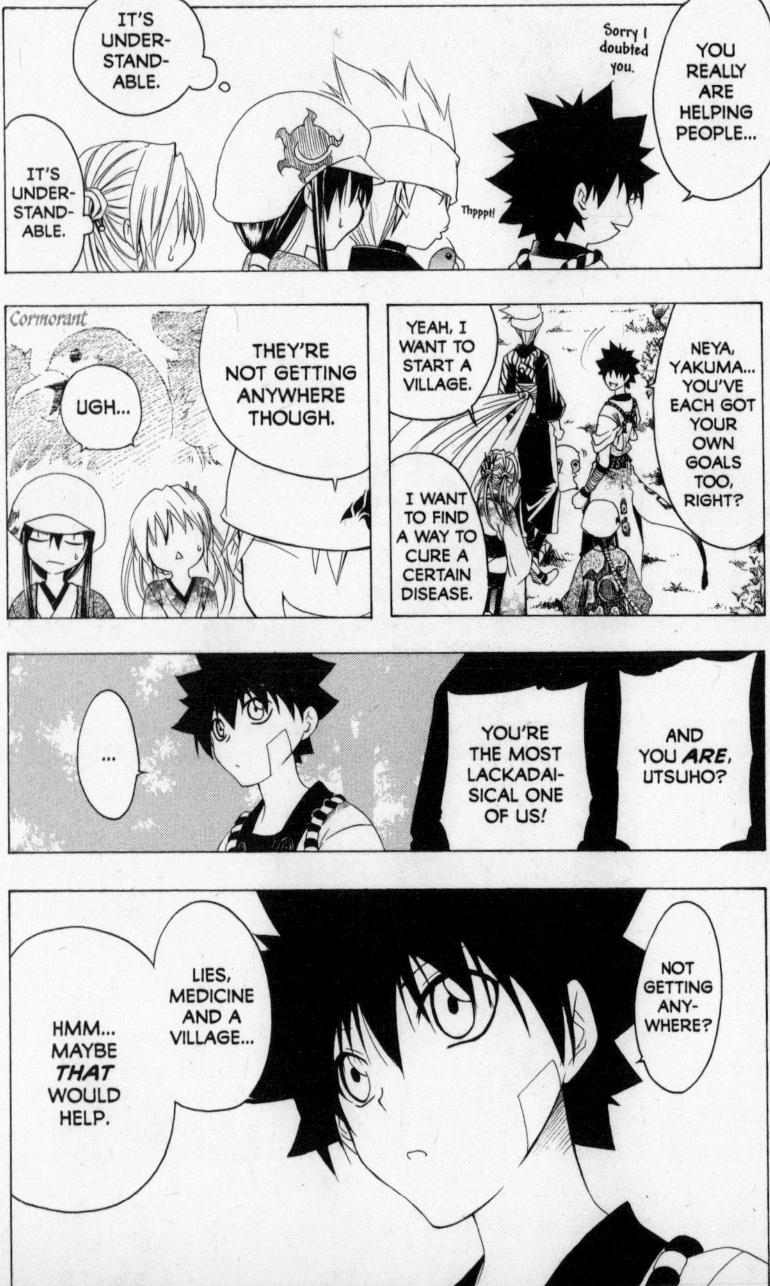
YOU REALLY ARE HELPING PEOPLE...
Sorry I doubted you.
Thpppt!
IT'S UNDERSTANDABLE.
IT'S UNDERSTANDABLE.
NEYA, YAKUMA... YOU'VE EACH GOT YOUR OWN GOALS TOO, RIGHT?
YEAH, I WANT TO START A VILLAGE.
I WANT TO FIND A WAY TO CURE A CERTAIN DISEASE.
THEY'RE NOT GETTING ANYWHERE THOUGH.
Cormorant
UGH...
AND YOU *ARE*, UTSUHO?
YOU'RE THE MOST LACKADAISICAL ONE OF US!
...
NOT GETTING ANYWHERE?
LIES, MEDICINE AND A VILLAGE...
HMM... MAYBE *THAT* WOULD HELP.

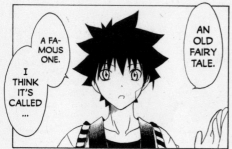

HUH?
WHAT'RE YOU TALKING ABOUT?

AN OLD FAIRY TALE.
A FA-MOUS ONE.
I THINK IT'S CALLED ...

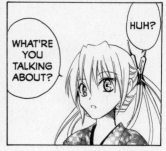

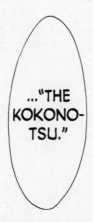

..."THE KOKONO-TSU."

Chapter 42
The Kokonotsu

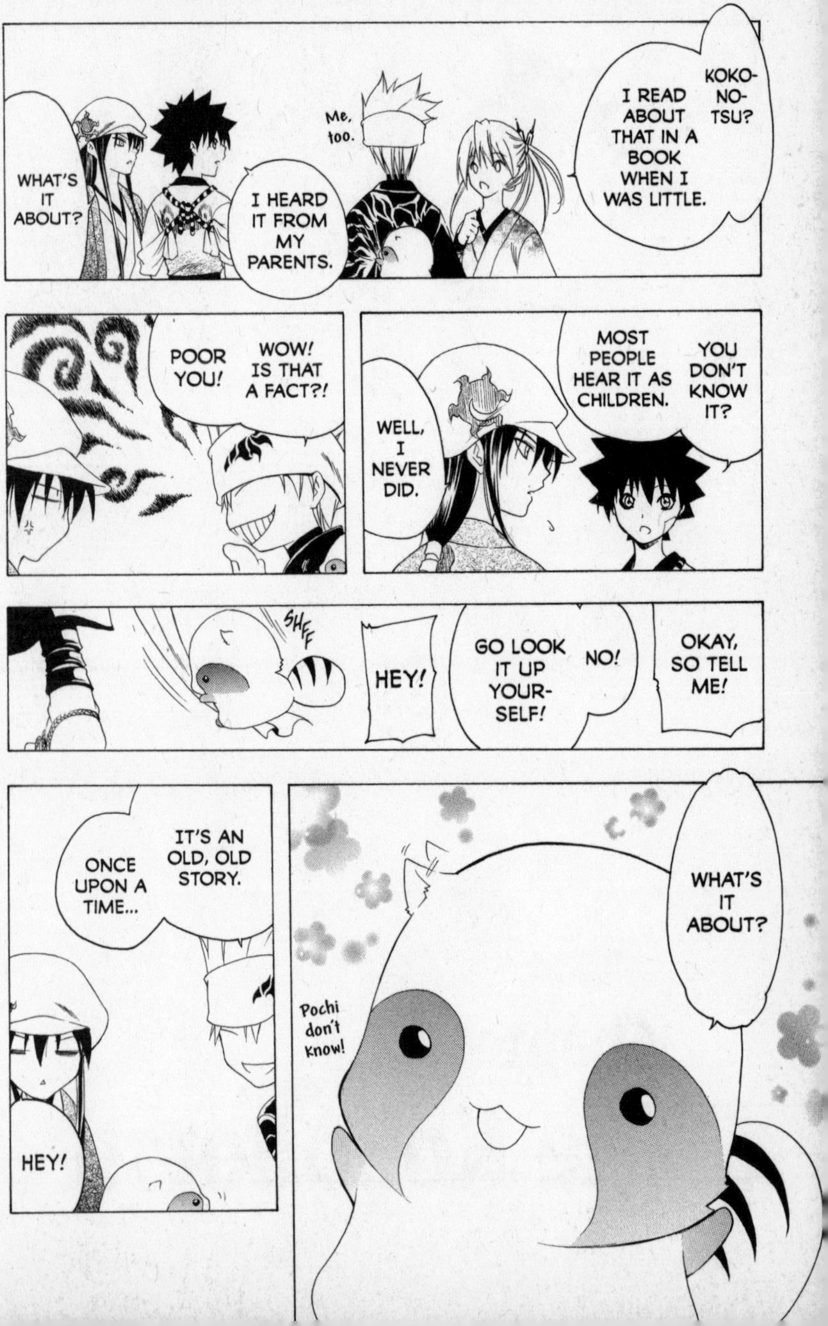
KOKO-NO-TSU?
I READ ABOUT THAT IN A BOOK WHEN I WAS LITTLE.
Me, too.
I HEARD IT FROM MY PARENTS.
WHAT'S IT ABOUT?
YOU DON'T KNOW IT?
MOST PEOPLE HEAR IT AS CHILDREN.
WELL, I NEVER DID.
WOW! IS THAT A FACT?!
POOR YOU!
OKAY, SO TELL ME!
NO!
GO LOOK IT UP YOUR-SELF!
HEY!
SHFF
WHAT'S IT ABOUT?
Pochi don't know!
IT'S AN OLD, OLD STORY.
ONCE UPON A TIME...
HEY!

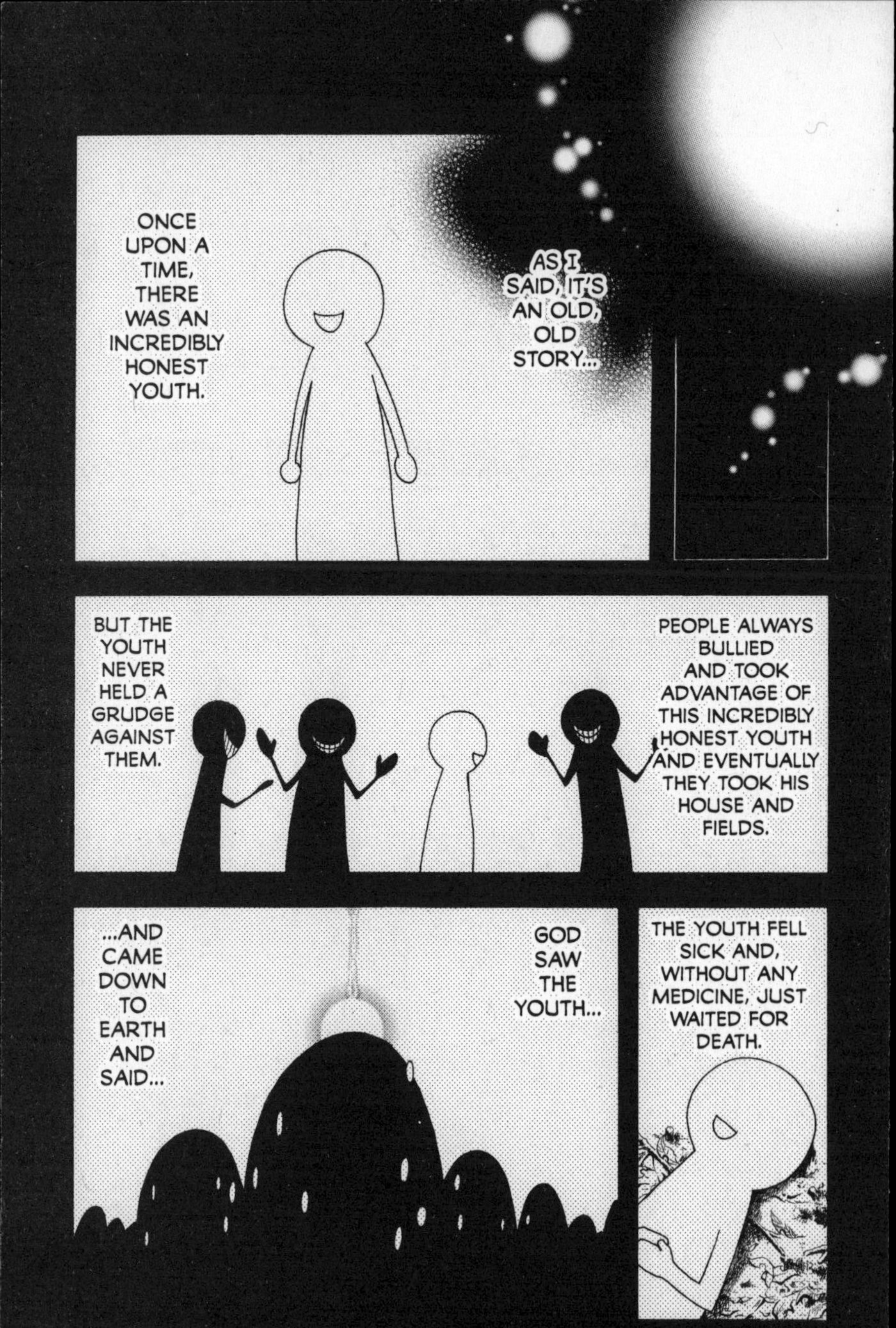
AS I SAID, IT'S AN OLD, OLD STORY...
ONCE UPON A TIME, THERE WAS AN INCREDIBLY HONEST YOUTH.
PEOPLE ALWAYS BULLIED AND TOOK ADVANTAGE OF THIS INCREDIBLY HONEST YOUTH AND EVENTUALLY THEY TOOK HIS HOUSE AND FIELDS.
BUT THE YOUTH NEVER HELD A GRUDGE AGAINST THEM.
THE YOUTH FELL SICK AND, WITHOUT ANY MEDICINE, JUST WAITED FOR DEATH.
GOD SAW THE YOUTH...
...AND CAME DOWN TO EARTH AND SAID...

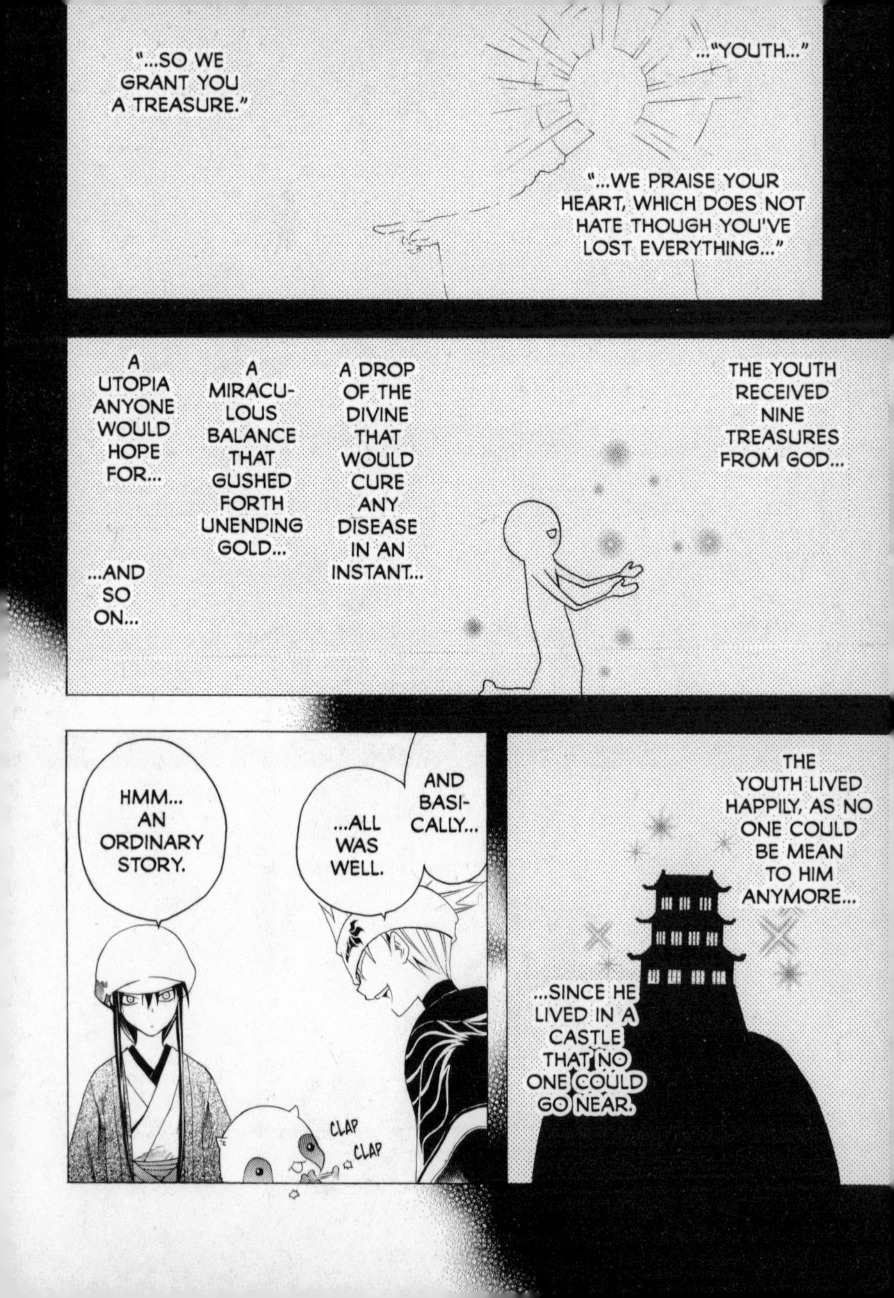
..."YOUTH..."
"...WE PRAISE YOUR HEART, WHICH DOES NOT HATE THOUGH YOU'VE LOST EVERYTHING..."
"...SO WE GRANT YOU A TREASURE."
THE YOUTH RECEIVED NINE TREASURES FROM GOD...
A DROP OF THE DIVINE THAT WOULD CURE ANY DISEASE IN AN INSTANT...
A MIRACULOUS BALANCE THAT GUSHED FORTH UNENDING GOLD...
A UTOPIA ANYONE WOULD HOPE FOR...
...AND SO ON...
THE YOUTH LIVED HAPPILY, AS NO ONE COULD BE MEAN TO HIM ANYMORE...
...SINCE HE LIVED IN A CASTLE THAT NO ONE COULD GO NEAR.
AND BASICALLY...
...ALL WAS WELL.
HMM... AN ORDINARY STORY.
CLAP
CLAP

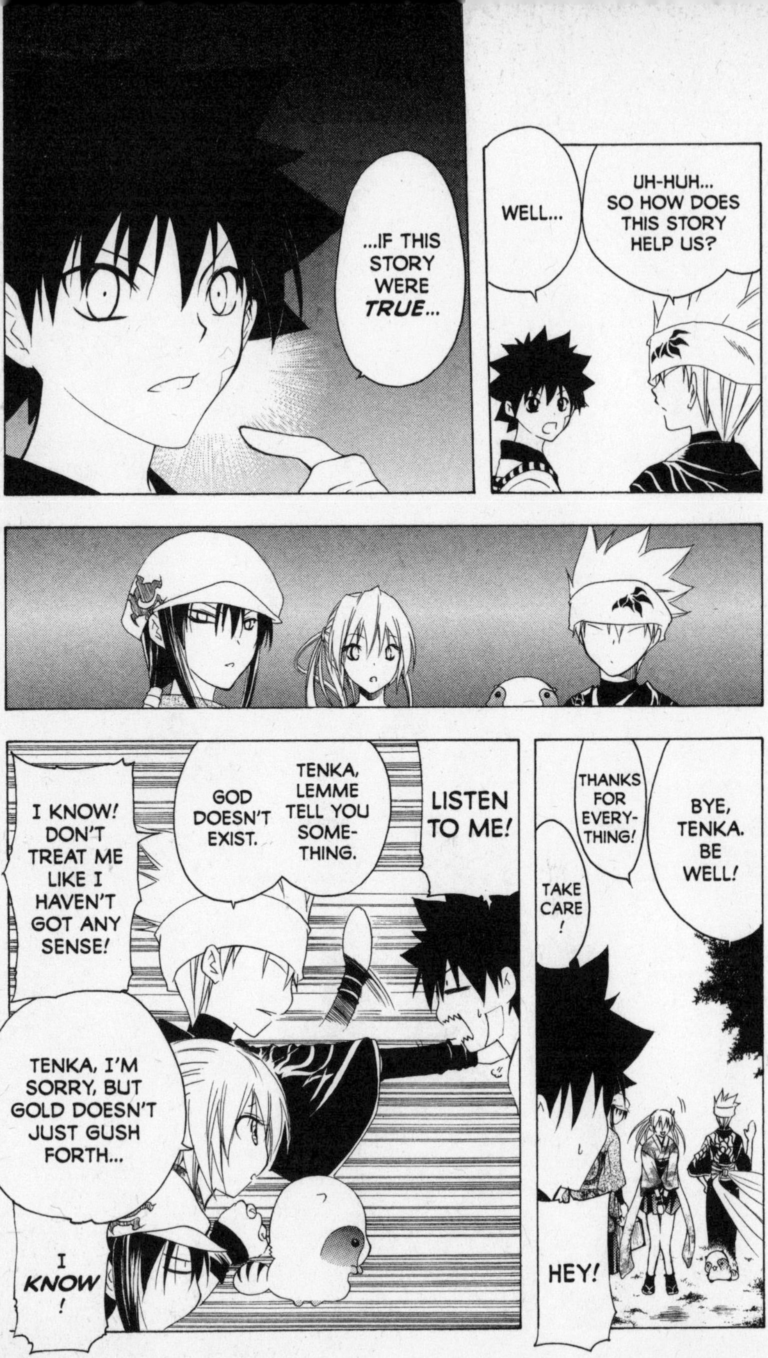
UH-HUH... SO HOW DOES THIS STORY HELP US?
WELL...
...IF THIS STORY WERE *TRUE*...
BYE, TENKA. BE WELL!
THANKS FOR EVERY-THING!
TAKE CARE!
HEY!
LISTEN TO ME!
TENKA, LEMME TELL YOU SOME-THING.
GOD DOESN'T EXIST.
I KNOW! DON'T TREAT ME LIKE I HAVEN'T GOT ANY SENSE!
TENKA, I'M SORRY, BUT GOLD DOESN'T JUST GUSH FORTH...
I *KNOW*!

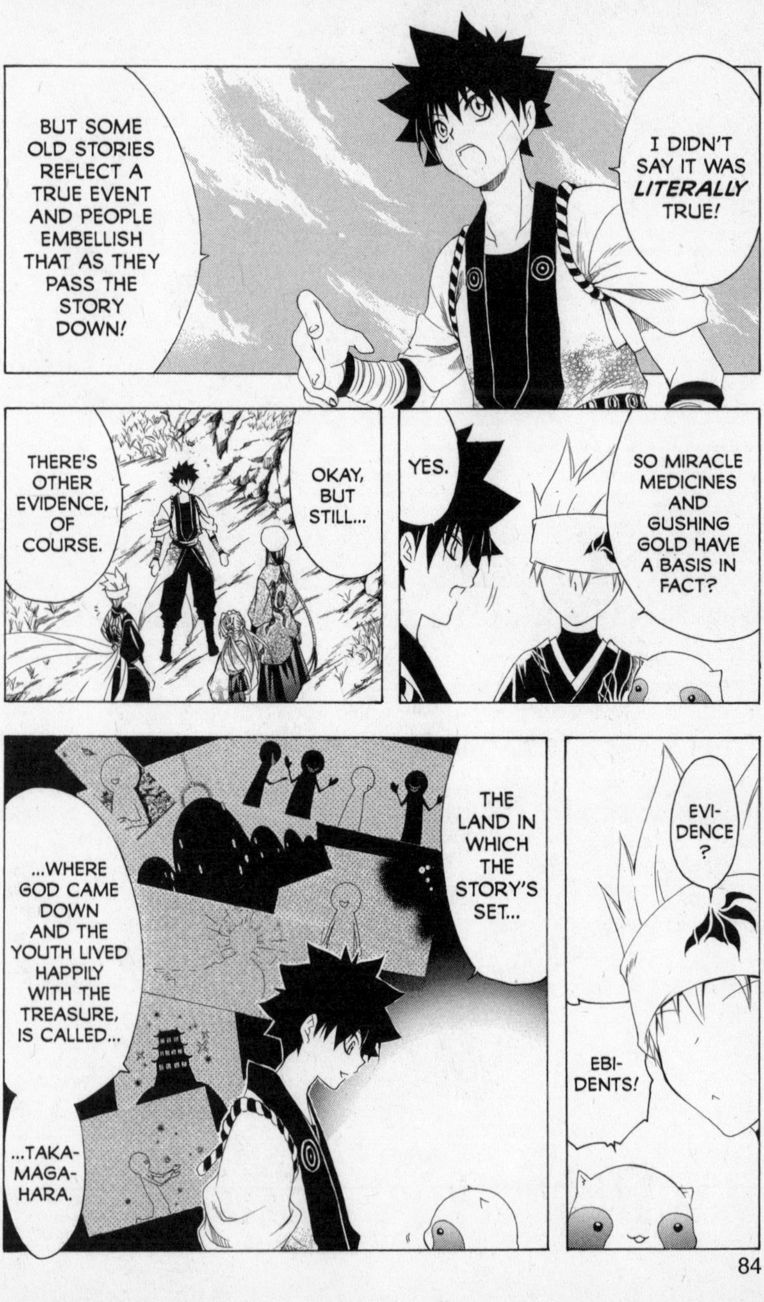
I DIDN'T SAY IT WAS *LITERALLY* TRUE!
BUT SOME OLD STORIES REFLECT A TRUE EVENT AND PEOPLE EMBELLISH THAT AS THEY PASS THE STORY DOWN!
SO MIRACLE MEDICINES AND GUSHING GOLD HAVE A BASIS IN FACT?
YES.
OKAY, BUT STILL...
THERE'S OTHER EVIDENCE, OF COURSE.
EVI-DENCE?
EBI-DENTS!
THE LAND IN WHICH THE STORY'S SET...
...WHERE GOD CAME DOWN AND THE YOUTH LIVED HAPPILY WITH THE TREASURE, IS CALLED...
...TAKA-MAGA-HARA.

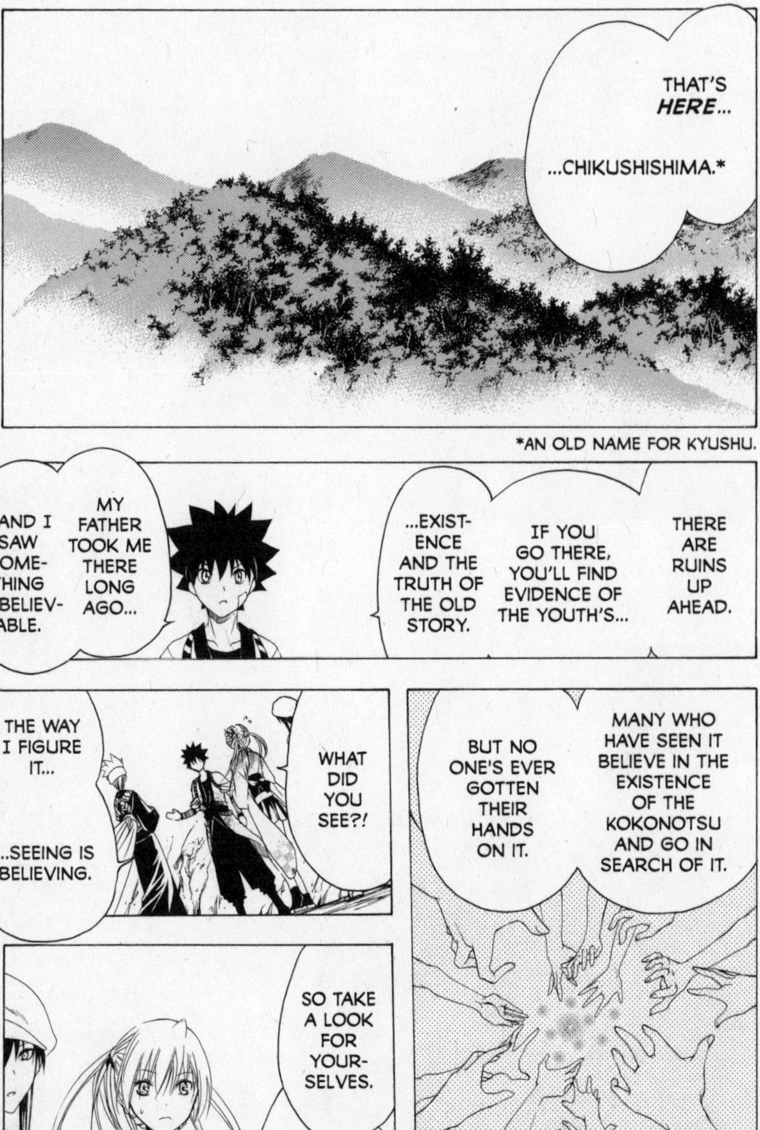
THAT'S *HERE*...
...CHIKUSHISHIMA.*
*AN OLD NAME FOR KYUSHU.
THERE ARE RUINS UP AHEAD.
IF YOU GO THERE, YOU'LL FIND EVIDENCE OF THE YOUTH'S...
...EXISTENCE AND THE TRUTH OF THE OLD STORY.
MY FATHER TOOK ME THERE LONG AGO...
...AND I SAW SOMETHING UNBELIEVABLE.
MANY WHO HAVE SEEN IT BELIEVE IN THE EXISTENCE OF THE KOKONOTSU AND GO IN SEARCH OF IT.
BUT NO ONE'S EVER GOTTEN THEIR HANDS ON IT.
WHAT DID YOU SEE?!
THE WAY I FIGURE IT...
...SEEING IS BELIEVING.
SO TAKE A LOOK FOR YOURSELVES.

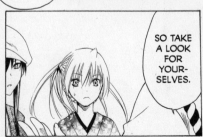

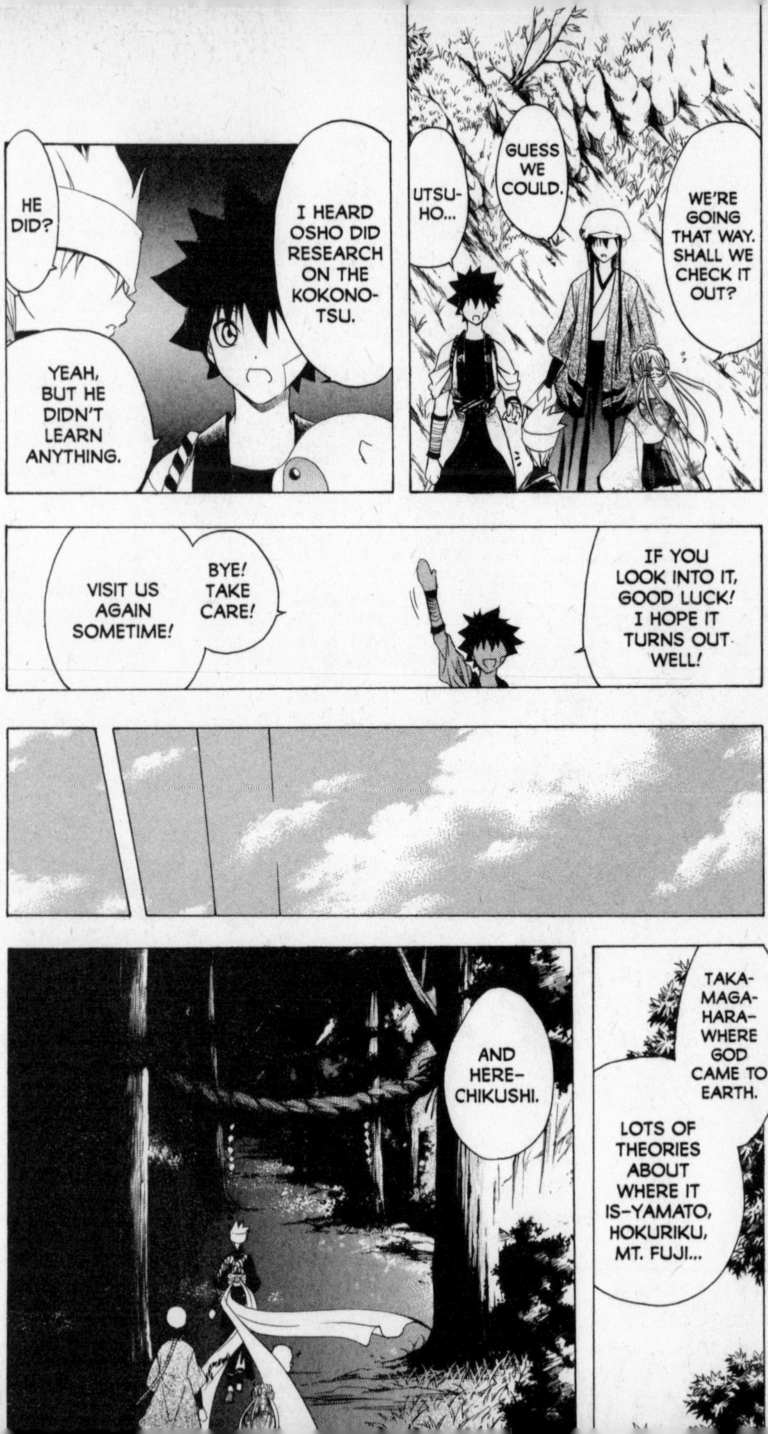
WE'RE GOING THAT WAY. SHALL WE CHECK IT OUT?
GUESS WE COULD.
UTSU-HO...
I HEARD OSHO DID RESEARCH ON THE KOKONO-TSU.
HE DID?
YEAH, BUT HE DIDN'T LEARN ANYTHING.
IF YOU LOOK INTO IT, GOOD LUCK! I HOPE IT TURNS OUT WELL!
BYE! TAKE CARE!
VISIT US AGAIN SOMETIME!
TAKA-MAGA-HARA-WHERE GOD CAME TO EARTH.
LOTS OF THEORIES ABOUT WHERE IT IS-YAMATO, HOKURIKU, MT. FUJI...
AND HERE-CHIKUSHI.

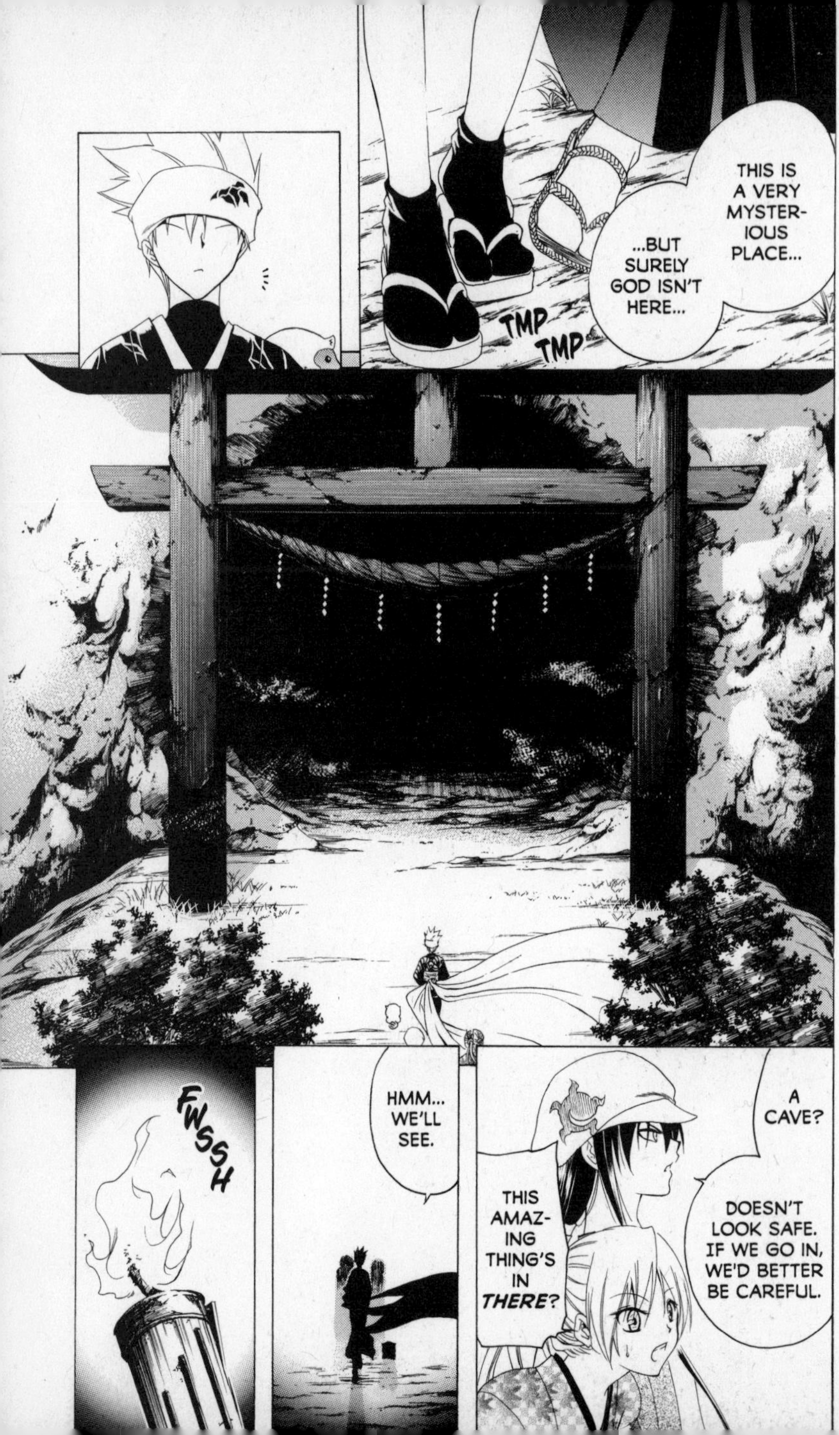
THIS IS A VERY MYSTER-IOUS PLACE...
...BUT SURELY GOD ISN'T HERE...
TMP TMP
A CAVE?
DOESN'T LOOK SAFE. IF WE GO IN, WE'D BETTER BE CAREFUL.
THIS AMAZ-ING THING'S IN *THERE*?
HMM... WE'LL SEE.
FWSSH

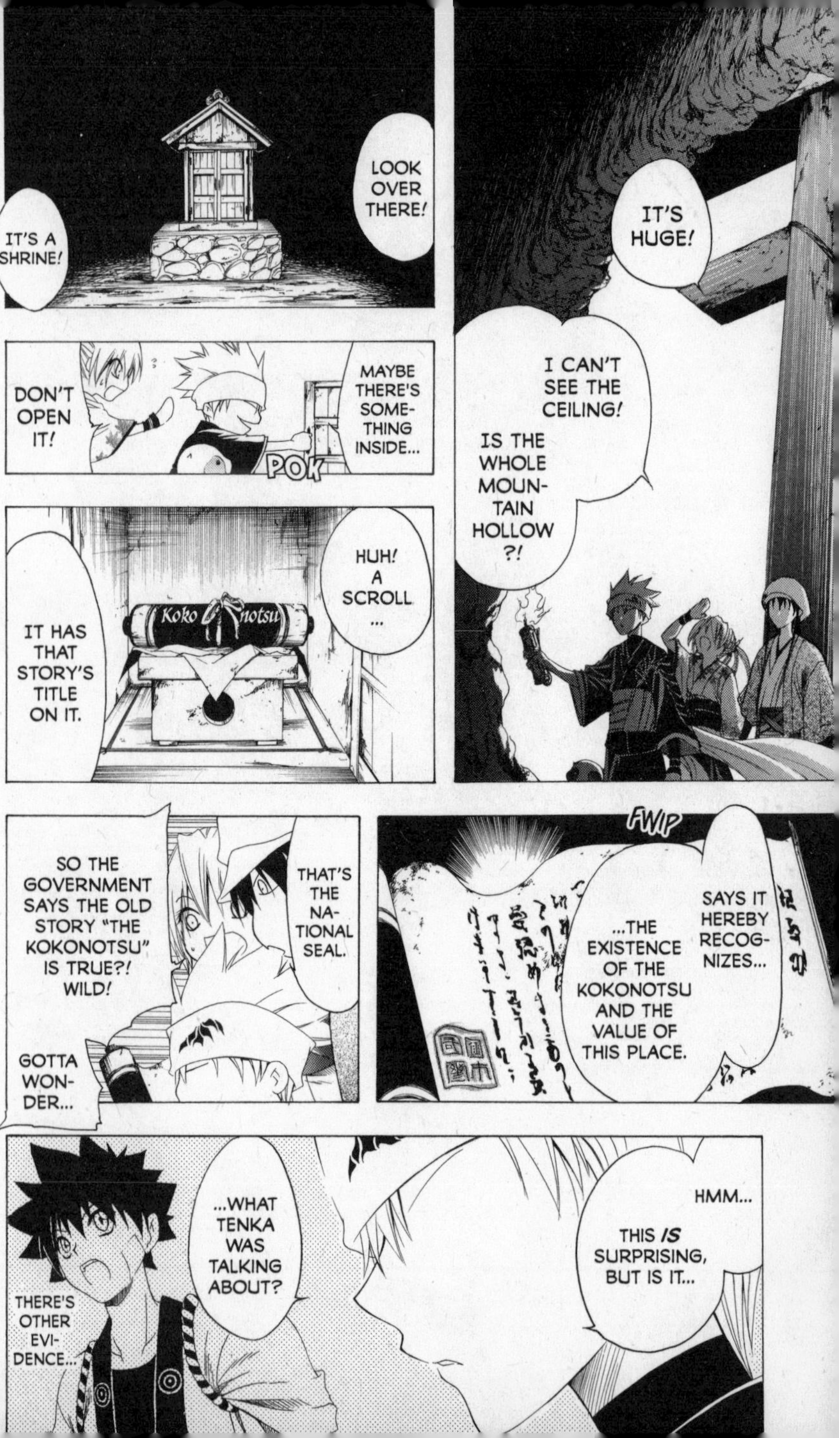
IT'S HUGE!
I CAN'T SEE THE CEILING!
IS THE WHOLE MOUNTAIN HOLLOW?!
LOOK OVER THERE!
IT'S A SHRINE!
MAYBE THERE'S SOMETHING INSIDE...
POK
DON'T OPEN IT!
HUH! A SCROLL...
IT HAS THAT STORY'S TITLE ON IT.
FWIP
SAYS IT HEREBY RECOGNIZES...
...THE EXISTENCE OF THE KOKONOTSU AND THE VALUE OF THIS PLACE.
THAT'S THE NATIONAL SEAL.
SO THE GOVERNMENT SAYS THE OLD STORY "THE KOKONOTSU" IS TRUE?! WILD!
GOTTA WONDER...
HMM...
THIS *IS* SURPRISING, BUT IS IT...
...WHAT TENKA WAS TALKING ABOUT?
THERE'S OTHER EVIDENCE...

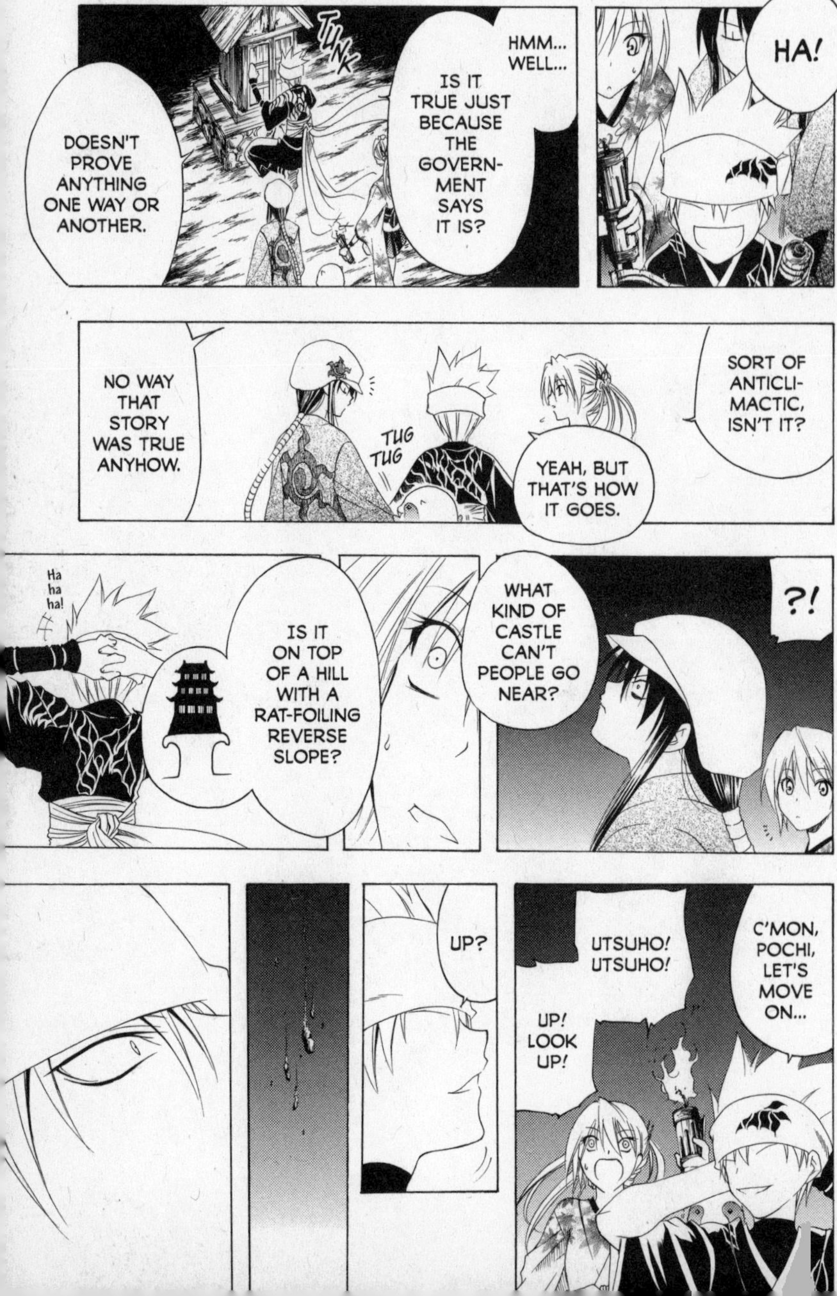
HA!
HMM... WELL...
IS IT TRUE JUST BECAUSE THE GOVERN-MENT SAYS IT IS?
TINK
DOESN'T PROVE ANYTHING ONE WAY OR ANOTHER.
SORT OF ANTICLI-MACTIC, ISN'T IT?
YEAH, BUT THAT'S HOW IT GOES.
TUG TUG
NO WAY THAT STORY WAS TRUE ANYHOW.
?!
WHAT KIND OF CASTLE CAN'T PEOPLE GO NEAR?
IS IT ON TOP OF A HILL WITH A RAT-FOILING REVERSE SLOPE?
Ha ha ha!
C'MON, POCHI, LET'S MOVE ON...
UTSUHO! UTSUHO!
UP! LOOK UP!
UP?

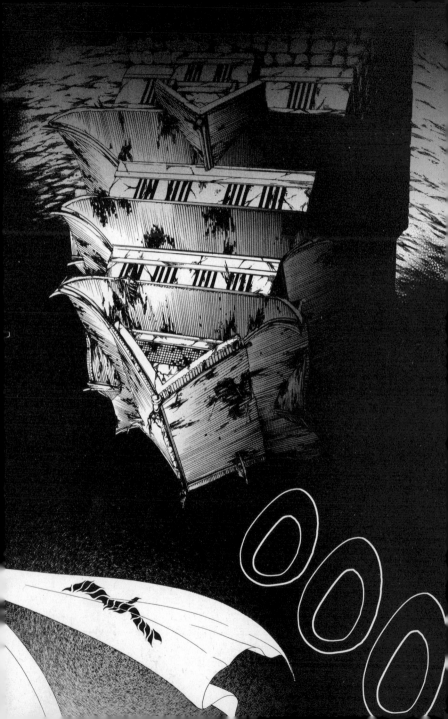

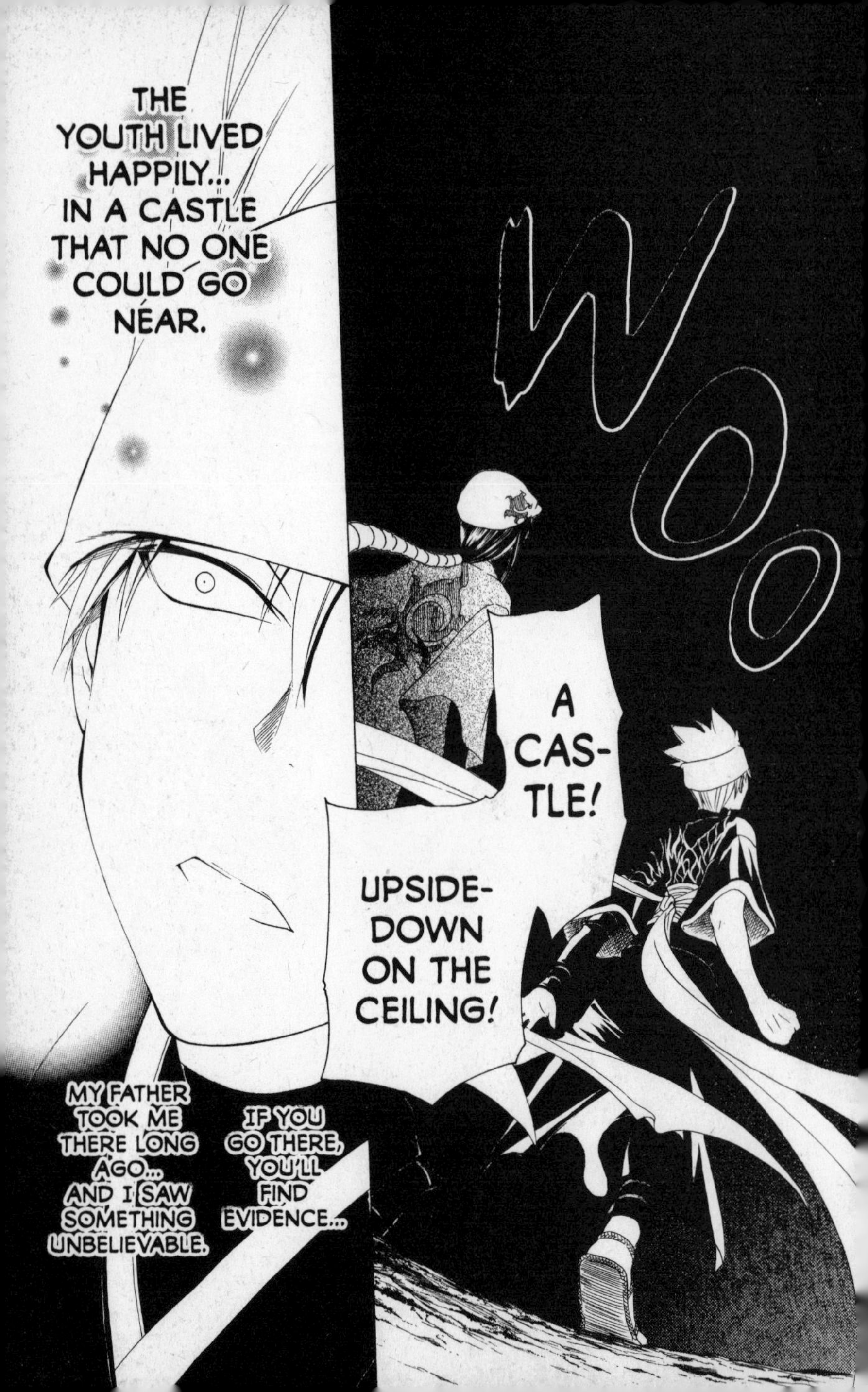
WOOO
A CASTLE!
UPSIDE-DOWN ON THE CEILING!
THE YOUTH LIVED HAPPILY... IN A CASTLE THAT NO ONE COULD GO NEAR.
IF YOU GO THERE, YOU'LL FIND EVIDENCE...
MY FATHER TOOK ME THERE LONG AGO... AND I SAW SOMETHING UNBELIEVABLE.

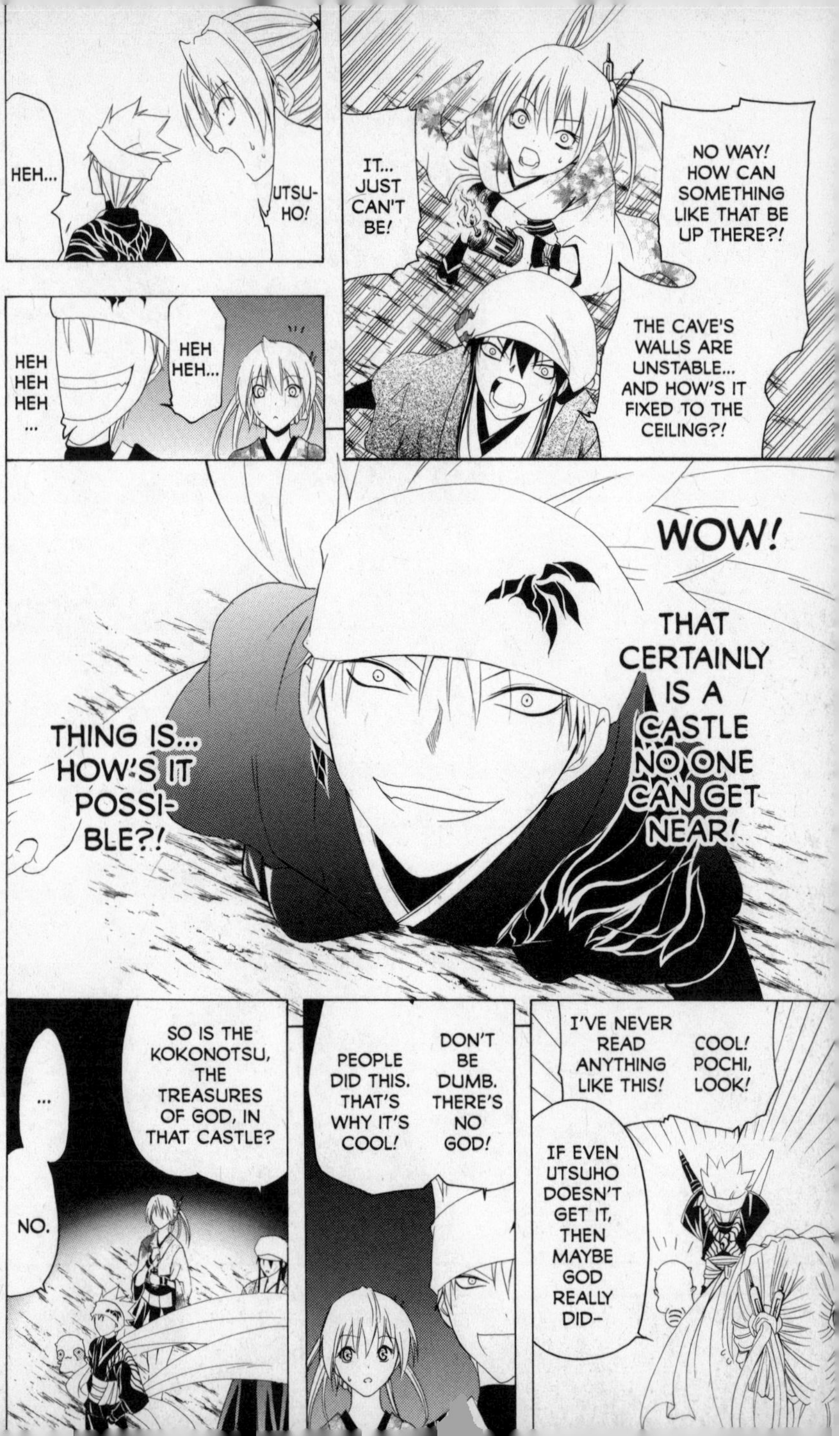
NO WAY! HOW CAN SOMETHING LIKE THAT BE UP THERE?!
IT... JUST CAN'T BE!
THE CAVE'S WALLS ARE UNSTABLE... AND HOW'S IT FIXED TO THE CEILING?!
UTSU-HO!
HEH...
HEH HEH...
HEH HEH HEH ...
WOW!
THAT CERTAINLY IS A CASTLE NO ONE CAN GET NEAR!
THING IS... HOW'S IT POSSIBLE?!
COOL! POCHI, LOOK!
I'VE NEVER READ ANYTHING LIKE THIS!
IF EVEN UTSUHO DOESN'T GET IT, THEN MAYBE GOD REALLY DID–
DON'T BE DUMB. THERE'S NO GOD!
PEOPLE DID THIS. THAT'S WHY IT'S COOL!
SO IS THE KOKONOTSU, THE TREASURES OF GOD, IN THAT CASTLE?
...
NO.

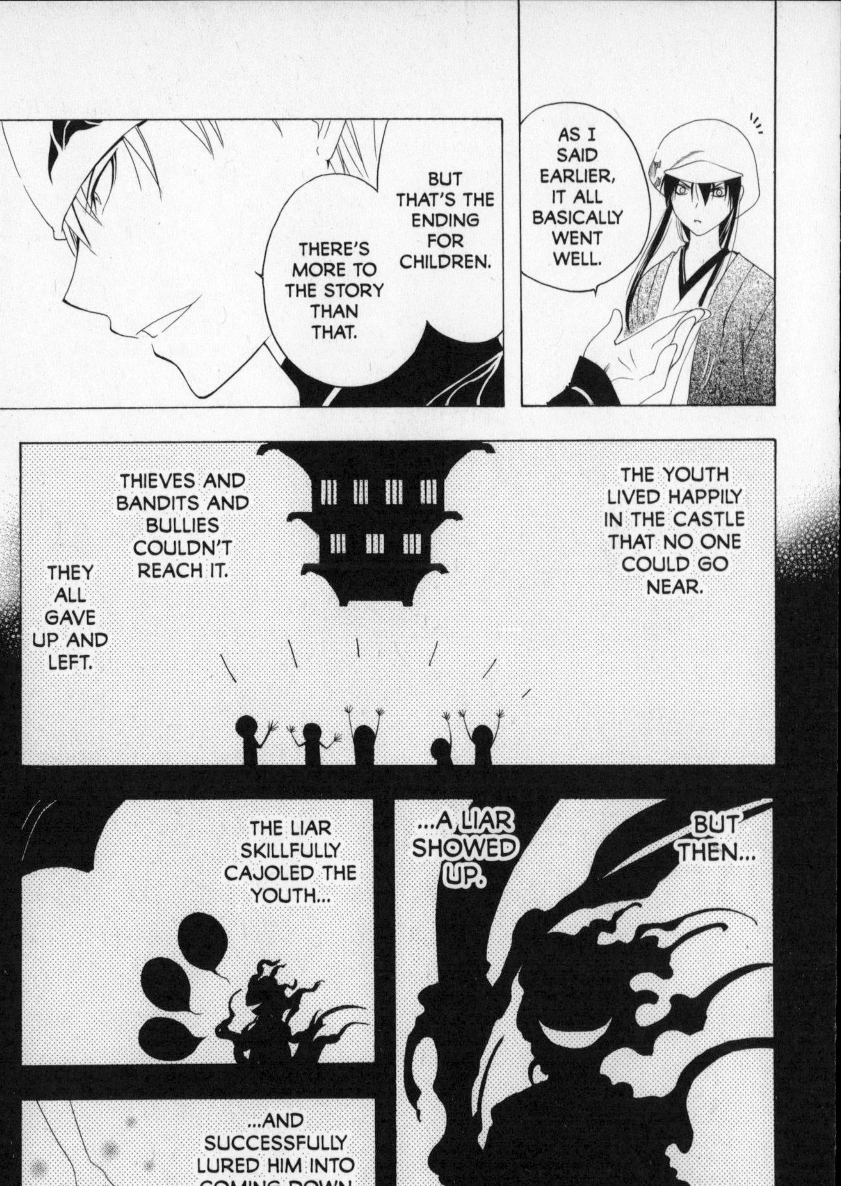
AS I SAID EARLIER, IT ALL BASICALLY WENT WELL.
BUT THAT'S THE ENDING FOR CHILDREN.
THERE'S MORE TO THE STORY THAN THAT.
THE YOUTH LIVED HAPPILY IN THE CASTLE THAT NO ONE COULD GO NEAR.
THIEVES AND BANDITS AND BULLIES COULDN'T REACH IT.
THEY ALL GAVE UP AND LEFT.
BUT THEN...
...A LIAR SHOWED UP.
THE LIAR SKILLFULLY CAJOLED THE YOUTH...
...AND SUCCESSFULLY LURED HIM INTO COMING DOWN WITH THE TREASURES.

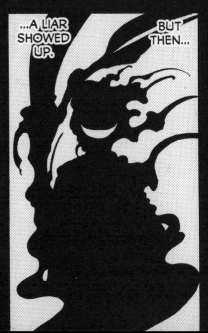

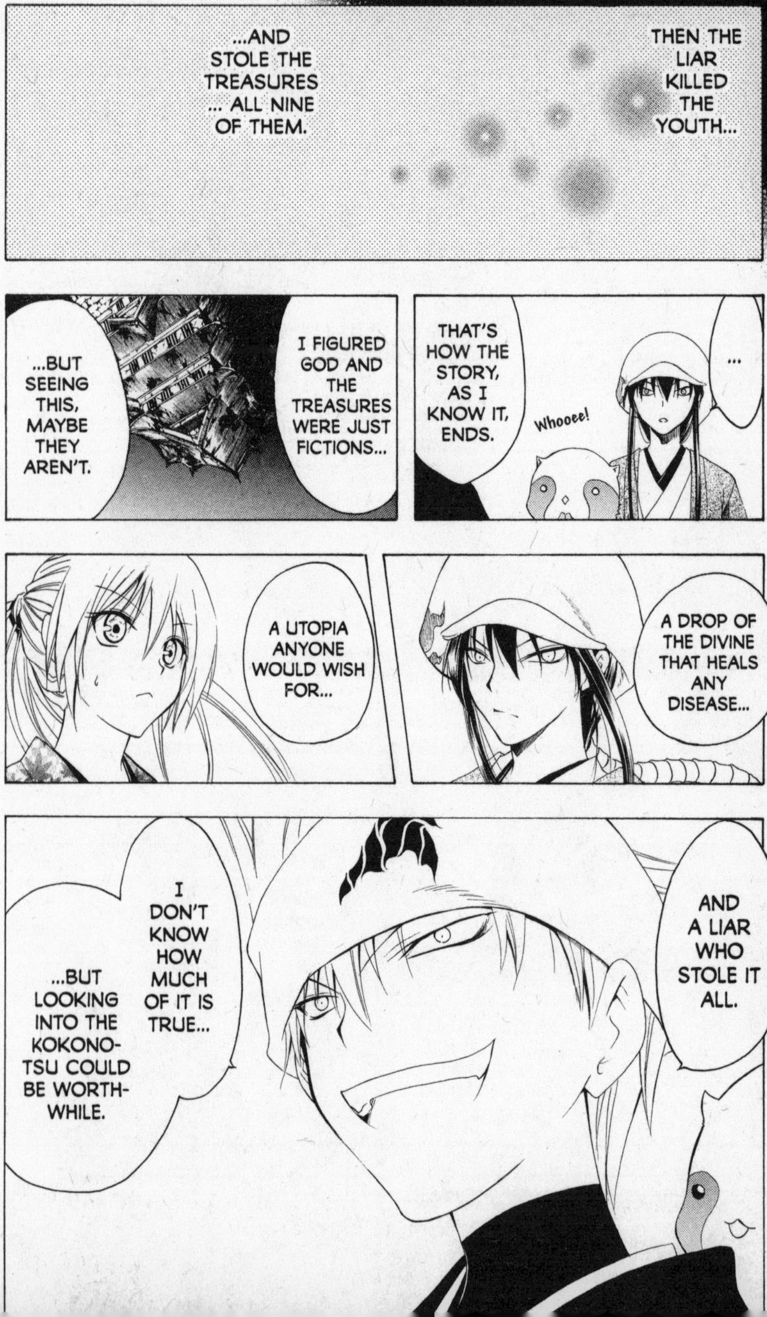
THEN THE LIAR KILLED THE YOUTH...
...AND STOLE THE TREASURES ... ALL NINE OF THEM.
...
THAT'S HOW THE STORY, AS I KNOW IT, ENDS.
Whooee!
I FIGURED GOD AND THE TREASURES WERE JUST FICTIONS...
...BUT SEEING THIS, MAYBE THEY AREN'T.
A DROP OF THE DIVINE THAT HEALS ANY DISEASE...
A UTOPIA ANYONE WOULD WISH FOR...
AND A LIAR WHO STOLE IT ALL.
I DON'T KNOW HOW MUCH OF IT IS TRUE...
...BUT LOOKING INTO THE KOKONO-TSU COULD BE WORTH-WHILE.

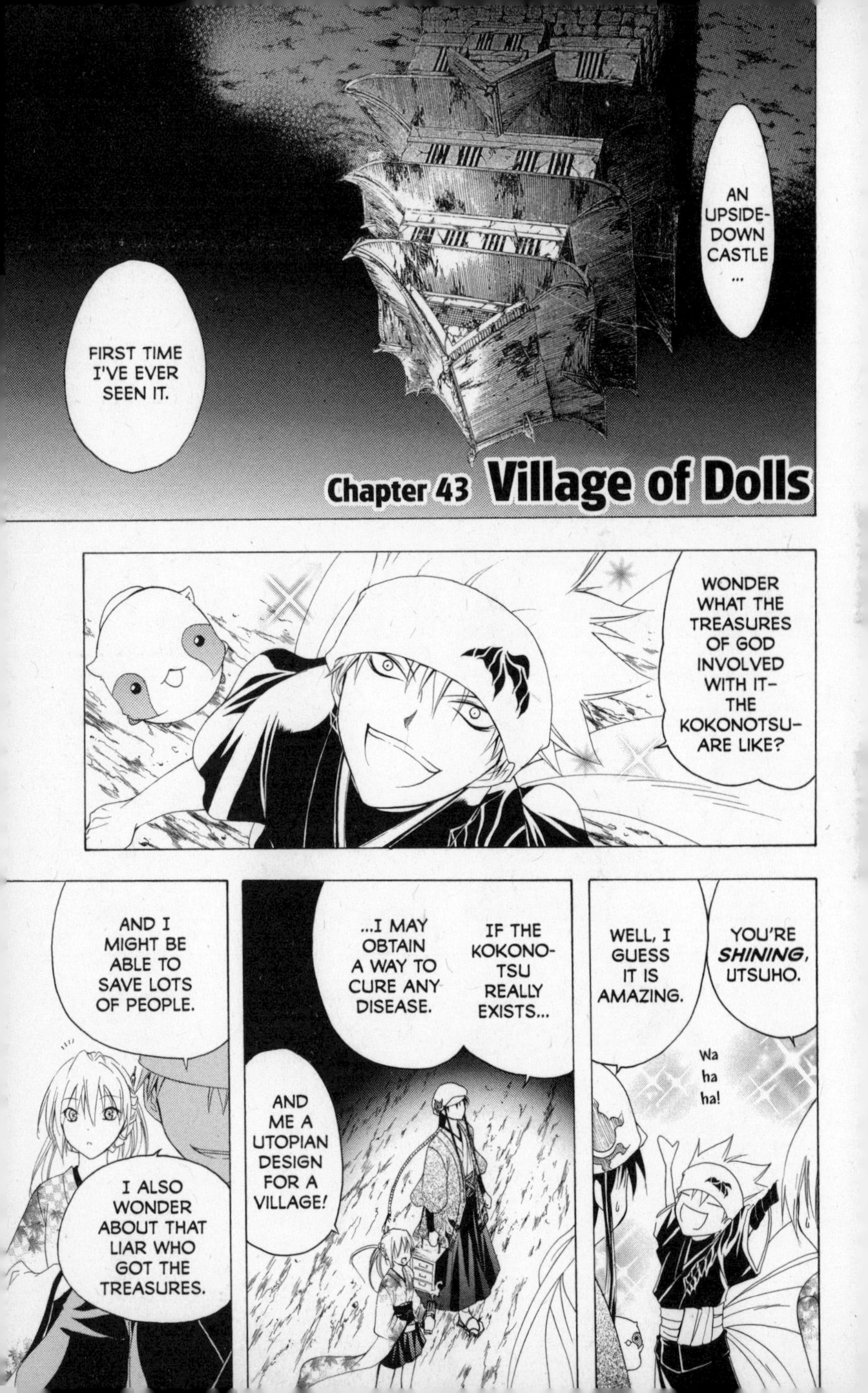
AN UPSIDE-DOWN CASTLE ...
FIRST TIME I'VE EVER SEEN IT.
Chapter 43 Village of Dolls
WONDER WHAT THE TREASURES OF GOD INVOLVED WITH IT–THE KOKONOTSU–ARE LIKE?
YOU'RE *SHINING*, UTSUHO.
WELL, I GUESS IT IS AMAZING.
Wa ha ha!
IF THE KOKONOTSU REALLY EXISTS...
...I MAY OBTAIN A WAY TO CURE ANY DISEASE.
AND ME A UTOPIAN DESIGN FOR A VILLAGE!
AND I MIGHT BE ABLE TO SAVE LOTS OF PEOPLE.
I ALSO WONDER ABOUT THAT LIAR WHO GOT THE TREASURES.

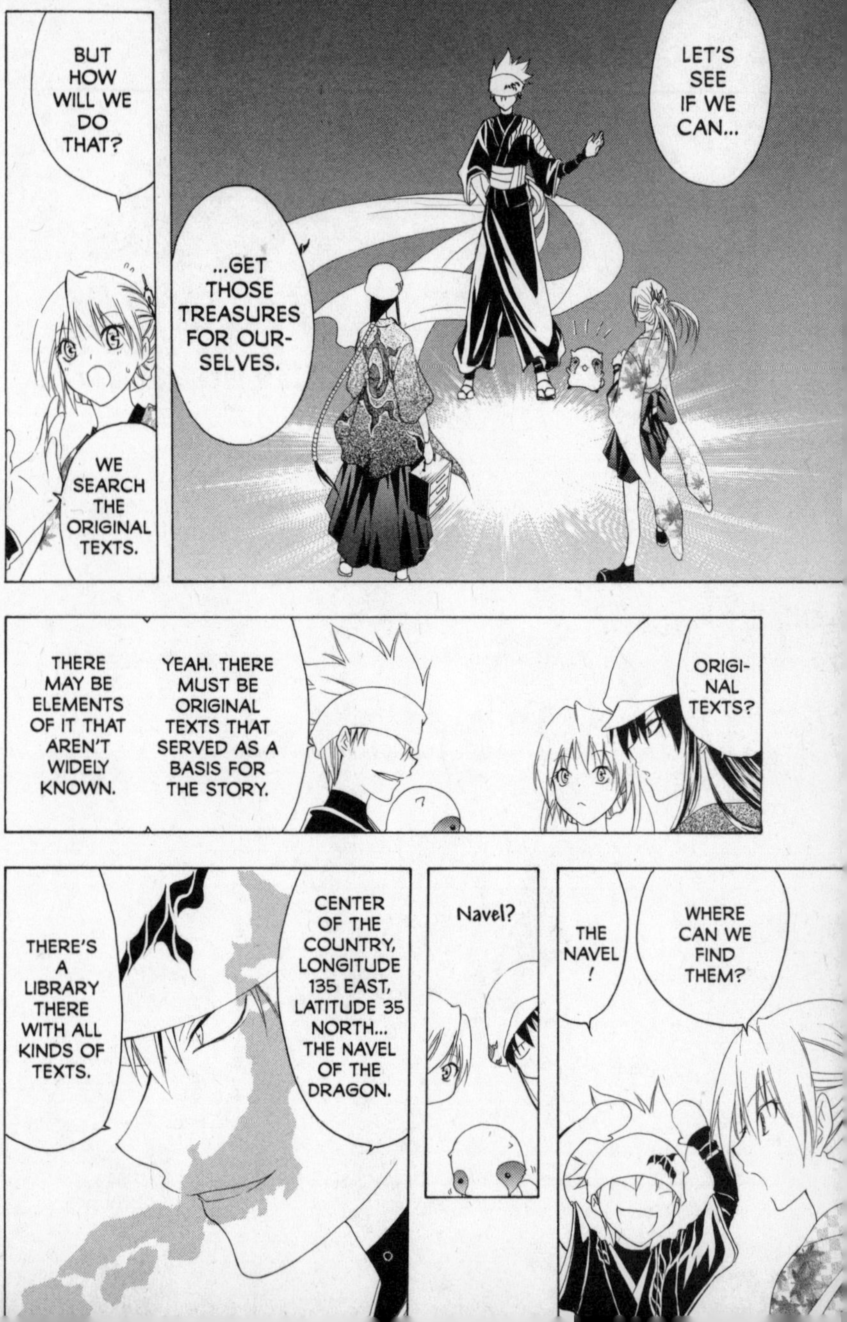
LET'S SEE IF WE CAN...
...GET THOSE TREASURES FOR OURSELVES.
BUT HOW WILL WE DO THAT?
WE SEARCH THE ORIGINAL TEXTS.
ORIGINAL TEXTS?
YEAH. THERE MUST BE ORIGINAL TEXTS THAT SERVED AS A BASIS FOR THE STORY.
THERE MAY BE ELEMENTS OF IT THAT AREN'T WIDELY KNOWN.
WHERE CAN WE FIND THEM?
THE NAVEL!
Navel?
CENTER OF THE COUNTRY, LONGITUDE 135 EAST, LATITUDE 35 NORTH... THE NAVEL OF THE DRAGON.
THERE'S A LIBRARY THERE WITH ALL KINDS OF TEXTS.

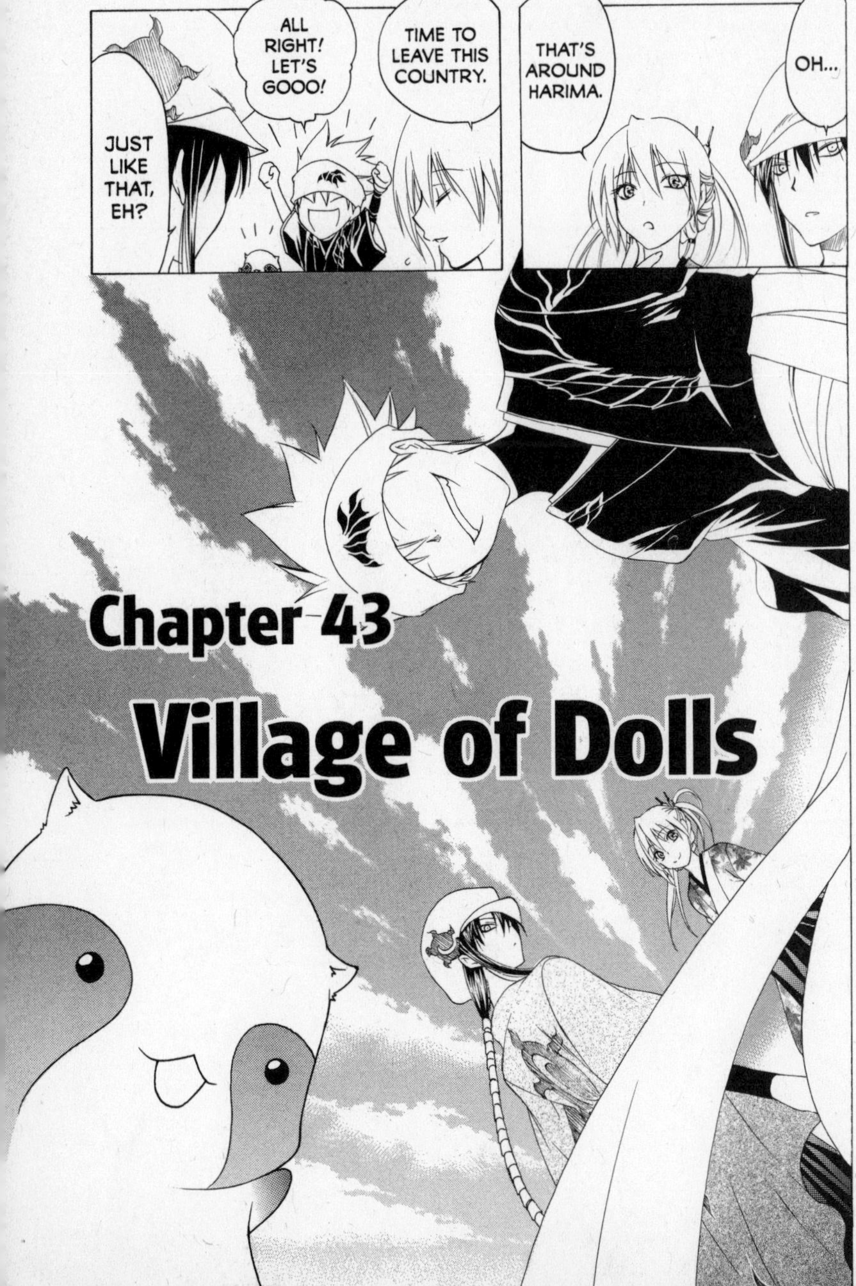
OH...
THAT'S AROUND HARIMA.
TIME TO LEAVE THIS COUNTRY.
ALL RIGHT! LET'S GOOO!
JUST LIKE THAT, EH?
Chapter 43
Village of Dolls

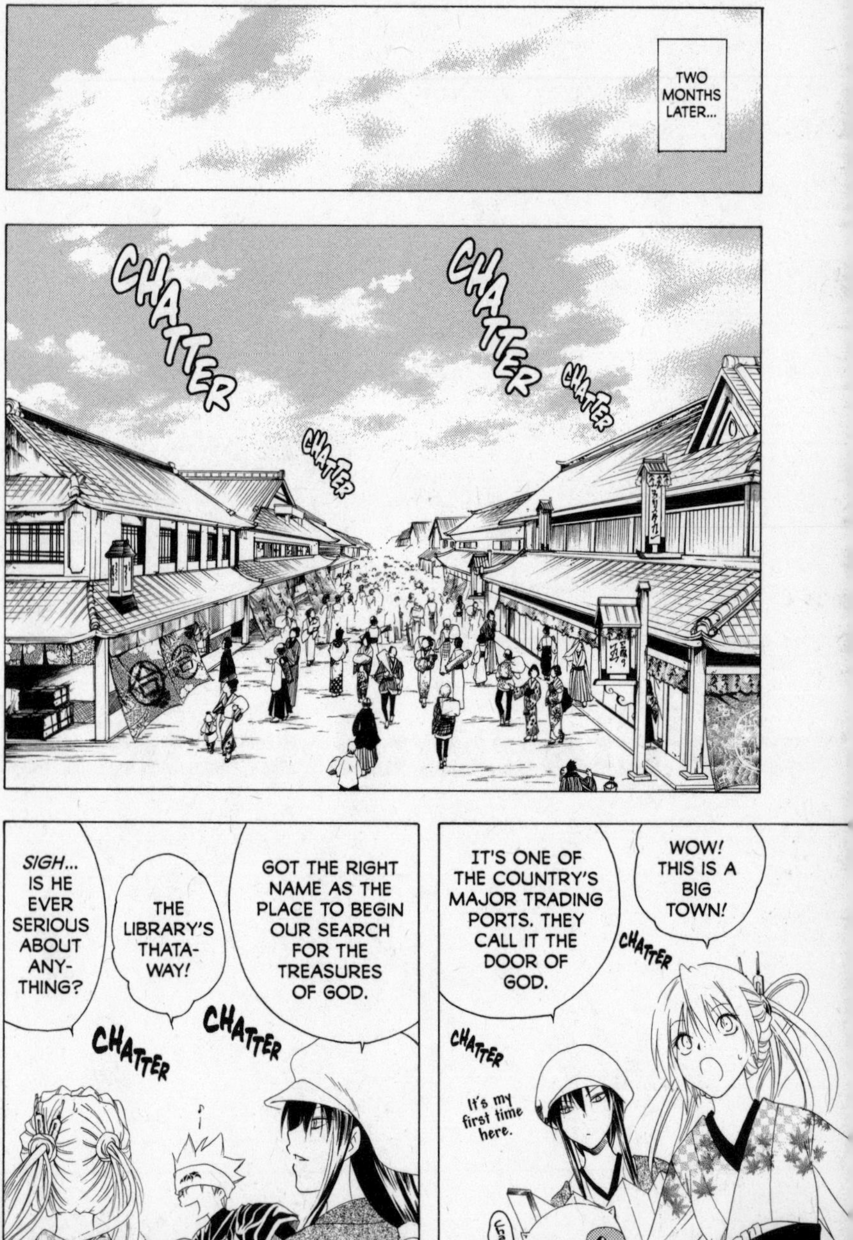
TWO MONTHS LATER...
CHATTER
CHATTER
CHATTER
CHATTER
WOW! THIS IS A BIG TOWN!
IT'S ONE OF THE COUNTRY'S MAJOR TRADING PORTS. THEY CALL IT THE DOOR OF GOD.
CHATTER
CHATTER
It's my first time here.
GOT THE RIGHT NAME AS THE PLACE TO BEGIN OUR SEARCH FOR THE TREASURES OF GOD.
THE LIBRARY'S THATA-WAY!
SIGH... IS HE EVER SERIOUS ABOUT ANY-THING?
CHATTER
CHATTER

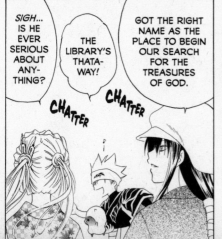

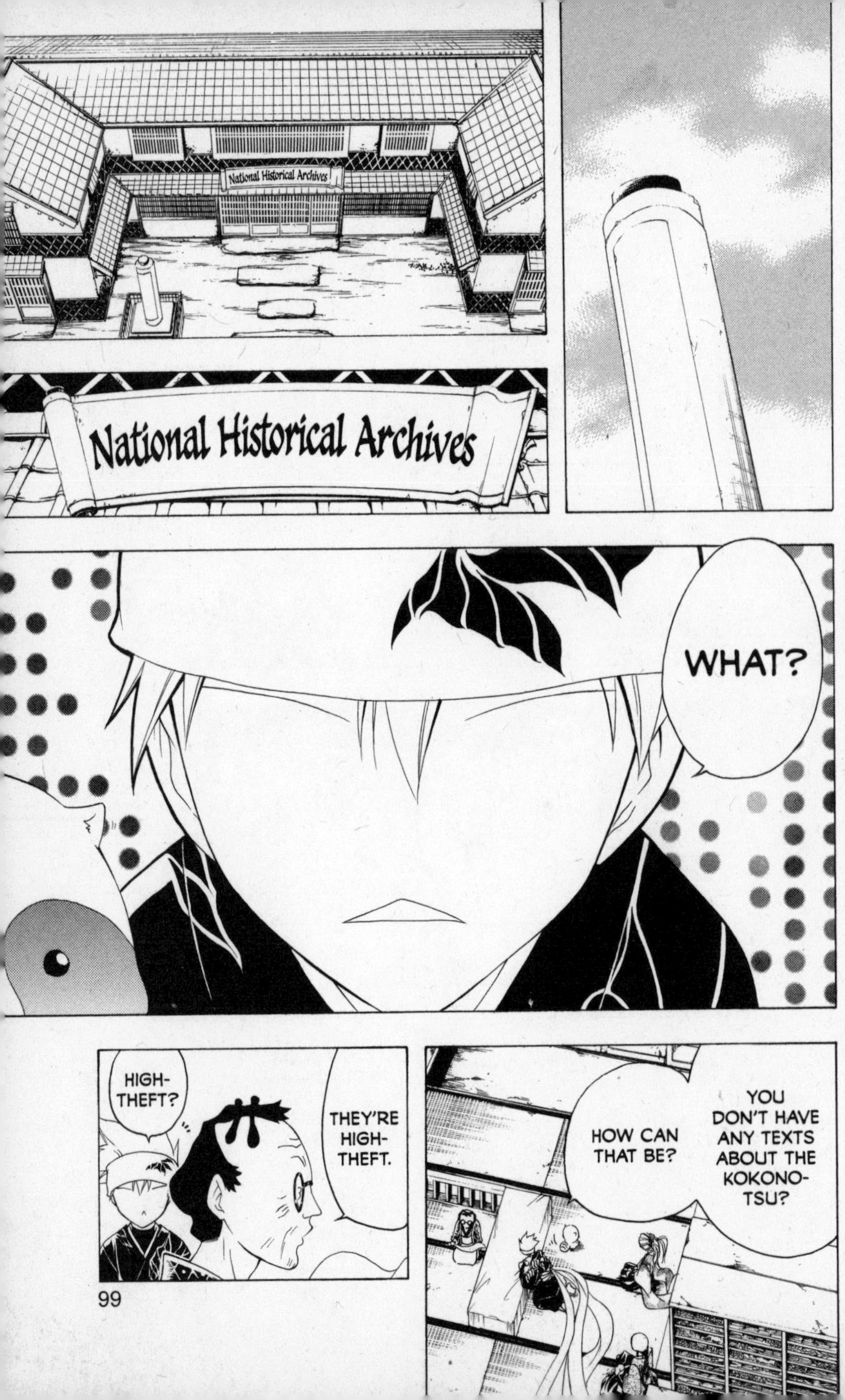
National Historical Archives
National Historical Archives
WHAT?
YOU DON'T HAVE ANY TEXTS ABOUT THE KOKONO-TSU?
HOW CAN THAT BE?
THEY'RE HIGH-THEFT.
HIGH-THEFT?

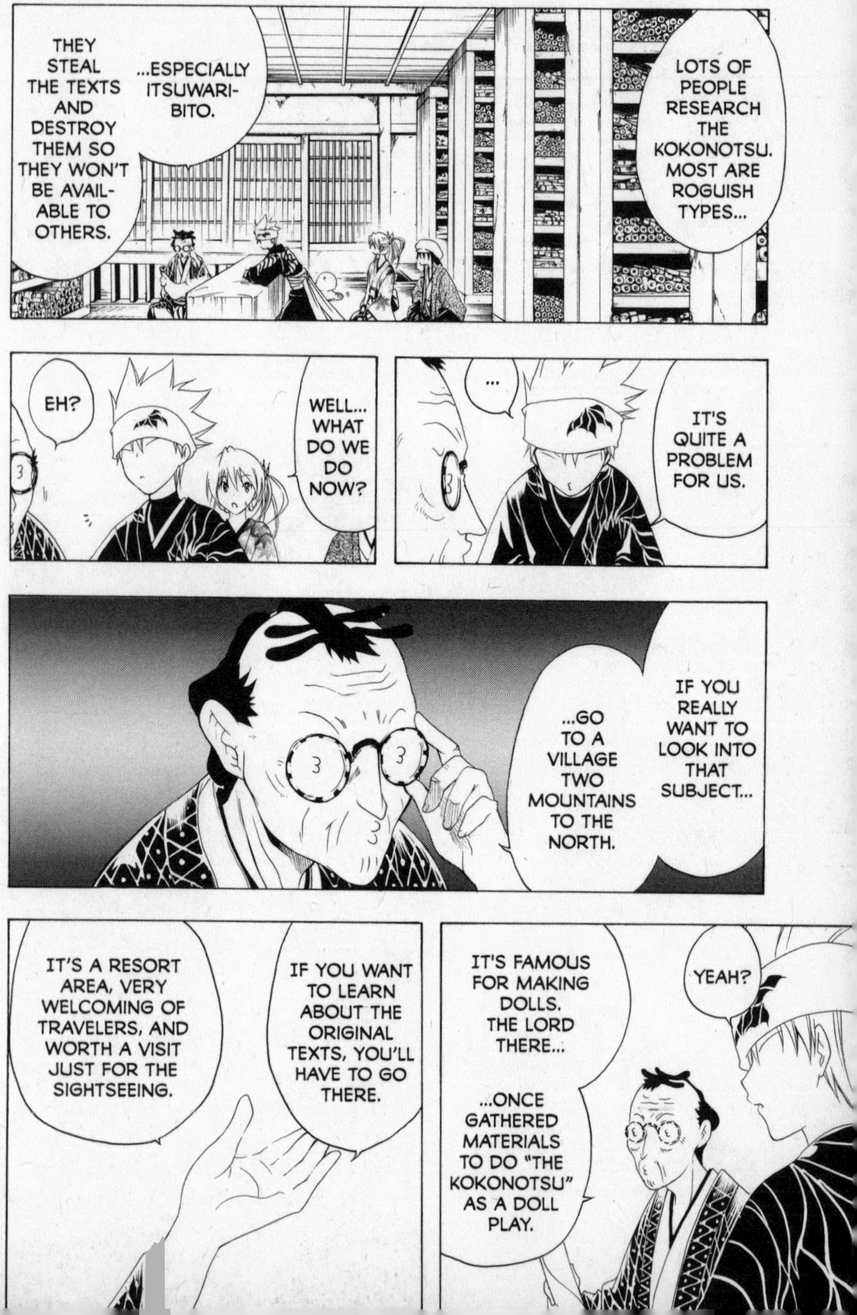
LOTS OF PEOPLE RESEARCH THE KOKONOTSU. MOST ARE ROGUISH TYPES...
...ESPECIALLY ITSUWARI-BITO.
THEY STEAL THE TEXTS AND DESTROY THEM SO THEY WON'T BE AVAIL-ABLE TO OTHERS.
IT'S QUITE A PROBLEM FOR US.
...
WELL... WHAT DO WE DO NOW?
EH?
IF YOU REALLY WANT TO LOOK INTO THAT SUBJECT...
...GO TO A VILLAGE TWO MOUNTAINS TO THE NORTH.
YEAH?
IT'S FAMOUS FOR MAKING DOLLS. THE LORD THERE...
...ONCE GATHERED MATERIALS TO DO "THE KOKONOTSU" AS A DOLL PLAY.
IF YOU WANT TO LEARN ABOUT THE ORIGINAL TEXTS, YOU'LL HAVE TO GO THERE.
IT'S A RESORT AREA, VERY WELCOMING OF TRAVELERS, AND WORTH A VISIT JUST FOR THE SIGHTSEEING.

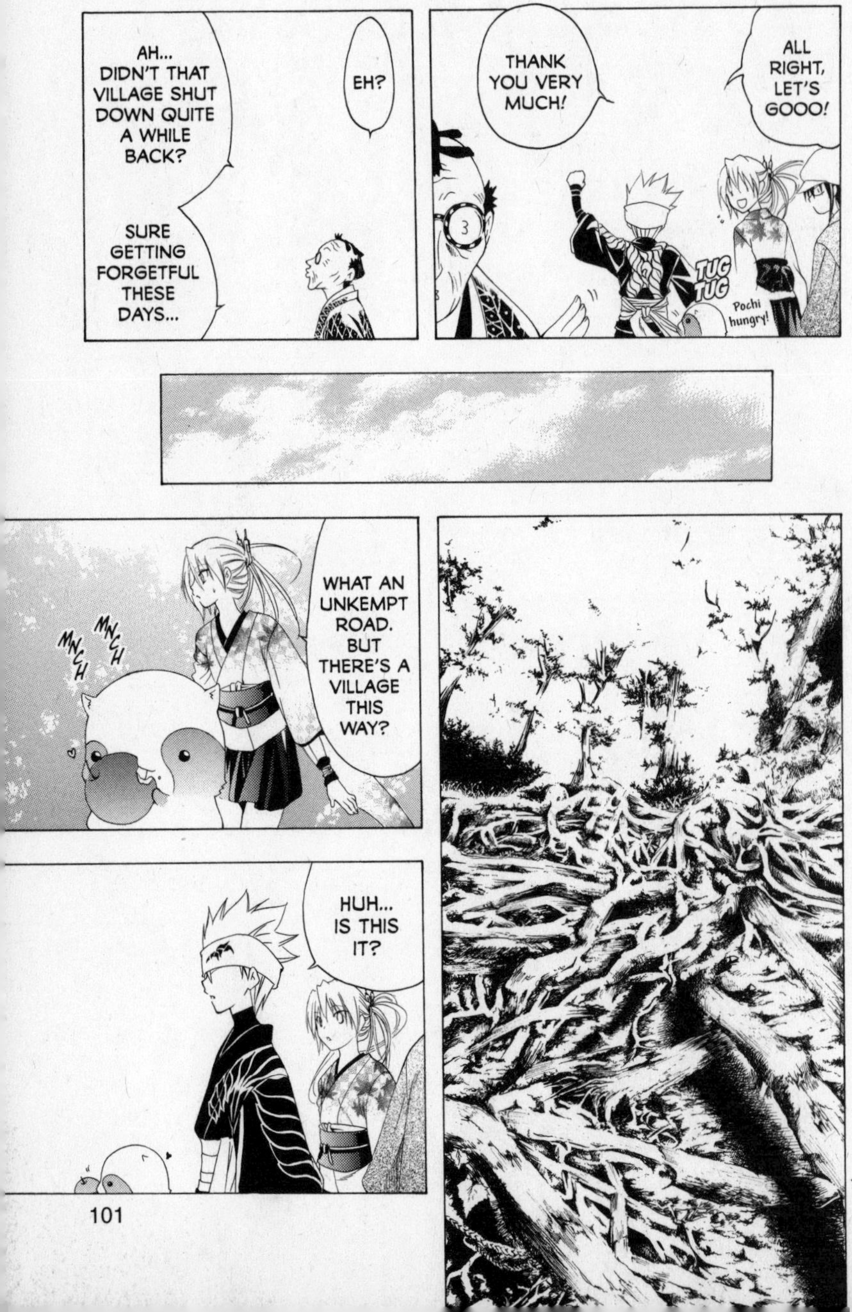
ALL RIGHT, LET'S GOOO!
TUG TUG
Pochi hungry!
THANK YOU VERY MUCH!
EH?
AH... DIDN'T THAT VILLAGE SHUT DOWN QUITE A WHILE BACK?
SURE GETTING FORGETFUL THESE DAYS...
WHAT AN UNKEMPT ROAD. BUT THERE'S A VILLAGE THIS WAY?
MNCH MNCH
HUH... IS THIS IT?

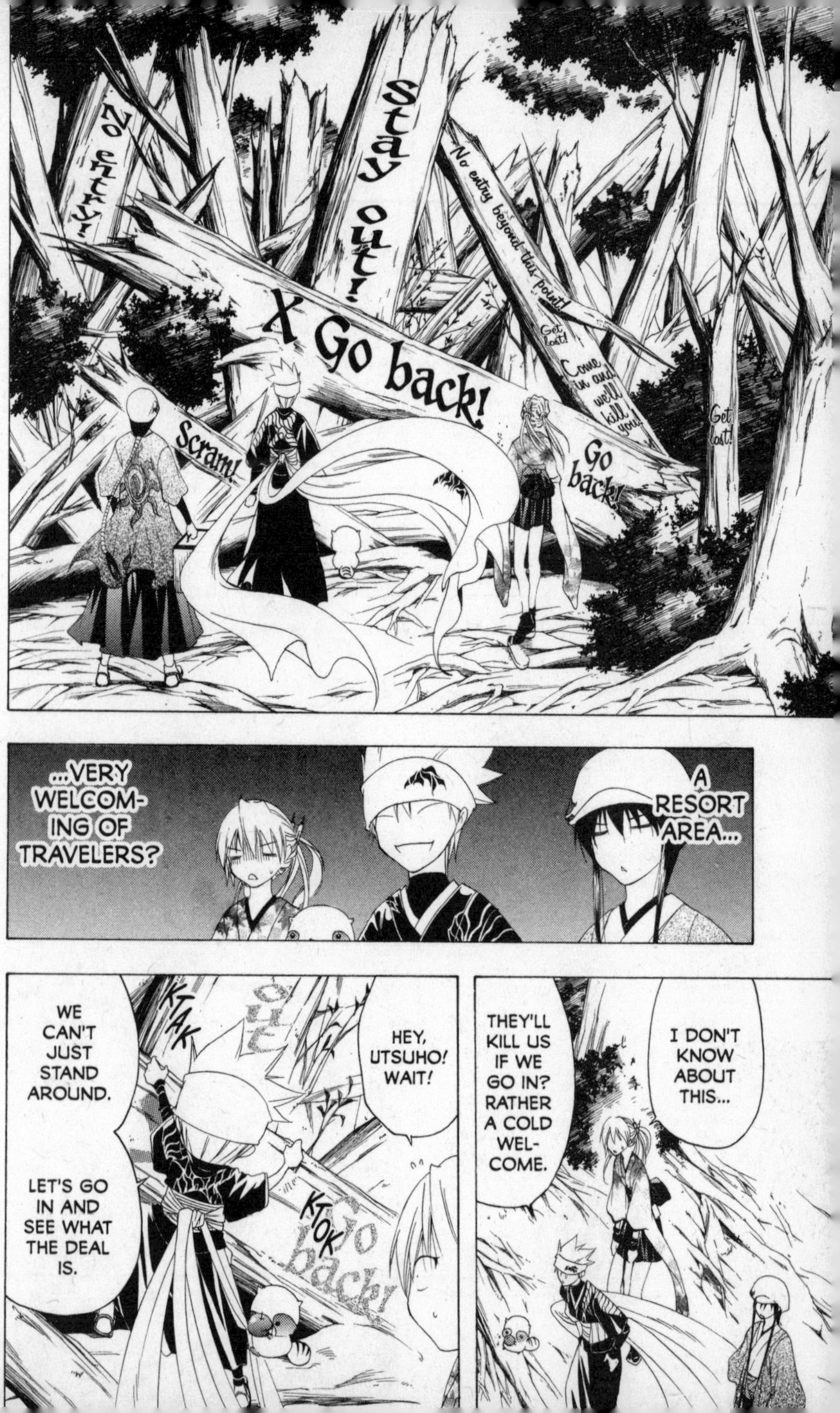
Get lost!
Go back!
Come in and well kill you!
Get lost!
No entry beyond this point!
X Go back!
Stay out!
Scram!
No entry!
A RESORT AREA...
...VERY WELCOM-ING OF TRAVELERS?
I DON'T KNOW ABOUT THIS...
THEY'LL KILL US IF WE GO IN? RATHER A COLD WEL-COME.
HEY, UTSUHO! WAIT!
out
KTAK
WE CAN'T JUST STAND AROUND.
KTOK
Go back!
LET'S GO IN AND SEE WHAT THE DEAL IS.

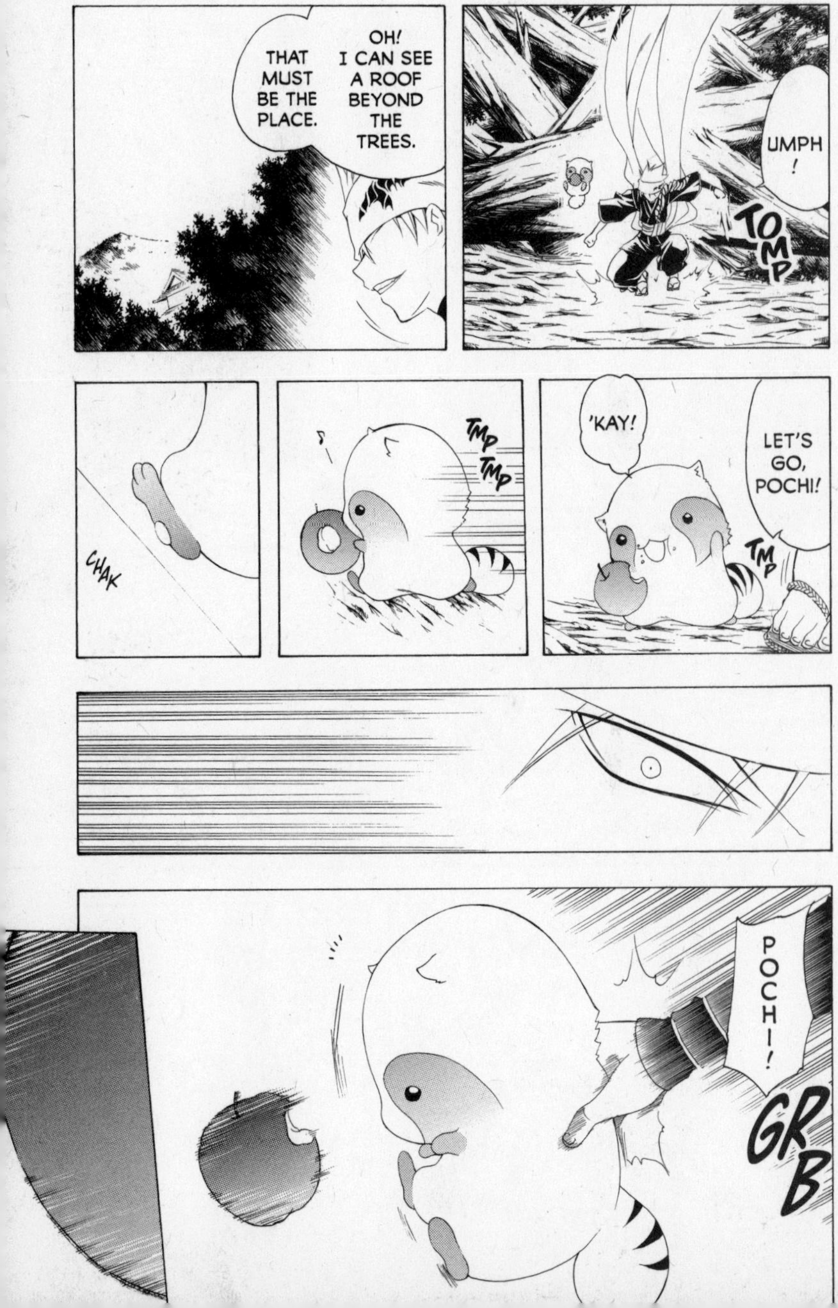
UMPH!
TOMP
OH! I CAN SEE A ROOF BEYOND THE TREES.
THAT MUST BE THE PLACE.
LET'S GO, POCHI!
TMP
'KAY!
TMP TMP
CHAK
POCHI!
GRB

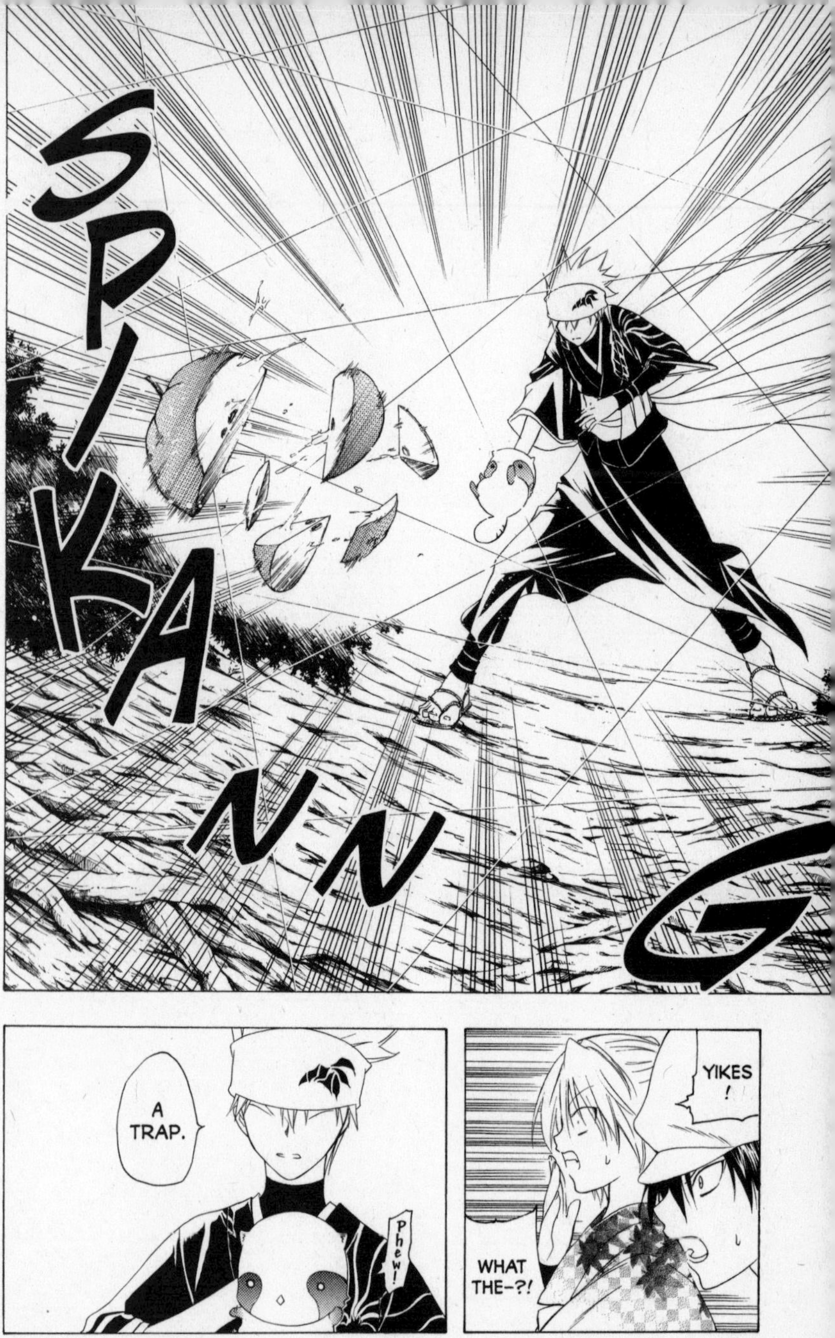
SPIKANNG
YIKES!
WHAT THE-?!
A TRAP.
Phew!

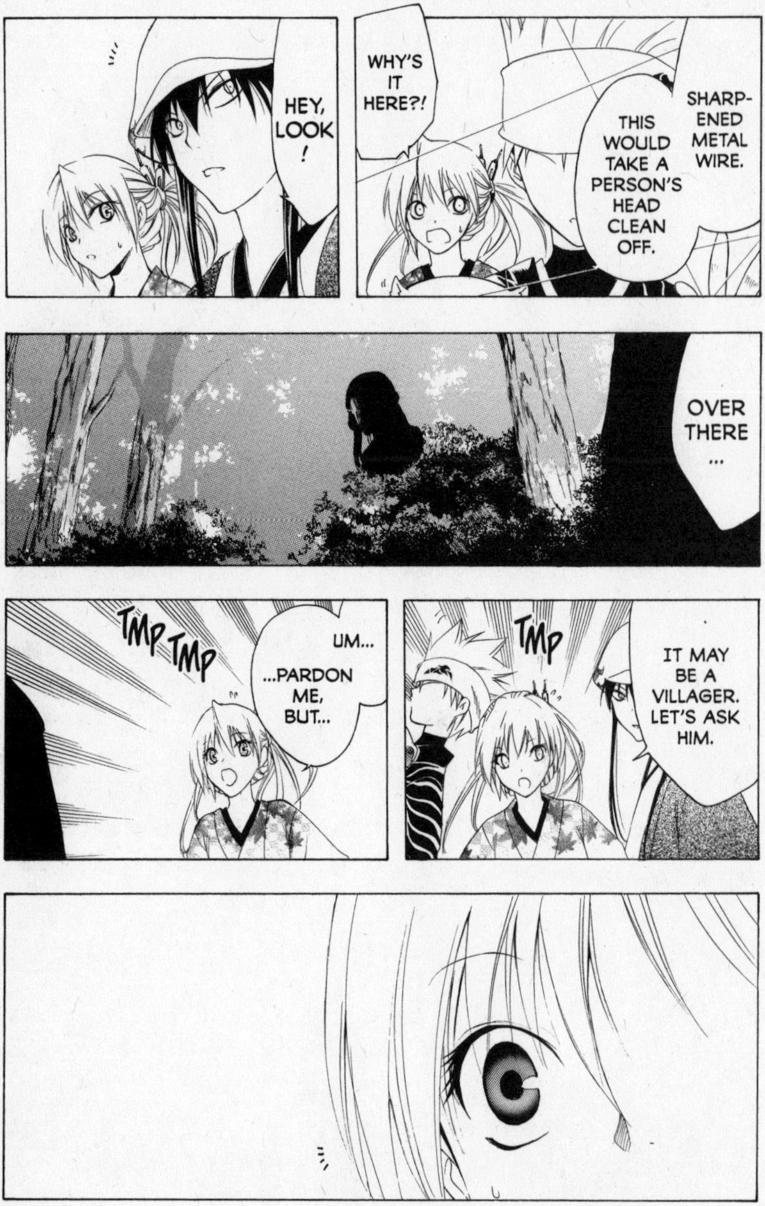
SHARPENED METAL WIRE.
THIS WOULD TAKE A PERSON'S HEAD CLEAN OFF.
WHY'S IT HERE?!
HEY, LOOK!
OVER THERE...
IT MAY BE A VILLAGER. LET'S ASK HIM.
TMP
UM... ...PARDON ME, BUT...
TMP TMP

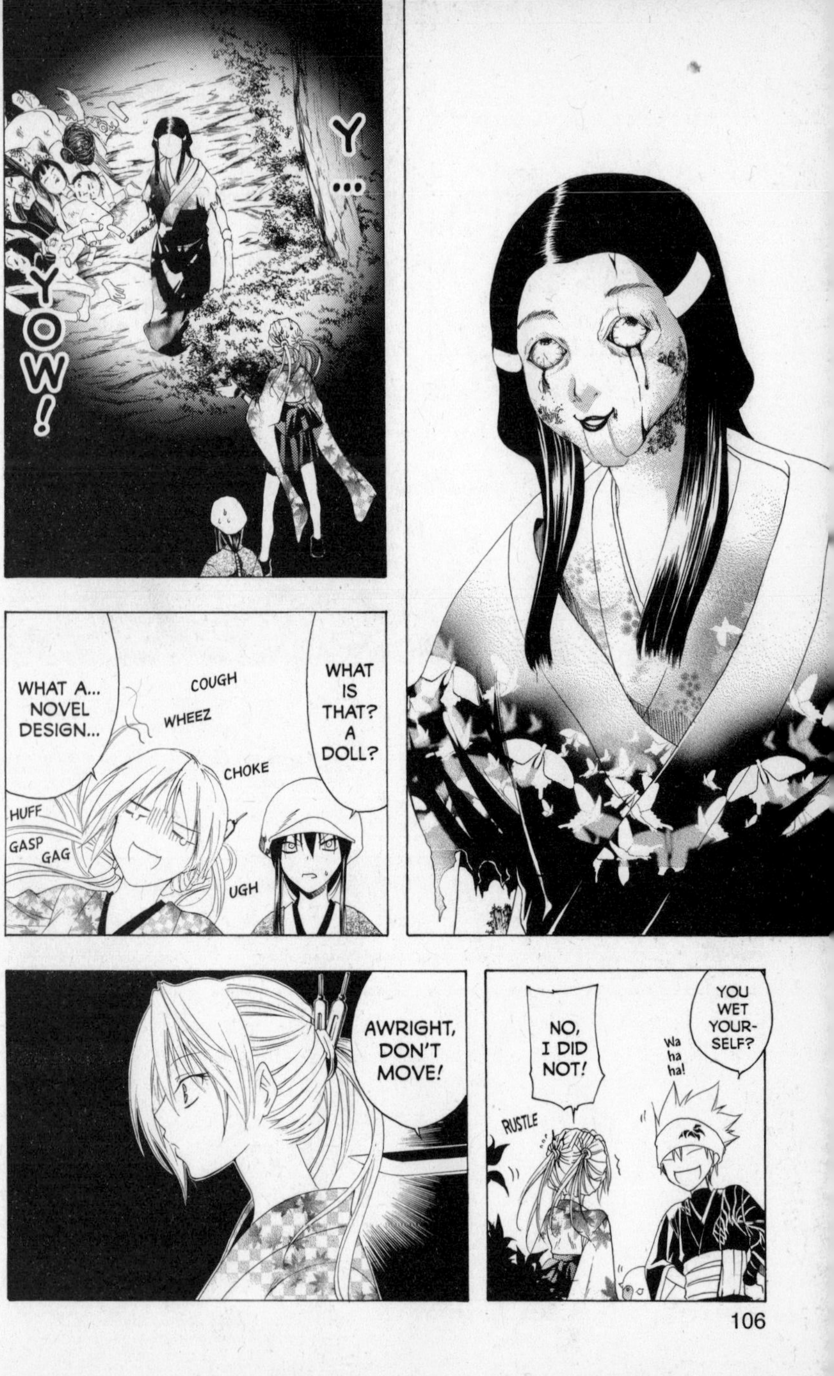
Y...
YOW!
WHAT IS THAT? A DOLL?
WHAT A... NOVEL DESIGN...
COUGH
WHEEZ
CHOKE
HUFF
GASP
GAG
UGH
YOU WET YOURSELF?
Wa ha ha!
NO, I DID NOT!
RUSTLE
AWRIGHT, DON'T MOVE!

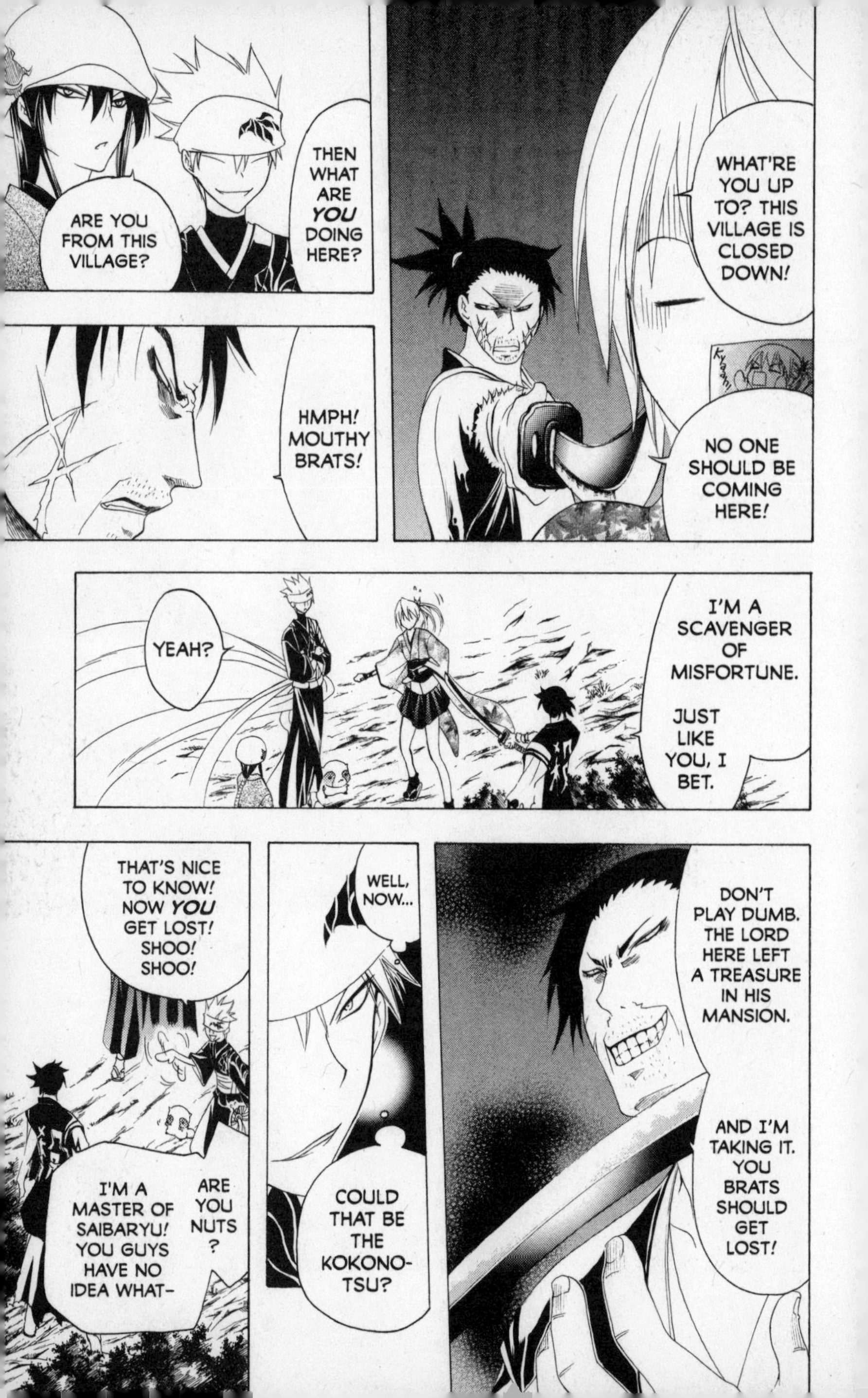
WHAT'RE YOU UP TO? THIS VILLAGE IS CLOSED DOWN!
NO ONE SHOULD BE COMING HERE!
THEN WHAT ARE *YOU* DOING HERE?
ARE YOU FROM THIS VILLAGE?
HMPH! MOUTHY BRATS!
I'M A SCAVENGER OF MISFORTUNE.
JUST LIKE YOU, I BET.
YEAH?
DON'T PLAY DUMB. THE LORD HERE LEFT A TREASURE IN HIS MANSION.
AND I'M TAKING IT. YOU BRATS SHOULD GET LOST!
WELL, NOW...
COULD THAT BE THE KOKONO-TSU?
THAT'S NICE TO KNOW! NOW *YOU* GET LOST! SHOO! SHOO!
ARE YOU NUTS?
I'M A MASTER OF SAIBARYU! YOU GUYS HAVE NO IDEA WHAT-

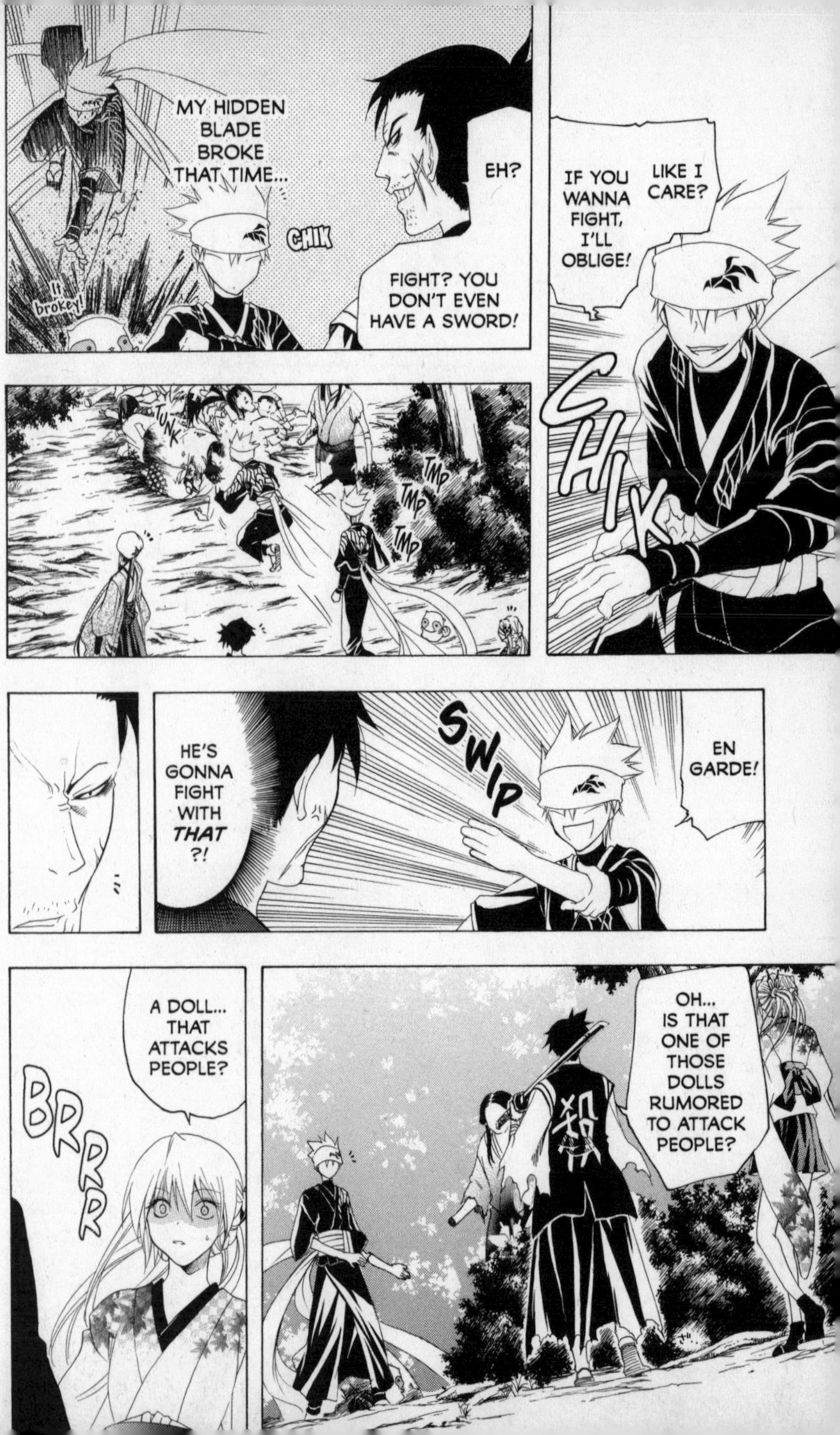
LIKE I CARE?
IF YOU WANNA FIGHT, I'LL OBLIGE!
CHIK
EH?
MY HIDDEN BLADE BROKE THAT TIME...
FIGHT? YOU DON'T EVEN HAVE A SWORD!
CHIK
It brokey!
TUNK
TMP TMP TMP TMP
EN GARDE!
SWIP
HE'S GONNA FIGHT WITH *THAT*?!
OH... IS THAT ONE OF THOSE DOLLS RUMORED TO ATTACK PEOPLE?
A DOLL... THAT ATTACKS PEOPLE?
BRRR

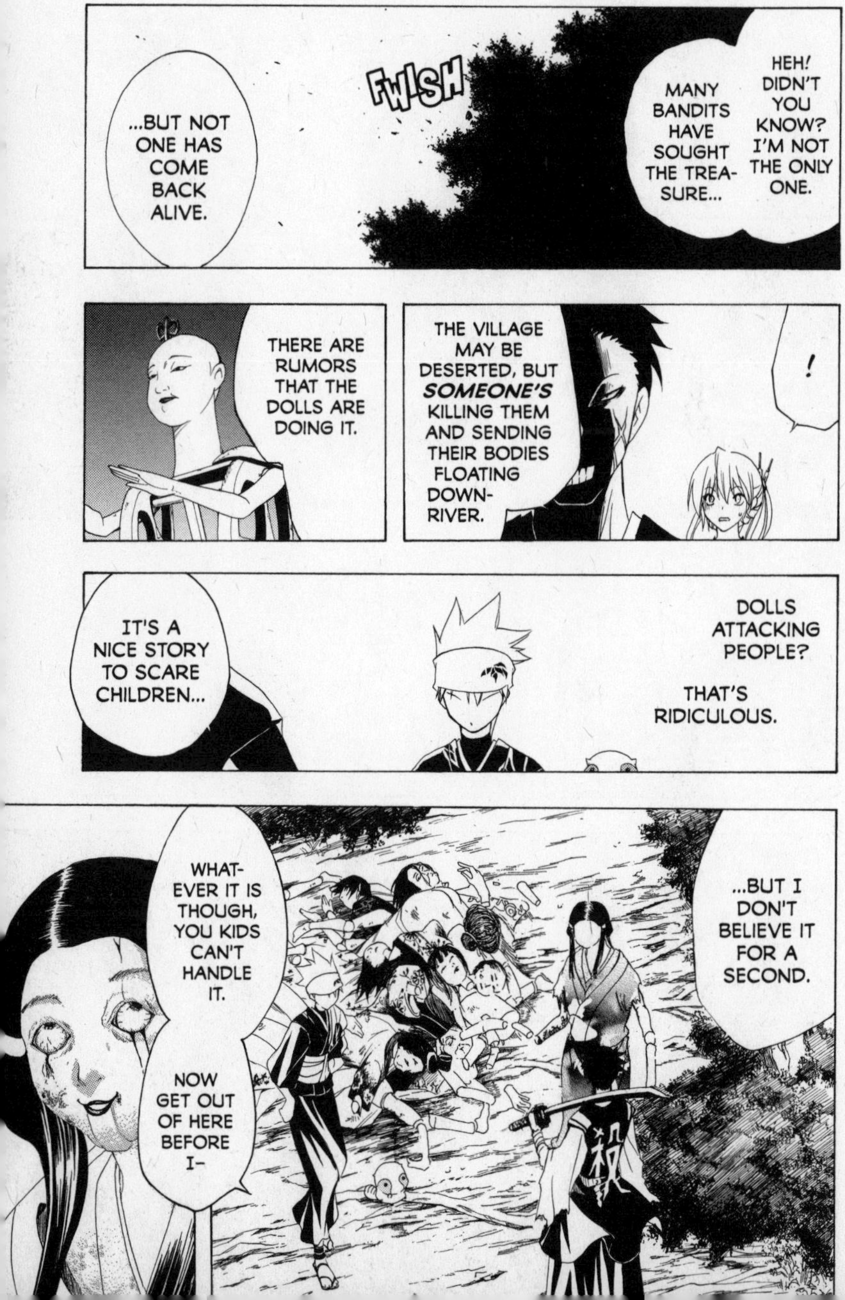
HEH! DIDN'T YOU KNOW? I'M NOT THE ONLY ONE.
MANY BANDITS HAVE SOUGHT THE TREA- SURE...
FWISH
...BUT NOT ONE HAS COME BACK ALIVE.
!
THE VILLAGE MAY BE DESERTED, BUT *SOMEONE'S* KILLING THEM AND SENDING THEIR BODIES FLOATING DOWN- RIVER.
THERE ARE RUMORS THAT THE DOLLS ARE DOING IT.
DOLLS ATTACKING PEOPLE?
THAT'S RIDICULOUS.
IT'S A NICE STORY TO SCARE CHILDREN...
...BUT I DON'T BELIEVE IT FOR A SECOND.
WHAT- EVER IT IS THOUGH, YOU KIDS CAN'T HANDLE IT.
NOW GET OUT OF HERE BEFORE I–

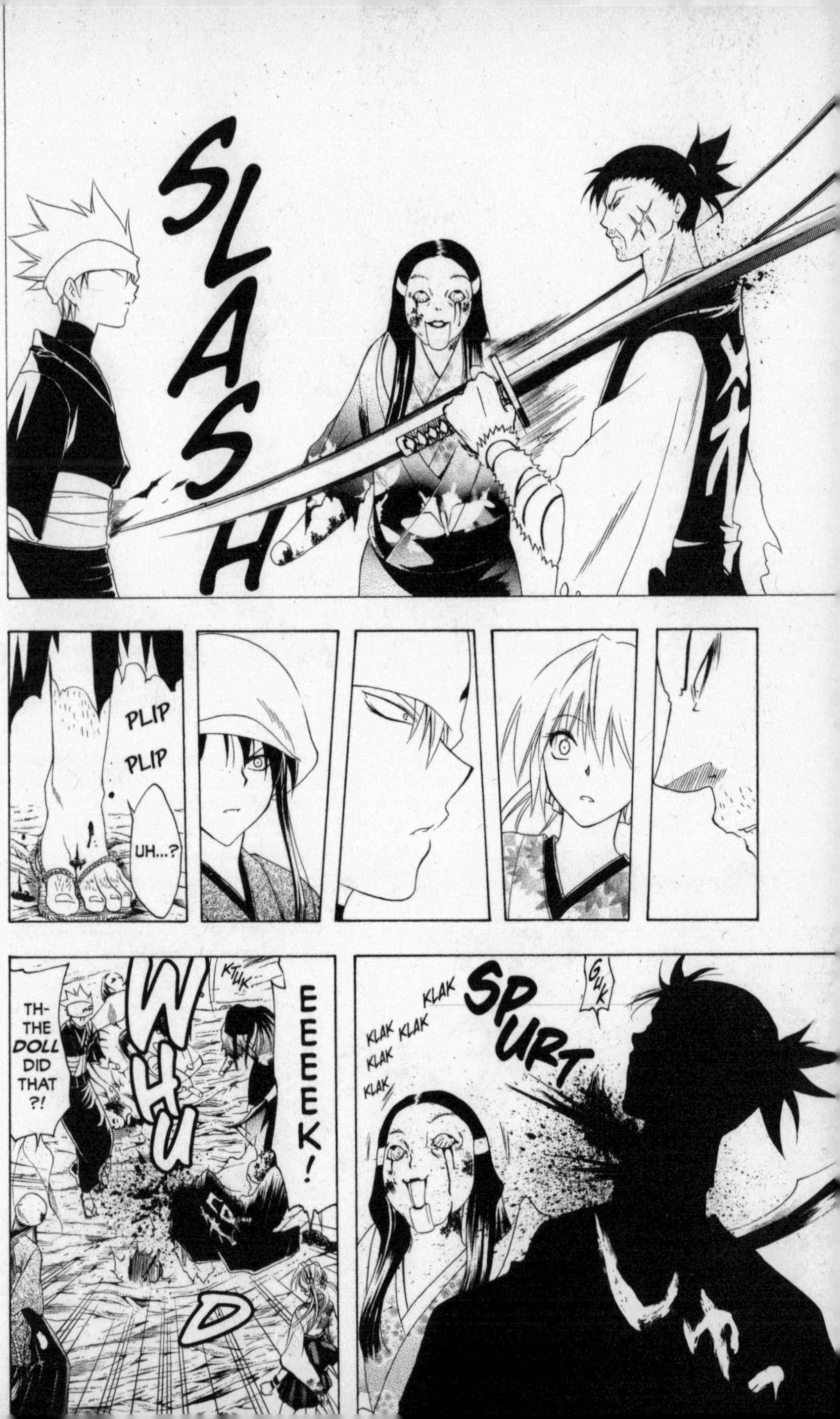
SLASH
PLIP
PLIP
UH...?
GUK
SPURT
KLAK
KLAK KLAK
KLAK
KLAK
KLAK
EEEEEK!
KTUK
WHUD
TH-THE DOLL DID THAT?!

SHLUK

STAGGER

UTSU-HO!

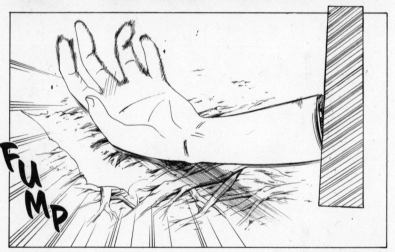

FUMP

UTSUHO! HAND... YOUR HAND!

YAAA-AAH!

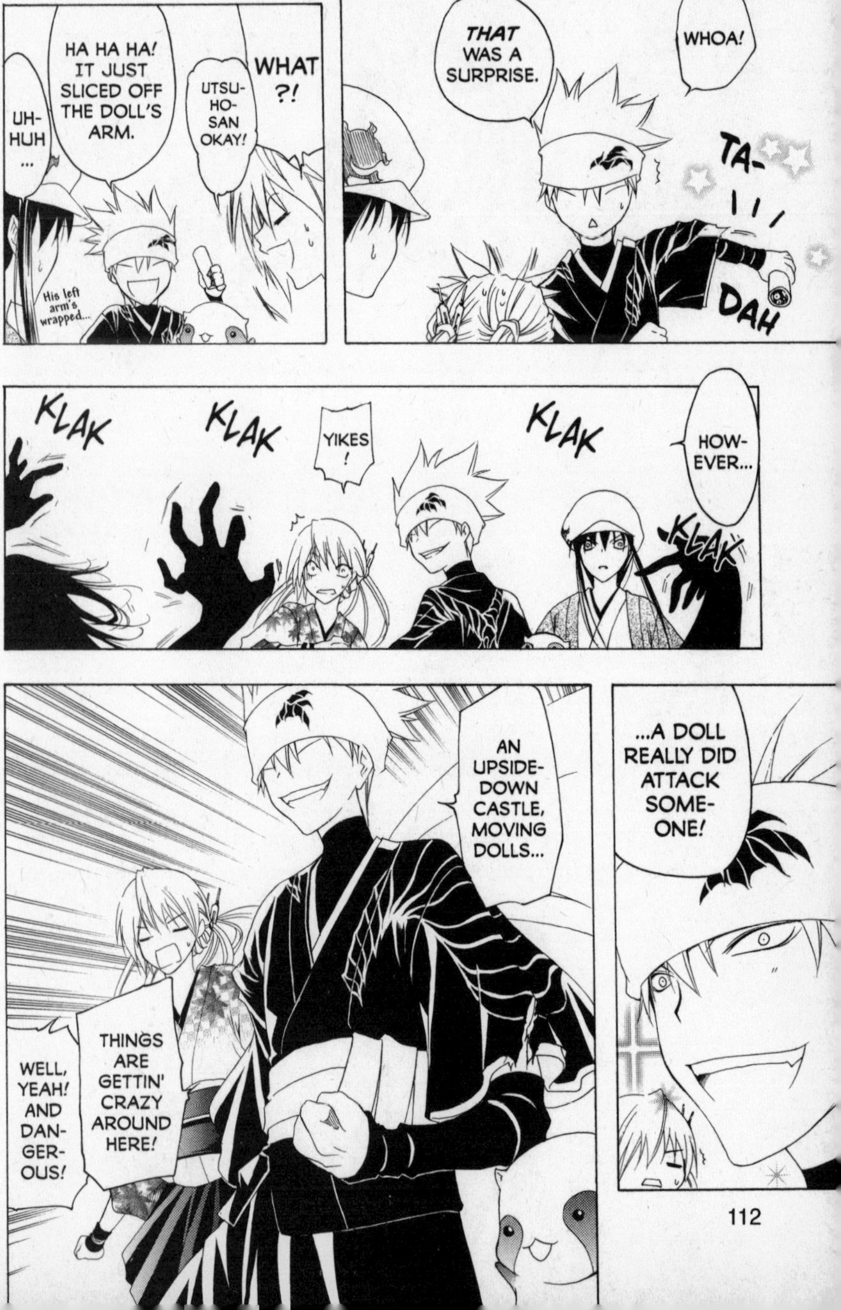
WHOA!
THAT WAS A SURPRISE.
TA-DAH
WHAT?!
UTSU-HO-SAN OKAY!
HA HA HA! IT JUST SLICED OFF THE DOLL'S ARM.
UH-HUH...
His left arm's wrapped...
HOW-EVER...
KLAK
KLAK
YIKES!
KLAK
KLAK
...A DOLL REALLY DID ATTACK SOME-ONE!
AN UPSIDE-DOWN CASTLE, MOVING DOLLS...
THINGS ARE GETTIN' CRAZY AROUND HERE!
WELL, YEAH! AND DAN-GER-OUS!

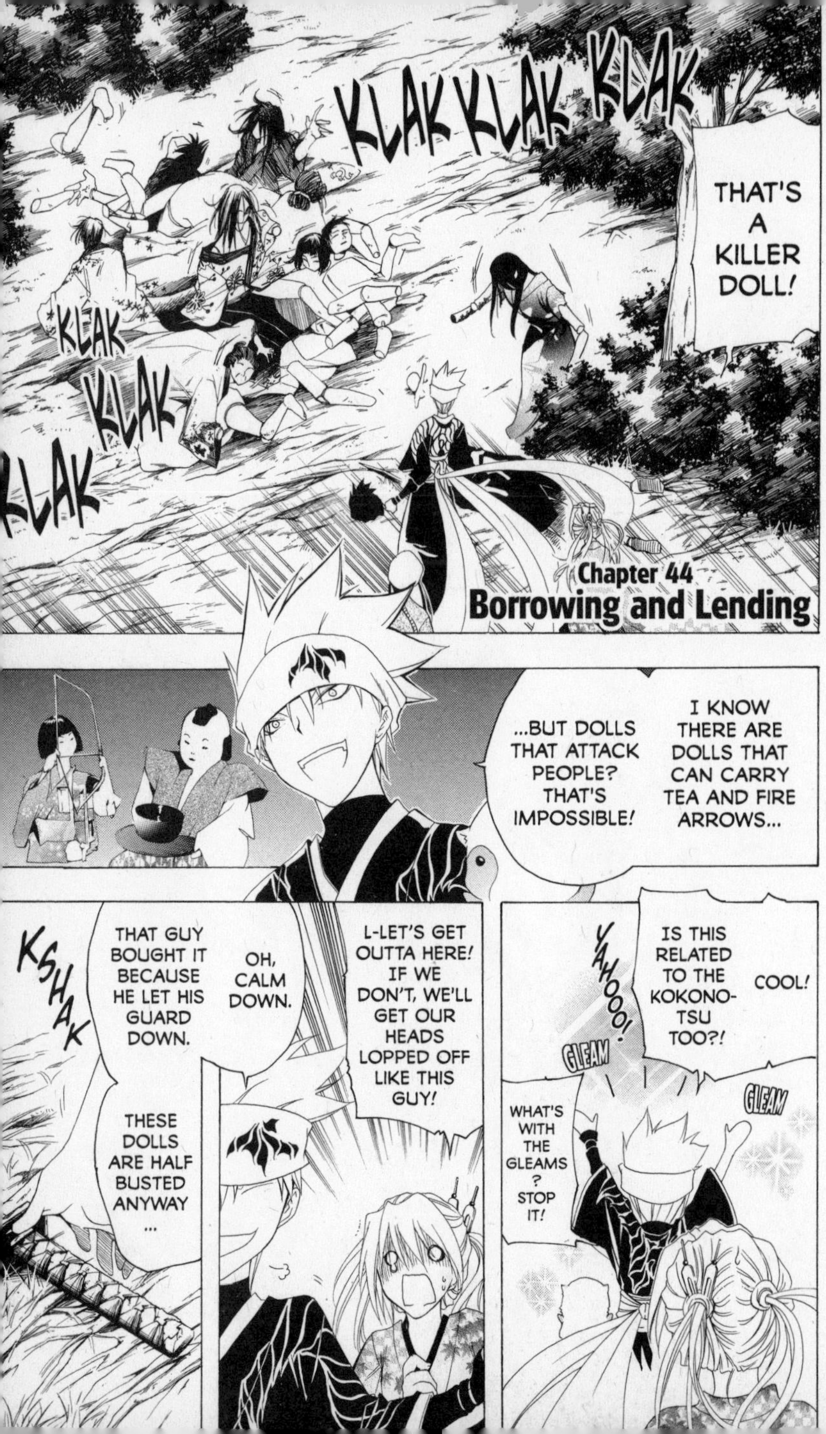
KLAK KLAK KLAK
THAT'S A KILLER DOLL!
KLAK KLAK KLAK
Chapter 44
Borrowing and Lending
I KNOW THERE ARE DOLLS THAT CAN CARRY TEA AND FIRE ARROWS...
...BUT DOLLS THAT ATTACK PEOPLE? THAT'S IMPOSSIBLE!
IS THIS RELATED TO THE KOKONO-TSU TOO?!
COOL!
YAHOOO!
GLEAM
GLEAM
WHAT'S WITH THE GLEAMS? STOP IT!
L-LET'S GET OUTTA HERE! IF WE DON'T, WE'LL GET OUR HEADS LOPPED OFF LIKE THIS GUY!
OH, CALM DOWN.
THAT GUY BOUGHT IT BECAUSE HE LET HIS GUARD DOWN.
THESE DOLLS ARE HALF BUSTED ANYWAY...
KSHAK

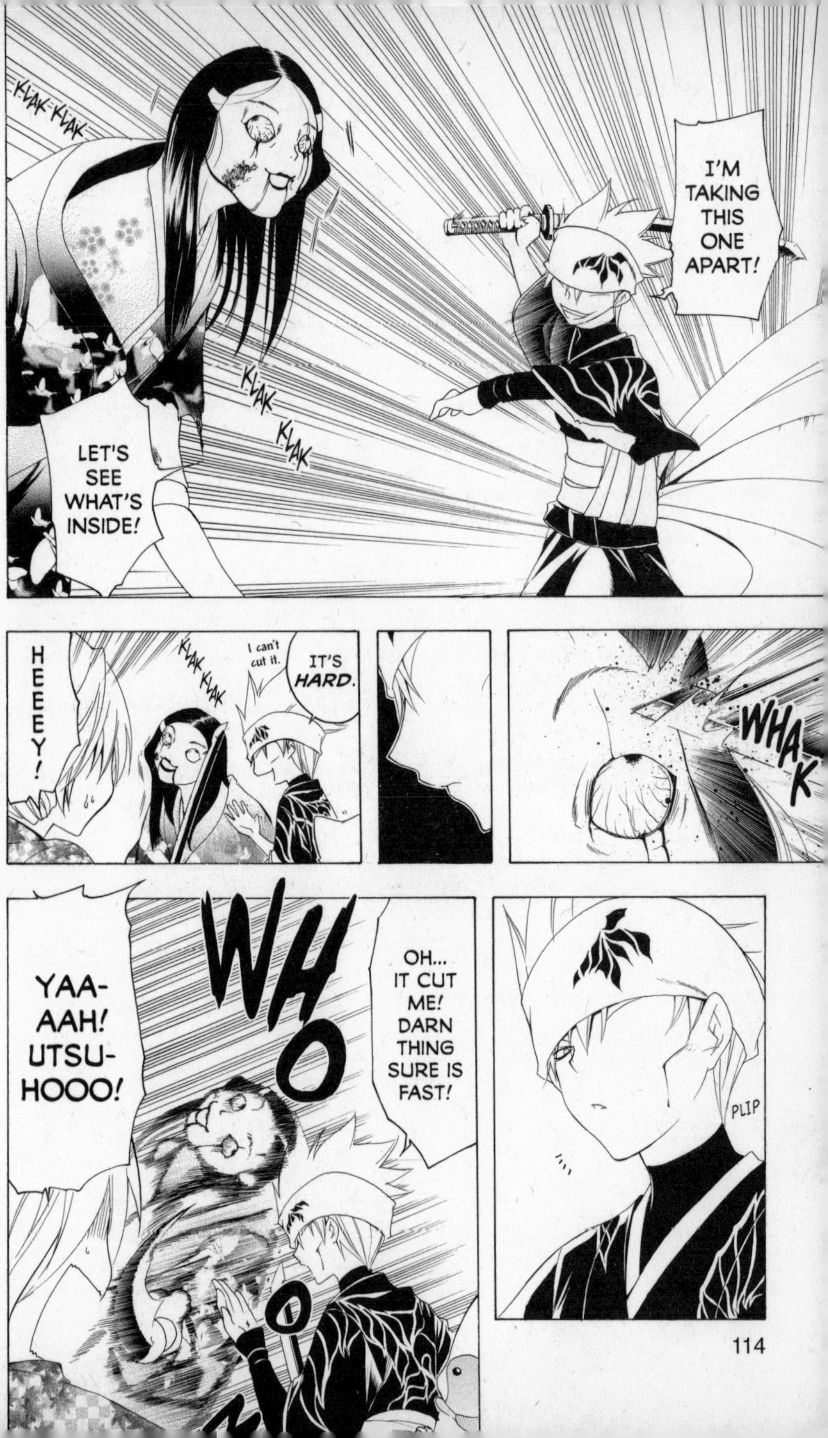

I'M TAKING THIS ONE APART!
KLAK KLAK
KLAK KLAK
LET'S SEE WHAT'S INSIDE!
WHAK
IT'S HARD.
I can't cut it.
KLAK KLAK
HEEEEY!
PLIP
OH... IT CUT ME! DARN THING SURE IS FAST!
WHOO
YAA-AAH! UTSU-HOOO!

Chapter 44
Borrowing and Lending

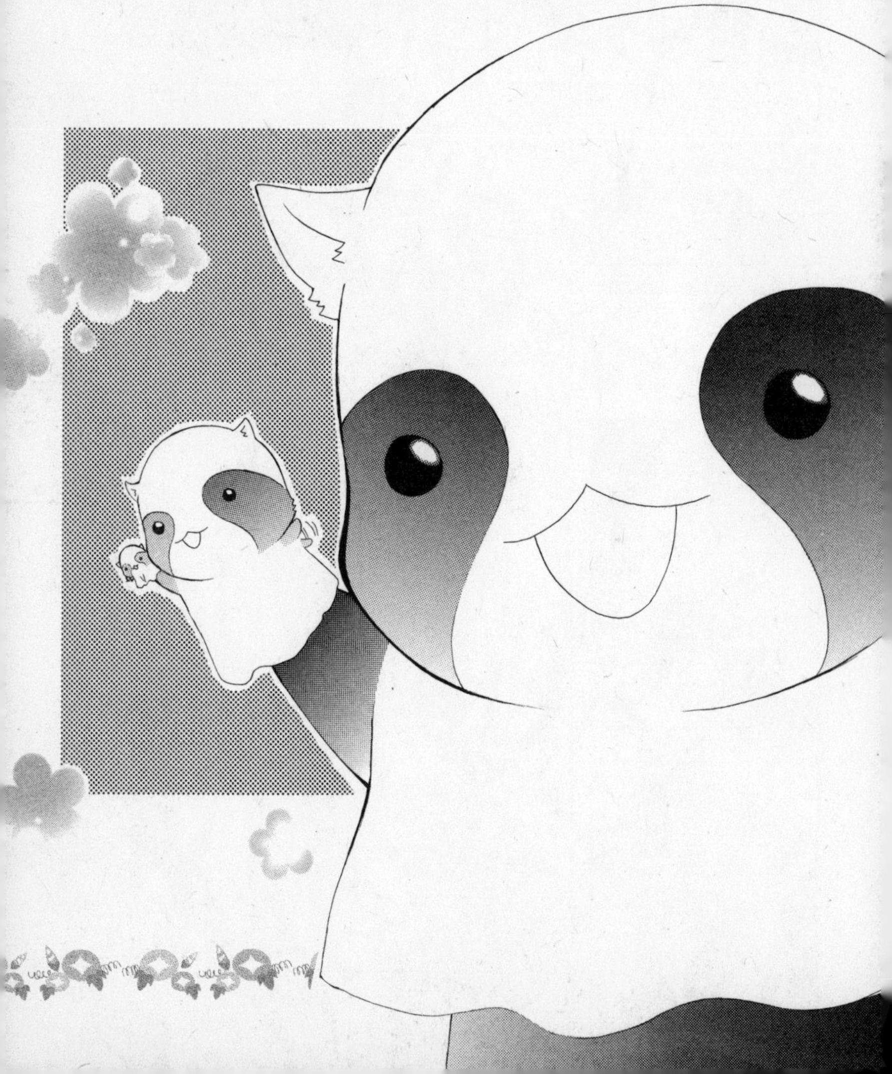

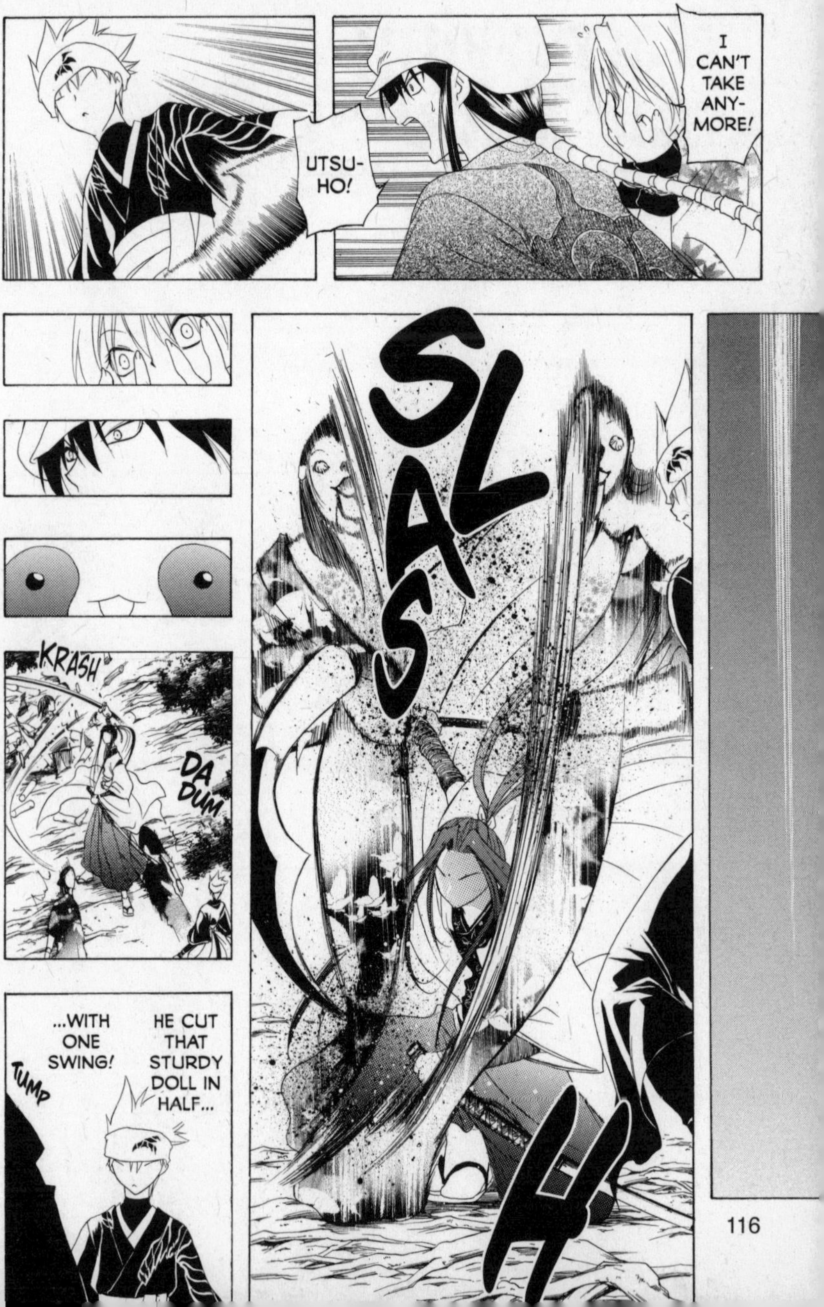
I CAN'T TAKE ANYMORE!
UTSU-HO!
SLASH
KRASH
DA DUM
HE CUT THAT STURDY DOLL IN HALF...
...WITH ONE SWING!
TUMP

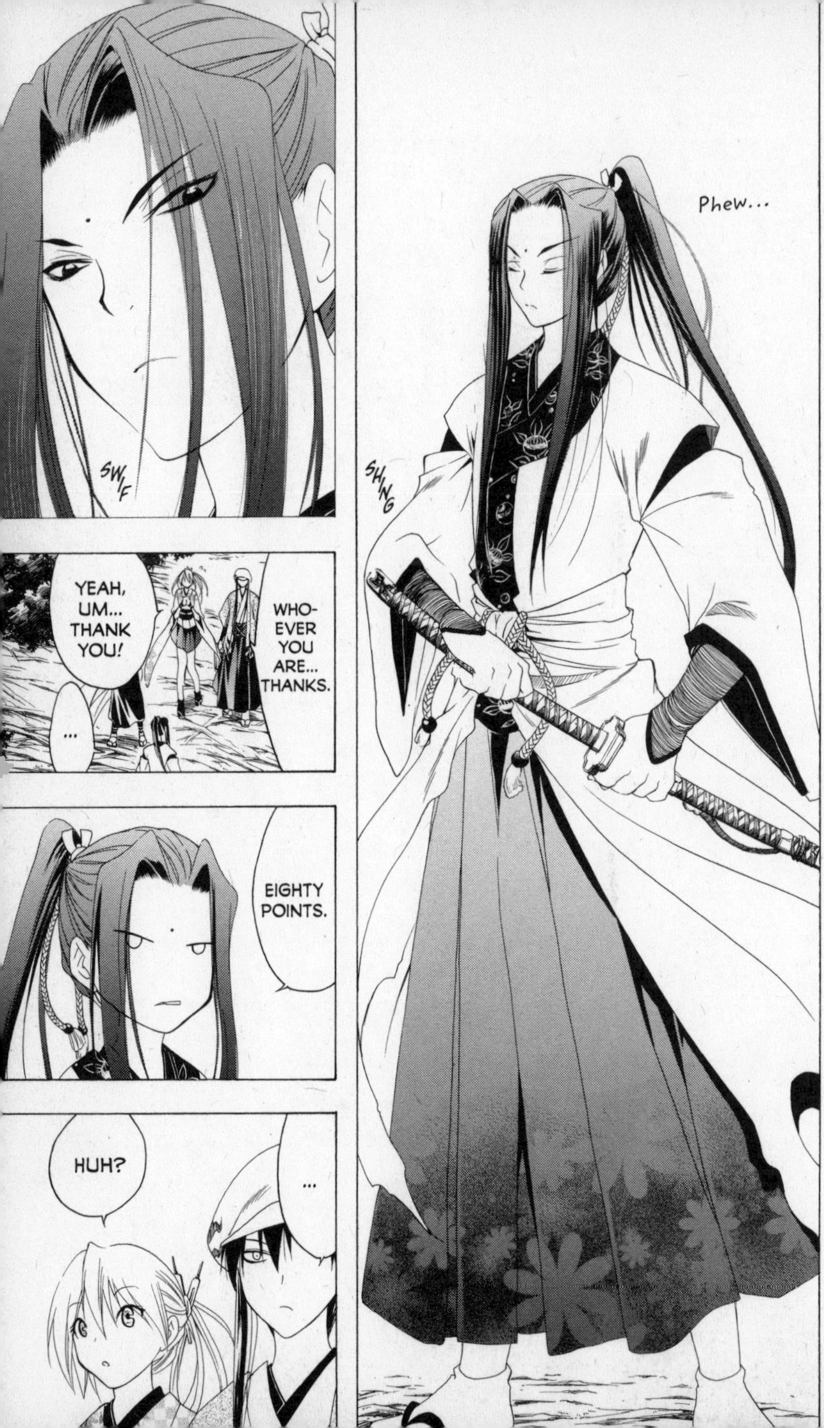

Phew...
SHING
SWIF
WHO-EVER YOU ARE... THANKS.
YEAH, UM... THANK YOU!
...
EIGHTY POINTS.
...
HUH?

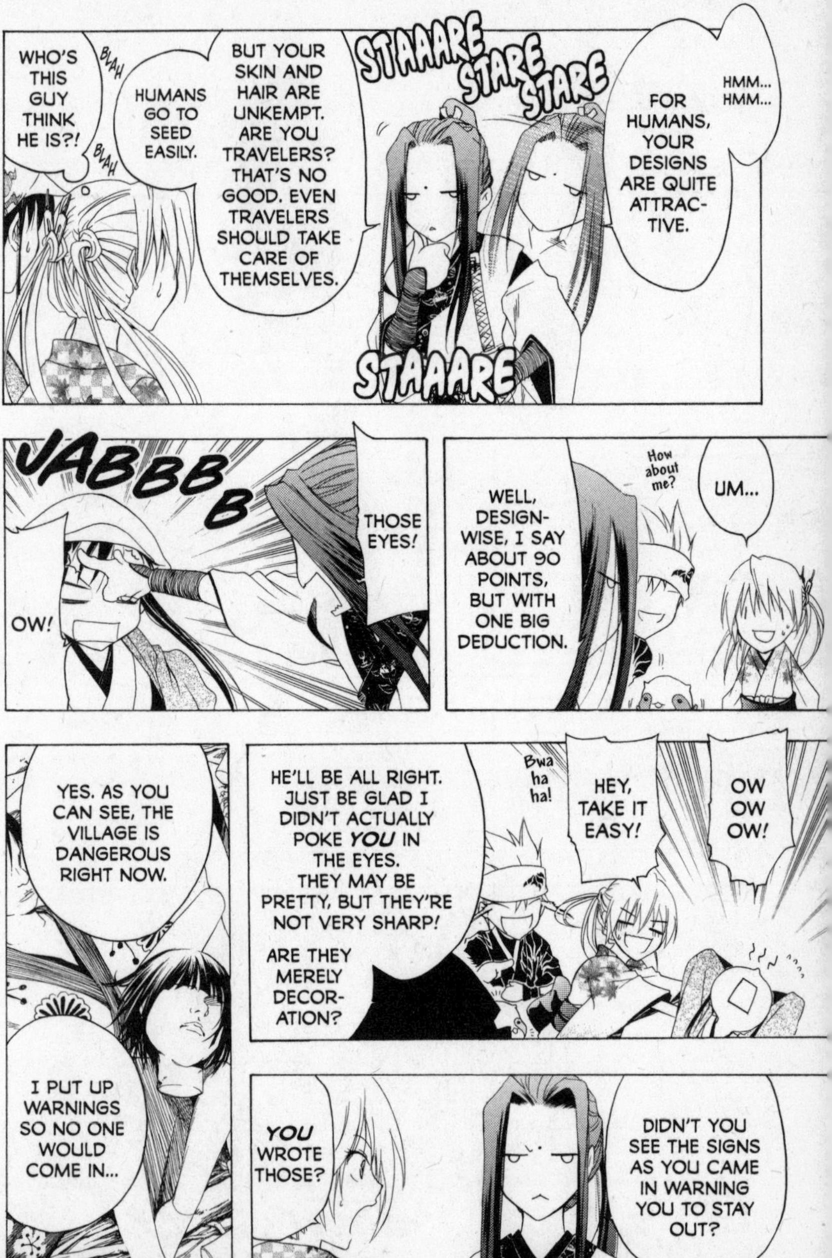
HMM... HMM...
FOR HUMANS, YOUR DESIGNS ARE QUITE ATTRACTIVE.
STAAARE STARE STARE
BUT YOUR SKIN AND HAIR ARE UNKEMPT. ARE YOU TRAVELERS? THAT'S NO GOOD. EVEN TRAVELERS SHOULD TAKE CARE OF THEMSELVES.
HUMANS GO TO SEED EASILY.
BLAH BLAH
WHO'S THIS GUY THINK HE IS?!
STAAARE
UM...
How about me?
WELL, DESIGN-WISE, I SAY ABOUT 90 POINTS, BUT WITH ONE BIG DEDUCTION.
THOSE EYES!
JABBBB B
OW!
OW OW OW!
HEY, TAKE IT EASY!
Bwa ha ha!
HE'LL BE ALL RIGHT. JUST BE GLAD I DIDN'T ACTUALLY POKE *YOU* IN THE EYES. THEY MAY BE PRETTY, BUT THEY'RE NOT VERY SHARP!
ARE THEY MERELY DECORATION?
DIDN'T YOU SEE THE SIGNS AS YOU CAME IN WARNING YOU TO STAY OUT?
YOU WROTE THOSE?
YES. AS YOU CAN SEE, THE VILLAGE IS DANGEROUS RIGHT NOW.
I PUT UP WARNINGS SO NO ONE WOULD COME IN...

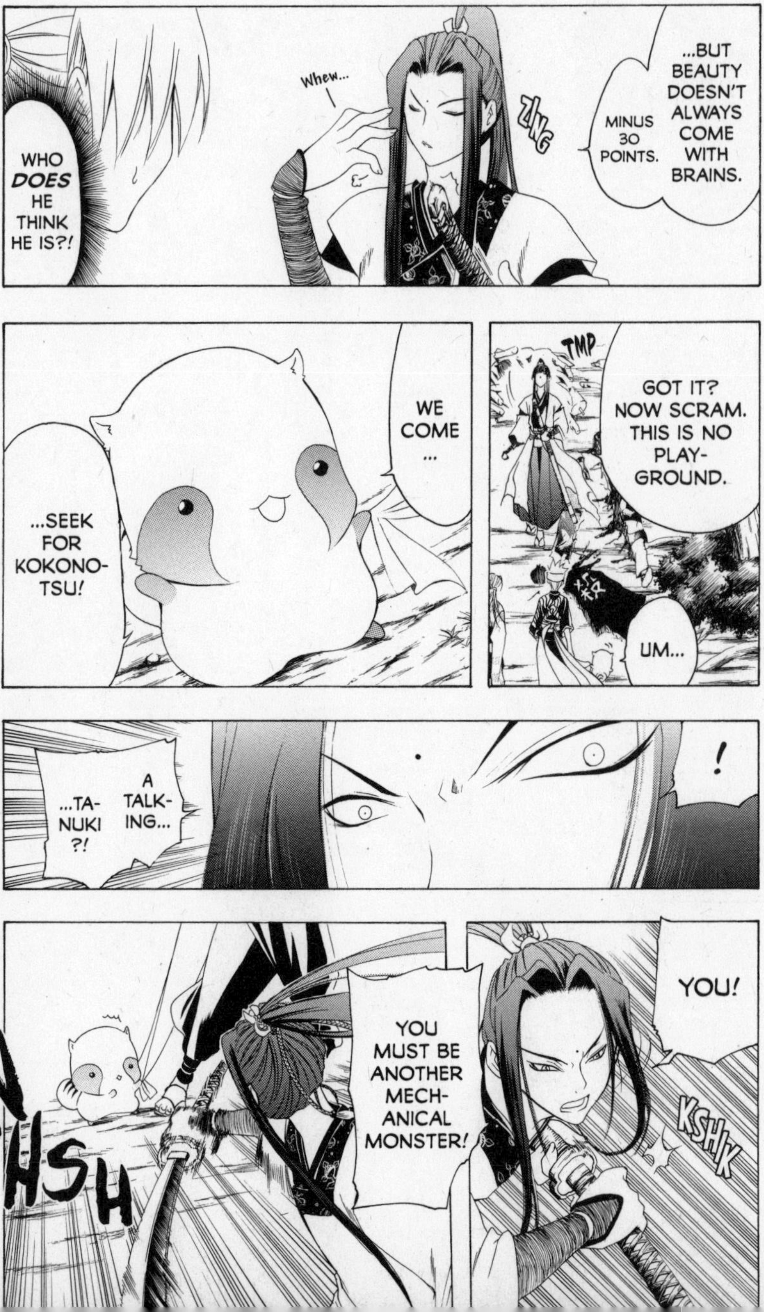
...BUT BEAUTY DOESN'T ALWAYS COME WITH BRAINS.
MINUS 30 POINTS.
ZING
Whew...
WHO **DOES** HE THINK HE IS?!
TMP
GOT IT? NOW SCRAM. THIS IS NO PLAY-GROUND.
UM...
WE COME ...
...SEEK FOR KOKONO-TSU!
!
A TALK-ING...
...TA-NUKI ?!
YOU!
KSHIK
YOU MUST BE ANOTHER MECH-ANICAL MONSTER!
WHSH

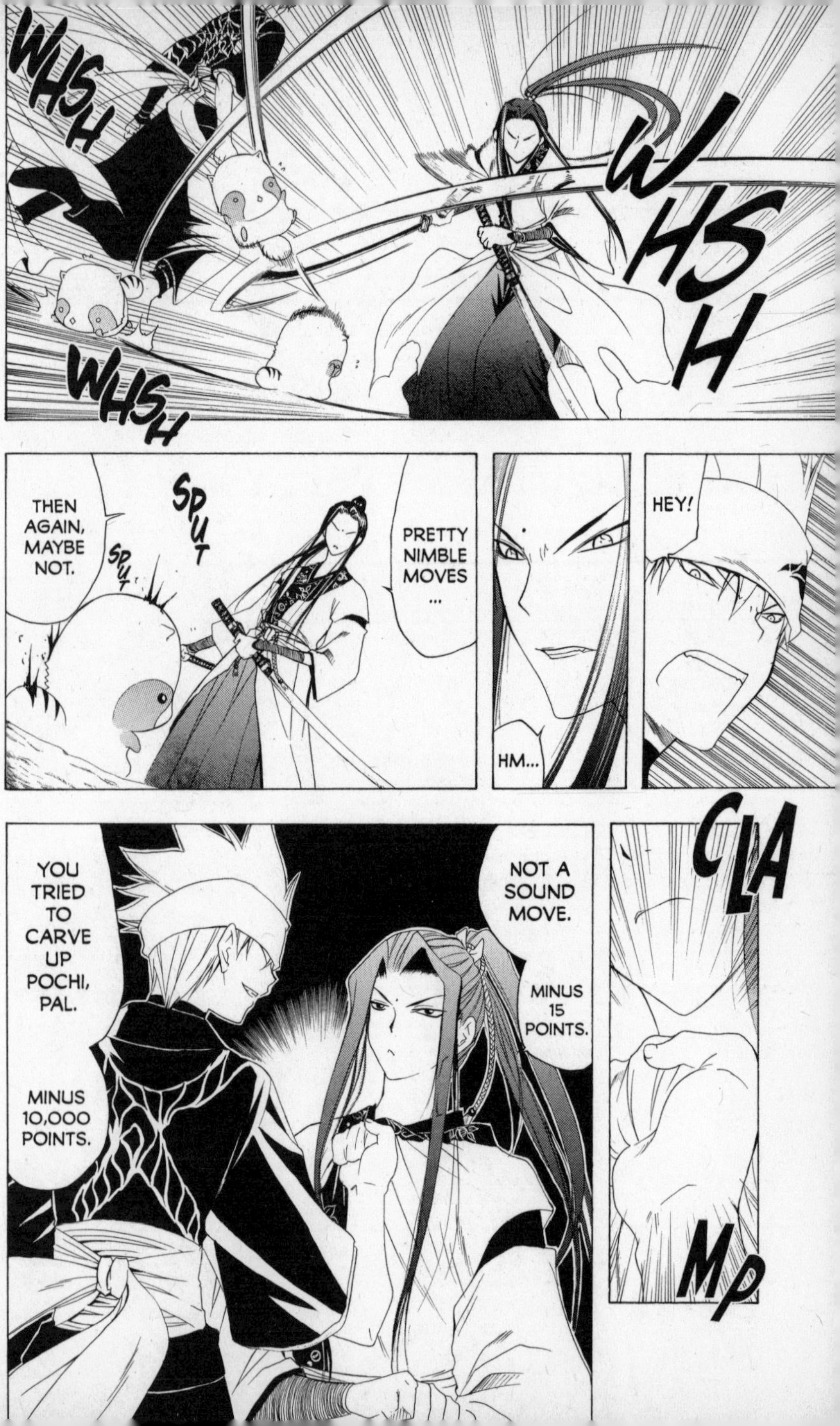
WHSH
WHSH
WHSH
HEY!
HM...
PRETTY NIMBLE MOVES ...
SPUT
THEN AGAIN, MAYBE NOT.
SPUT
CLAMP
NOT A SOUND MOVE.
MINUS 15 POINTS.
YOU TRIED TO CARVE UP POCHI, PAL.
MINUS 10,000 POINTS.

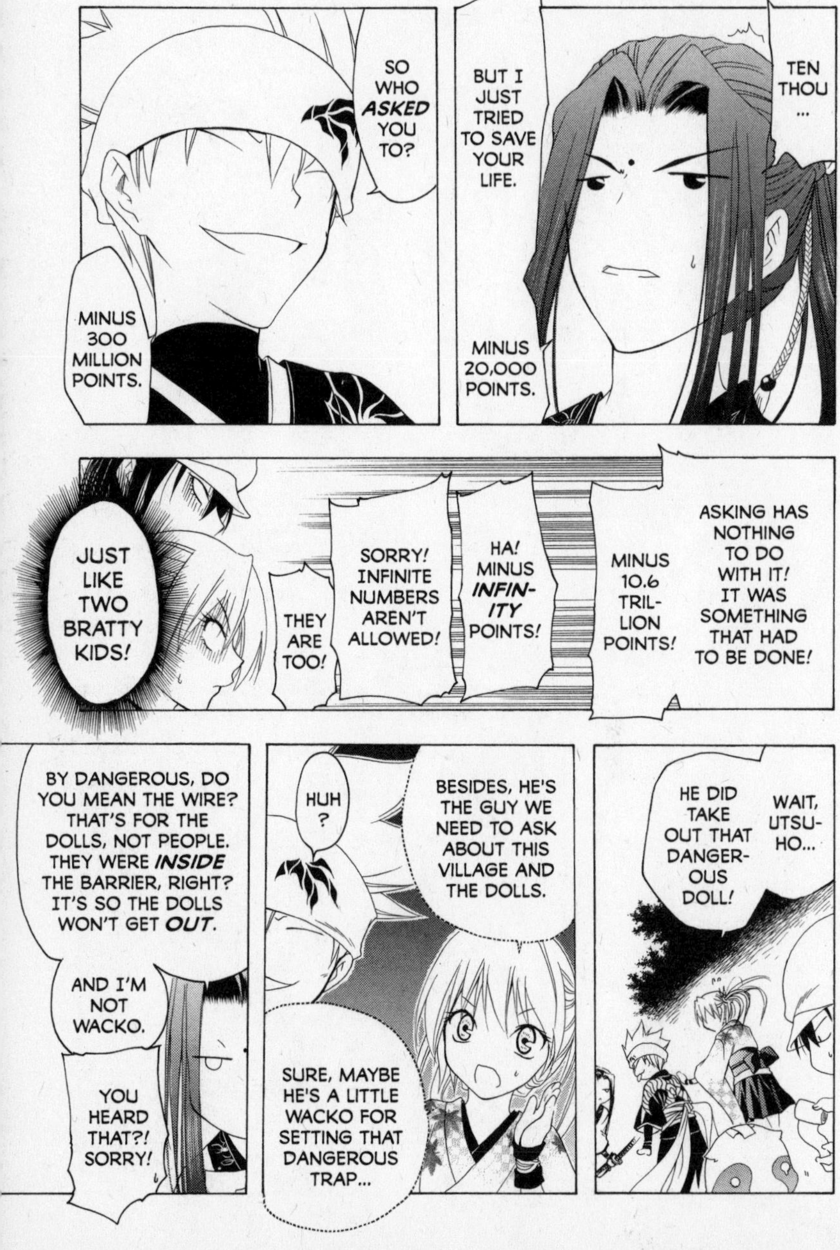
TEN THOU ...
BUT I JUST TRIED TO SAVE YOUR LIFE.
MINUS 20,000 POINTS.
SO WHO *ASKED* YOU TO?
MINUS 300 MILLION POINTS.
ASKING HAS NOTHING TO DO WITH IT! IT WAS SOMETHING THAT HAD TO BE DONE!
MINUS 10.6 TRILLION POINTS!
HA! MINUS *INFINITY* POINTS!
SORRY! INFINITE NUMBERS AREN'T ALLOWED!
THEY ARE TOO!
JUST LIKE TWO BRATTY KIDS!
WAIT, UTSUHO...
HE DID TAKE OUT THAT DANGEROUS DOLL!
HUH?
BESIDES, HE'S THE GUY WE NEED TO ASK ABOUT THIS VILLAGE AND THE DOLLS.
SURE, MAYBE HE'S A LITTLE WACKO FOR SETTING THAT DANGEROUS TRAP...
BY DANGEROUS, DO YOU MEAN THE WIRE? THAT'S FOR THE DOLLS, NOT PEOPLE. THEY WERE *INSIDE* THE BARRIER, RIGHT? IT'S SO THE DOLLS WON'T GET *OUT*.
AND I'M NOT WACKO.
YOU HEARD THAT?! SORRY!

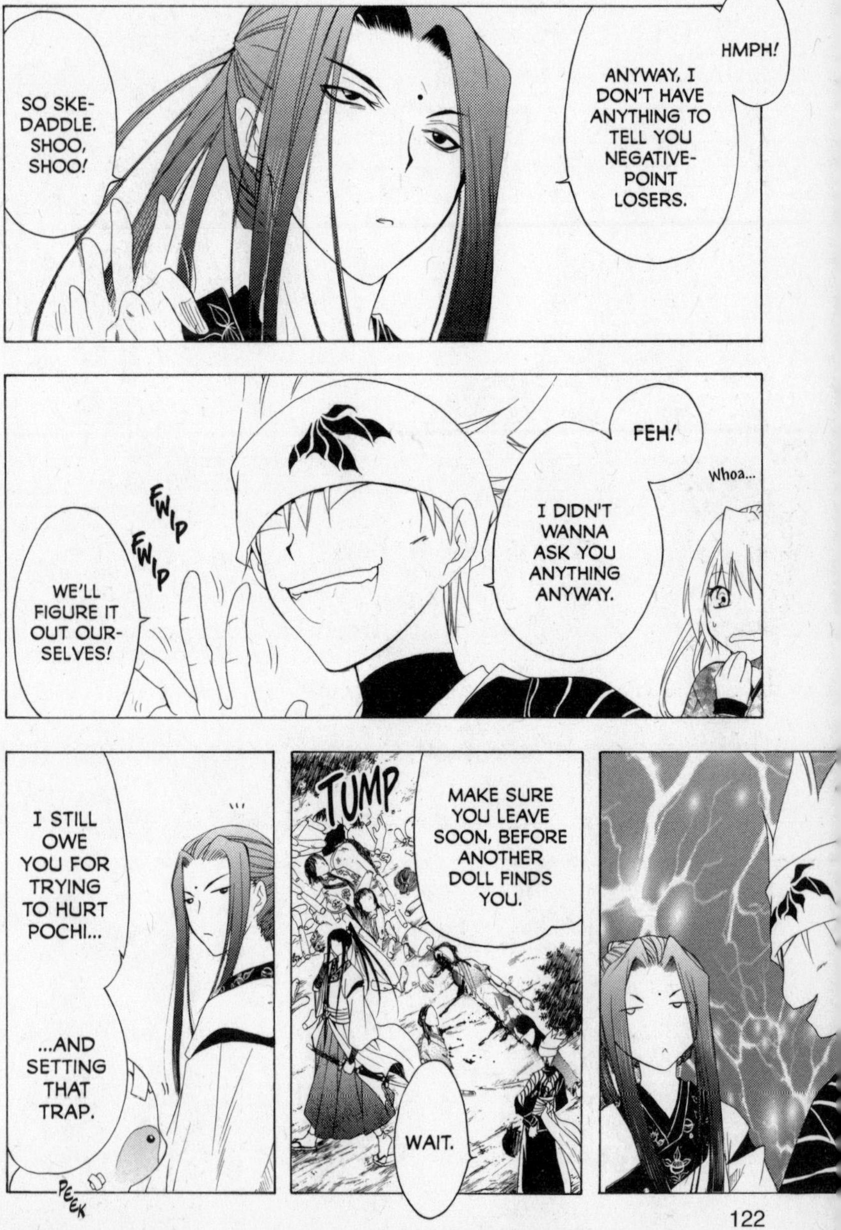
HMPH!
ANYWAY, I DON'T HAVE ANYTHING TO TELL YOU NEGATIVE-POINT LOSERS.
SO SKE-DADDLE. SHOO, SHOO!
FEH!
I DIDN'T WANNA ASK YOU ANYTHING ANYWAY.
Whoa...
FWIP
FWIP
WE'LL FIGURE IT OUT OUR-SELVES!
TUMP
MAKE SURE YOU LEAVE SOON, BEFORE ANOTHER DOLL FINDS YOU.
WAIT.
I STILL OWE YOU FOR TRYING TO HURT POCHI...
...AND SETTING THAT TRAP.
PEEK

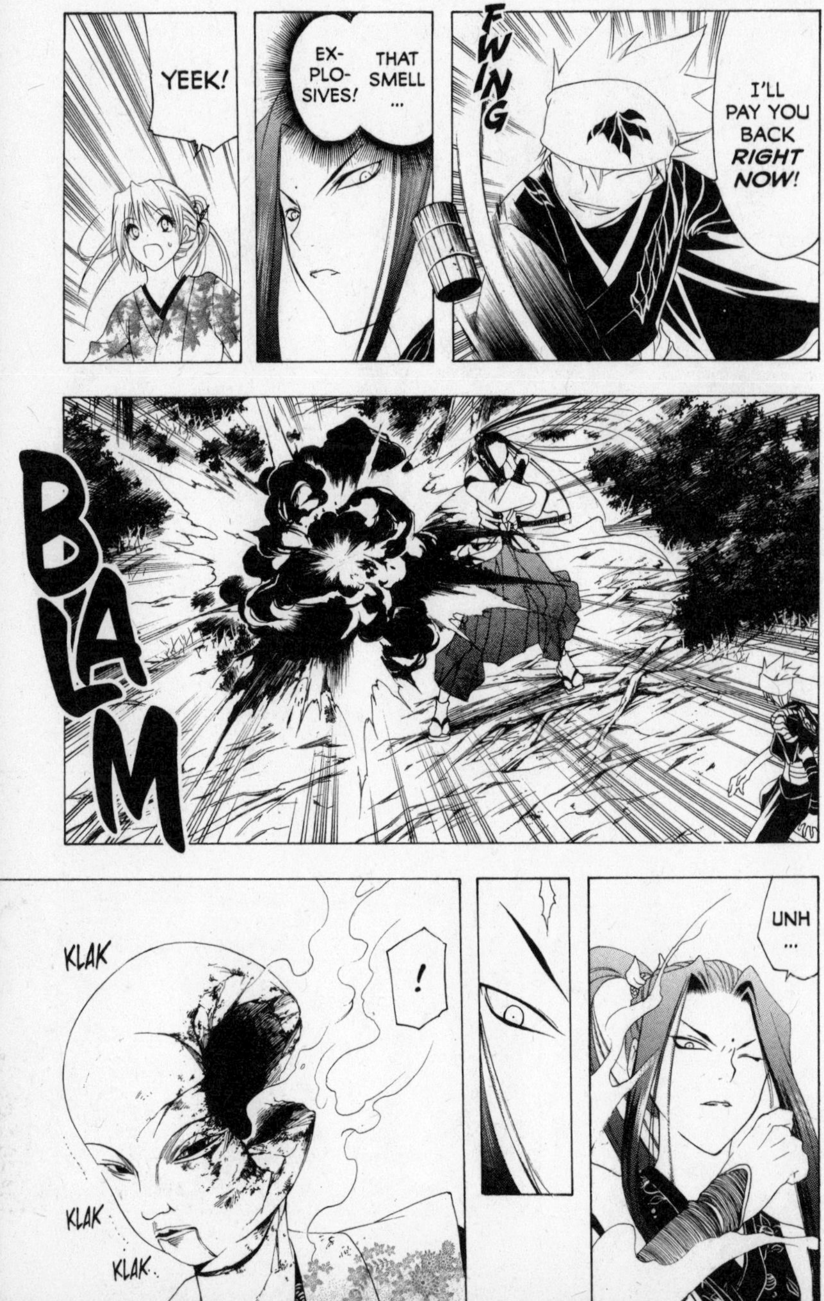
FWING
I'LL PAY YOU BACK RIGHT NOW!
THAT SMELL ...
EXPLOSIVES!
YEEK!
BLAM
UNH ...
!
KLAK
KLAK
KLAK

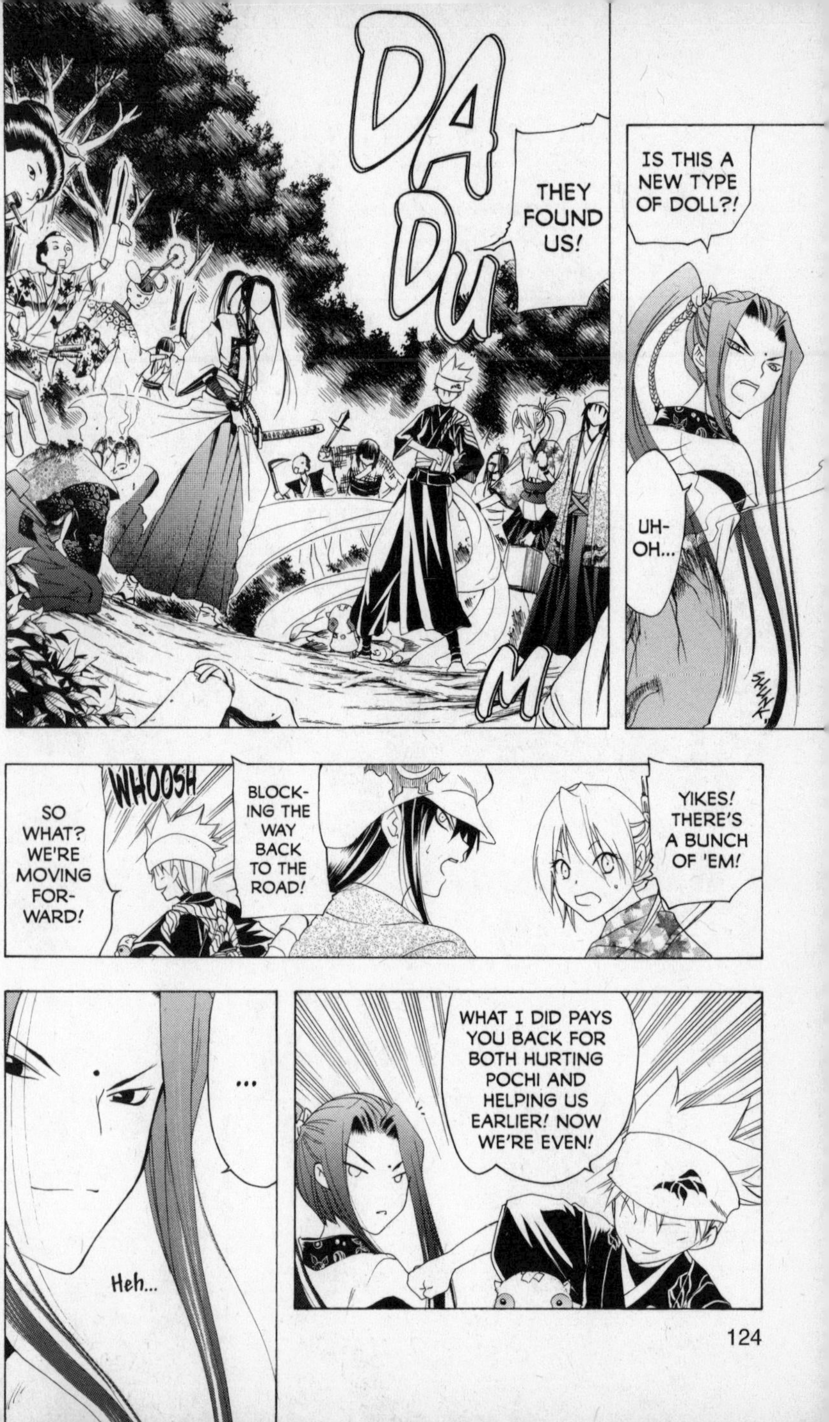
IS THIS A NEW TYPE OF DOLL?!
UH-OH...
SHUNK
THEY FOUND US!
DADUM
YIKES! THERE'S A BUNCH OF 'EM!
BLOCKING THE WAY BACK TO THE ROAD!
WHOOSH
SO WHAT? WE'RE MOVING FORWARD!
WHAT I DID PAYS YOU BACK FOR BOTH HURTING POCHI AND HELPING US EARLIER! NOW WE'RE EVEN!
...
Heh...

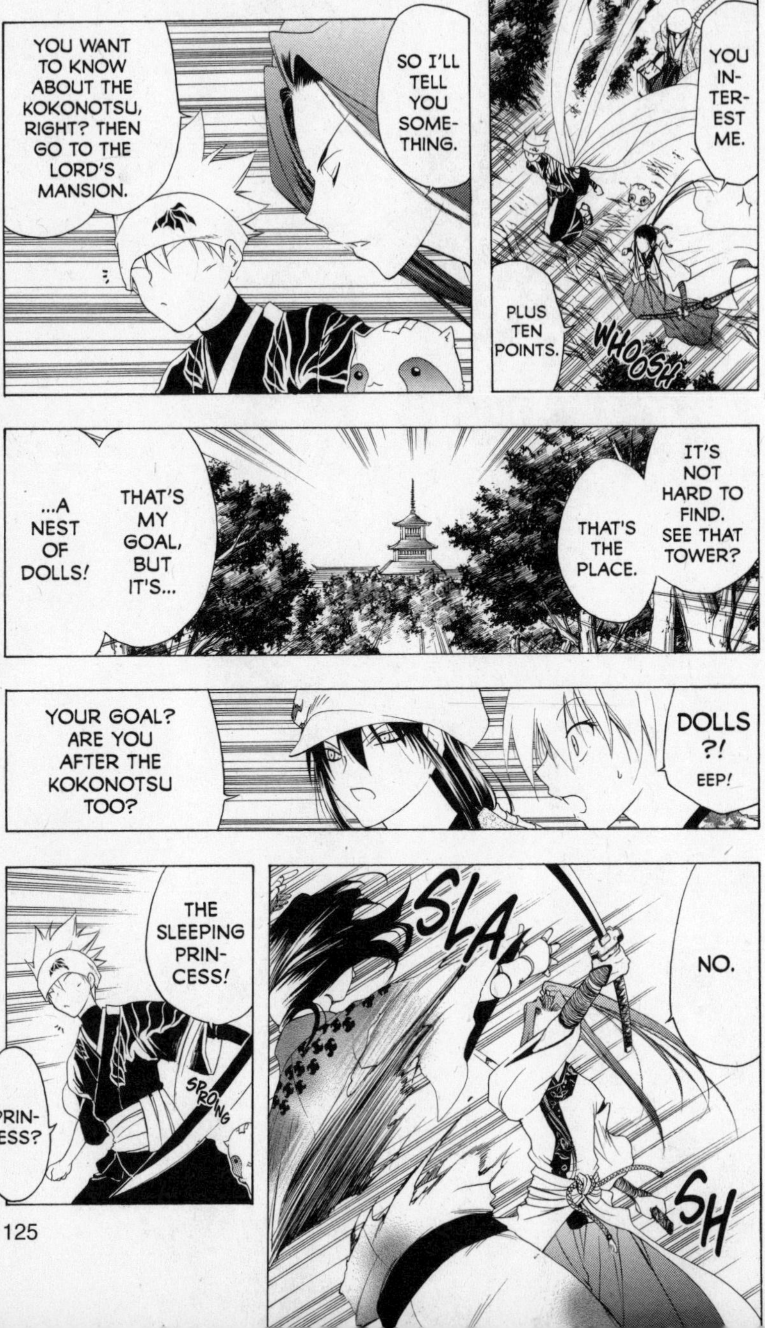
YOU INTEREST ME.
PLUS TEN POINTS.
WHOOSH
SO I'LL TELL YOU SOMETHING.
YOU WANT TO KNOW ABOUT THE KOKONOTSU, RIGHT? THEN GO TO THE LORD'S MANSION.
IT'S NOT HARD TO FIND. SEE THAT TOWER?
THAT'S THE PLACE.
THAT'S MY GOAL, BUT IT'S...
...A NEST OF DOLLS!
DOLLS?!
EEP!
YOUR GOAL? ARE YOU AFTER THE KOKONOTSU TOO?
SLA
SH
NO.
THE SLEEPING PRINCESS!
SPRONG
PRINCESS?

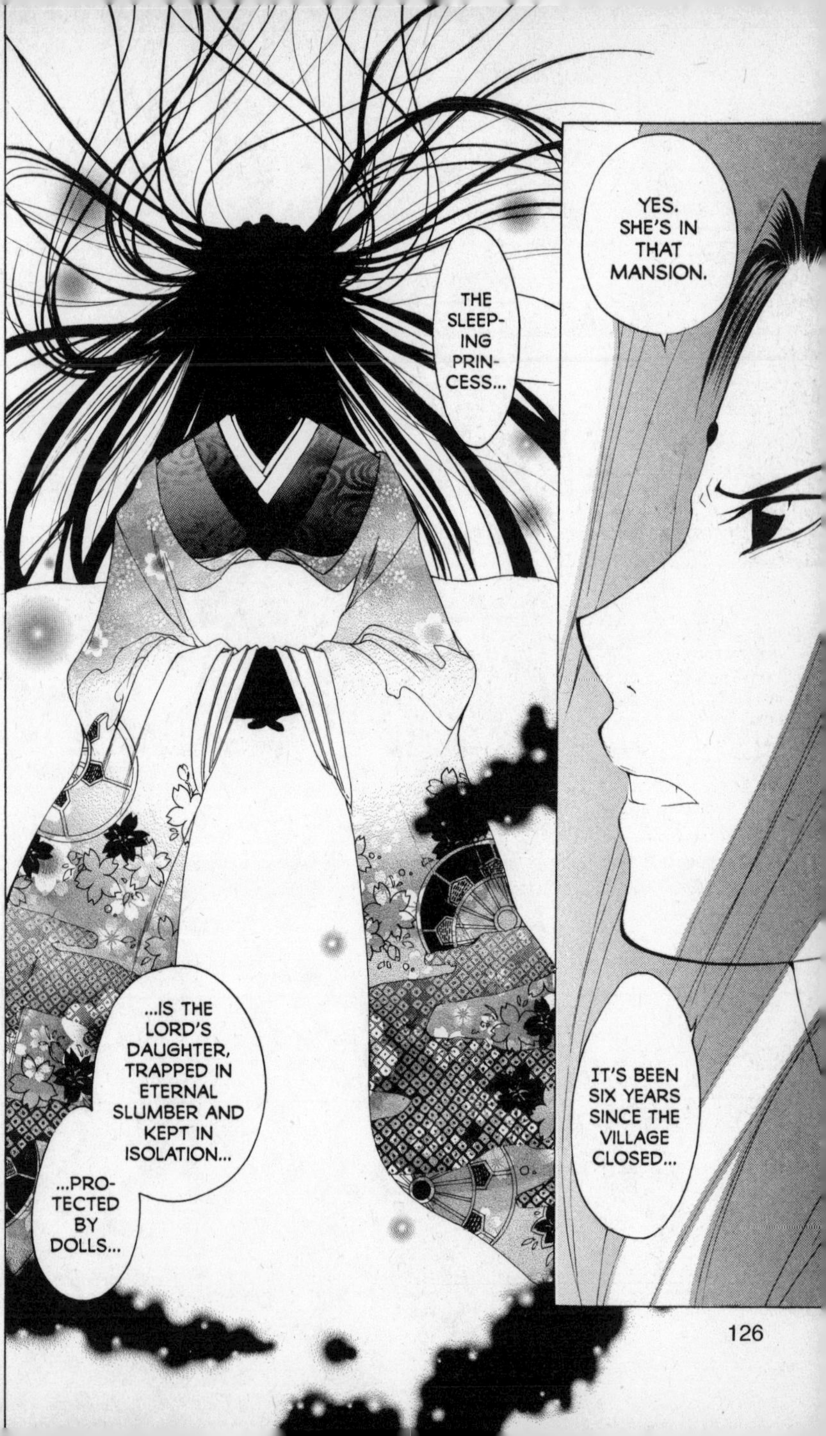
YES. SHE'S IN THAT MANSION.
IT'S BEEN SIX YEARS SINCE THE VILLAGE CLOSED...
THE SLEEPING PRINCESS...
...IS THE LORD'S DAUGHTER, TRAPPED IN ETERNAL SLUMBER AND KEPT IN ISOLATION...
...PROTECTED BY DOLLS...

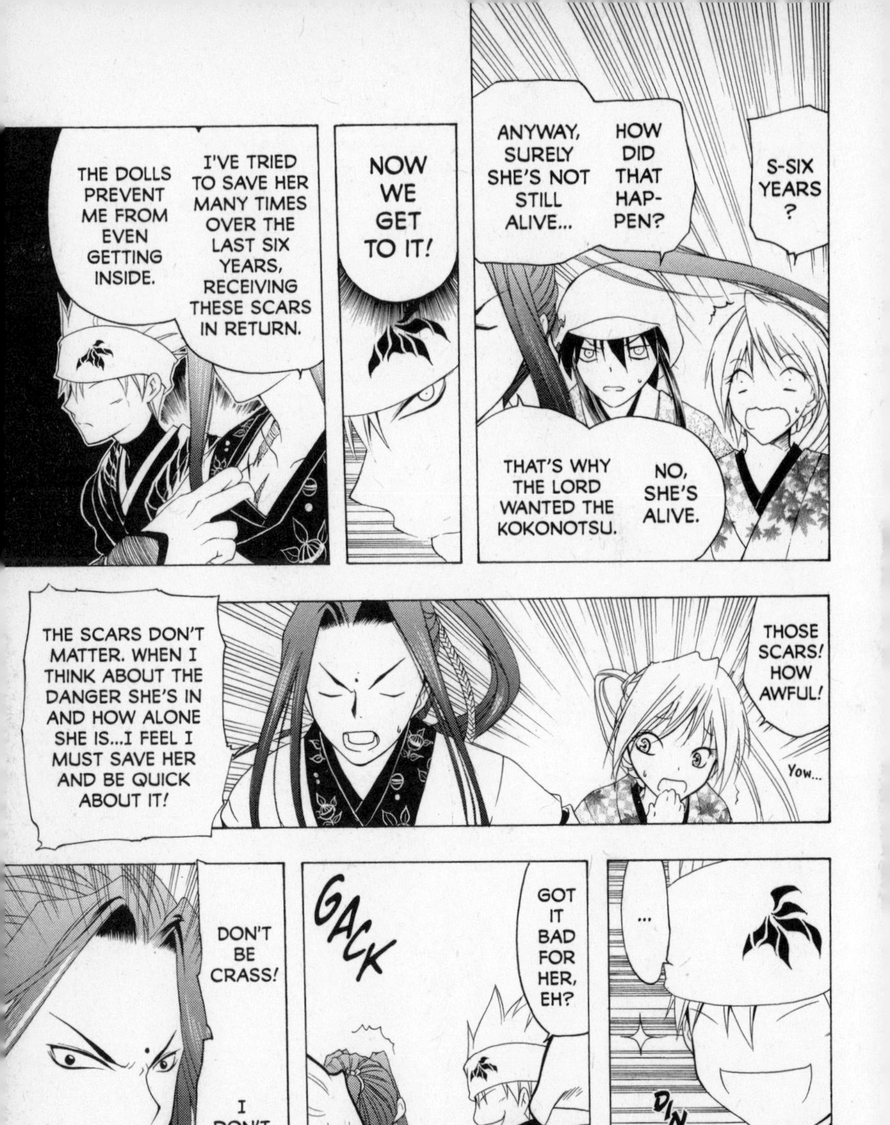
S-SIX YEARS?
HOW DID THAT HAP-PEN?
ANYWAY, SURELY SHE'S NOT STILL ALIVE...
NO, SHE'S ALIVE.
THAT'S WHY THE LORD WANTED THE KOKONOTSU.
NOW WE GET TO IT!
I'VE TRIED TO SAVE HER MANY TIMES OVER THE LAST SIX YEARS, RECEIVING THESE SCARS IN RETURN.
THE DOLLS PREVENT ME FROM EVEN GETTING INSIDE.
THOSE SCARS! HOW AWFUL!
Yow...
THE SCARS DON'T MATTER. WHEN I THINK ABOUT THE DANGER SHE'S IN AND HOW ALONE SHE IS...I FEEL I MUST SAVE HER AND BE QUICK ABOUT IT!
...
DING
GOT IT BAD FOR HER, EH?
GACK
Yippee! Yippee!
DON'T BE CRASS!
I DON'T "GOT IT BAD"...

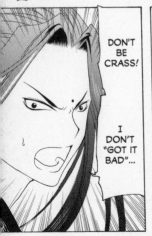

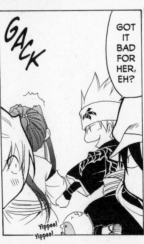

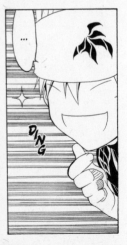

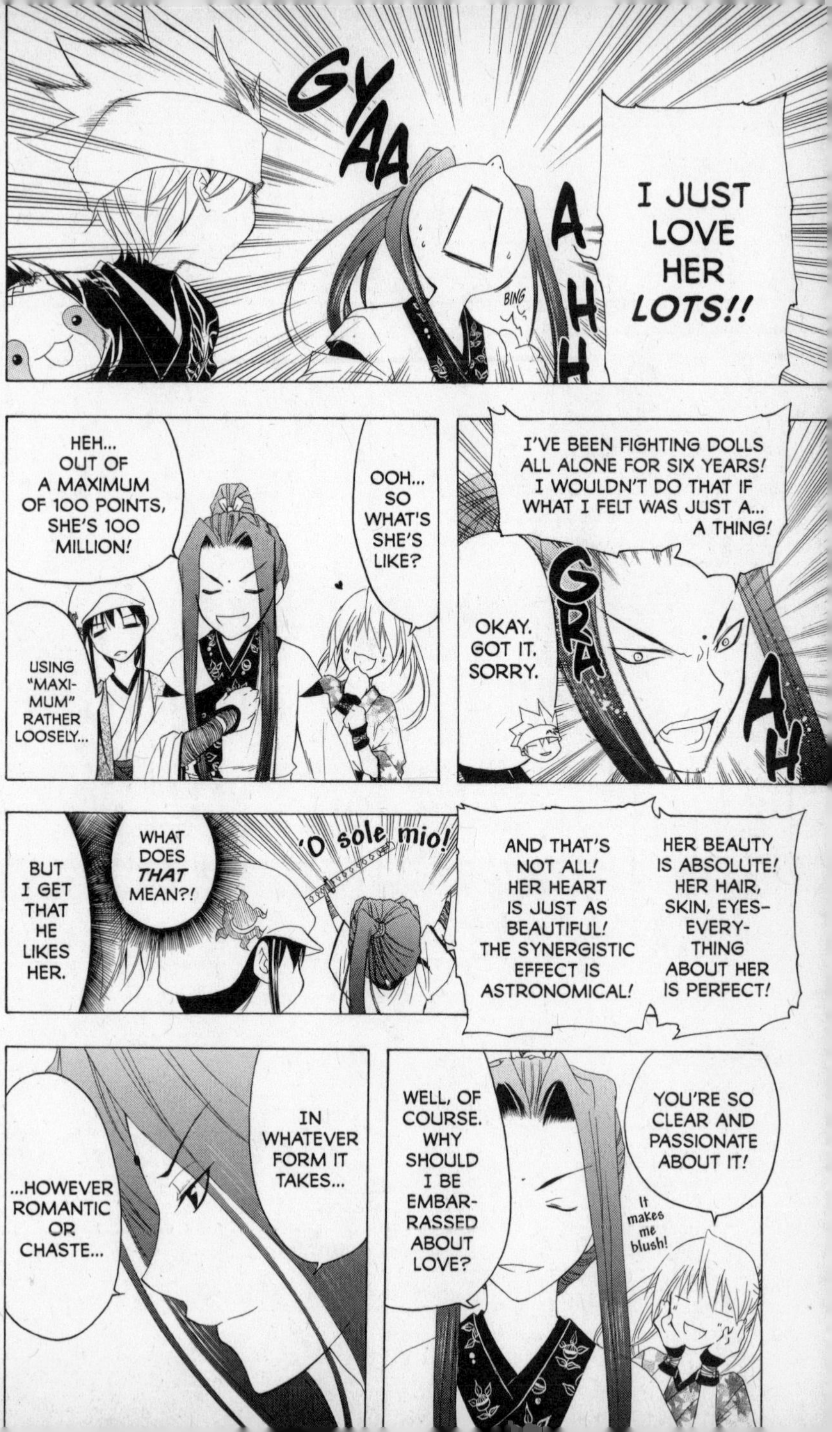
I JUST LOVE HER LOTS!!
GYAAAAHH
BING
I'VE BEEN FIGHTING DOLLS ALL ALONE FOR SIX YEARS! I WOULDN'T DO THAT IF WHAT I FELT WAS JUST A... A THING!
GRAAH
OKAY. GOT IT. SORRY.
OOH... SO WHAT'S SHE'S LIKE?
HEH... OUT OF A MAXIMUM OF 100 POINTS, SHE'S 100 MILLION!
USING "MAXIMUM" RATHER LOOSELY...
HER BEAUTY IS ABSOLUTE! HER HAIR, SKIN, EYES—EVERYTHING ABOUT HER IS PERFECT!
AND THAT'S NOT ALL! HER HEART IS JUST AS BEAUTIFUL! THE SYNERGISTIC EFFECT IS ASTRONOMICAL!
'O sole mio!
WHAT DOES THAT MEAN?!
BUT I GET THAT HE LIKES HER.
YOU'RE SO CLEAR AND PASSIONATE ABOUT IT!
It makes me blush!
WELL, OF COURSE. WHY SHOULD I BE EMBARRASSED ABOUT LOVE?
IN WHATEVER FORM IT TAKES...
...HOWEVER ROMANTIC OR CHASTE...

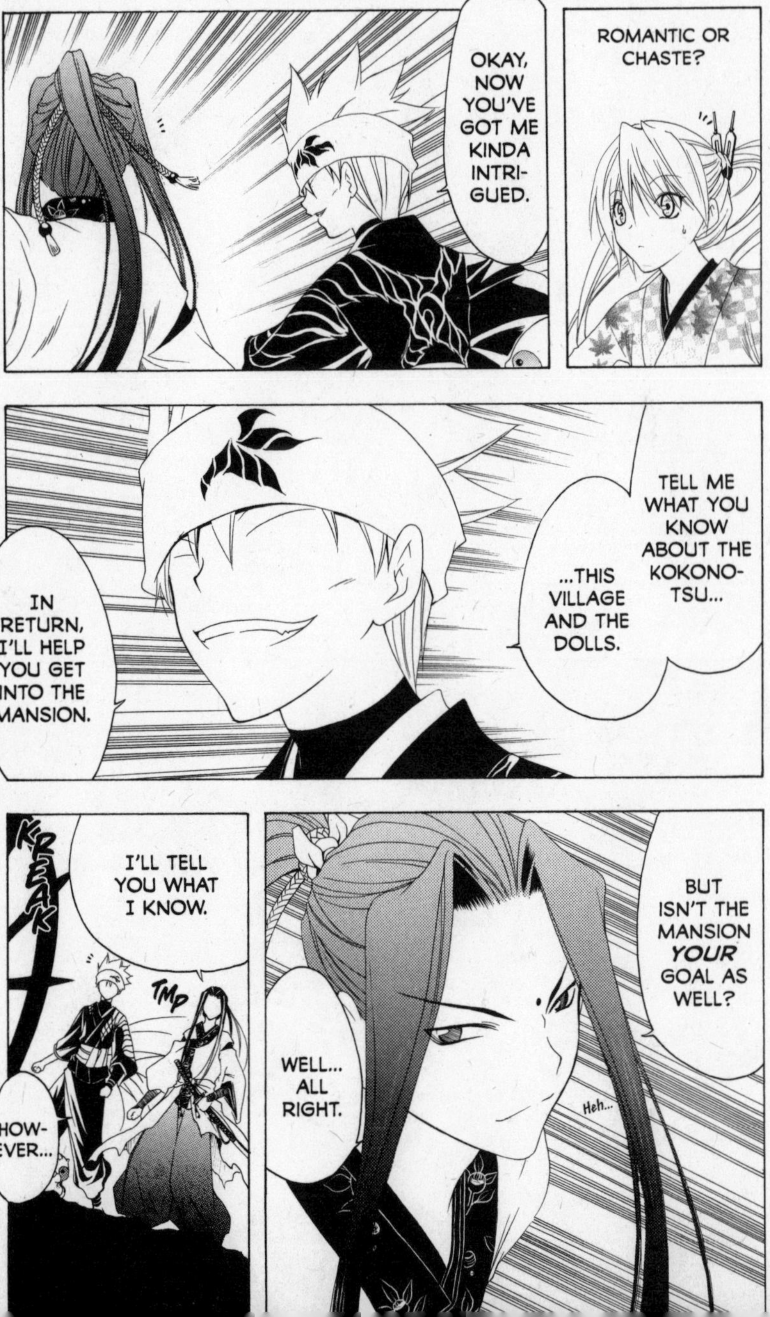
ROMANTIC OR CHASTE?
OKAY, NOW YOU'VE GOT ME KINDA INTRIGUED.
TELL ME WHAT YOU KNOW ABOUT THE KOKONOTSU...
...THIS VILLAGE AND THE DOLLS.
IN RETURN, I'LL HELP YOU GET INTO THE MANSION.
BUT ISN'T THE MANSION *YOUR* GOAL AS WELL?
Heh...
WELL... ALL RIGHT.
I'LL TELL YOU WHAT I KNOW.
KREAK
TMP
HOWEVER...

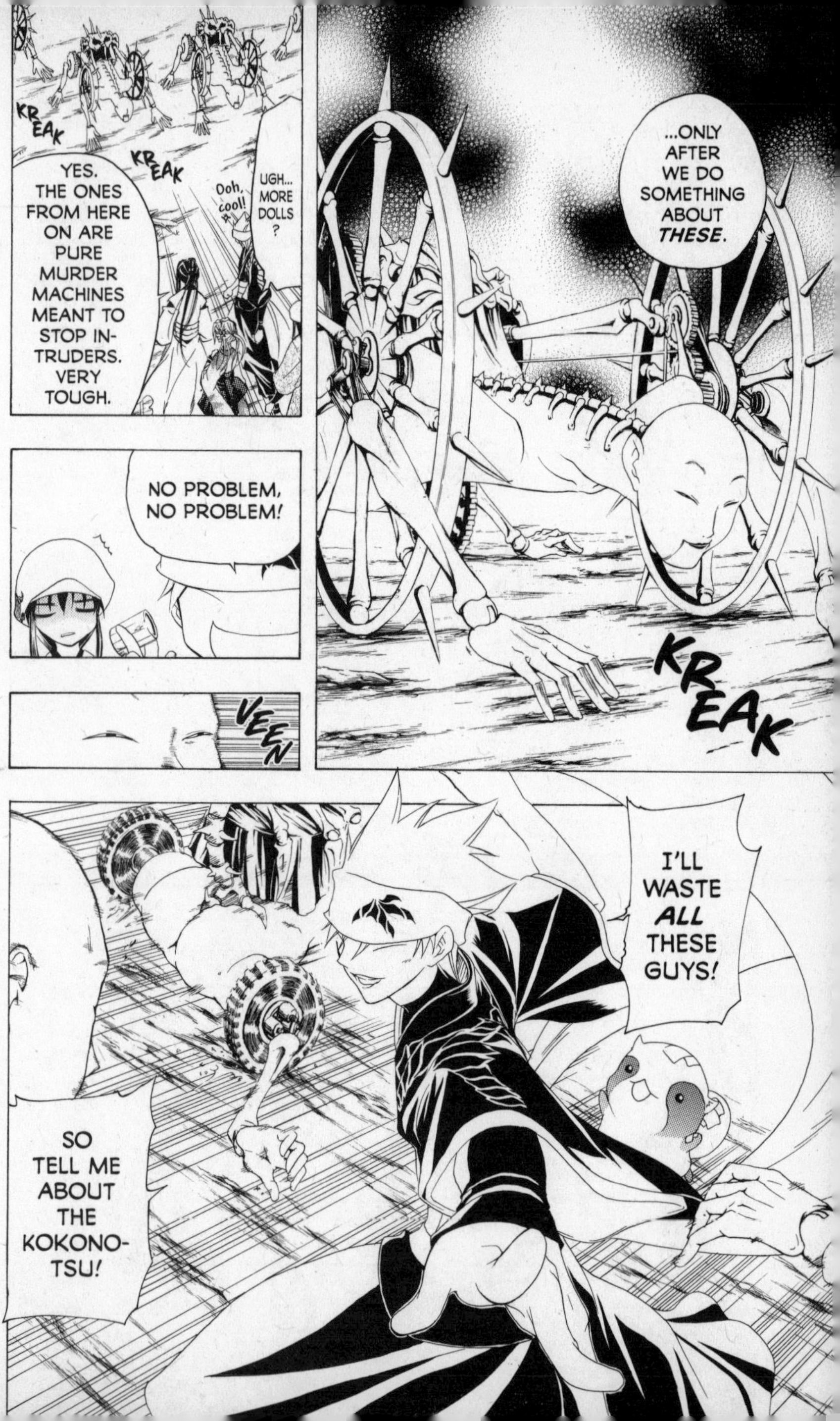
...ONLY AFTER WE DO SOMETHING ABOUT *THESE*.
KREAK
UGH... MORE DOLLS?
Ooh, cool!
KREAK
YES. THE ONES FROM HERE ON ARE PURE MURDER MACHINES MEANT TO STOP IN-TRUDERS. VERY TOUGH.
KREAK
NO PROBLEM, NO PROBLEM!
VEEN
I'LL WASTE *ALL* THESE GUYS!
SO TELL ME ABOUT THE KOKONO-TSU!

Chapter 45
The Lord's Dolls

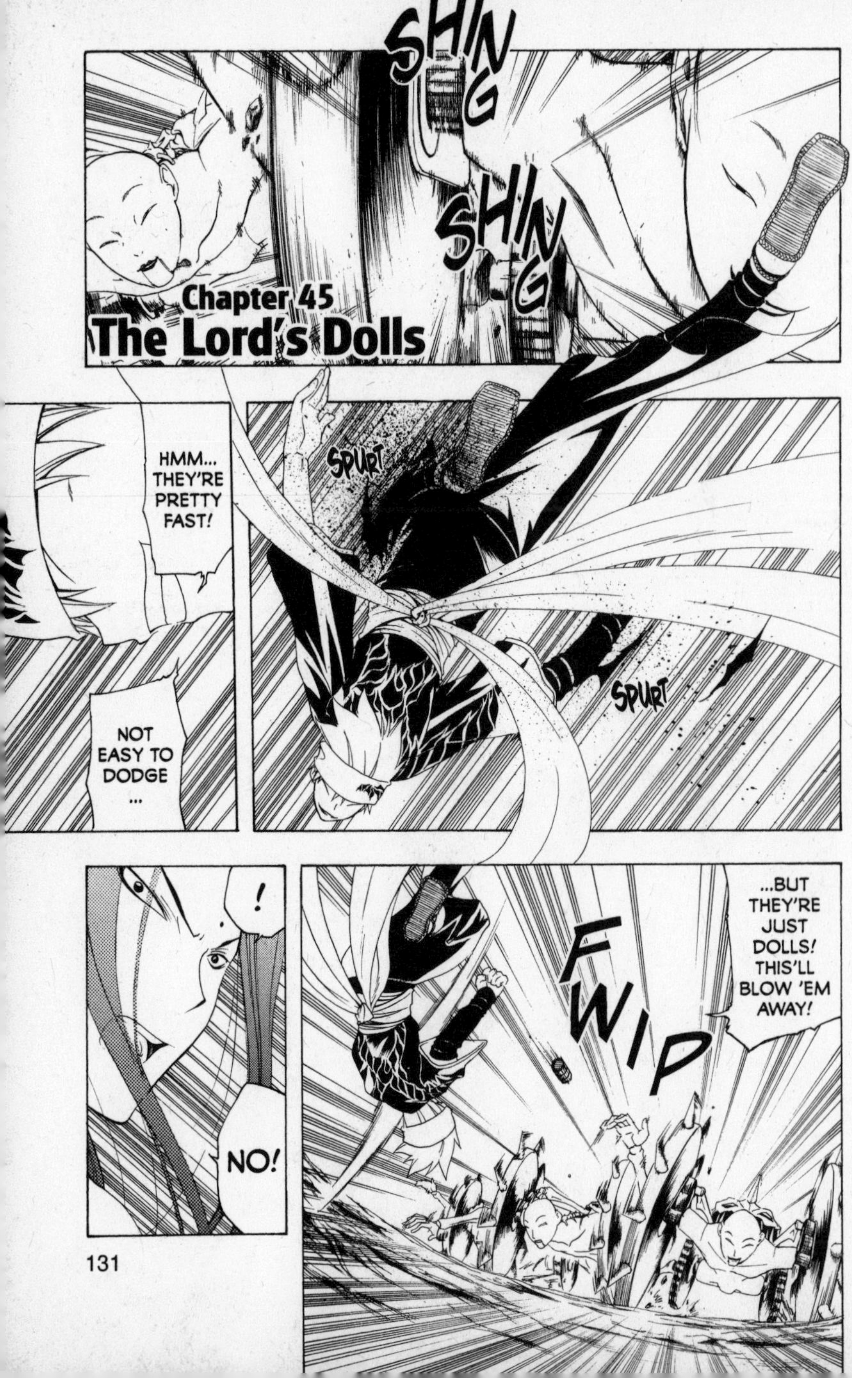
SHING
SHING
SPURT
SPURT
HMM... THEY'RE PRETTY FAST!
NOT EASY TO DODGE ...
...BUT THEY'RE JUST DOLLS! THIS'LL BLOW 'EM AWAY!
FWIP
!
NO!

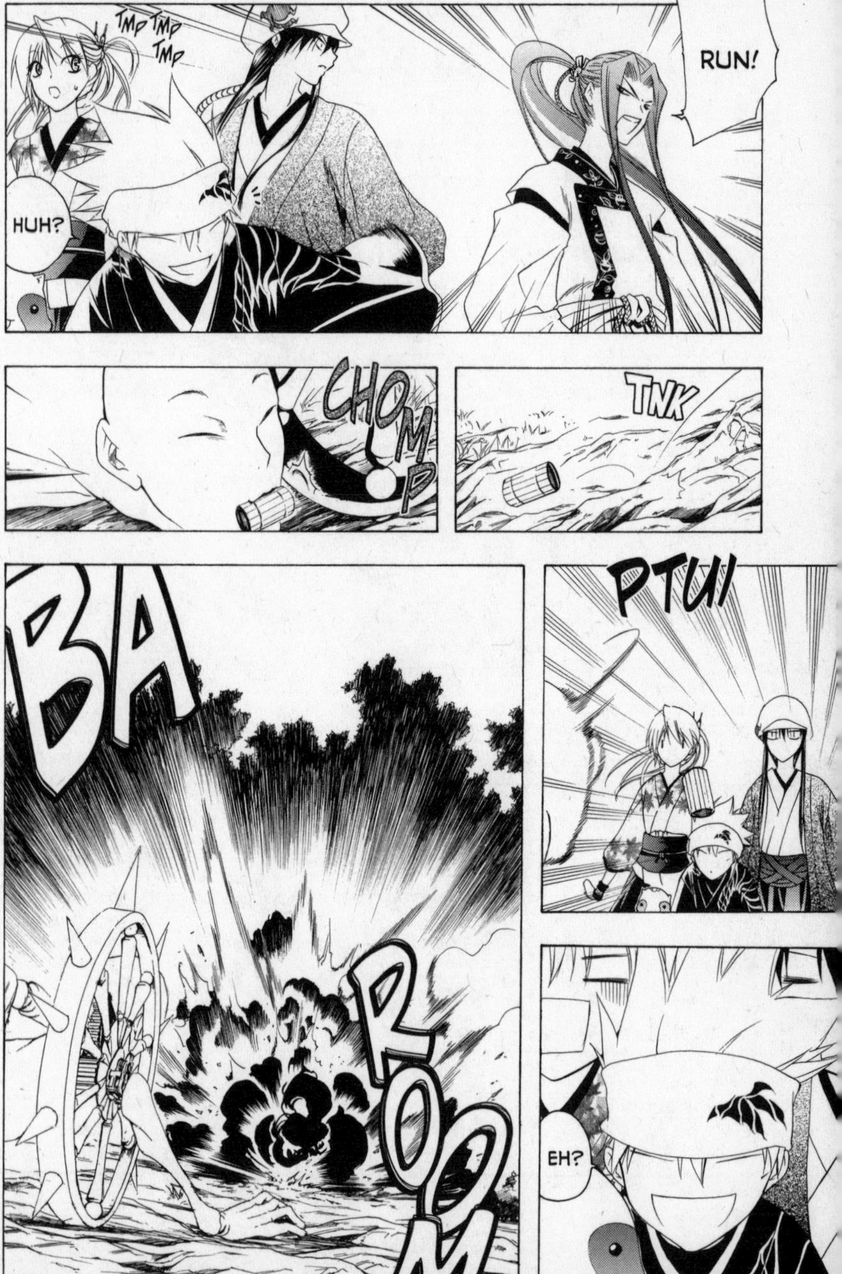
RUN!
TMP TMP
TMP
HUH?
TNK
CHOMP
PTUI
EH?
BA
ROOOM

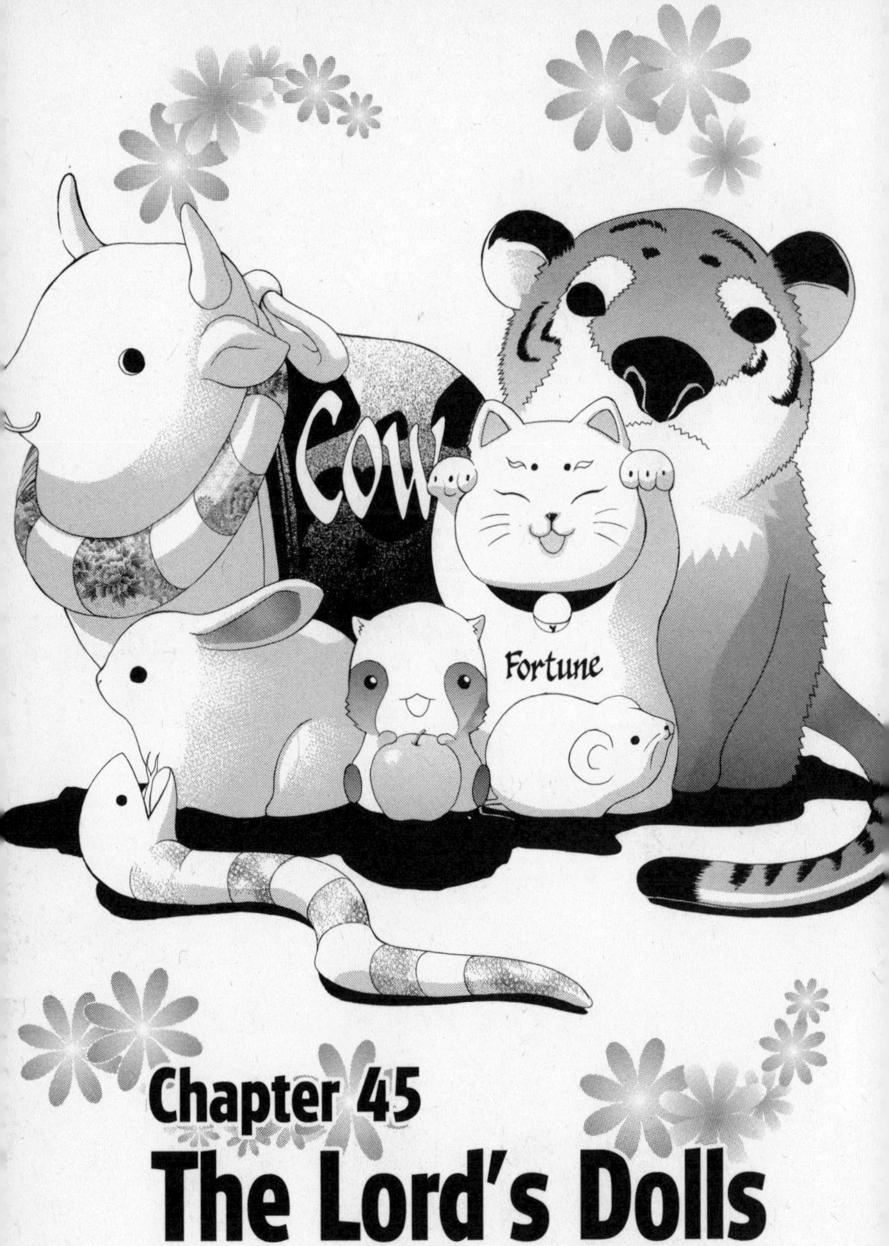
COW
Fortune

Chapter 45
The Lord's Dolls

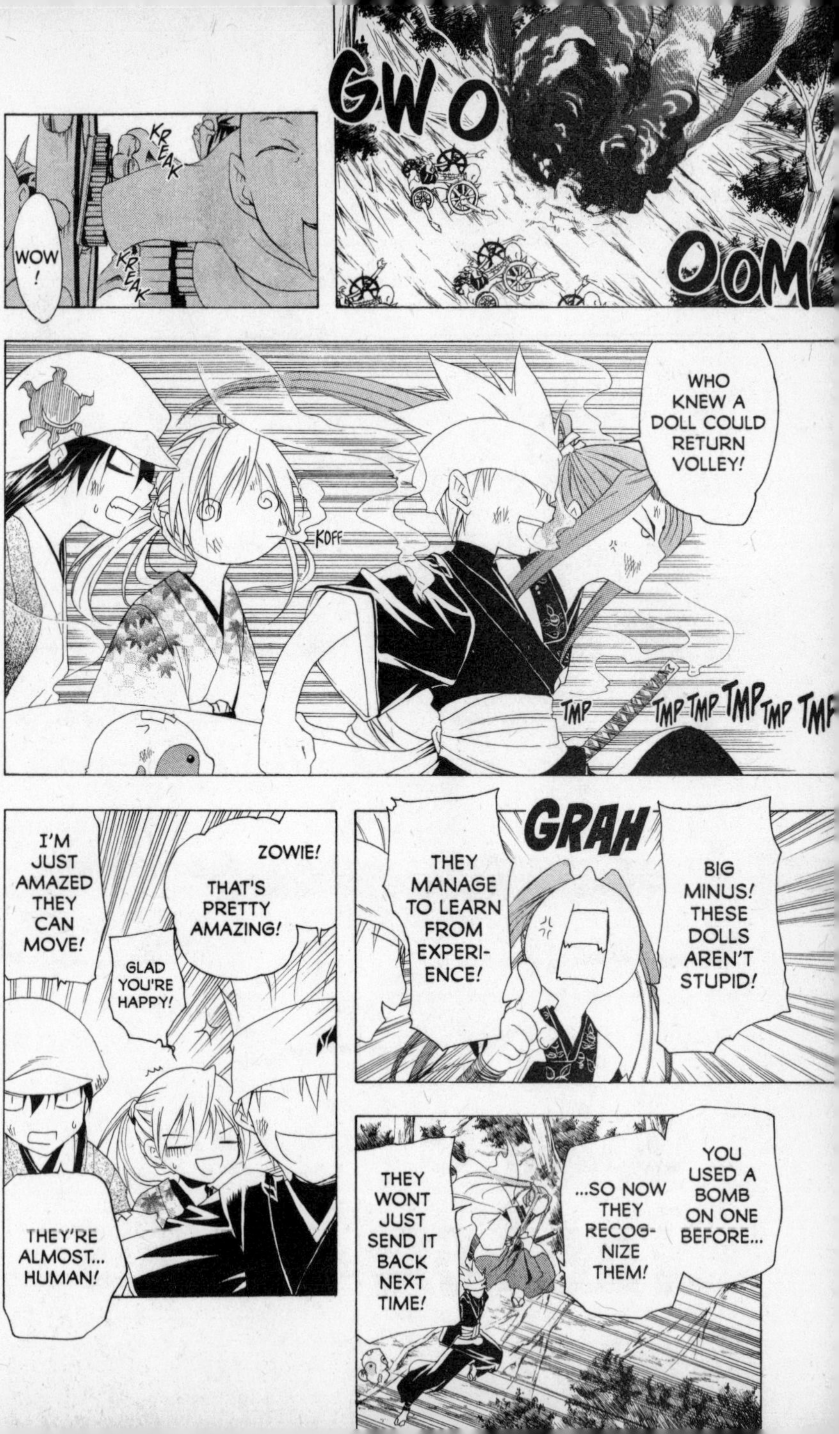
GWO
OOM
KREAK
KREAK
WOW!
WHO KNEW A DOLL COULD RETURN VOLLEY!
KOFF
TMP TMP TMP TMP TMP TMP
BIG MINUS! THESE DOLLS AREN'T STUPID!
GRAH
THEY MANAGE TO LEARN FROM EXPERIENCE!
YOU USED A BOMB ON ONE BEFORE...
...SO NOW THEY RECOGNIZE THEM!
THEY WONT JUST SEND IT BACK NEXT TIME!
ZOWIE! THAT'S PRETTY AMAZING!
I'M JUST AMAZED THEY CAN MOVE!
GLAD YOU'RE HAPPY!
THEY'RE ALMOST... HUMAN!

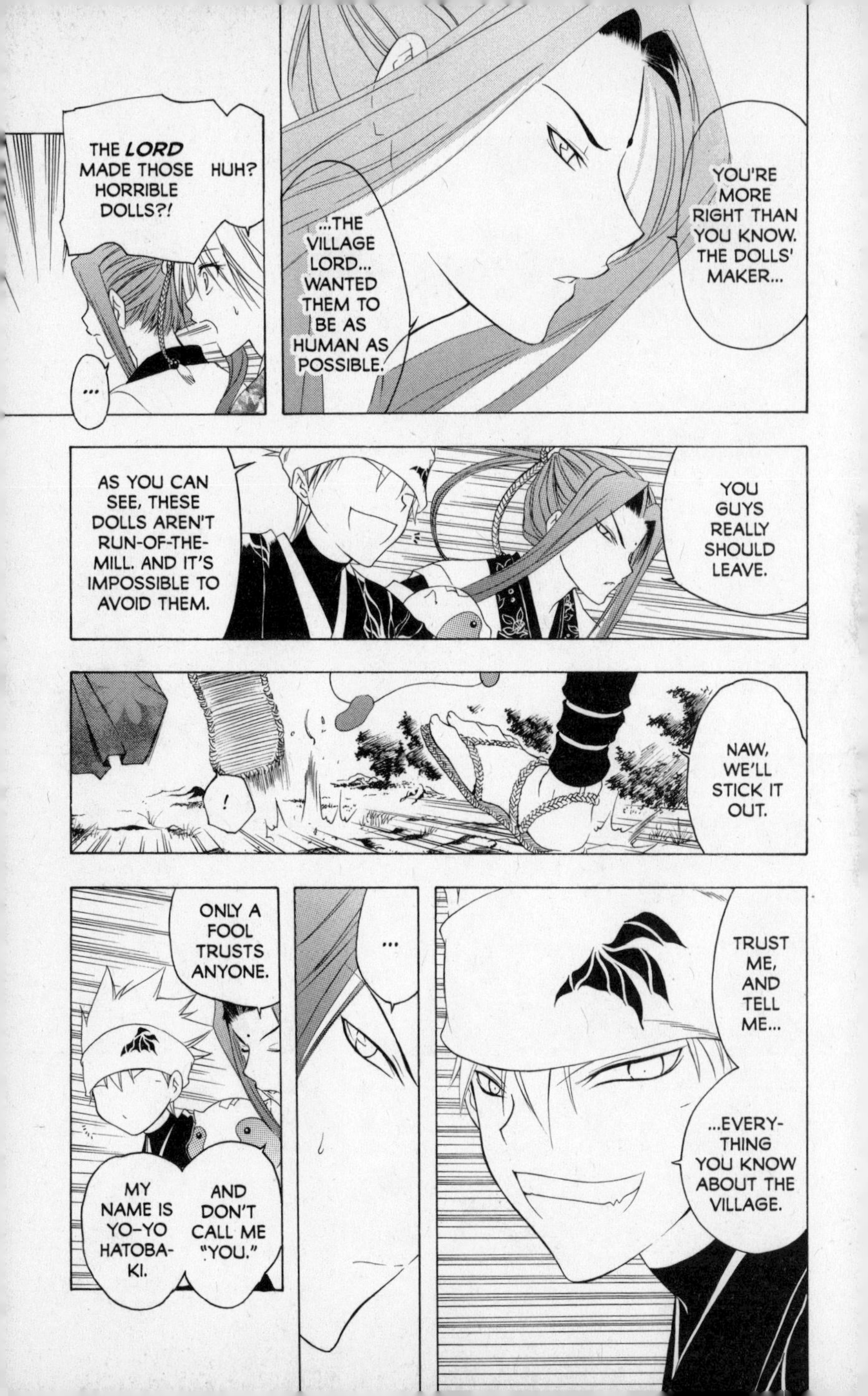
YOU'RE MORE RIGHT THAN YOU KNOW. THE DOLLS' MAKER...
...THE VILLAGE LORD... WANTED THEM TO BE AS HUMAN AS POSSIBLE.
HUH?
THE *LORD* MADE THOSE HORRIBLE DOLLS?!
...
YOU GUYS REALLY SHOULD LEAVE.
AS YOU CAN SEE, THESE DOLLS AREN'T RUN-OF-THE-MILL. AND IT'S IMPOSSIBLE TO AVOID THEM.
NAW, WE'LL STICK IT OUT.
!
TRUST ME, AND TELL ME...
...EVERYTHING YOU KNOW ABOUT THE VILLAGE.
...
ONLY A FOOL TRUSTS ANYONE.
AND DON'T CALL ME "YOU."
MY NAME IS YO-YO HATOBAKI.

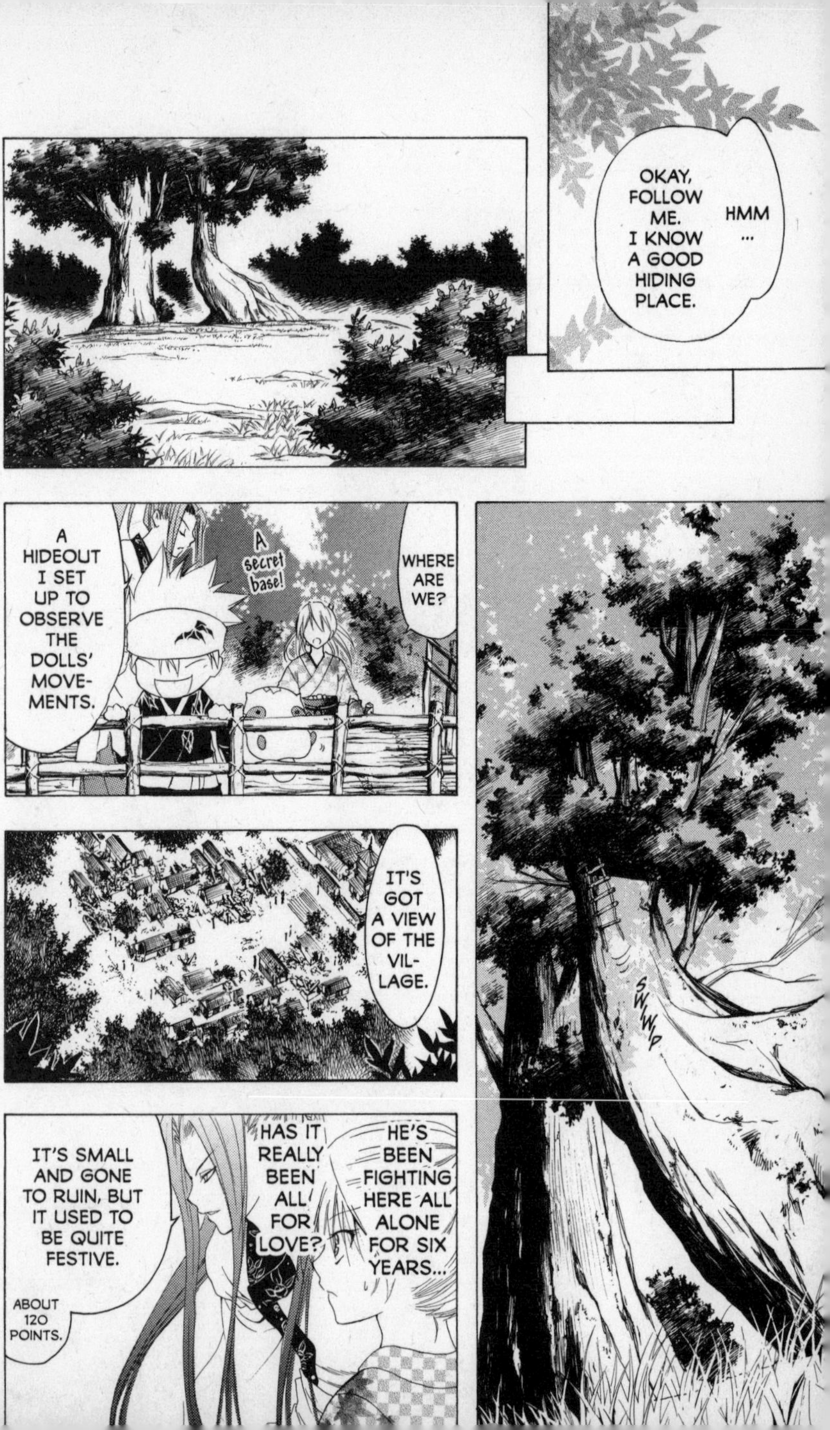
HMM ...
OKAY, FOLLOW ME. I KNOW A GOOD HIDING PLACE.
SWIWIP
WHERE ARE WE?
A secret base!
A HIDEOUT I SET UP TO OBSERVE THE DOLLS' MOVEMENTS.
IT'S GOT A VIEW OF THE VIL-LAGE.
HE'S BEEN FIGHTING HERE ALL ALONE FOR SIX YEARS...
HAS IT REALLY BEEN ALL FOR LOVE?
IT'S SMALL AND GONE TO RUIN, BUT IT USED TO BE QUITE FESTIVE.
ABOUT 120 POINTS.

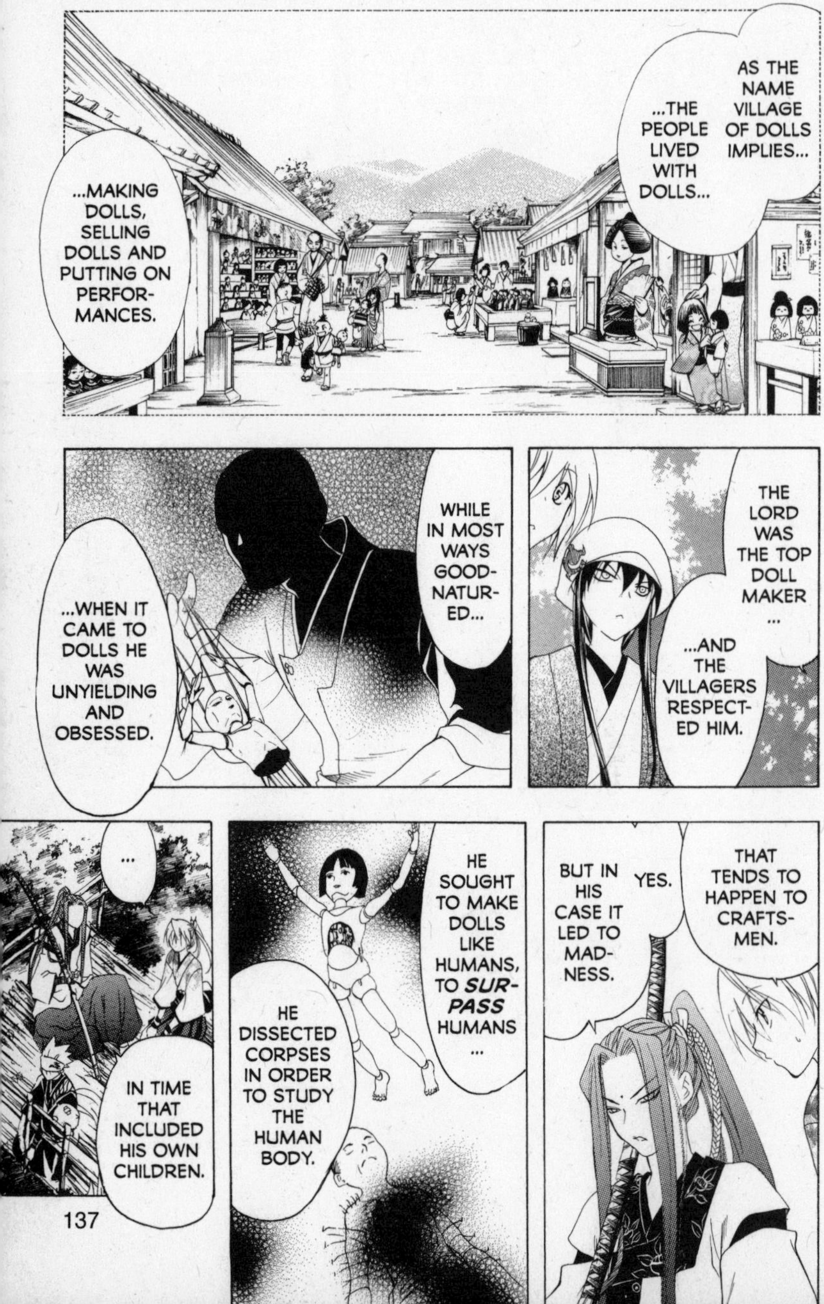
AS THE NAME VILLAGE OF DOLLS IMPLIES...
...THE PEOPLE LIVED WITH DOLLS...
...MAKING DOLLS, SELLING DOLLS AND PUTTING ON PERFORMANCES.
THE LORD WAS THE TOP DOLL MAKER ...
...AND THE VILLAGERS RESPECTED HIM.
WHILE IN MOST WAYS GOOD-NATURED...
...WHEN IT CAME TO DOLLS HE WAS UNYIELDING AND OBSESSED.
THAT TENDS TO HAPPEN TO CRAFTSMEN.
YES.
BUT IN HIS CASE IT LED TO MADNESS.
HE SOUGHT TO MAKE DOLLS LIKE HUMANS, TO *SURPASS* HUMANS ...
HE DISSECTED CORPSES IN ORDER TO STUDY THE HUMAN BODY.
...
IN TIME THAT INCLUDED HIS OWN CHILDREN.

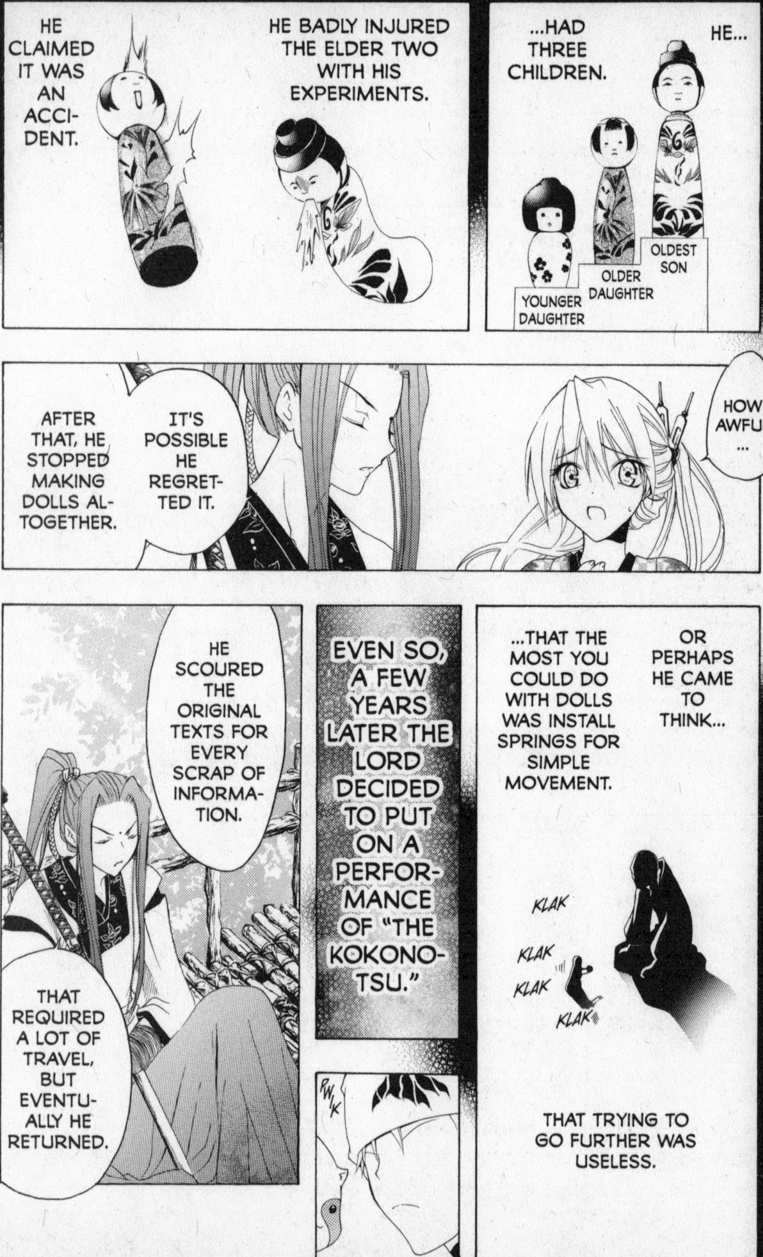
HE...
...HAD THREE CHILDREN.
OLDEST SON
OLDER DAUGHTER
YOUNGER DAUGHTER
HE BADLY INJURED THE ELDER TWO WITH HIS EXPERIMENTS.
HE CLAIMED IT WAS AN ACCI-DENT.
HOW AWFUL ...
IT'S POSSIBLE HE REGRET-TED IT.
AFTER THAT, HE STOPPED MAKING DOLLS AL-TOGETHER.
OR PERHAPS HE CAME TO THINK...
...THAT THE MOST YOU COULD DO WITH DOLLS WAS INSTALL SPRINGS FOR SIMPLE MOVEMENT.
KLAK
KLAK
KLAK
KLAK
THAT TRYING TO GO FURTHER WAS USELESS.
EVEN SO, A FEW YEARS LATER THE LORD DECIDED TO PUT ON A PERFOR-MANCE OF "THE KOKONO-TSU."
PWIK
HE SCOURED THE ORIGINAL TEXTS FOR EVERY SCRAP OF INFORMA-TION.
THAT REQUIRED A LOT OF TRAVEL, BUT EVENTU-ALLY HE RETURNED.

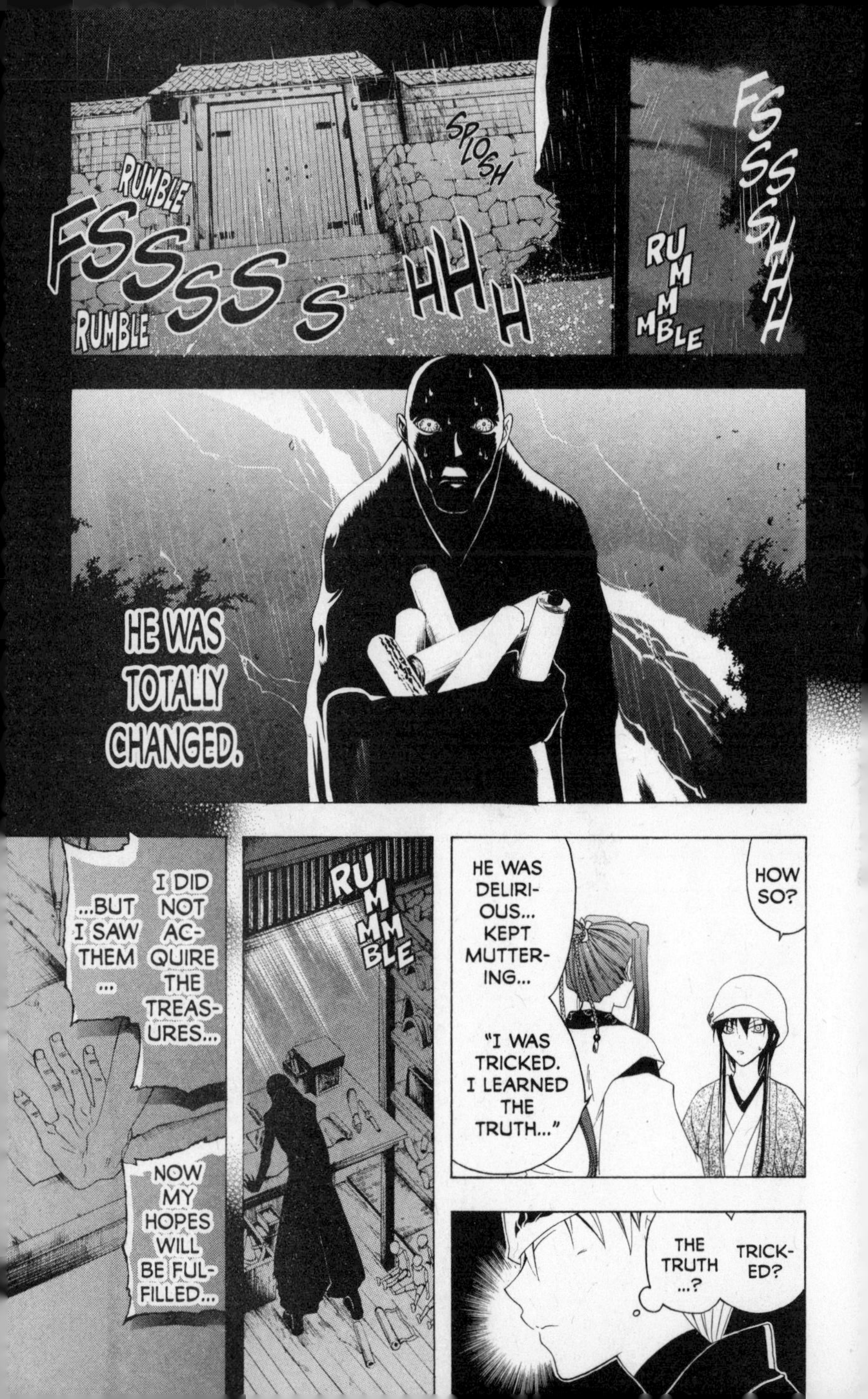
FSSSHHH
RUMMMBLE
SPLOSH
RUMBLE
FSSSSSHHHH
RUMBLE
HE WAS TOTALLY CHANGED.
HOW SO?
HE WAS DELIRIOUS... KEPT MUTTERING...
"I WAS TRICKED. I LEARNED THE TRUTH..."
TRICKED?
THE TRUTH...?
RUMMMBLE
I DID NOT ACQUIRE THE TREASURES...
...BUT I SAW THEM...
NOW MY HOPES WILL BE FULFILLED...

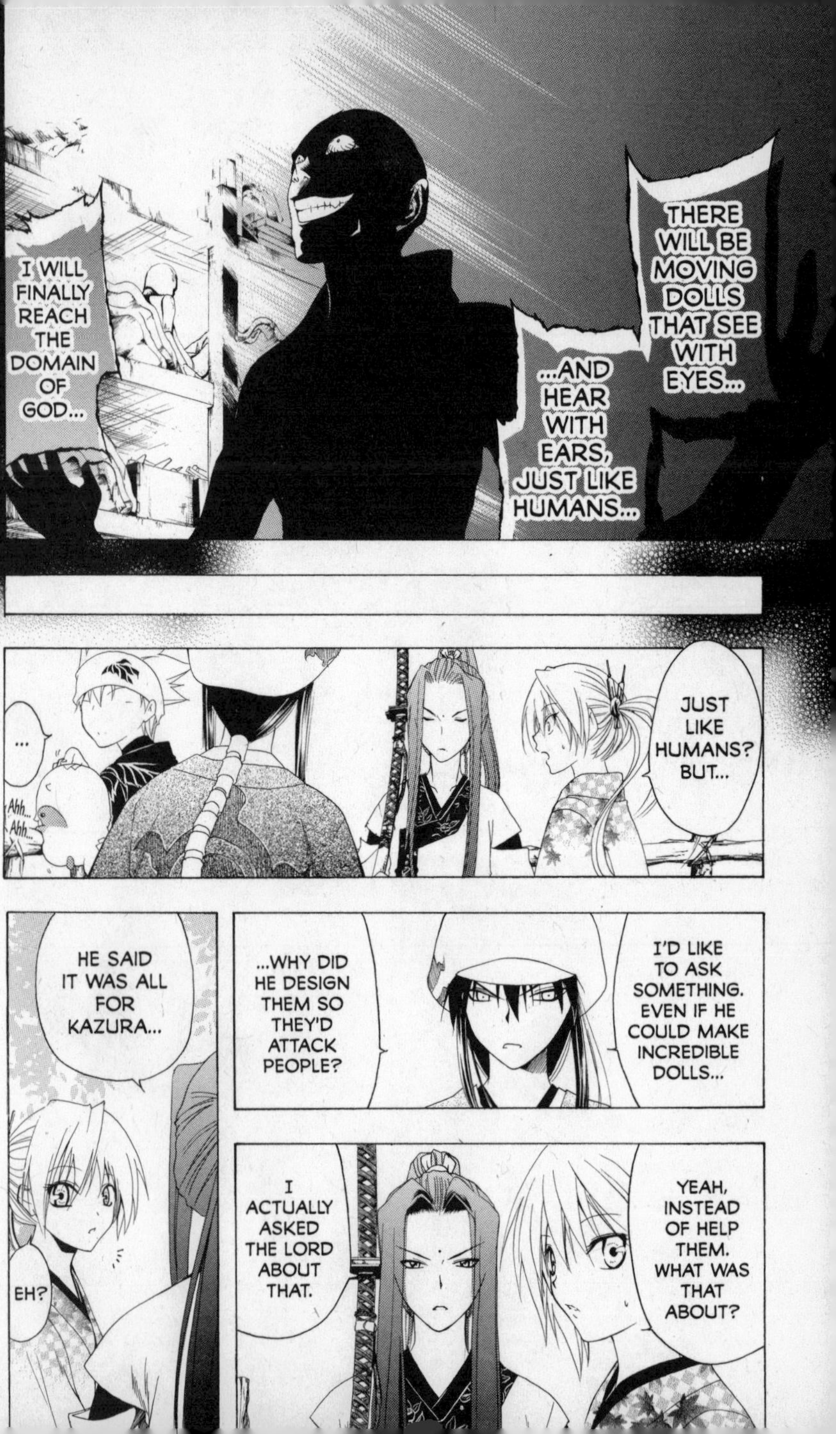
THERE WILL BE MOVING DOLLS THAT SEE WITH EYES...
...AND HEAR WITH EARS, JUST LIKE HUMANS...
I WILL FINALLY REACH THE DOMAIN OF GOD...
JUST LIKE HUMANS? BUT...
...
Ahh... Ahh...
I'D LIKE TO ASK SOMETHING. EVEN IF HE COULD MAKE INCREDIBLE DOLLS...
...WHY DID HE DESIGN THEM SO THEY'D ATTACK PEOPLE?
YEAH, INSTEAD OF HELP THEM. WHAT WAS THAT ABOUT?
I ACTUALLY ASKED THE LORD ABOUT THAT.
HE SAID IT WAS ALL FOR KAZURA...
EH?

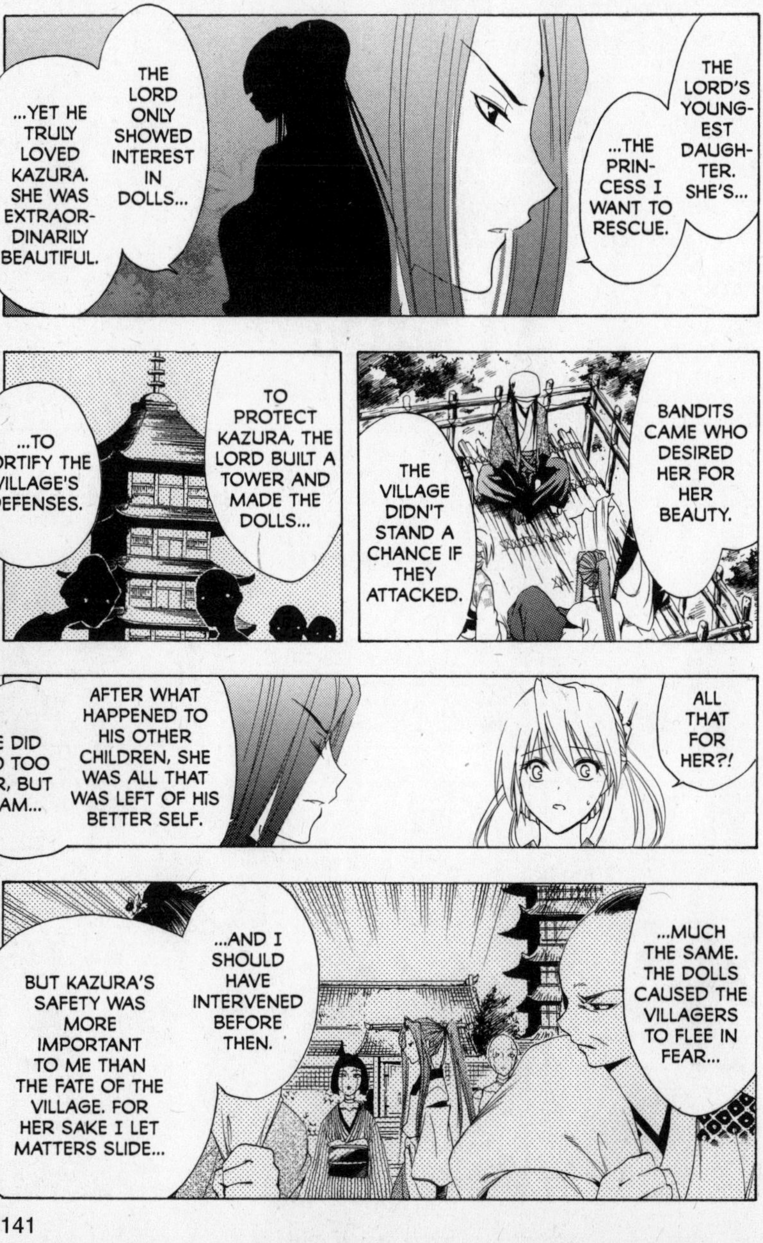
THE LORD'S YOUNGEST DAUGHTER. SHE'S...
...THE PRINCESS I WANT TO RESCUE.
THE LORD ONLY SHOWED INTEREST IN DOLLS...
...YET HE TRULY LOVED KAZURA. SHE WAS EXTRAORDINARILY BEAUTIFUL.
BANDITS CAME WHO DESIRED HER FOR HER BEAUTY.
THE VILLAGE DIDN'T STAND A CHANCE IF THEY ATTACKED.
TO PROTECT KAZURA, THE LORD BUILT A TOWER AND MADE THE DOLLS...
...TO FORTIFY THE VILLAGE'S DEFENSES.
ALL THAT FOR HER?!
AFTER WHAT HAPPENED TO HIS OTHER CHILDREN, SHE WAS ALL THAT WAS LEFT OF HIS BETTER SELF.
HE DID GO TOO FAR, BUT I AM...
...MUCH THE SAME. THE DOLLS CAUSED THE VILLAGERS TO FLEE IN FEAR...
...AND I SHOULD HAVE INTERVENED BEFORE THEN.
BUT KAZURA'S SAFETY WAS MORE IMPORTANT TO ME THAN THE FATE OF THE VILLAGE. FOR HER SAKE I LET MATTERS SLIDE...

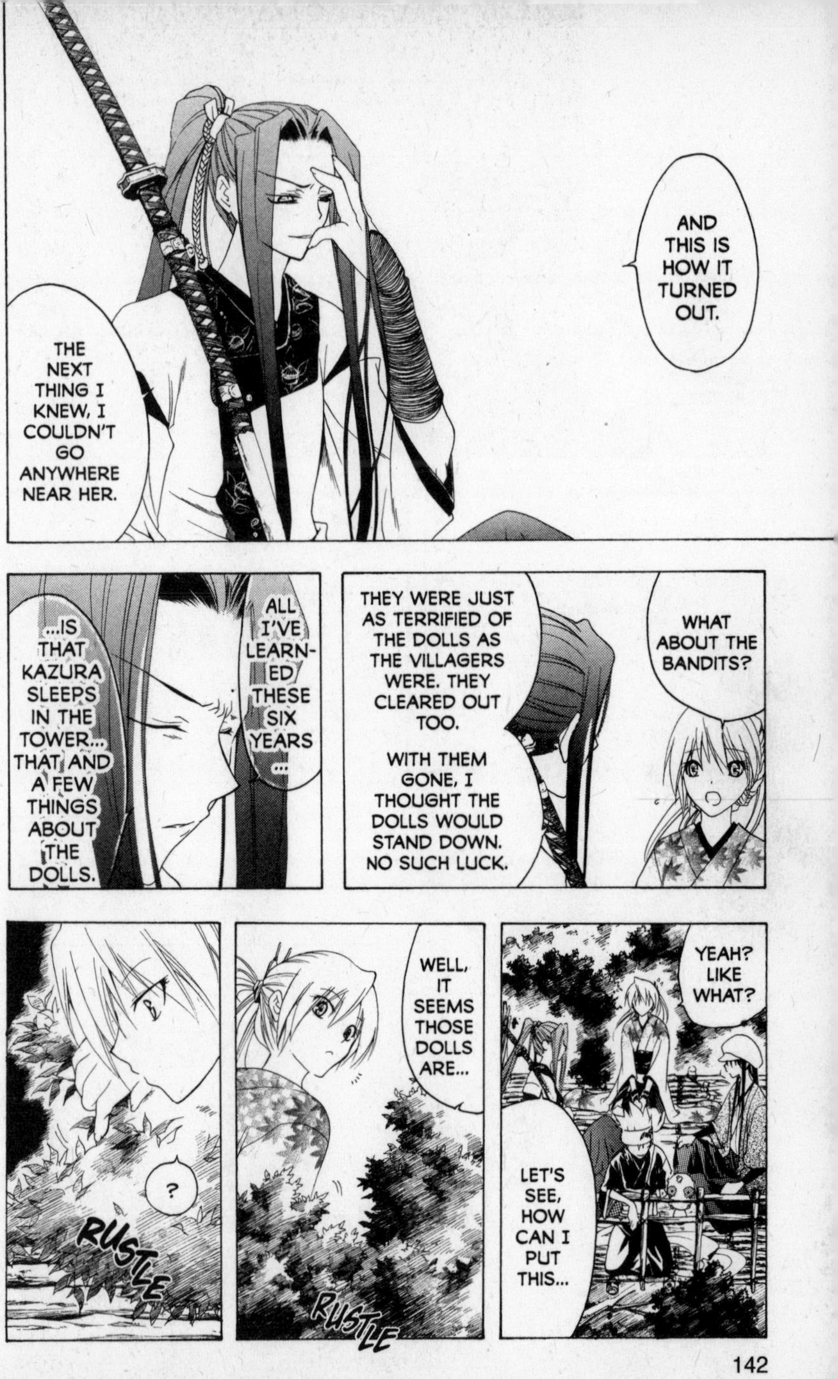
AND THIS IS HOW IT TURNED OUT.
THE NEXT THING I KNEW, I COULDN'T GO ANYWHERE NEAR HER.
WHAT ABOUT THE BANDITS?
THEY WERE JUST AS TERRIFIED OF THE DOLLS AS THE VILLAGERS WERE. THEY CLEARED OUT TOO.
WITH THEM GONE, I THOUGHT THE DOLLS WOULD STAND DOWN. NO SUCH LUCK.
ALL I'VE LEARN-ED THESE SIX YEARS...
...IS THAT KAZURA SLEEPS IN THE TOWER... THAT AND A FEW THINGS ABOUT THE DOLLS.
YEAH? LIKE WHAT?
LET'S SEE, HOW CAN I PUT THIS...
WELL, IT SEEMS THOSE DOLLS ARE...
RUSTLE
?
RUSTLE

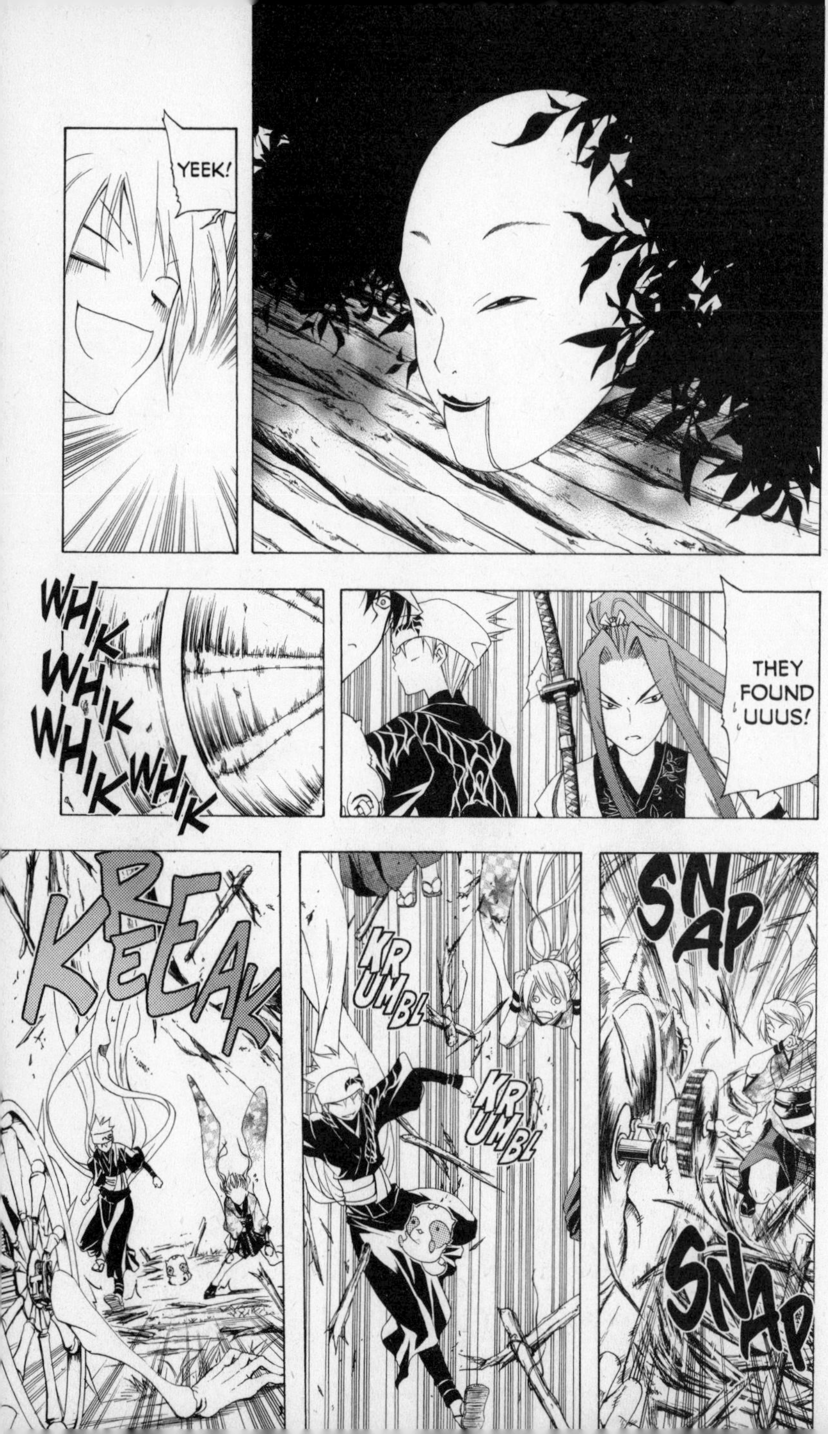
YEEK!
THEY FOUND UUUS!
WHIK WHIK WHIK WHIK WHIK
SNAP
SNAP
KRUMBL
KRUMBL
KREEAK

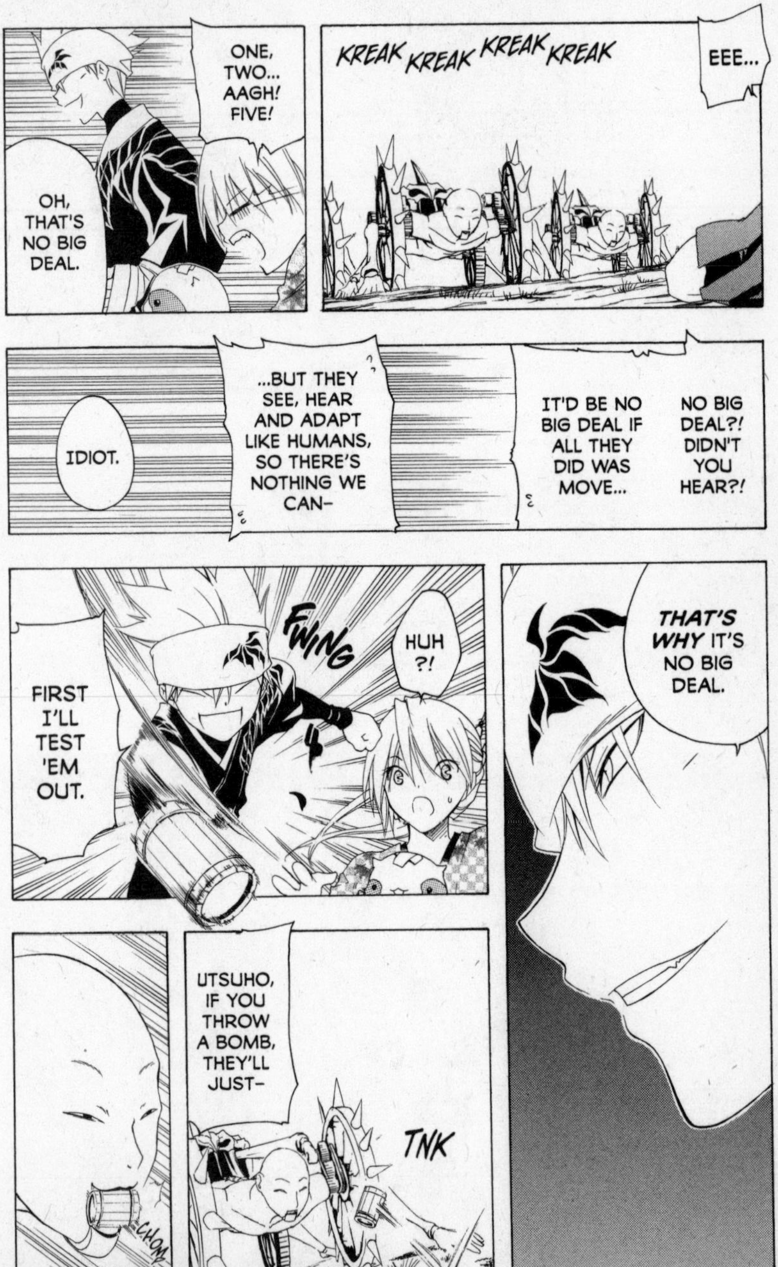
EEE...
KREAK KREAK KREAK KREAK
ONE, TWO... AAGH! FIVE!
OH, THAT'S NO BIG DEAL.
NO BIG DEAL?! DIDN'T YOU HEAR?!
IT'D BE NO BIG DEAL IF ALL THEY DID WAS MOVE...
...BUT THEY SEE, HEAR AND ADAPT LIKE HUMANS, SO THERE'S NOTHING WE CAN–
IDIOT.
THAT'S WHY IT'S NO BIG DEAL.
HUH ?!
FWING
FIRST I'LL TEST 'EM OUT.
UTSUHO, IF YOU THROW A BOMB, THEY'LL JUST–
TNK
CHOM

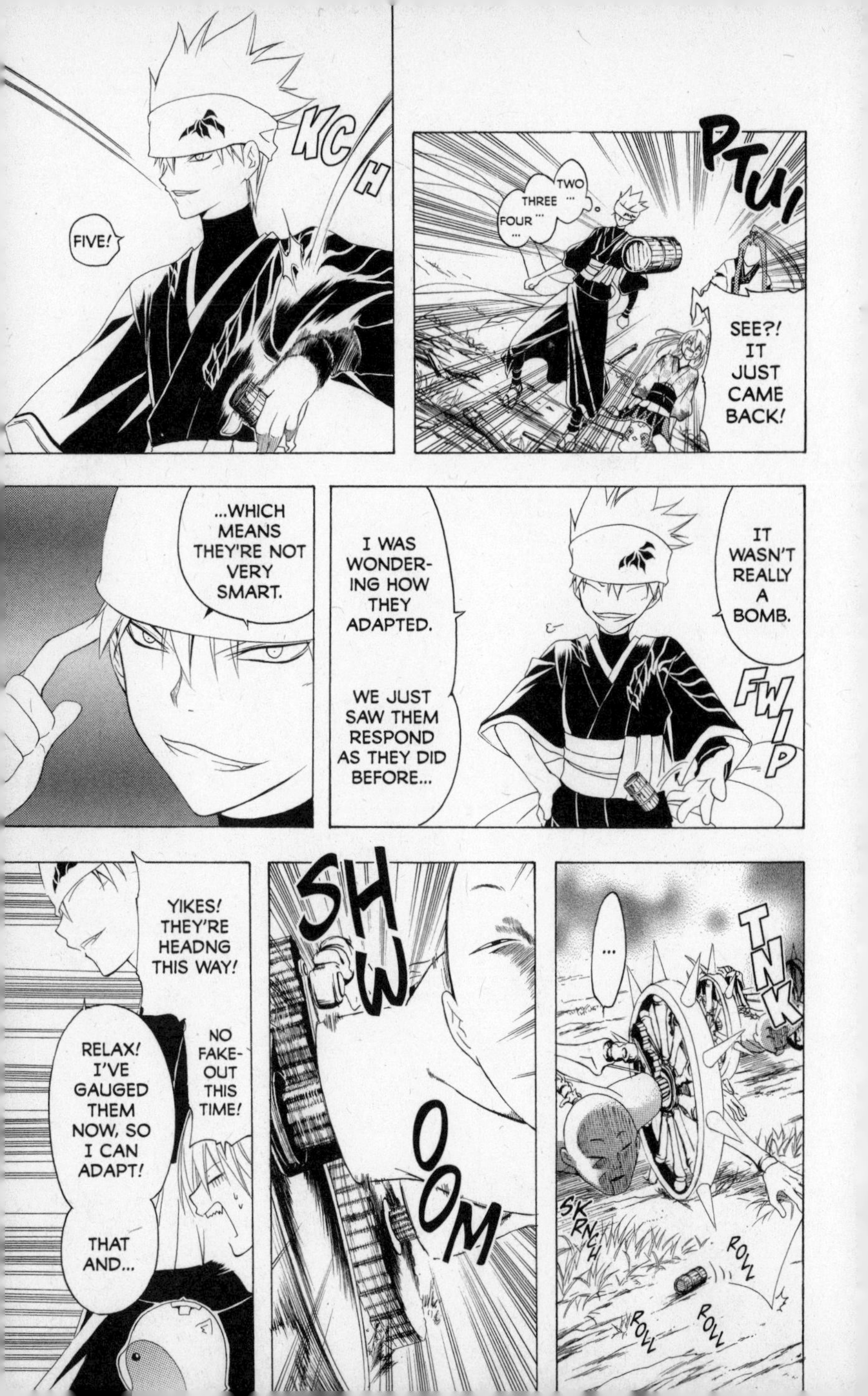
PTUI
TWO ... THREE ... FOUR ...
SEE?! IT JUST CAME BACK!
KCH
FIVE!
IT WASN'T REALLY A BOMB.
FWIP
I WAS WONDERING HOW THEY ADAPTED.
WE JUST SAW THEM RESPOND AS THEY DID BEFORE...
...WHICH MEANS THEY'RE NOT VERY SMART.
TNK
...
SKRNCH
ROLL ROLL ROLL
SHWOOM
YIKES! THEY'RE HEADNG THIS WAY!
NO FAKE-OUT THIS TIME!
RELAX! I'VE GAUGED THEM NOW, SO I CAN ADAPT!
THAT AND...

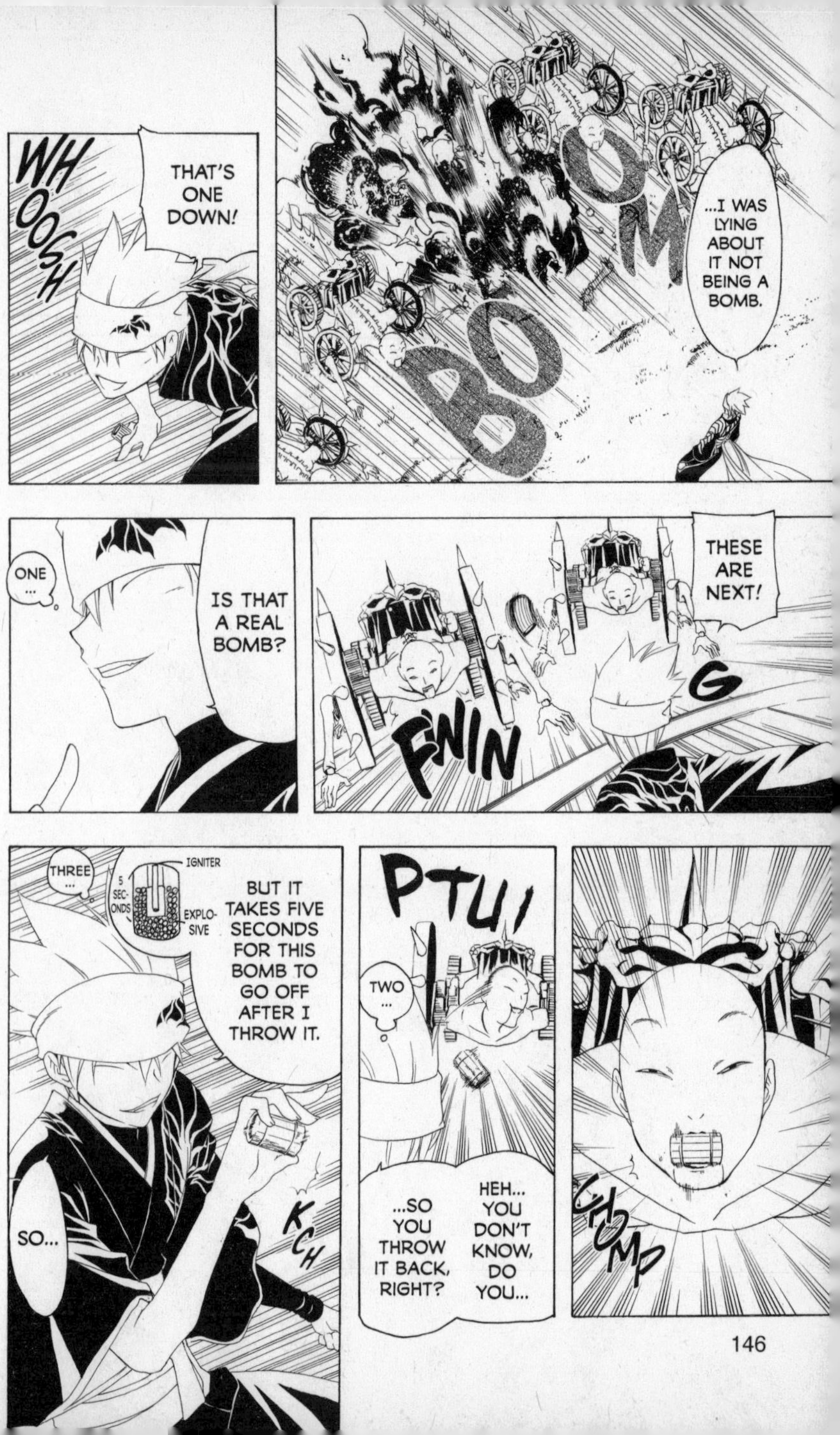
BOOM
...I WAS LYING ABOUT IT NOT BEING A BOMB.
THAT'S ONE DOWN!
WHOOSH
THESE ARE NEXT!
FWING
ONE...
IS THAT A REAL BOMB?
CHOMP
PTUI
TWO...
HEH... YOU DON'T KNOW, DO YOU...
...SO YOU THROW IT BACK, RIGHT?
THREE...
IGNITER
5 SECONDS
EXPLOSIVE
BUT IT TAKES FIVE SECONDS FOR THIS BOMB TO GO OFF AFTER I THROW IT.
KCH
SO...

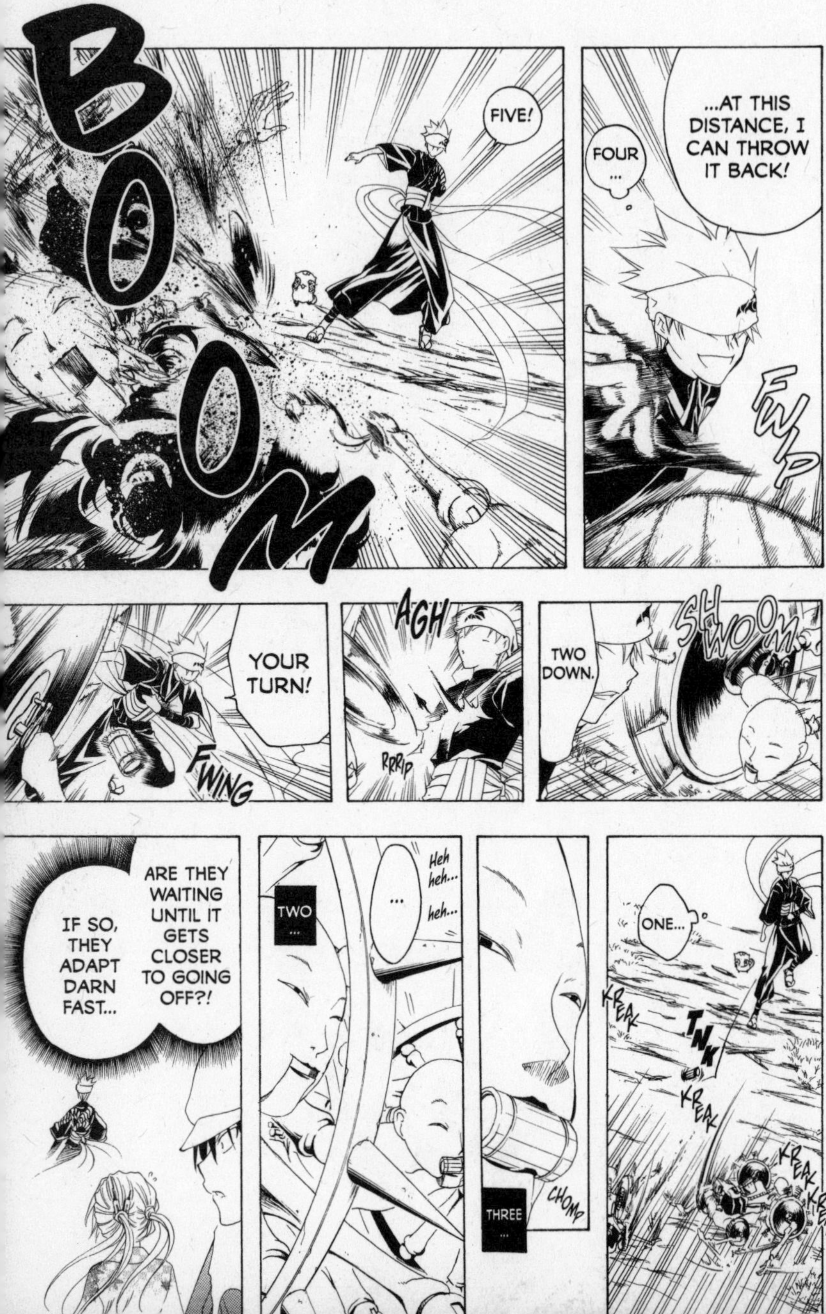
...AT THIS DISTANCE, I CAN THROW IT BACK!
FOUR ...
FWIP
FIVE!
BOOM
SHWOOM
TWO DOWN.
AGH
RRRIP
YOUR TURN!
FWING
ONE...
KREAK
TNK
KREAK
KREAK
KREAK
THREE ...
CHOMP
Heh heh... heh...
...
TWO ...
ARE THEY WAITING UNTIL IT GETS CLOSER TO GOING OFF?!
IF SO, THEY ADAPT DARN FAST...

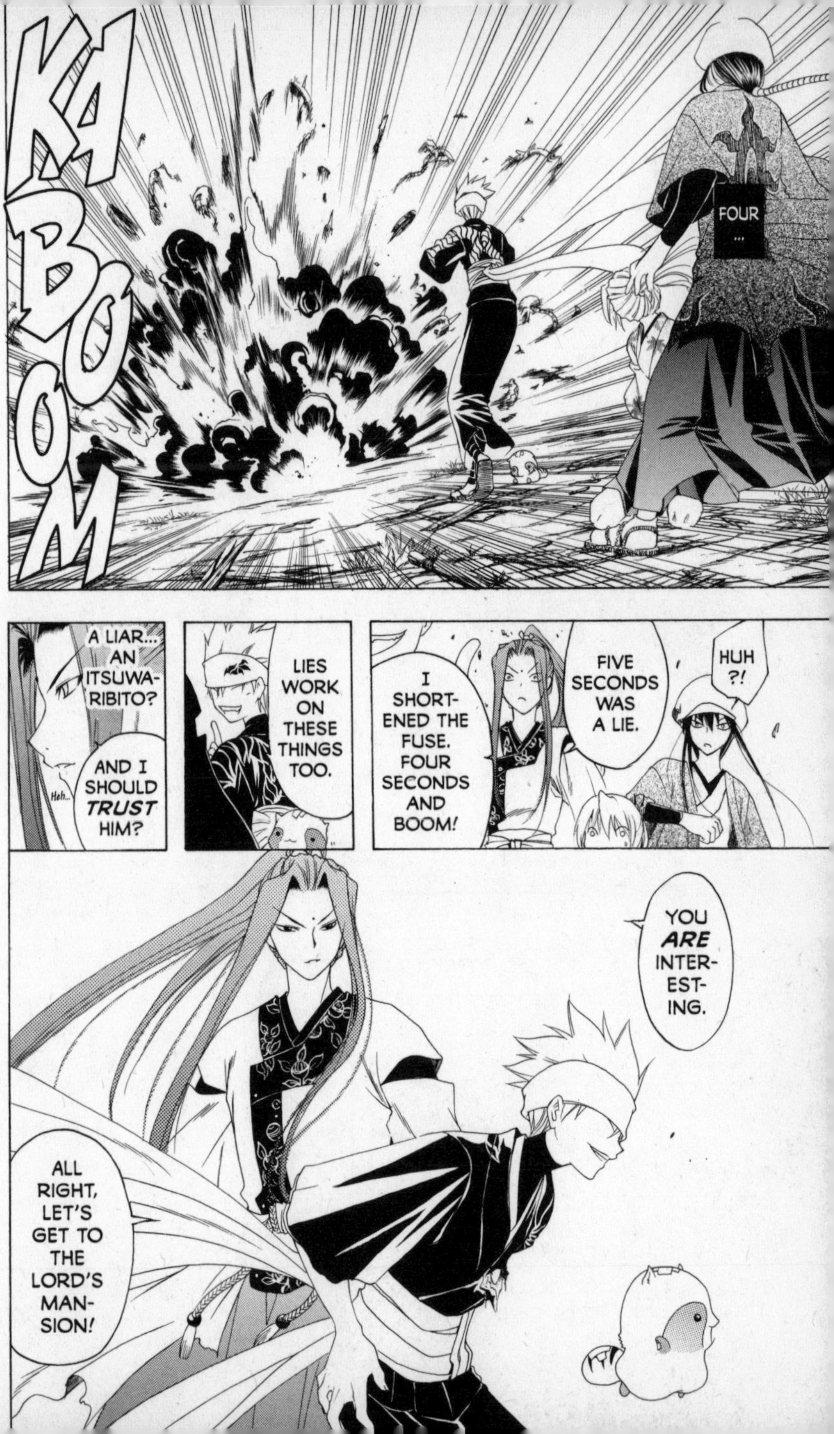
FOUR ...
KABOOM
HUH ?!
FIVE SECONDS WAS A LIE.
I SHORTENED THE FUSE. FOUR SECONDS AND BOOM!
LIES WORK ON THESE THINGS TOO.
A LIAR... AN ITSUWARIBITO?
Heh...
AND I SHOULD *TRUST* HIM?
YOU *ARE* INTERESTING.
ALL RIGHT, LET'S GET TO THE LORD'S MANSION!

Chapter 46 The Cursed Doll

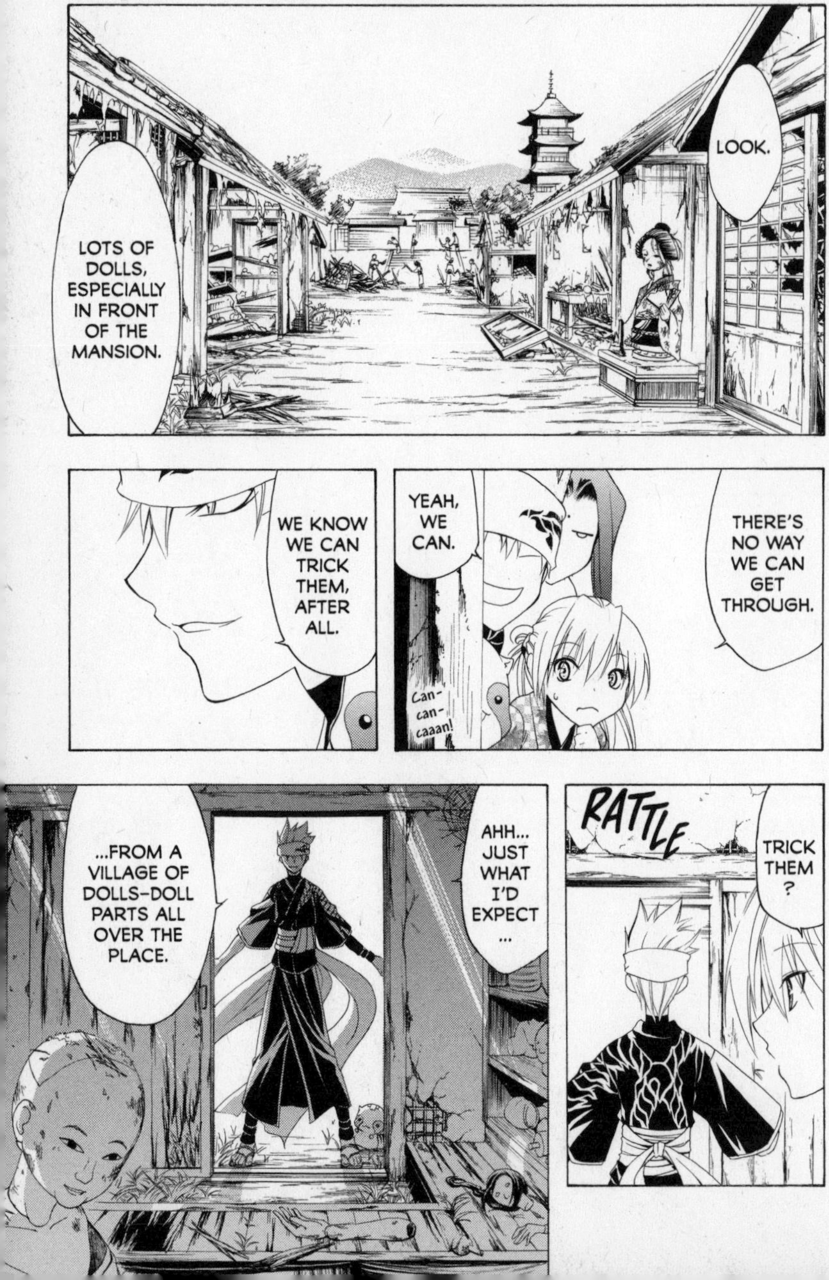
LOOK.
LOTS OF DOLLS, ESPECIALLY IN FRONT OF THE MANSION.
THERE'S NO WAY WE CAN GET THROUGH.
YEAH, WE CAN.
Can-can-caaan!
WE KNOW WE CAN TRICK THEM, AFTER ALL.
RATTLE
TRICK THEM?
AHH... JUST WHAT I'D EXPECT...
...FROM A VILLAGE OF DOLLS–DOLL PARTS ALL OVER THE PLACE.

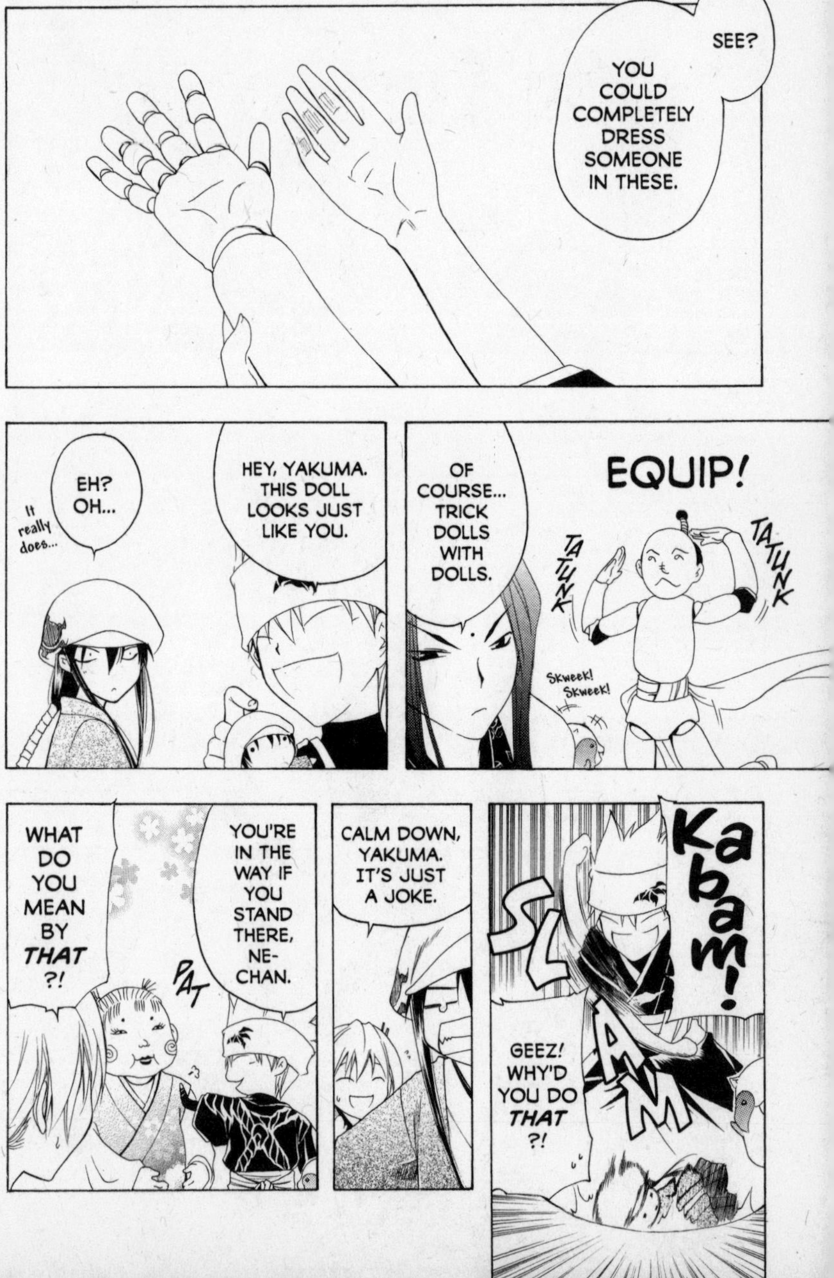
SEE?
YOU COULD COMPLETELY DRESS SOMEONE IN THESE.
EQUIP!
TATUNK
OF COURSE... TRICK DOLLS WITH DOLLS.
TATUNK
Skweek! Skweek!
HEY, YAKUMA. THIS DOLL LOOKS JUST LIKE YOU.
EH? OH...
It really does...
Kabam!
SLAM
GEEZ! WHY'D YOU DO *THAT* ?!
CALM DOWN, YAKUMA. IT'S JUST A JOKE.
YOU'RE IN THE WAY IF YOU STAND THERE, NE-CHAN.
PAT
WHAT DO YOU MEAN BY *THAT* ?!

Chapter 46
The Cursed Doll

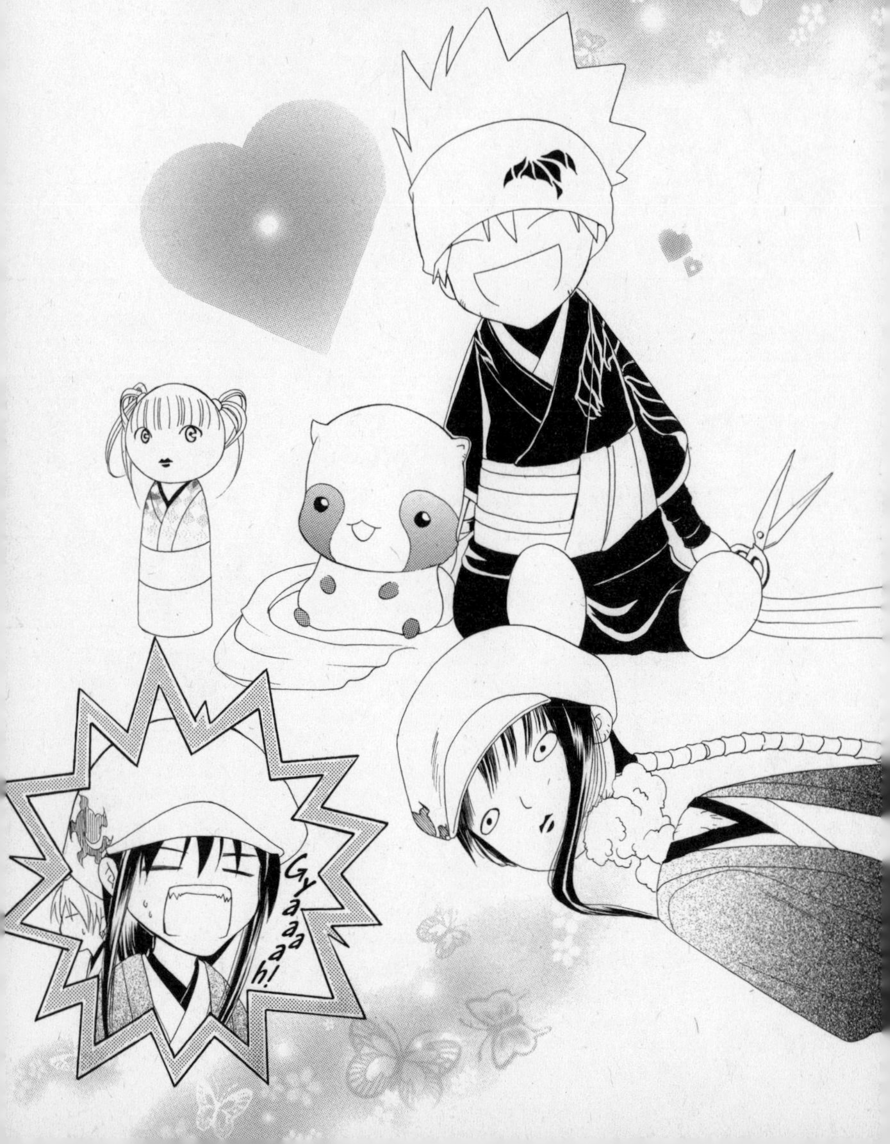
Gyaaaaah!

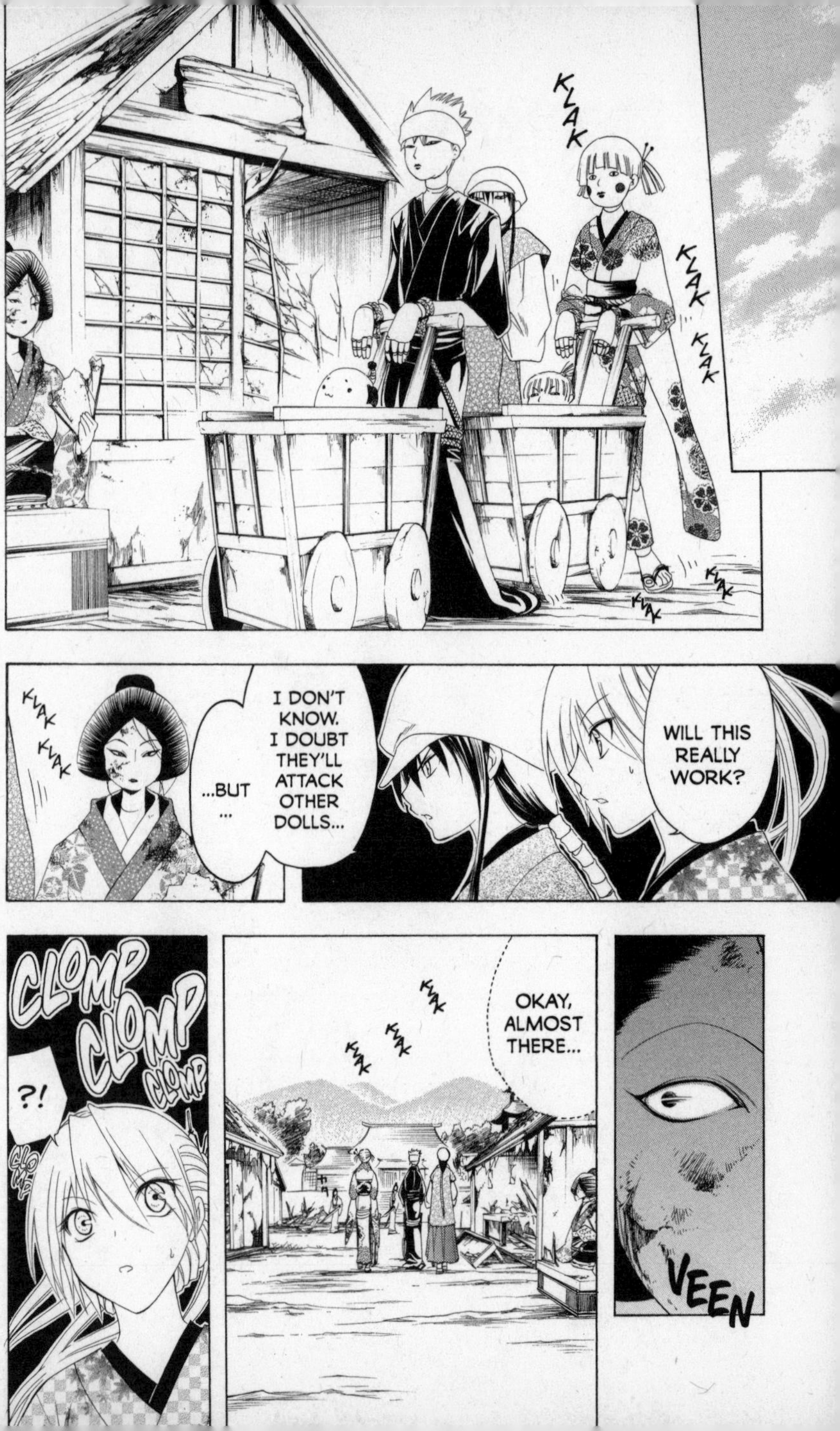
KLAK
KLAK
KLAK
KVAK
KVAK
WILL THIS REALLY WORK?
I DON'T KNOW. I DOUBT THEY'LL ATTACK OTHER DOLLS...
...BUT ...
KVAK
KVAK
VEEN
OKAY, ALMOST THERE...
KVAK
KVAK
KVAK
CLOMP
CLOMP
CLOMP
CLOMP
?!

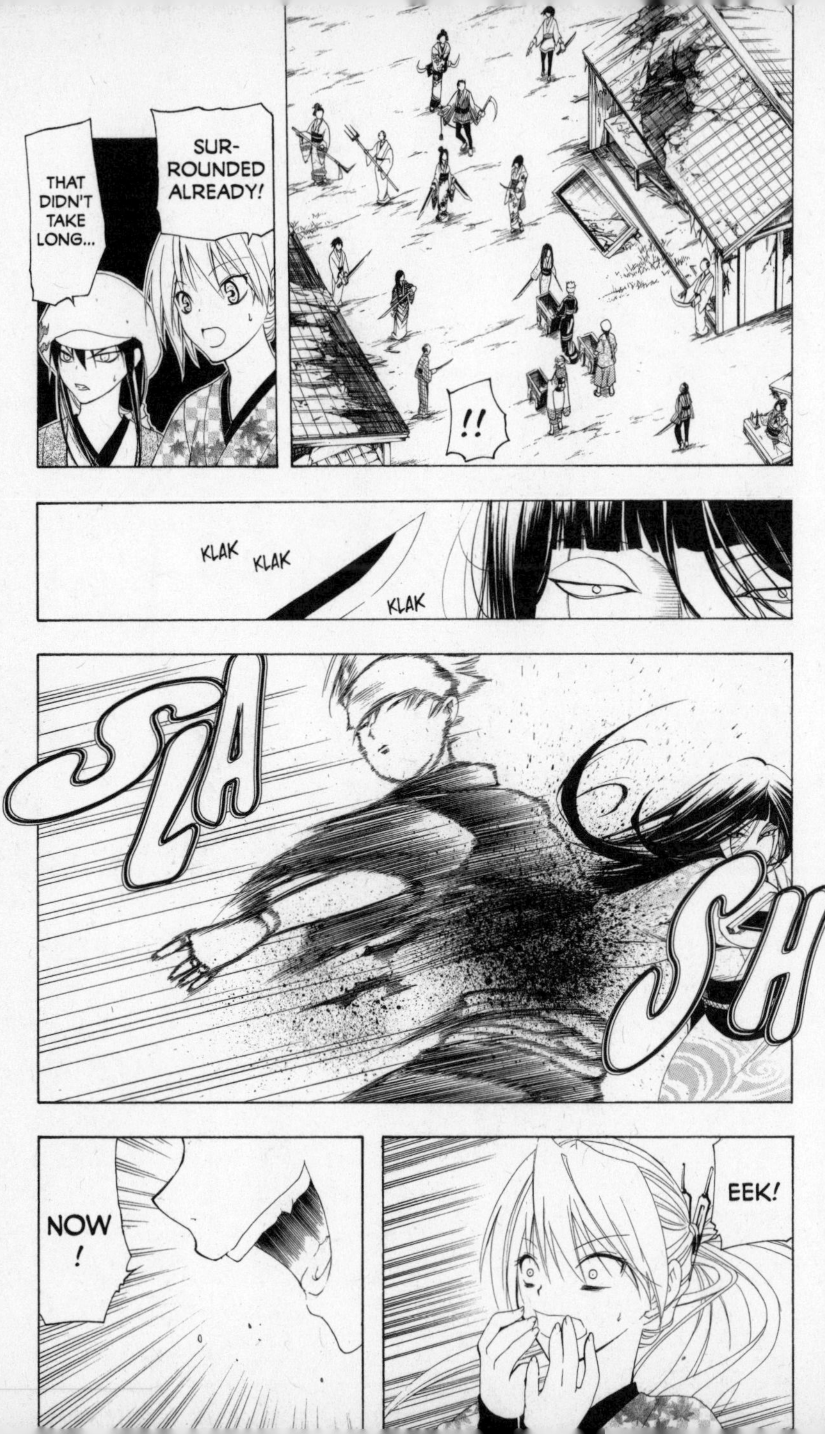
!!
SUR-ROUNDED ALREADY!
THAT DIDN'T TAKE LONG...
KLAK KLAK
KLAK
SLASH
EEK!
NOW!

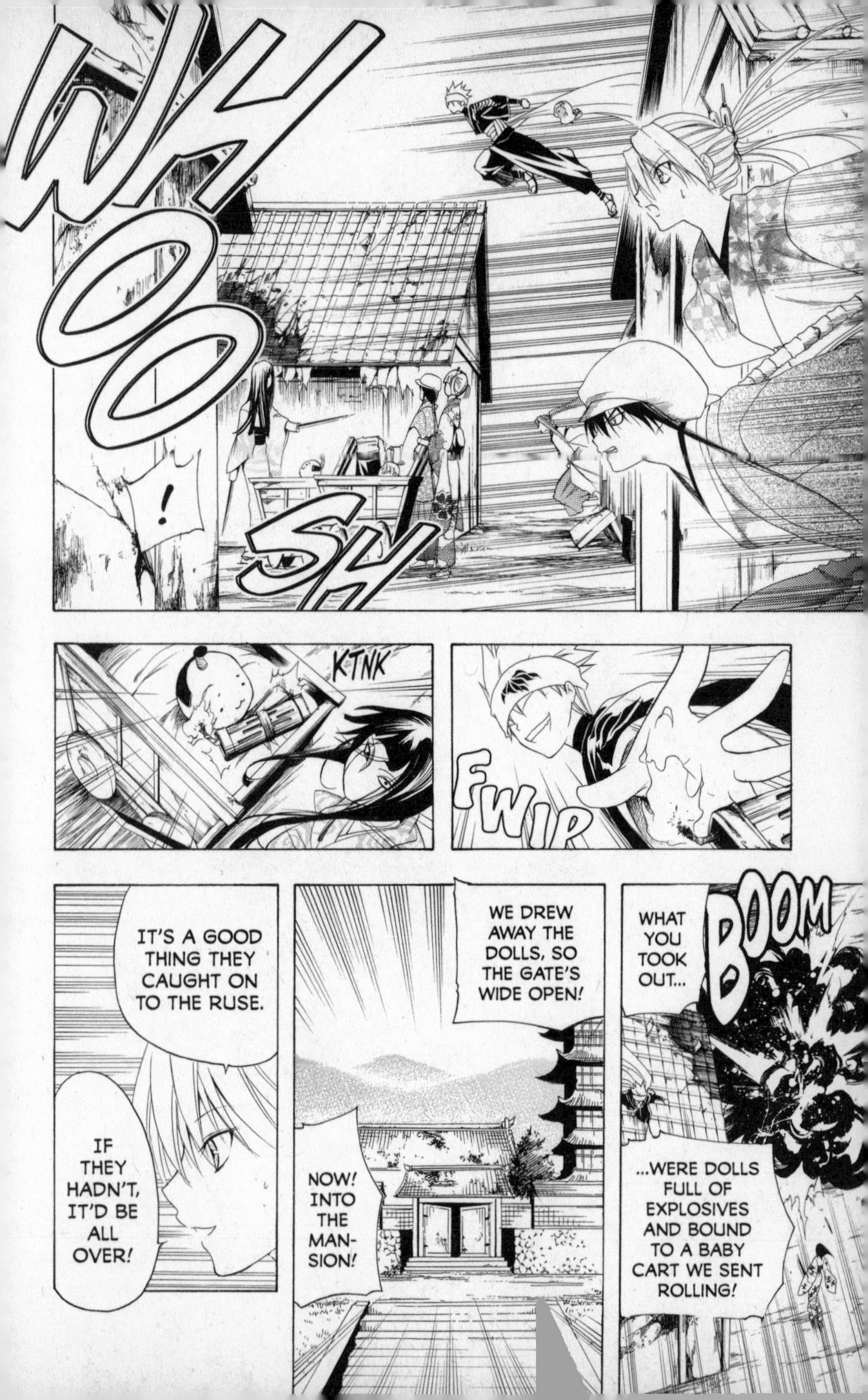
WHOO
!
SH
FWIP
KTNK
WHAT YOU TOOK OUT...
BOOM
...WERE DOLLS FULL OF EXPLOSIVES AND BOUND TO A BABY CART WE SENT ROLLING!
WE DREW AWAY THE DOLLS, SO THE GATE'S WIDE OPEN!
NOW! INTO THE MAN-SION!
IT'S A GOOD THING THEY CAUGHT ON TO THE RUSE.
IF THEY HADN'T, IT'D BE ALL OVER!

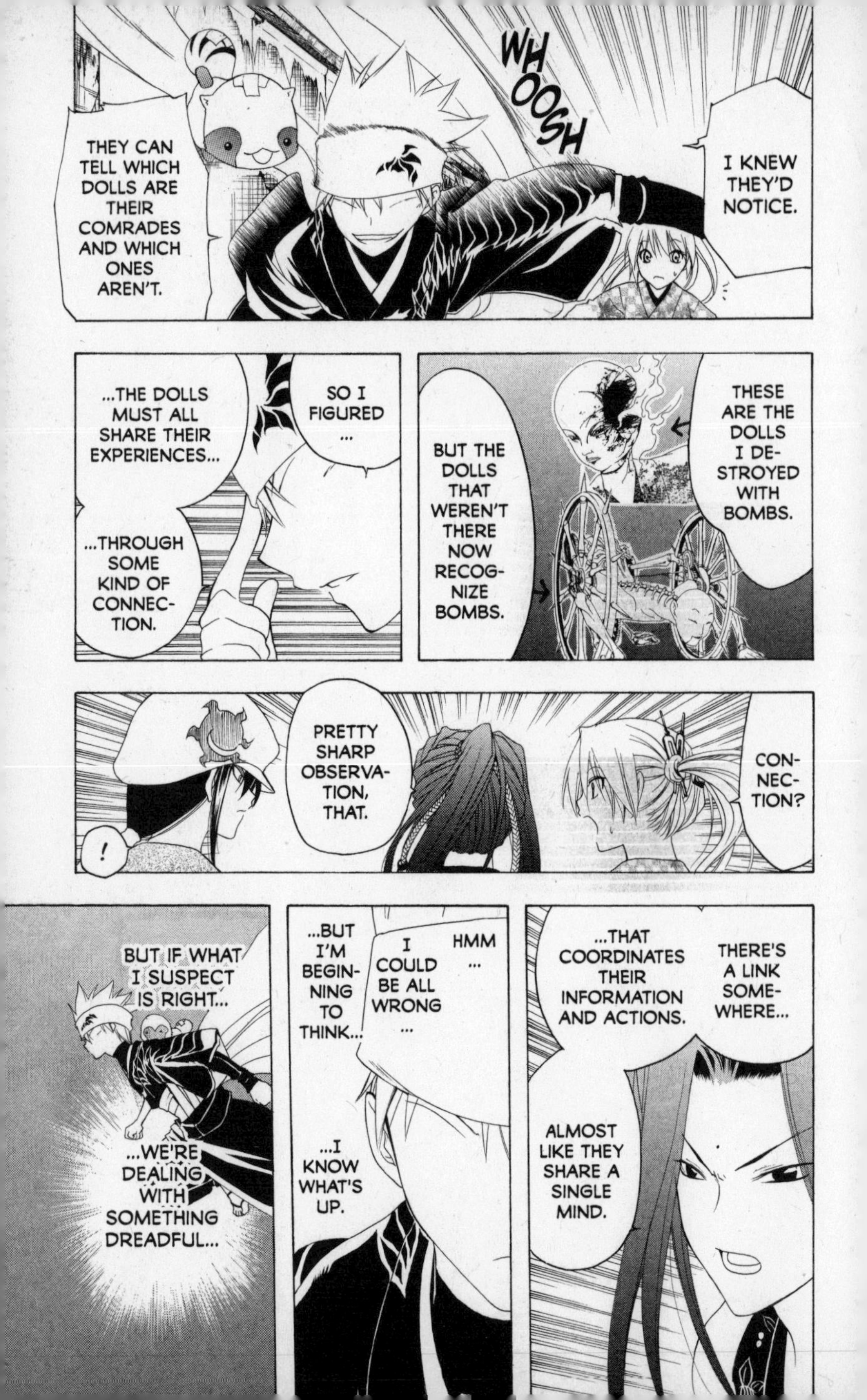
WHOOSH
I KNEW THEY'D NOTICE.
THEY CAN TELL WHICH DOLLS ARE THEIR COMRADES AND WHICH ONES AREN'T.
THESE ARE THE DOLLS I DESTROYED WITH BOMBS.
BUT THE DOLLS THAT WEREN'T THERE NOW RECOGNIZE BOMBS.
SO I FIGURED...
...THE DOLLS MUST ALL SHARE THEIR EXPERIENCES...
...THROUGH SOME KIND OF CONNECTION.
CONNECTION?
PRETTY SHARP OBSERVATION, THAT.
!
THERE'S A LINK SOMEWHERE...
...THAT COORDINATES THEIR INFORMATION AND ACTIONS.
ALMOST LIKE THEY SHARE A SINGLE MIND.
HMM...
I COULD BE ALL WRONG...
...BUT I'M BEGINNING TO THINK...
...I KNOW WHAT'S UP.
BUT IF WHAT I SUSPECT IS RIGHT...
...WE'RE DEALING WITH SOMETHING DREADFUL...

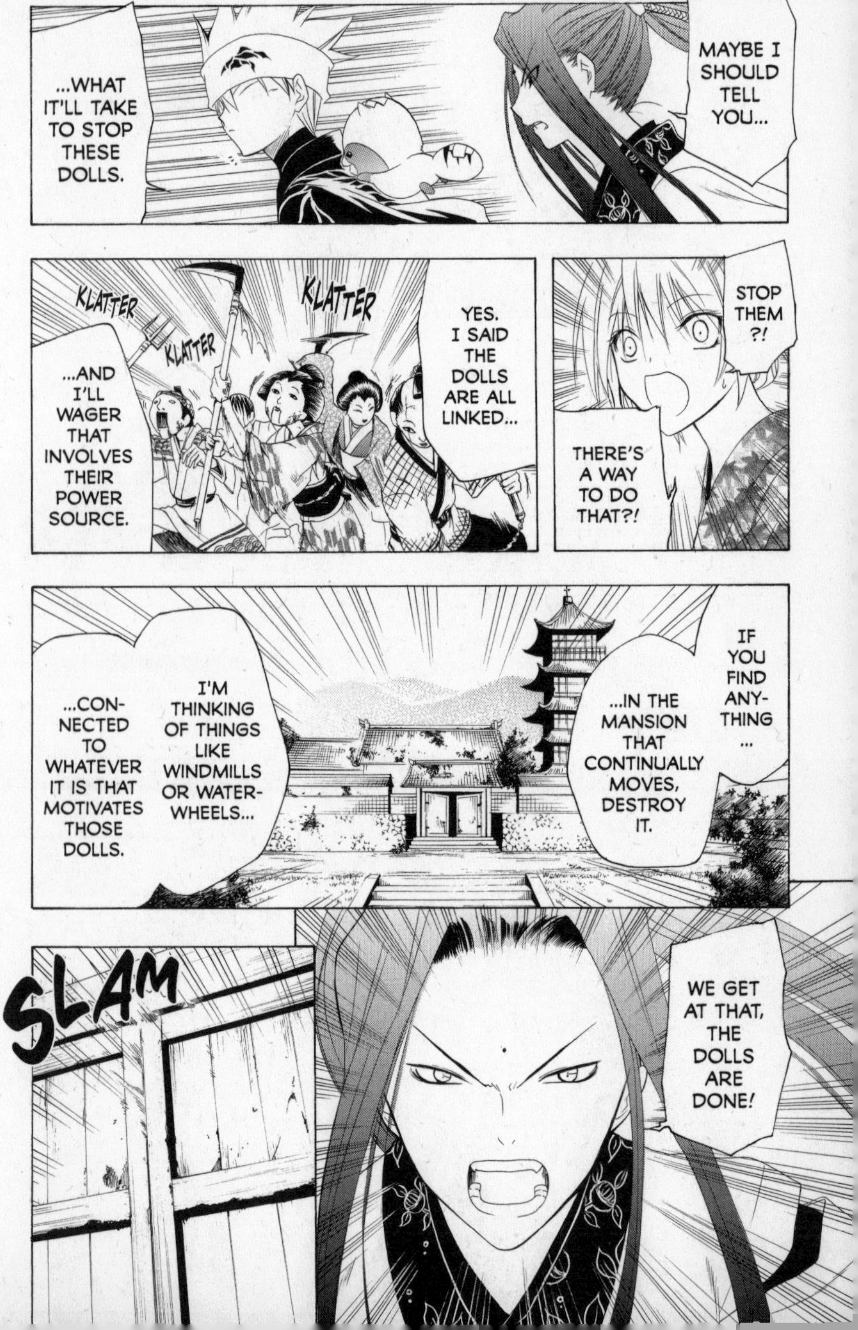
MAYBE I SHOULD TELL YOU...
...WHAT IT'LL TAKE TO STOP THESE DOLLS.
STOP THEM?!
THERE'S A WAY TO DO THAT?!
KLATTER
YES. I SAID THE DOLLS ARE ALL LINKED...
KLATTER
KLATTER
...AND I'LL WAGER THAT INVOLVES THEIR POWER SOURCE.
IF YOU FIND ANY-THING...
...IN THE MANSION THAT CONTINUALLY MOVES, DESTROY IT.
I'M THINKING OF THINGS LIKE WINDMILLS OR WATER-WHEELS...
...CON-NECTED TO WHATEVER IT IS THAT MOTIVATES THOSE DOLLS.
WE GET AT THAT, THE DOLLS ARE DONE!
SLAM

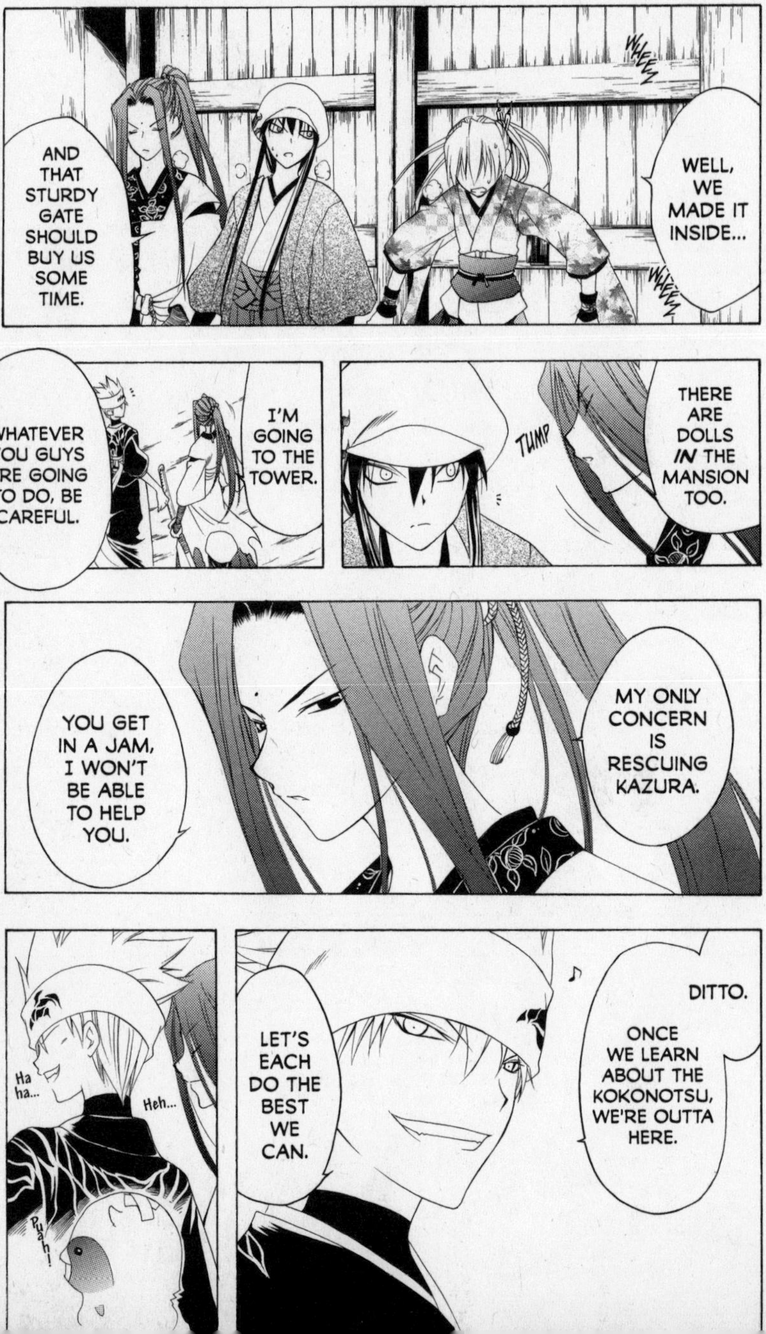
WHEEZ
WELL, WE MADE IT INSIDE...
WHEEZ
AND THAT STURDY GATE SHOULD BUY US SOME TIME.
THERE ARE DOLLS *IN* THE MANSION TOO.
TUMP
I'M GOING TO THE TOWER.
WHATEVER YOU GUYS ARE GOING TO DO, BE CAREFUL.
MY ONLY CONCERN IS RESCUING KAZURA.
YOU GET IN A JAM, I WON'T BE ABLE TO HELP YOU.
DITTO.
ONCE WE LEARN ABOUT THE KOKONOTSU, WE'RE OUTTA HERE.
LET'S EACH DO THE BEST WE CAN.
Heh...
Ha ha...
Puah!

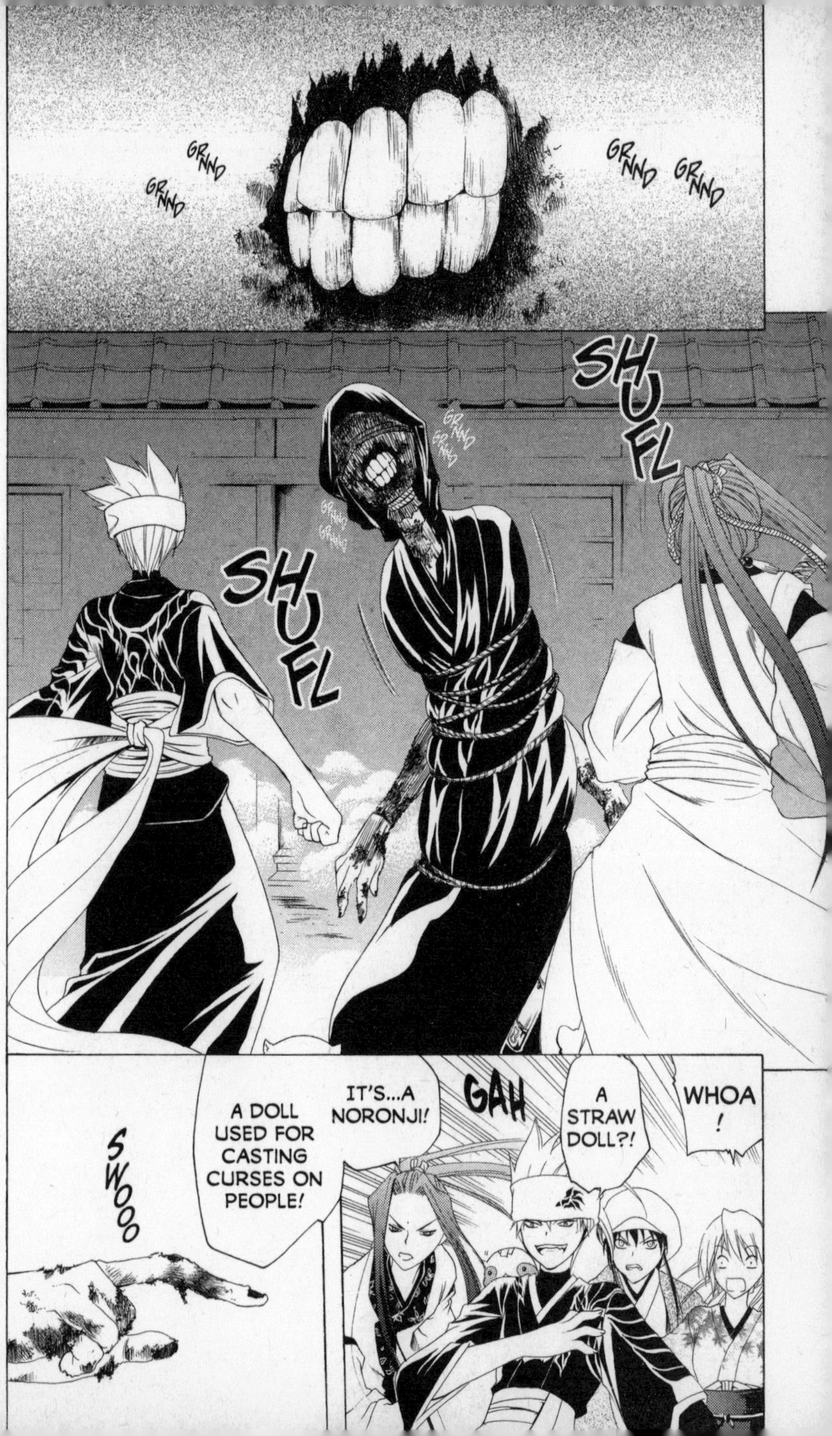
GRNND GRNND
GRNND
GRNND
SHUFL
GRNND GRNND
GRNND GRNND
SHUFL
WHOA!
A STRAW DOLL?!
GAH
IT'S...A NORONJI!
A DOLL USED FOR CASTING CURSES ON PEOPLE!
SWOOO

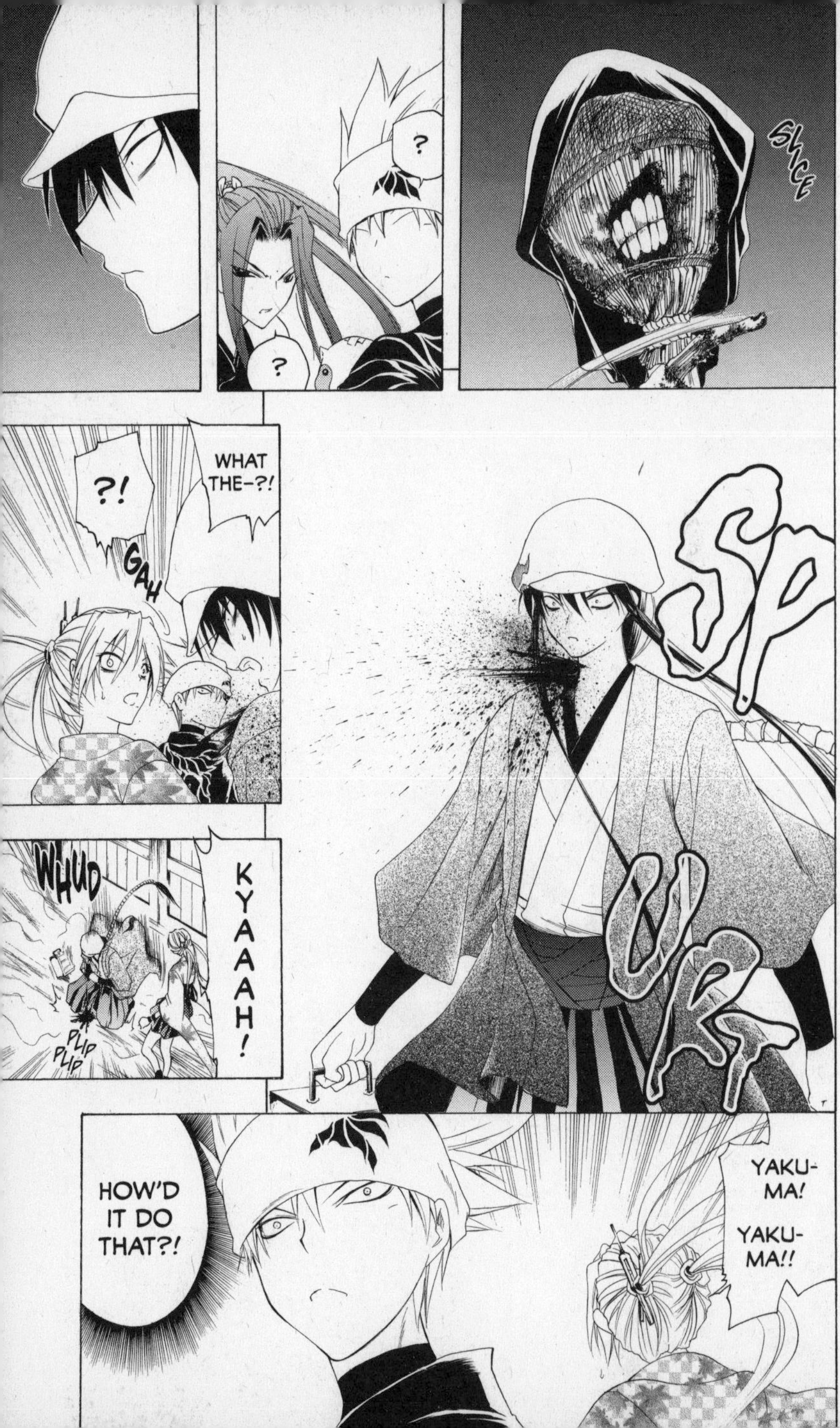
SLICE
?
?
SPURT
WHAT THE-?!
?!
GAH
KYAAAH!
WHUD
PLIP PLIP
YAKU-MA! YAKU-MA!!
HOW'D IT DO THAT?!

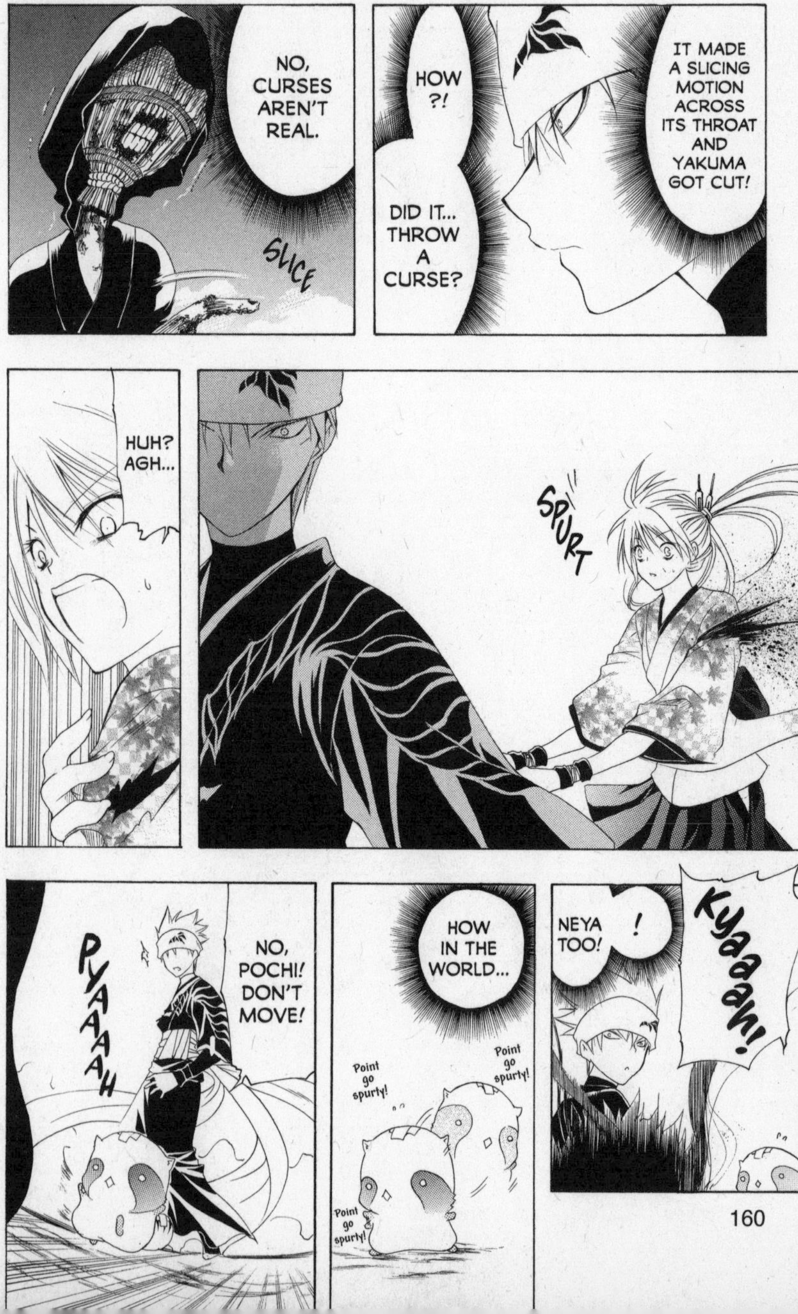

IT MADE A SLICING MOTION ACROSS ITS THROAT AND YAKUMA GOT CUT!
HOW ?!
DID IT... THROW A CURSE?
NO, CURSES AREN'T REAL.
SLICE
SPURT
HUH? AGH...
Kyaaaah!
NEYA TOO!
!
HOW IN THE WORLD...
Point go spurty!
Point go spurty!
Point go spurty!
NO, POCHI! DON'T MOVE!
PYAAAAH

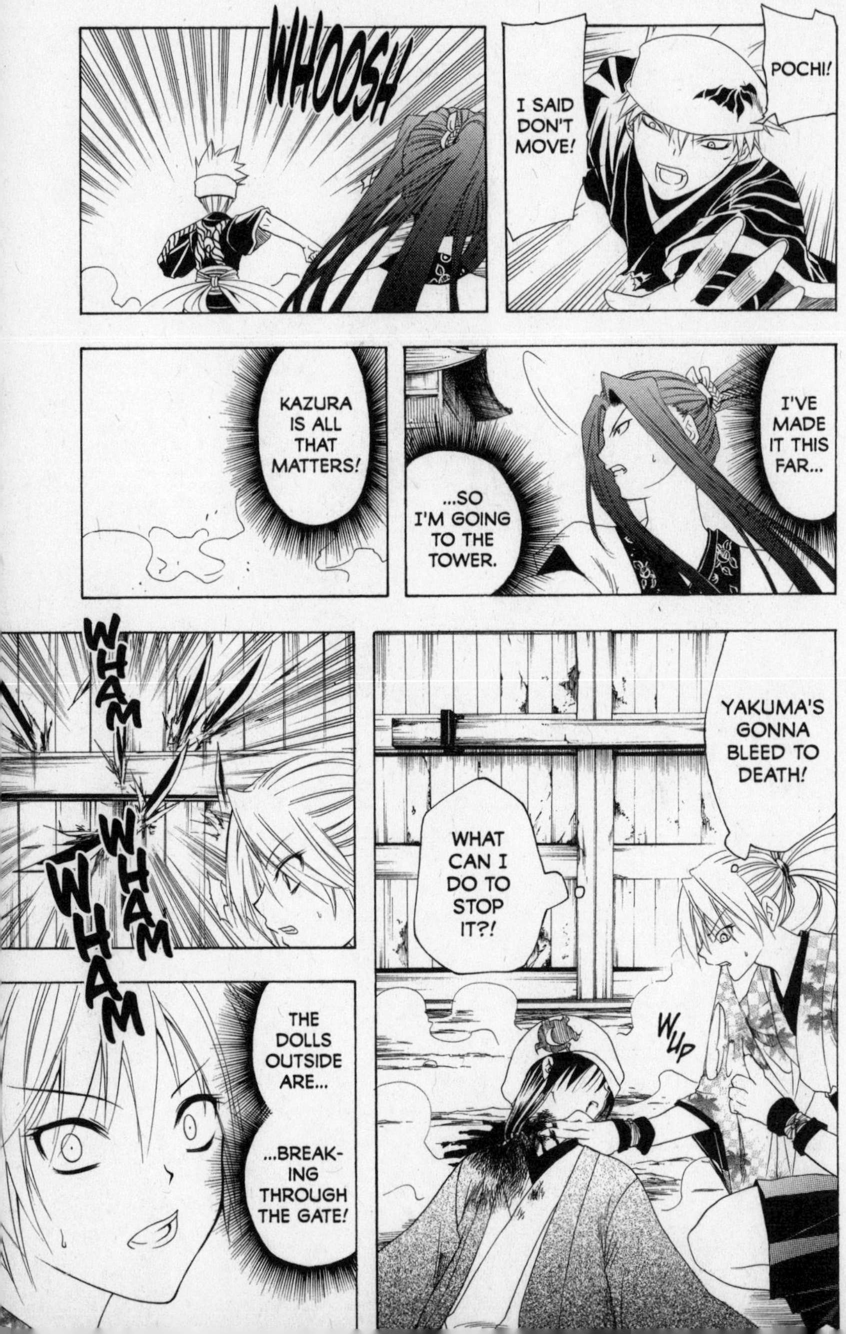
POCHI!
I SAID DON'T MOVE!
WHOOSH
I'VE MADE IT THIS FAR...
...SO I'M GOING TO THE TOWER.
KAZURA IS ALL THAT MATTERS!
YAKUMA'S GONNA BLEED TO DEATH!
WHAT CAN I DO TO STOP IT?!
WUP
WHAM
WHAM
WHAM
WHAM
THE DOLLS OUTSIDE ARE...
...BREAK-ING THROUGH THE GATE!

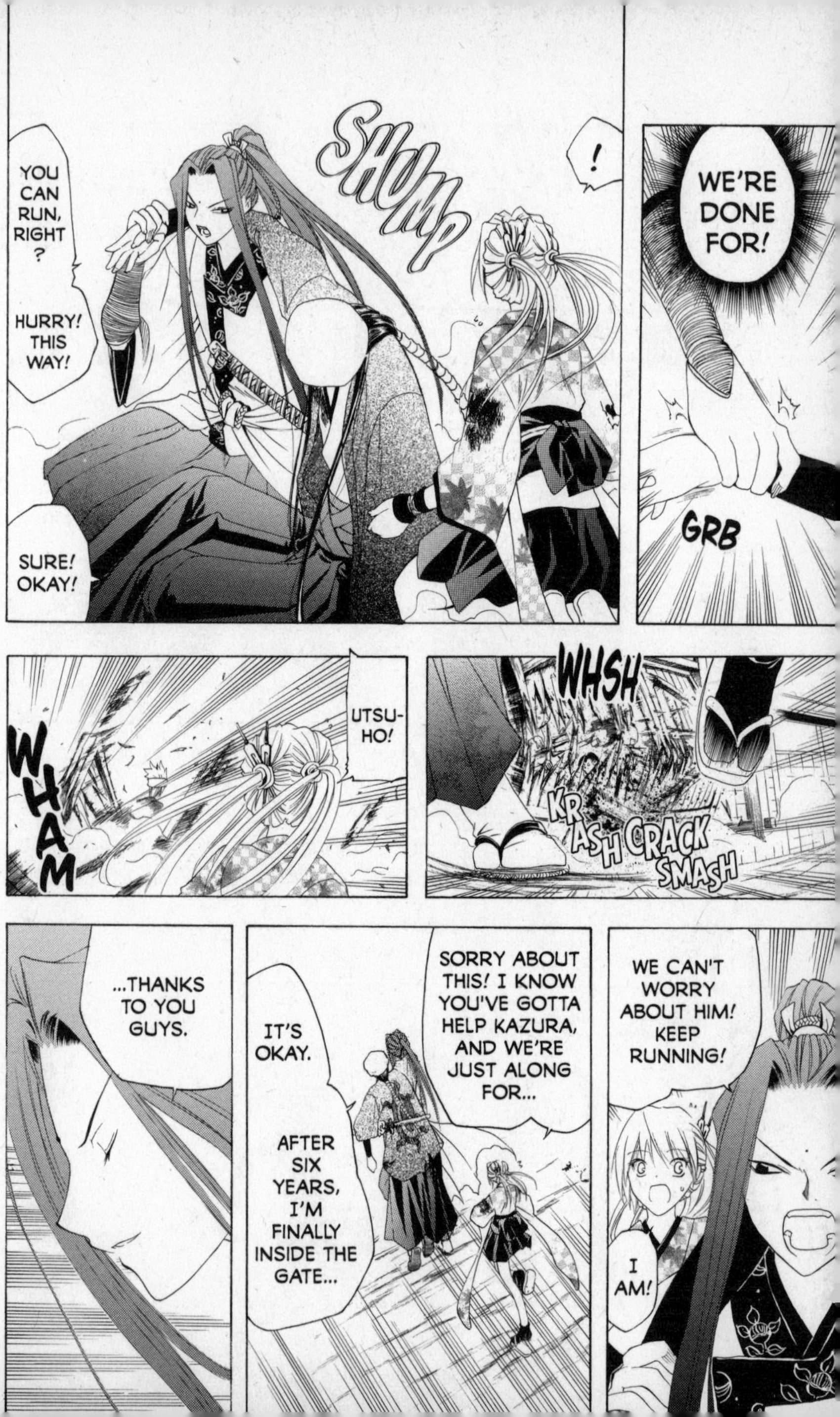
WE'RE DONE FOR!
GRB
!
SHUMP
YOU CAN RUN, RIGHT?
HURRY! THIS WAY!
SURE! OKAY!
WHSH
KRASH CRACK SMASH
UTSU-HO!
WHAM
WE CAN'T WORRY ABOUT HIM! KEEP RUNNING!
I AM!
SORRY ABOUT THIS! I KNOW YOU'VE GOTTA HELP KAZURA, AND WE'RE JUST ALONG FOR...
IT'S OKAY.
AFTER SIX YEARS, I'M FINALLY INSIDE THE GATE...
...THANKS TO YOU GUYS.

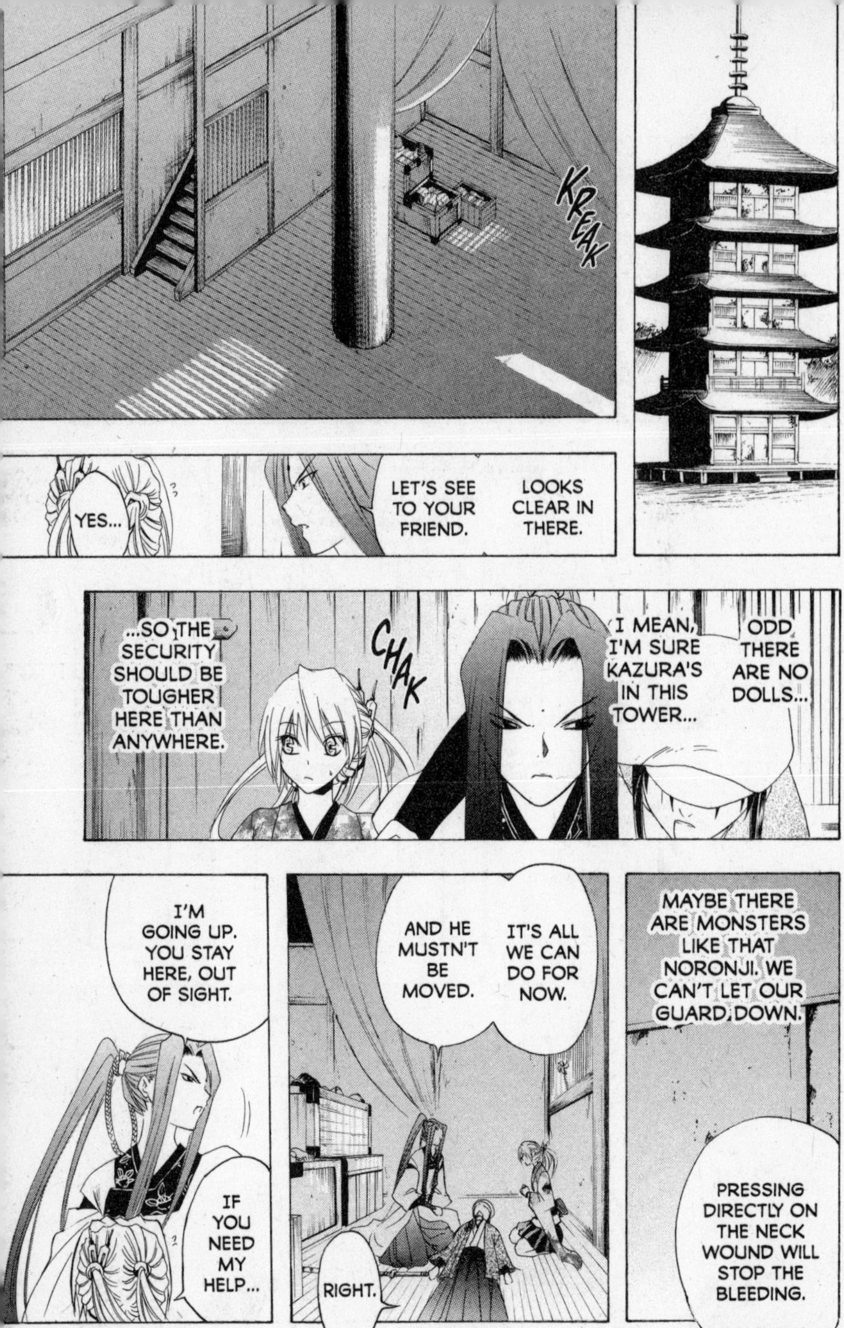
KREAK
LOOKS CLEAR IN THERE.
LET'S SEE TO YOUR FRIEND.
YES...
ODD THERE ARE NO DOLLS...
I MEAN, I'M SURE KAZURA'S IN THIS TOWER...
CHAK
...SO THE SECURITY SHOULD BE TOUGHER HERE THAN ANYWHERE.
MAYBE THERE ARE MONSTERS LIKE THAT NORONJI. WE CAN'T LET OUR GUARD DOWN.
PRESSING DIRECTLY ON THE NECK WOUND WILL STOP THE BLEEDING.
IT'S ALL WE CAN DO FOR NOW.
AND HE MUSTN'T BE MOVED.
RIGHT.
I'M GOING UP. YOU STAY HERE, OUT OF SIGHT.
IF YOU NEED MY HELP...

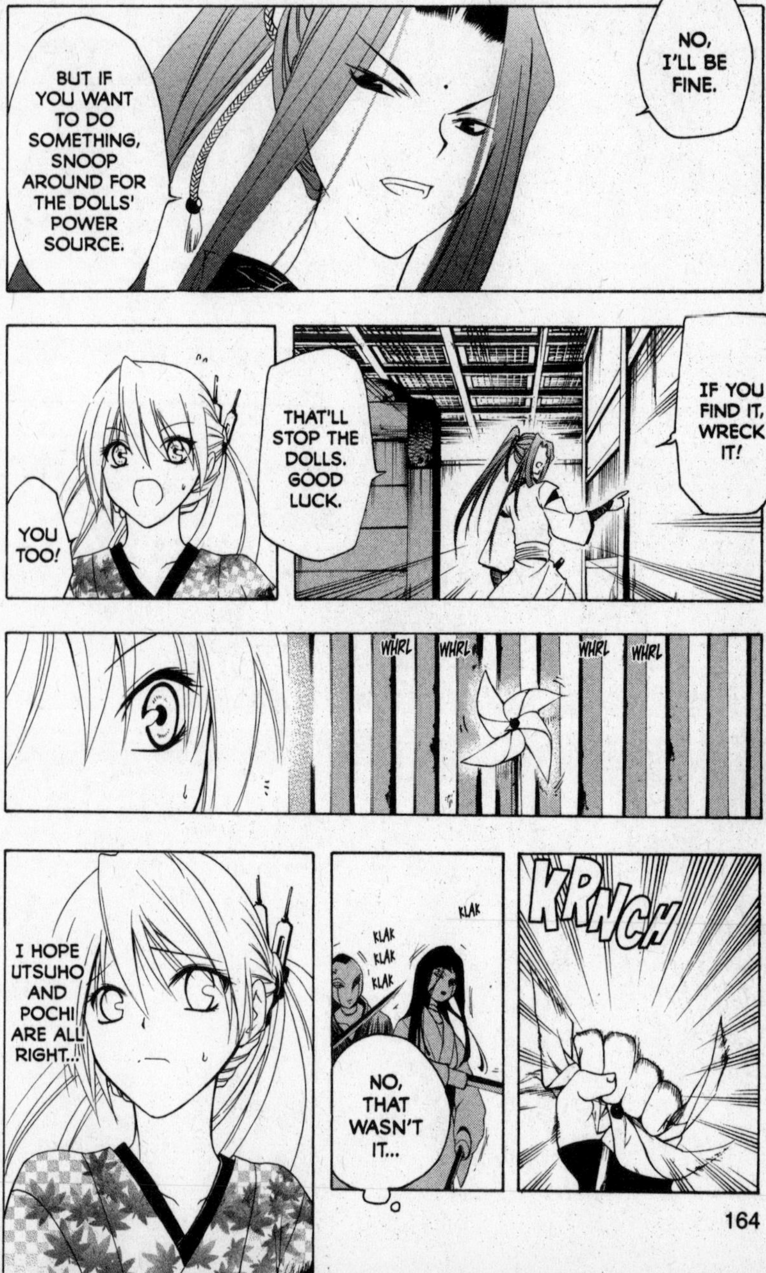
NO, I'LL BE FINE.
BUT IF YOU WANT TO DO SOMETHING, SNOOP AROUND FOR THE DOLLS' POWER SOURCE.
IF YOU FIND IT, WRECK IT!
THAT'LL STOP THE DOLLS. GOOD LUCK.
YOU TOO!
WHRL
WHRL
WHRL
WHRL
KRNCH
KLAK
KLAK
KLAK
KLAK
NO, THAT WASN'T IT...
I HOPE UTSUHO AND POCHI ARE ALL RIGHT...

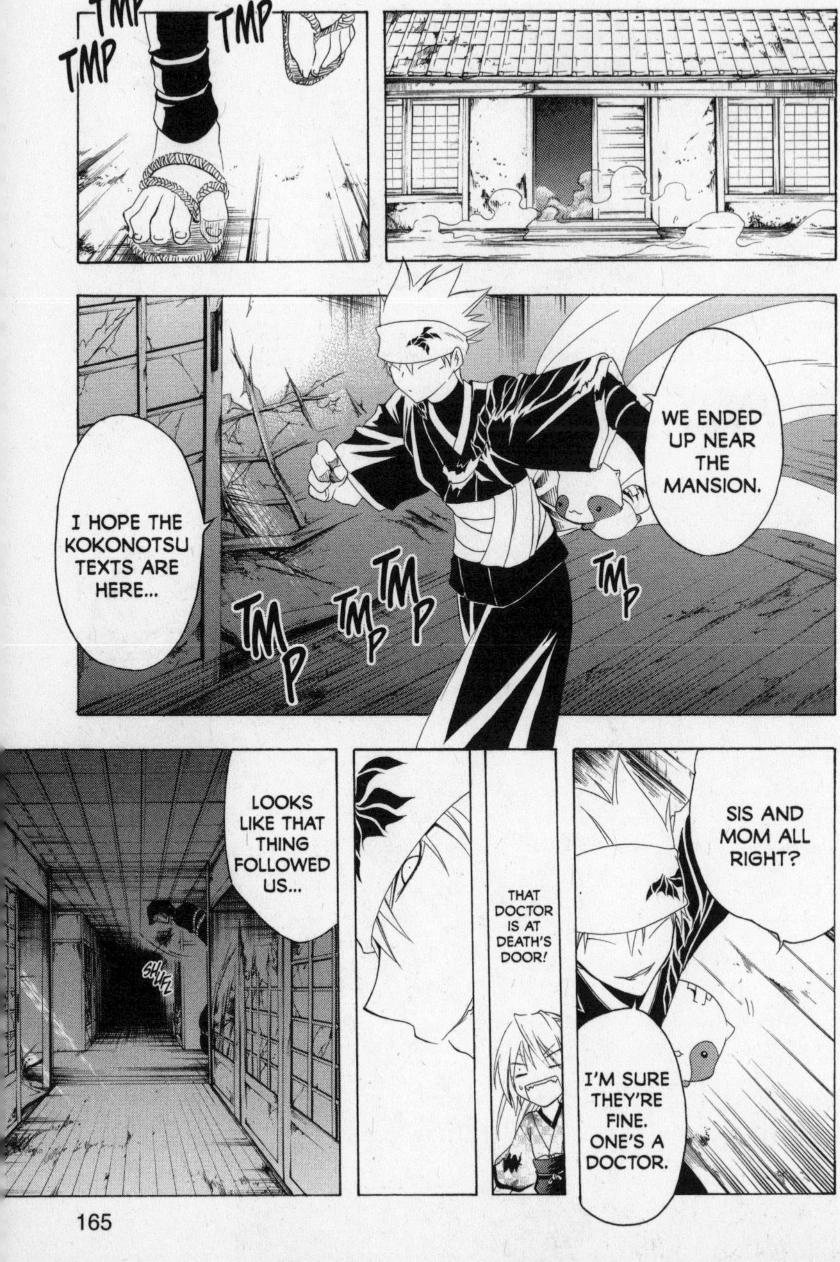
TMP
TMP
TMP
WE ENDED UP NEAR THE MANSION.
TMP
TMP
TMP
TMP
I HOPE THE KOKONOTSU TEXTS ARE HERE...
SIS AND MOM ALL RIGHT?
I'M SURE THEY'RE FINE. ONE'S A DOCTOR.
THAT DOCTOR IS AT DEATH'S DOOR!
LOOKS LIKE THAT THING FOLLOWED US...

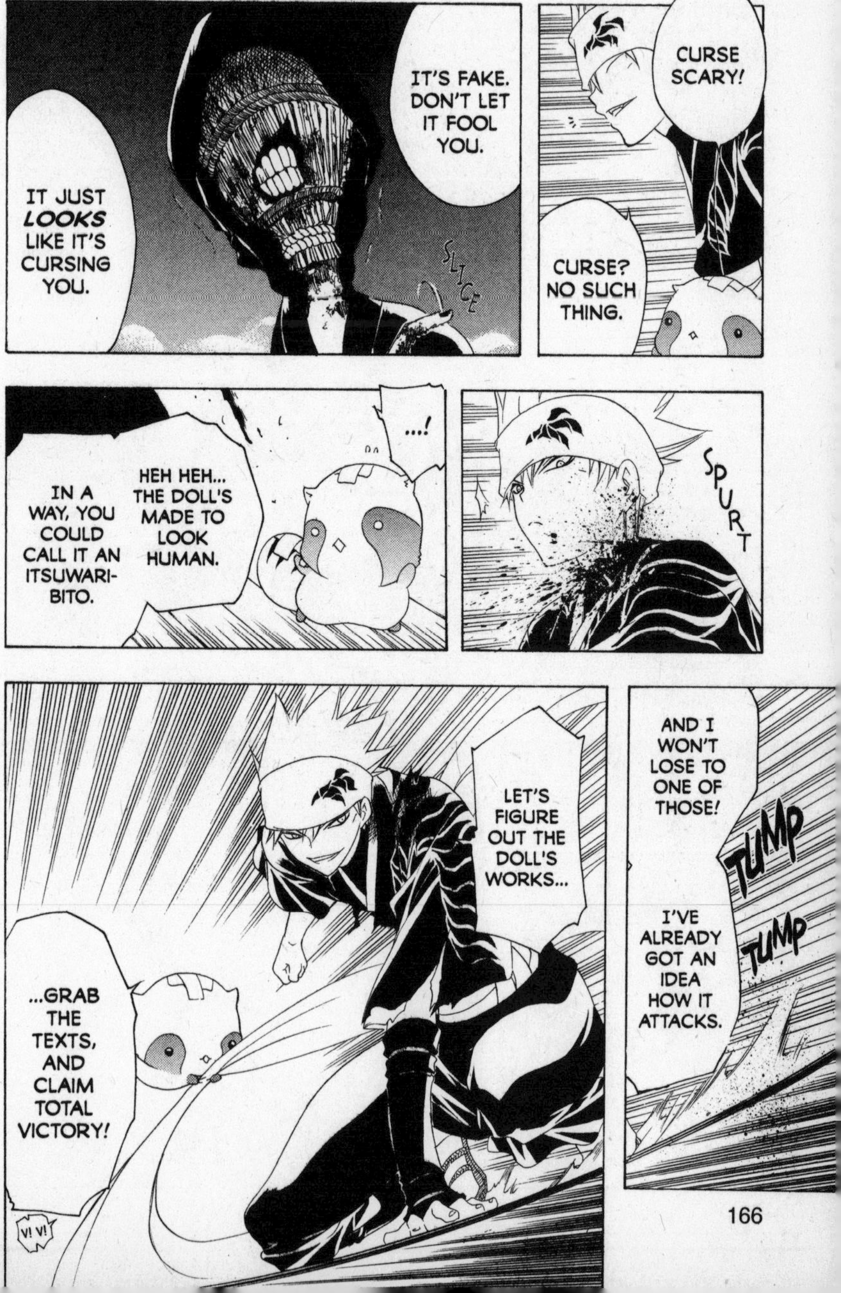
CURSE SCARY!
CURSE? NO SUCH THING.
IT'S FAKE. DON'T LET IT FOOL YOU.
SLICE
IT JUST ***LOOKS*** LIKE IT'S CURSING YOU.
SPURT
...!
HEH HEH... THE DOLL'S MADE TO LOOK HUMAN.
IN A WAY, YOU COULD CALL IT AN ITSUWARI-BITO.
AND I WON'T LOSE TO ONE OF THOSE!
TUMP
TUMP
I'VE ALREADY GOT AN IDEA HOW IT ATTACKS.
LET'S FIGURE OUT THE DOLL'S WORKS...
...GRAB THE TEXTS, AND CLAIM TOTAL VICTORY!
V! V!

Chapter 47 Sleeping Princess

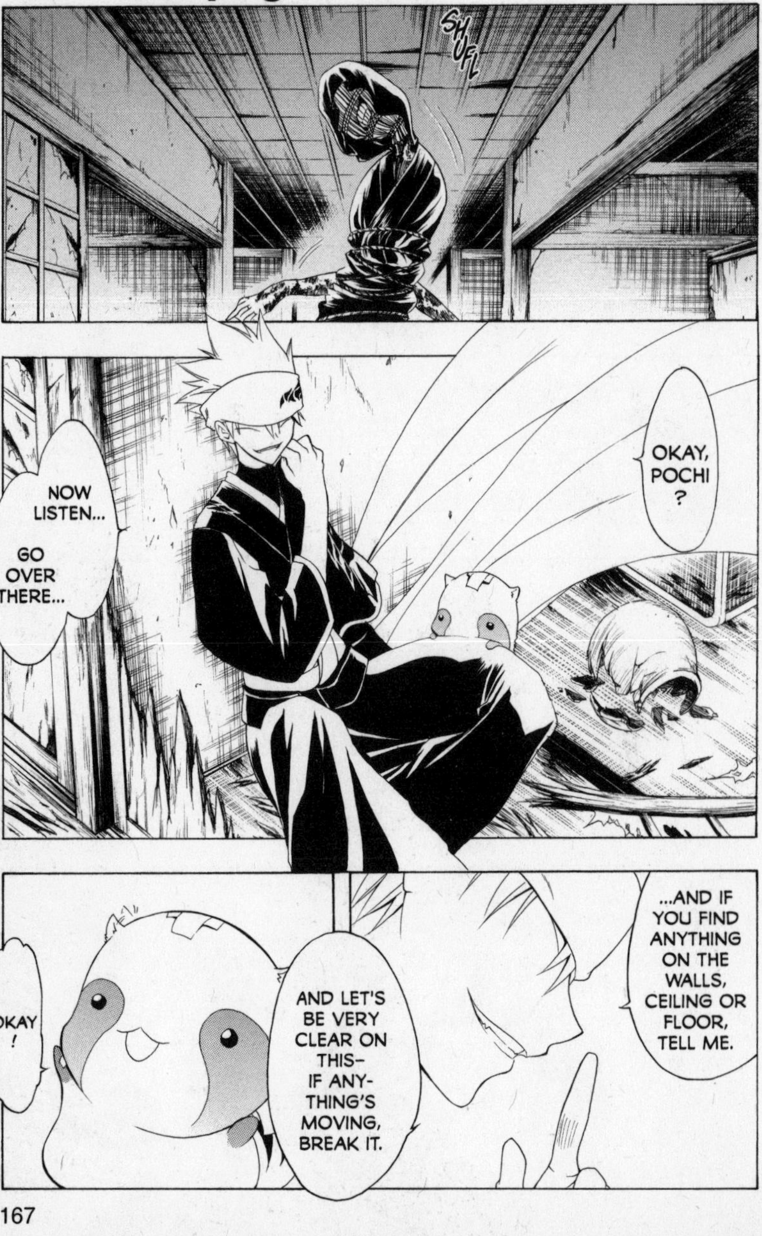
SHUFL
OKAY, POCHI?
NOW LISTEN... GO OVER THERE...
...AND IF YOU FIND ANYTHING ON THE WALLS, CEILING OR FLOOR, TELL ME.
AND LET'S BE VERY CLEAR ON THIS– IF ANY-THING'S MOVING, BREAK IT.
OKAY!

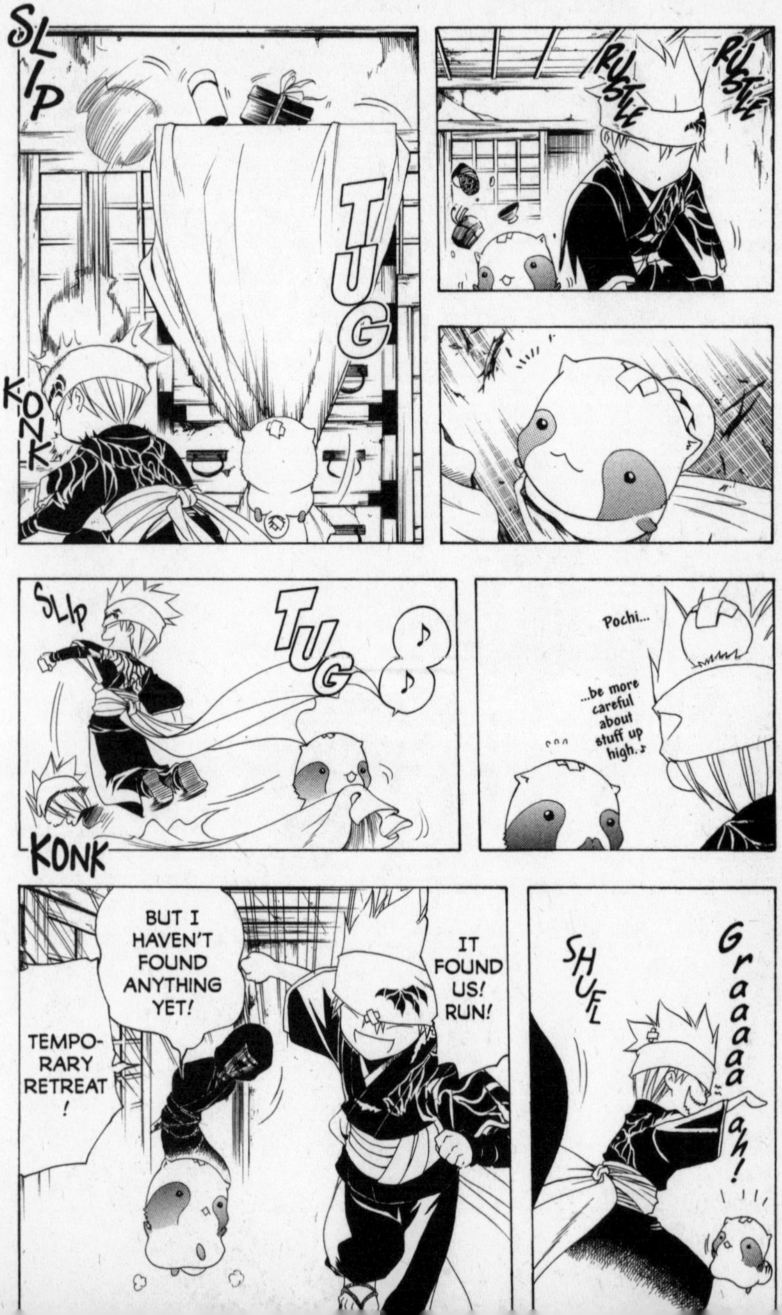
RUSTLE
RUSTLE
SLIP
TUG
KONK
Pochi...
...be more careful about stuff up high. ♪
SLIP
TUG
♪ ♪
KONK
Graaaaaah!
SHUFL
IT FOUND US! RUN!
BUT I HAVEN'T FOUND ANYTHING YET!
TEMPORARY RETREAT!

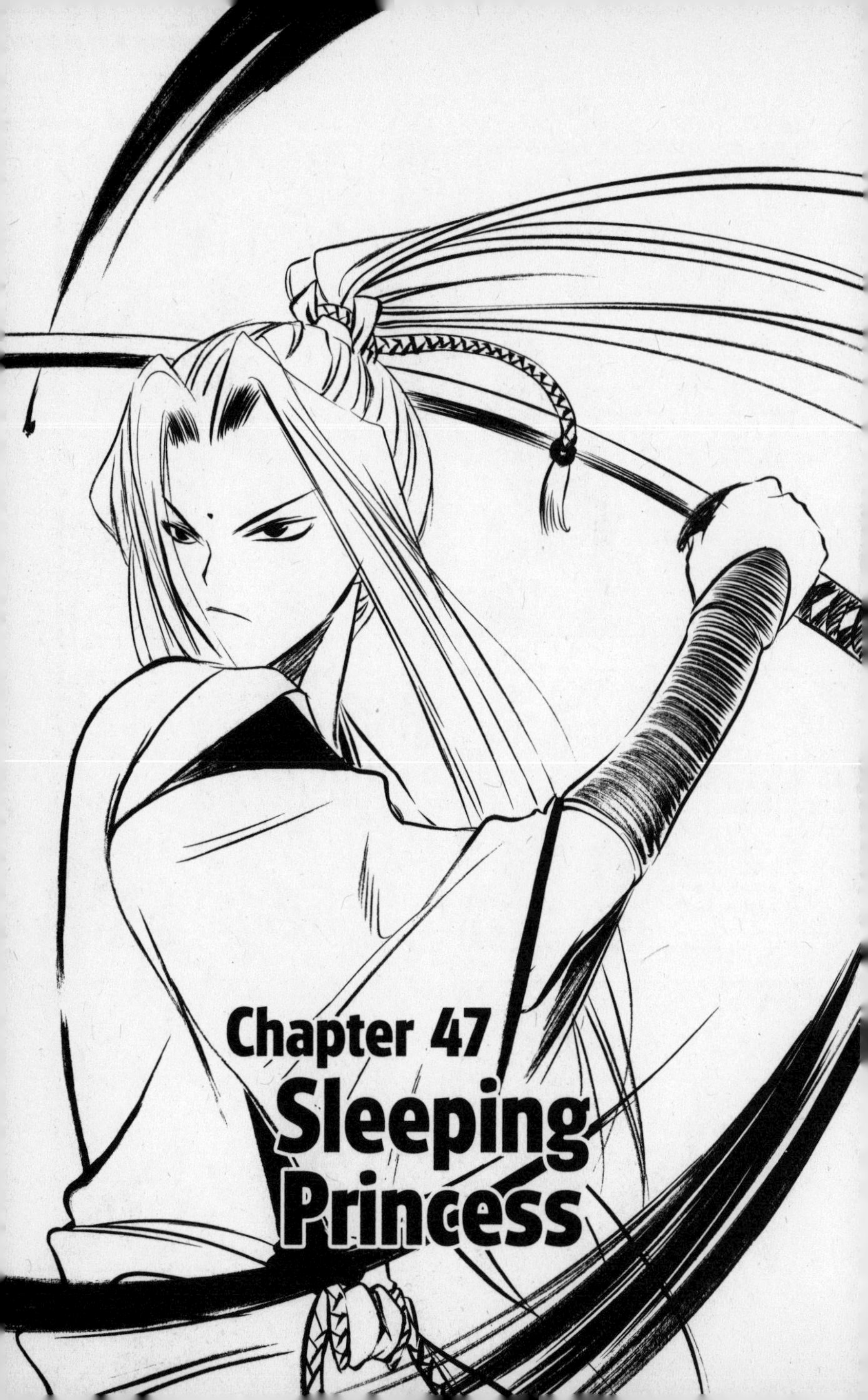
Chapter 47
Sleeping Princess

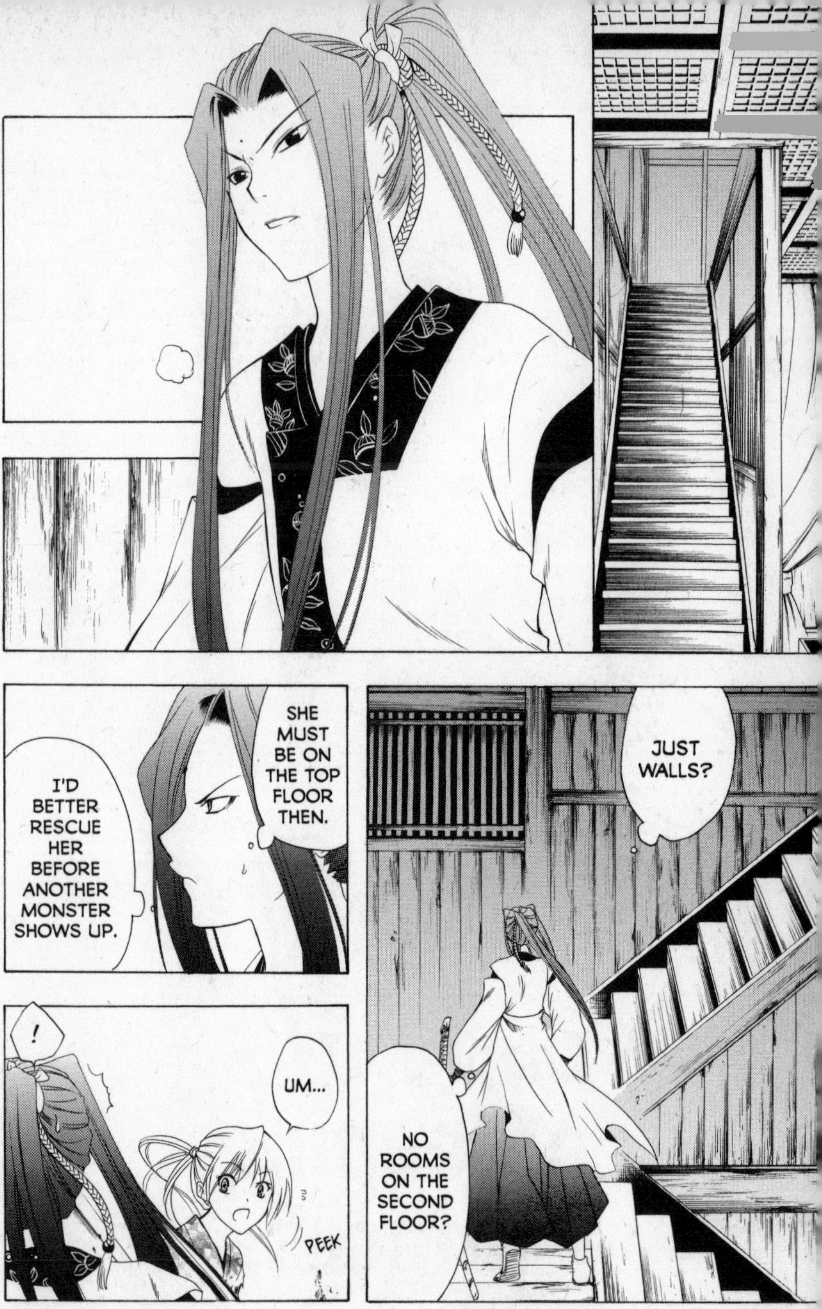
JUST WALLS?
NO ROOMS ON THE SECOND FLOOR?
SHE MUST BE ON THE TOP FLOOR THEN.
I'D BETTER RESCUE HER BEFORE ANOTHER MONSTER SHOWS UP.
!
UM...
PEEK

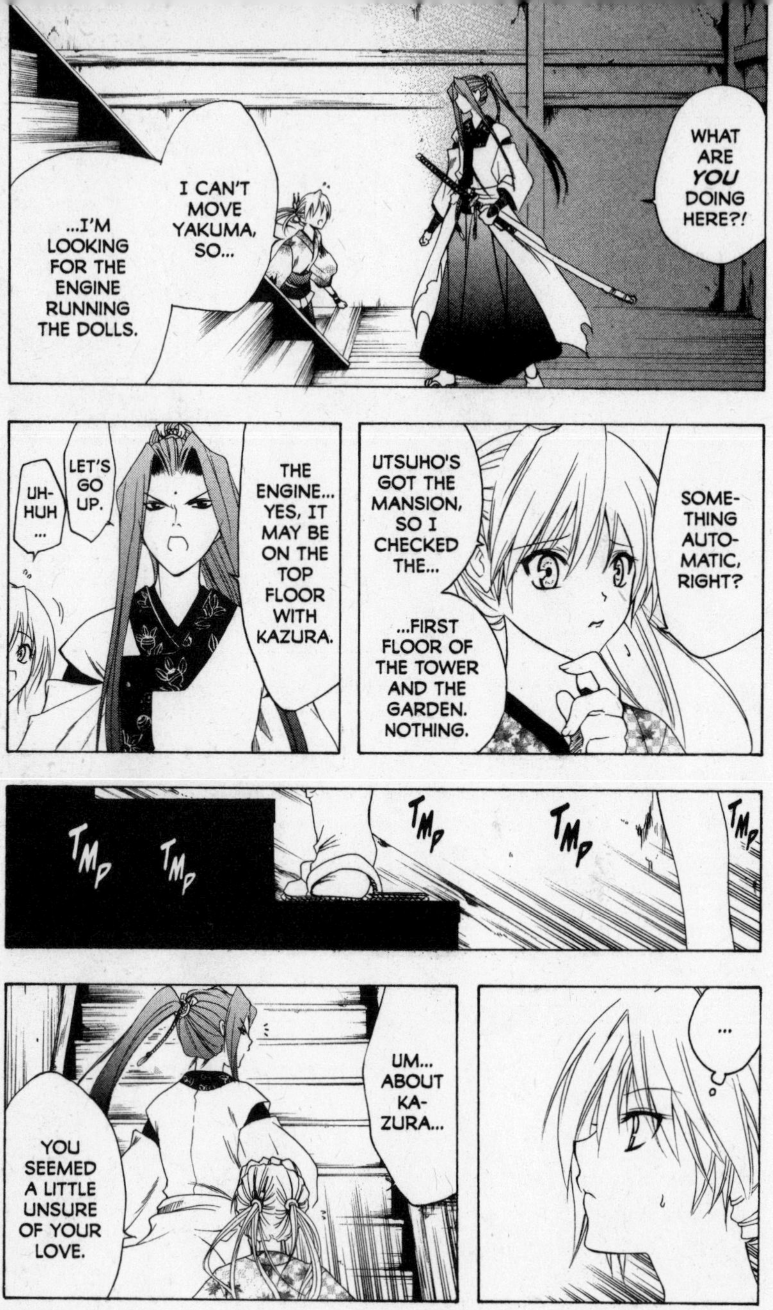
WHAT ARE ***YOU*** DOING HERE?!
I CAN'T MOVE YAKUMA, SO...
...I'M LOOKING FOR THE ENGINE RUNNING THE DOLLS.
SOME-THING AUTO-MATIC, RIGHT?
UTSUHO'S GOT THE MANSION, SO I CHECKED THE...
...FIRST FLOOR OF THE TOWER AND THE GARDEN. NOTHING.
THE ENGINE... YES, IT MAY BE ON THE TOP FLOOR WITH KAZURA.
LET'S GO UP.
UH-HUH...
TMP
TMP
TMP
TMP
TMP
...
UM... ABOUT KA-ZURA...
YOU SEEMED A LITTLE UNSURE OF YOUR LOVE.

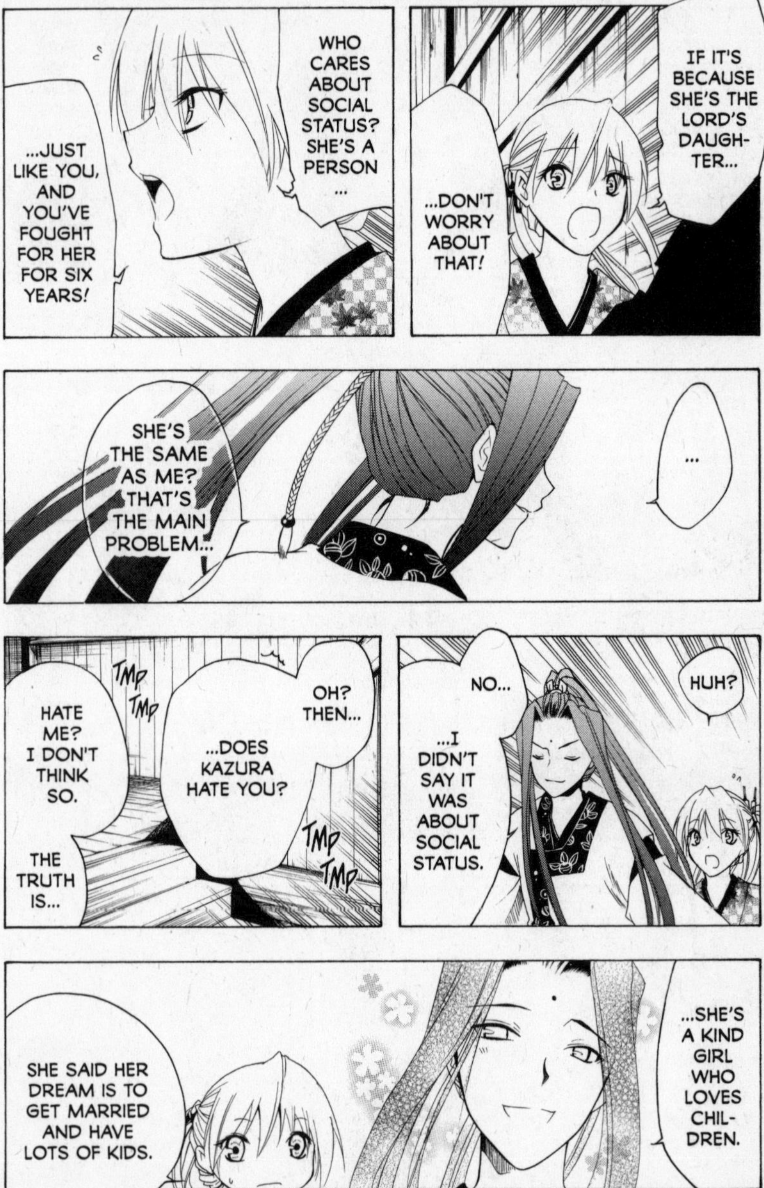
IF IT'S BECAUSE SHE'S THE LORD'S DAUGHTER...
...DON'T WORRY ABOUT THAT!
WHO CARES ABOUT SOCIAL STATUS? SHE'S A PERSON ...
...JUST LIKE YOU, AND YOU'VE FOUGHT FOR HER FOR SIX YEARS!
...
SHE'S THE SAME AS ME? THAT'S THE MAIN PROBLEM...
HUH?
NO...
...I DIDN'T SAY IT WAS ABOUT SOCIAL STATUS.
OH? THEN...
...DOES KAZURA HATE YOU?
TMP TMP
TMP TMP
HATE ME? I DON'T THINK SO.
THE TRUTH IS...
...SHE'S A KIND GIRL WHO LOVES CHIL- DREN.
SHE SAID HER DREAM IS TO GET MARRIED AND HAVE LOTS OF KIDS.

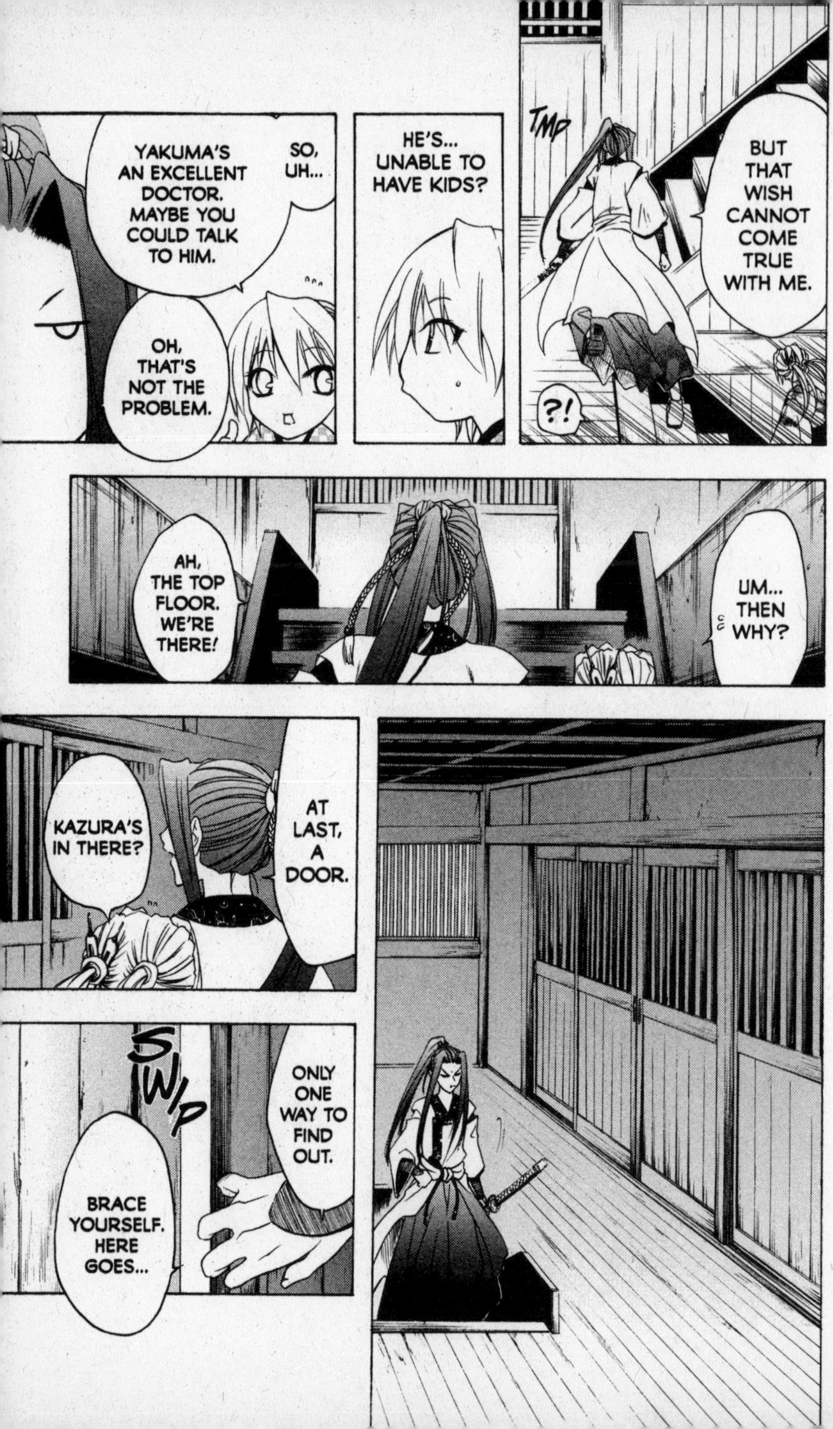
TMP
BUT THAT WISH CANNOT COME TRUE WITH ME.
?!
HE'S... UNABLE TO HAVE KIDS?
SO, UH...
YAKUMA'S AN EXCELLENT DOCTOR. MAYBE YOU COULD TALK TO HIM.
OH, THAT'S NOT THE PROBLEM.
UM... THEN WHY?
AH, THE TOP FLOOR. WE'RE THERE!
AT LAST, A DOOR.
KAZURA'S IN THERE?
SWIP
ONLY ONE WAY TO FIND OUT.
BRACE YOURSELF. HERE GOES...

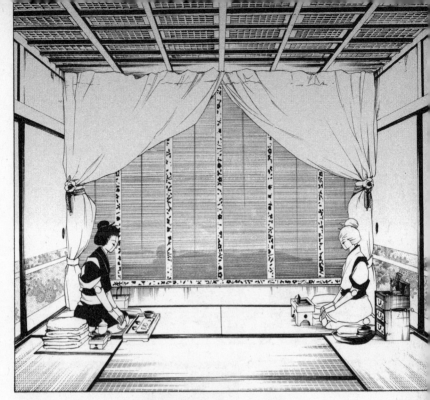

VEEN

IS SHE ASLEEP
BEHIND THAT
CURTAIN?

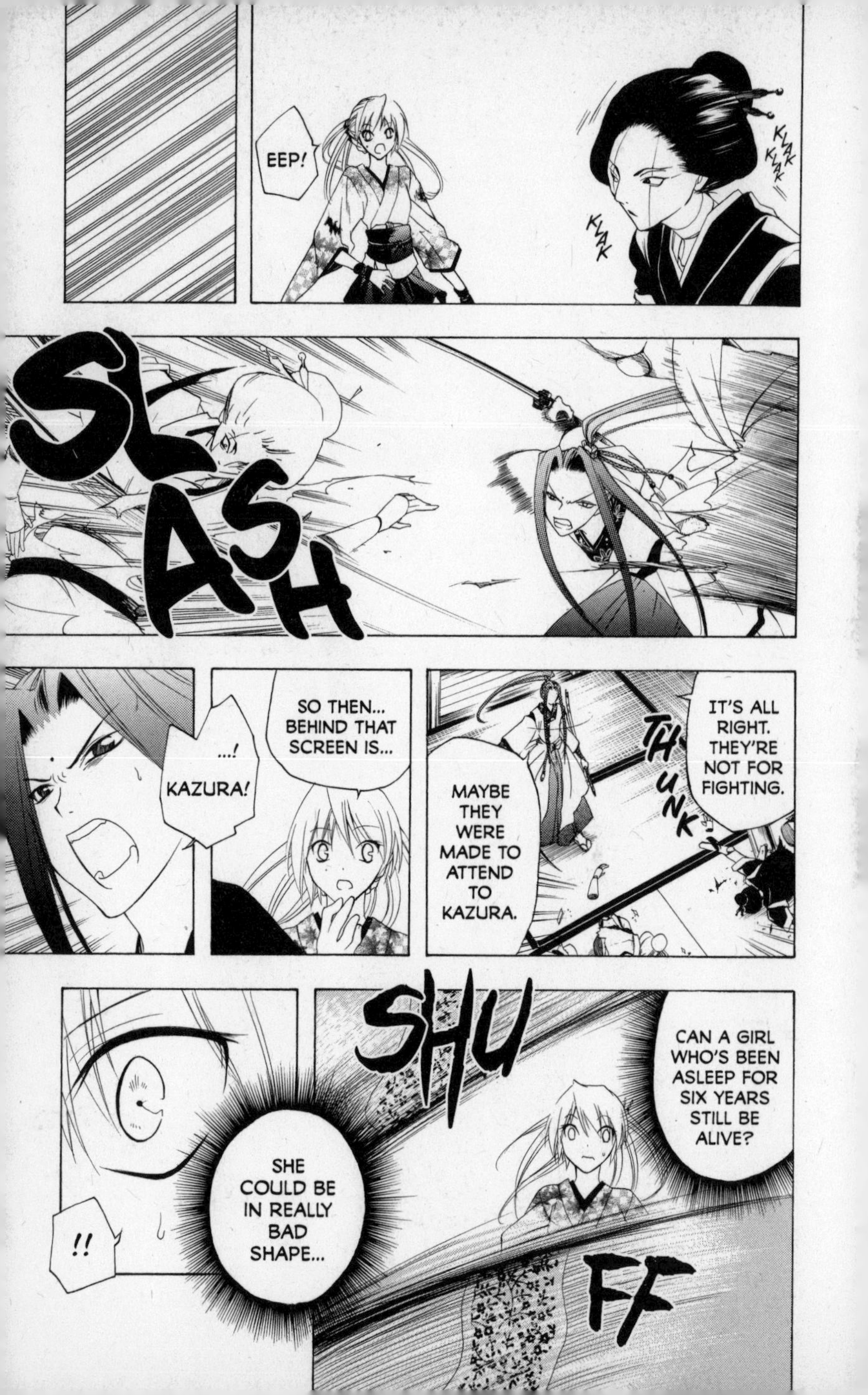
KLAK KLAK
KLAK
EEP!
SLASH
IT'S ALL RIGHT. THEY'RE NOT FOR FIGHTING.
THUNK
MAYBE THEY WERE MADE TO ATTEND TO KAZURA.
SO THEN... BEHIND THAT SCREEN IS...
...!
KAZURA!
CAN A GIRL WHO'S BEEN ASLEEP FOR SIX YEARS STILL BE ALIVE?
SHUFF
SHE COULD BE IN REALLY BAD SHAPE...
!!

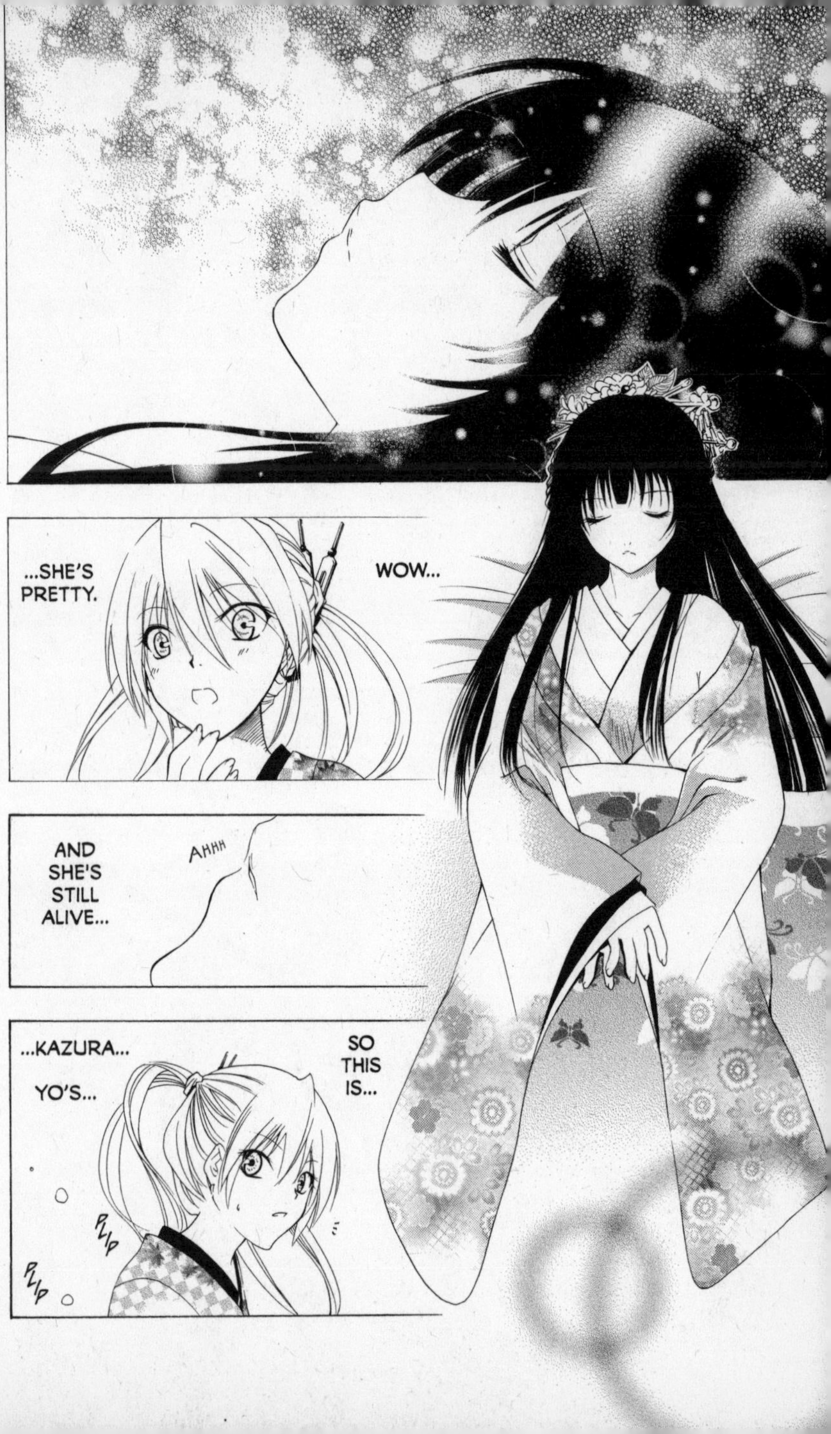
WOW...
...SHE'S PRETTY.
AHHH
AND SHE'S STILL ALIVE...
SO THIS IS...
...KAZURA...
YO'S...
PLIP
PLIP

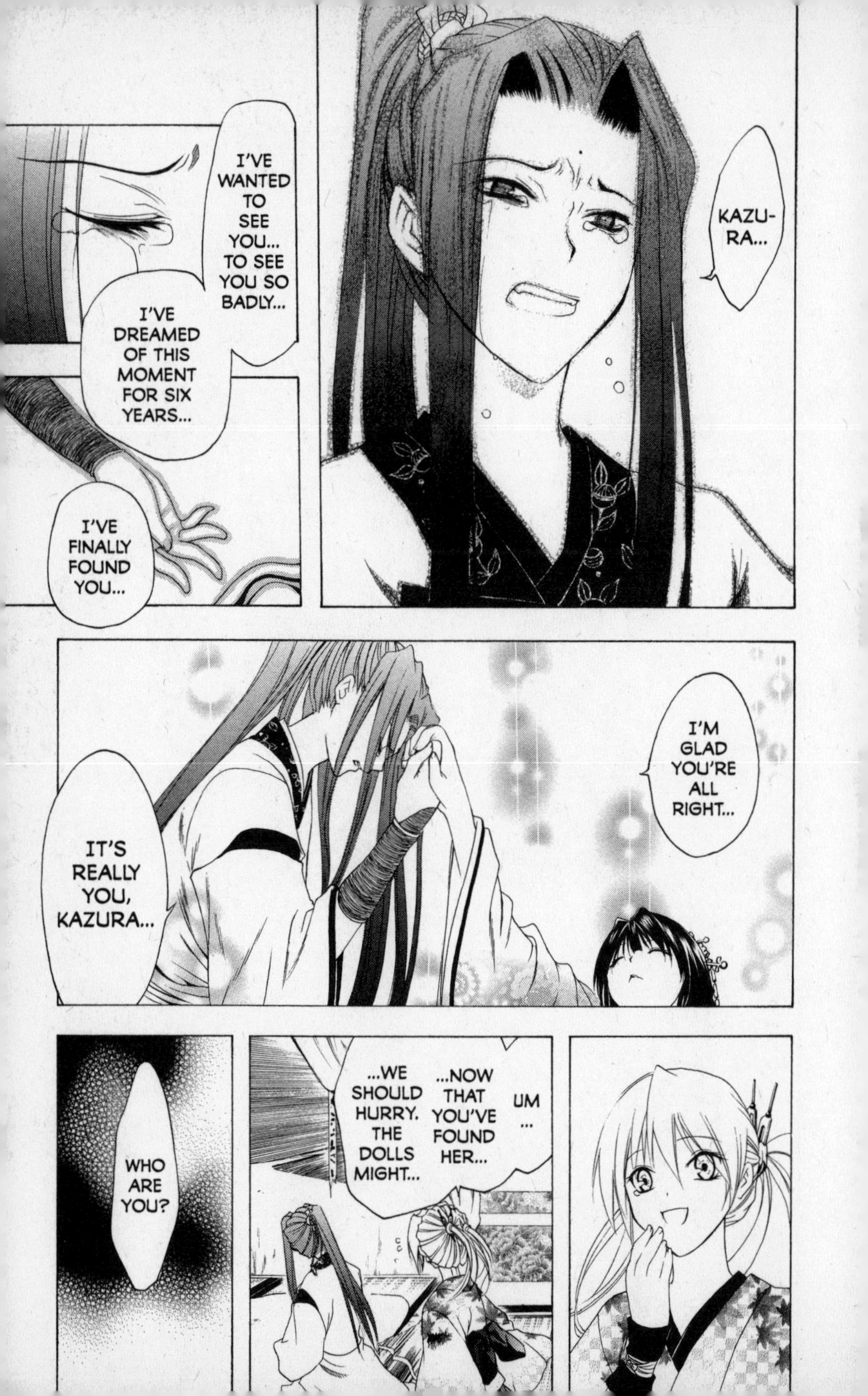
KAZU-RA...
I'VE WANTED TO SEE YOU... TO SEE YOU SO BADLY...
I'VE DREAMED OF THIS MOMENT FOR SIX YEARS...
I'VE FINALLY FOUND YOU...
I'M GLAD YOU'RE ALL RIGHT...
IT'S REALLY YOU, KAZURA...
UM ...
...NOW THAT YOU'VE FOUND HER...
...WE SHOULD HURRY. THE DOLLS MIGHT...
WHO ARE YOU?

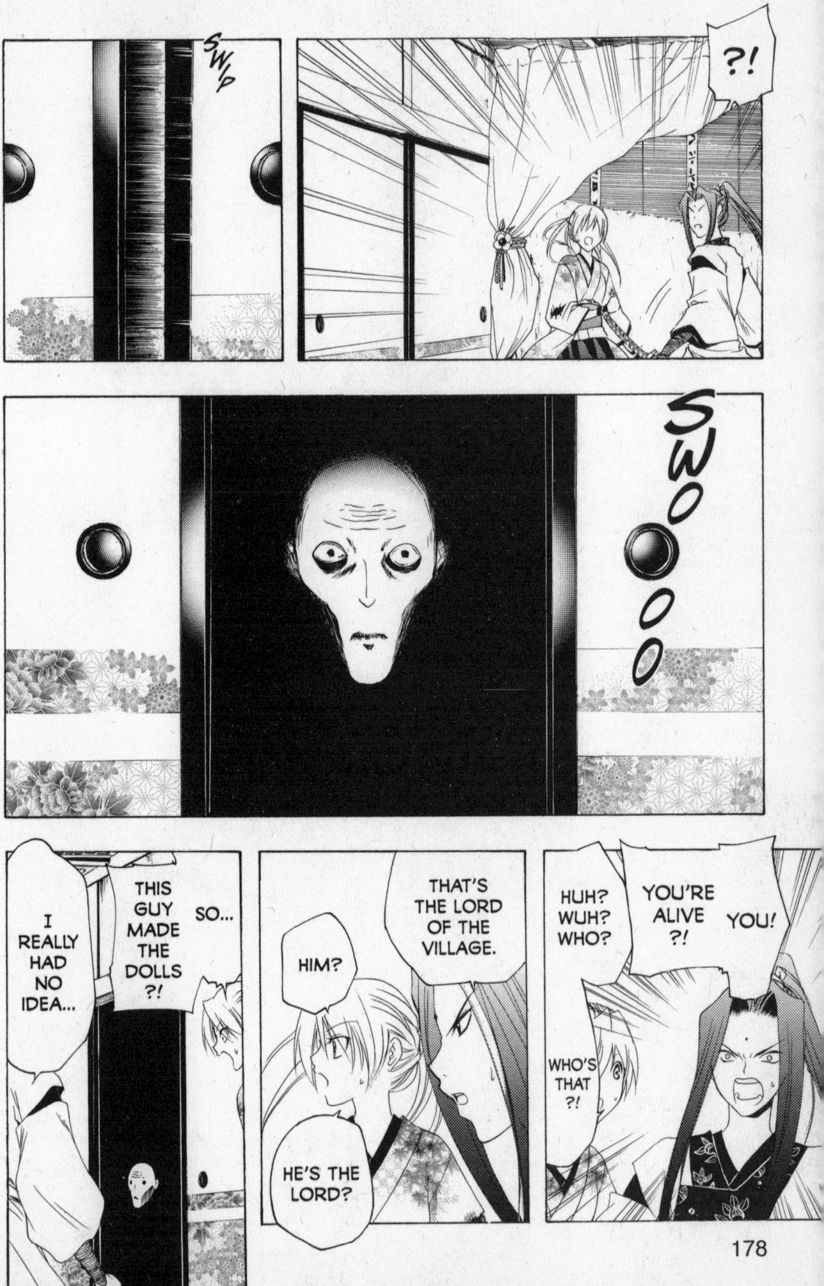
?!
SWIP
SWOOOOO
YOU!
YOU'RE ALIVE ?!
HUH? WUH? WHO?
WHO'S THAT ?!
THAT'S THE LORD OF THE VILLAGE.
HIM?
HE'S THE LORD?
SO...
THIS GUY MADE THE DOLLS ?!
I REALLY HAD NO IDEA...

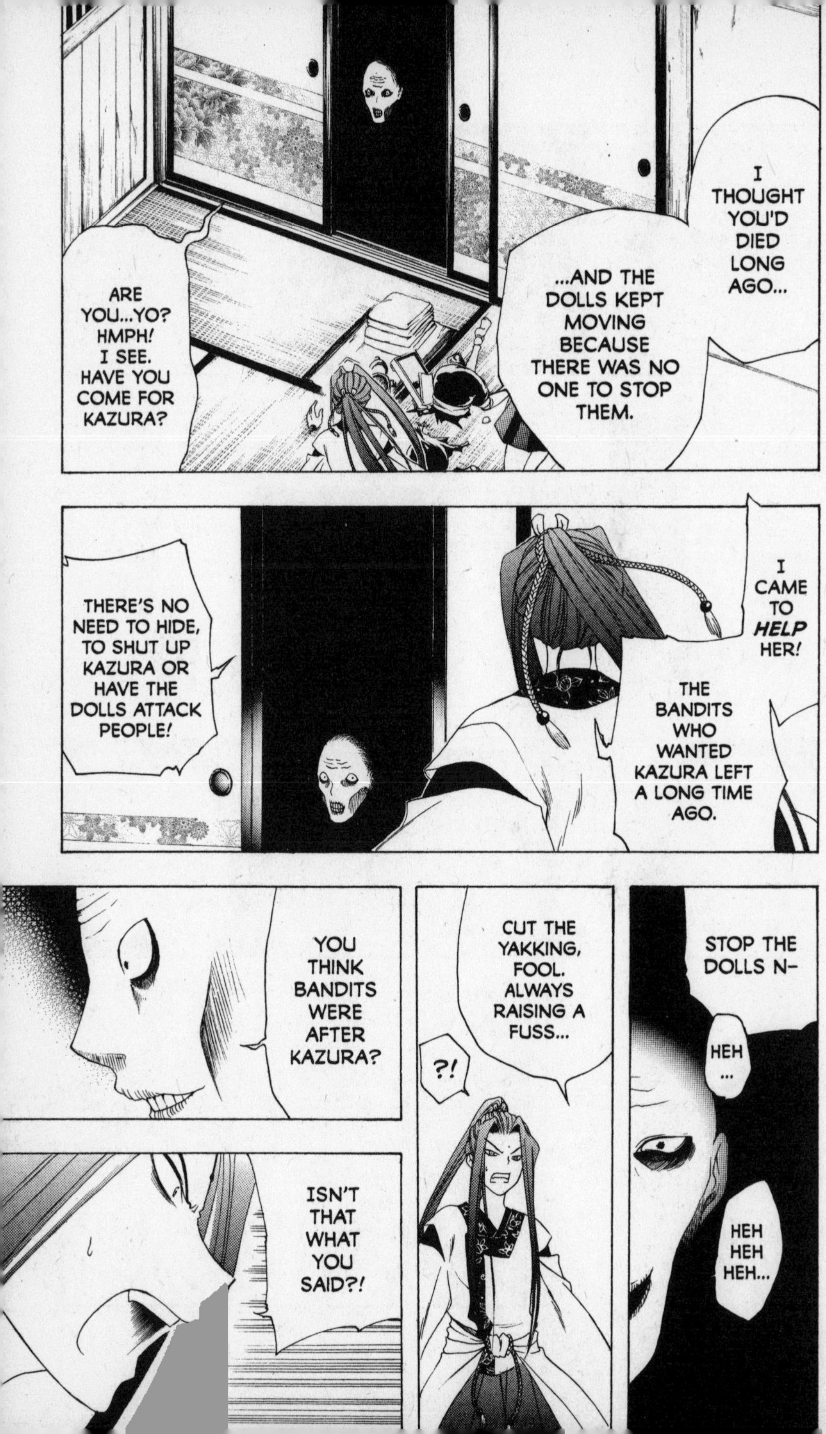
I THOUGHT YOU'D DIED LONG AGO...
...AND THE DOLLS KEPT MOVING BECAUSE THERE WAS NO ONE TO STOP THEM.
ARE YOU...YO? HMPH! I SEE. HAVE YOU COME FOR KAZURA?
I CAME TO *HELP* HER!
THE BANDITS WHO WANTED KAZURA LEFT A LONG TIME AGO.
THERE'S NO NEED TO HIDE, TO SHUT UP KAZURA OR HAVE THE DOLLS ATTACK PEOPLE!
STOP THE DOLLS N–
HEH...
HEH HEH HEH...
CUT THE YAKKING, FOOL. ALWAYS RAISING A FUSS...
?!
YOU THINK BANDITS WERE AFTER KAZURA?
ISN'T THAT WHAT YOU SAID?!

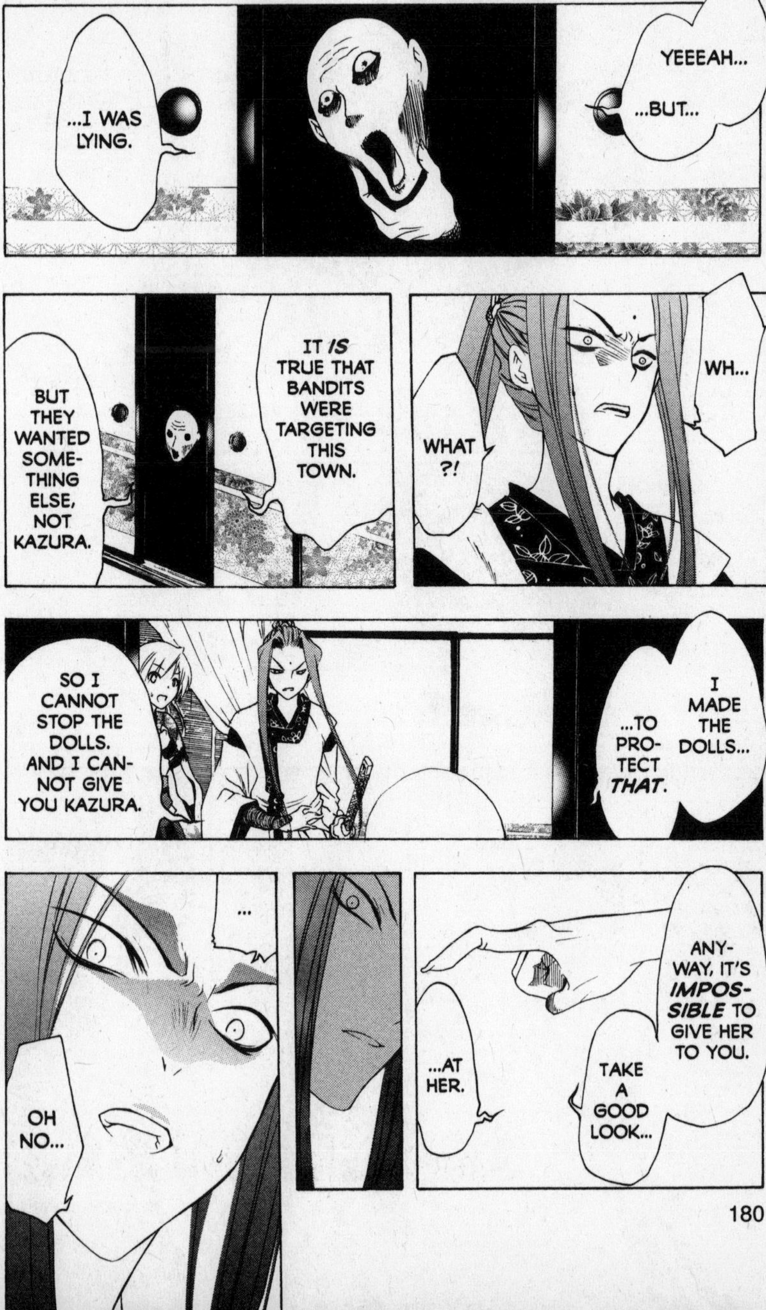
YEEEAH...
...BUT...
...I WAS LYING.
WH...
WHAT?!
IT *IS* TRUE THAT BANDITS WERE TARGETING THIS TOWN.
BUT THEY WANTED SOMETHING ELSE, NOT KAZURA.
I MADE THE DOLLS...
...TO PROTECT *THAT*.
SO I CANNOT STOP THE DOLLS. AND I CANNOT GIVE YOU KAZURA.
ANYWAY, IT'S ***IMPOSSIBLE*** TO GIVE HER TO YOU.
TAKE A GOOD LOOK...
...AT HER.
...
OH NO...

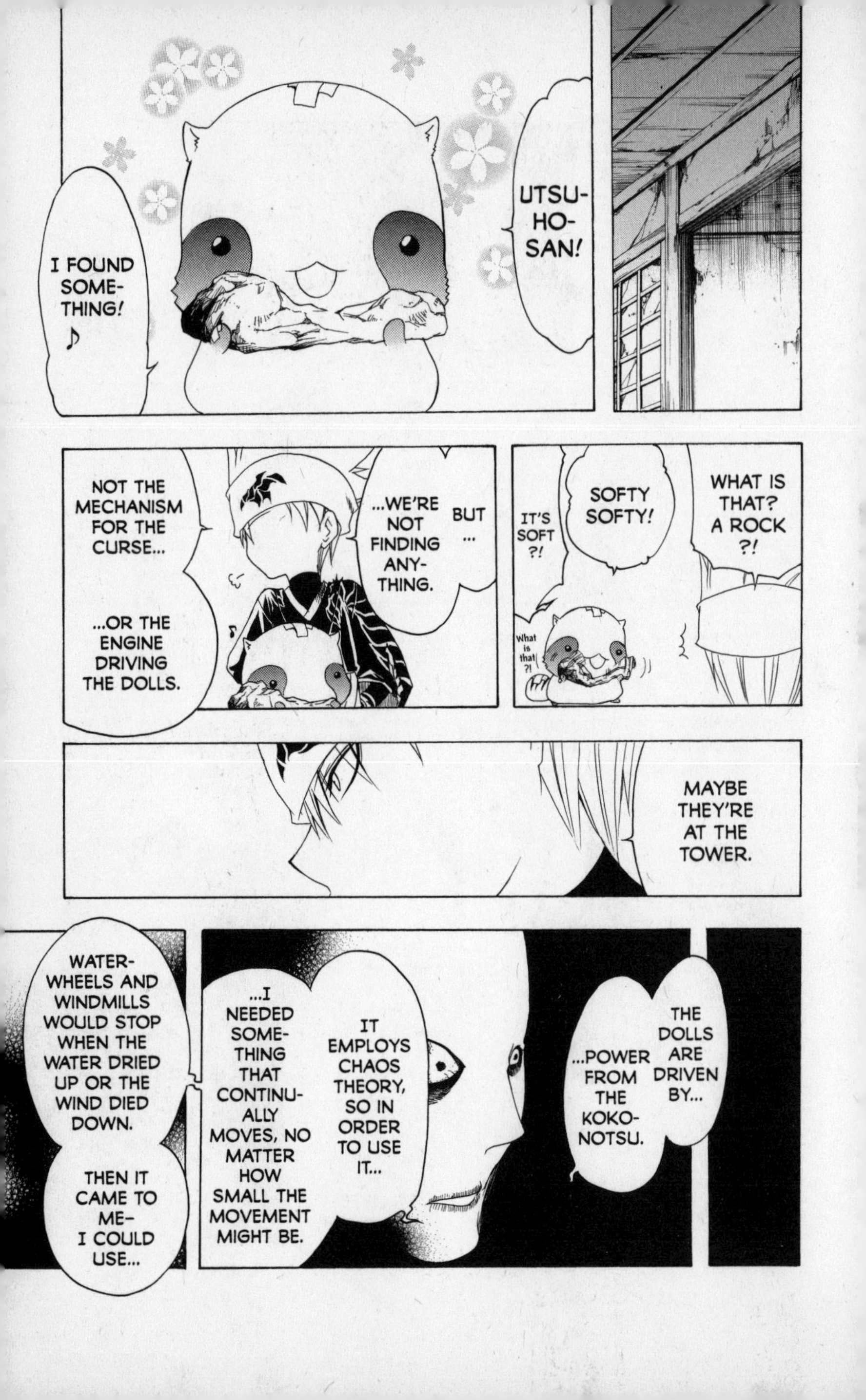
UTSU-HO-SAN!
I FOUND SOME-THING! ♪
WHAT IS THAT? A ROCK?!
SOFTY SOFTY!
IT'S SOFT?!
What is that?!
BUT...
...WE'RE NOT FINDING ANY-THING.
NOT THE MECHANISM FOR THE CURSE...
...OR THE ENGINE DRIVING THE DOLLS.
MAYBE THEY'RE AT THE TOWER.
THE DOLLS ARE DRIVEN BY...
...POWER FROM THE KOKO-NOTSU.
IT EMPLOYS CHAOS THEORY, SO IN ORDER TO USE IT...
...I NEEDED SOME-THING THAT CONTINU-ALLY MOVES, NO MATTER HOW SMALL THE MOVEMENT MIGHT BE.
WATER-WHEELS AND WINDMILLS WOULD STOP WHEN THE WATER DRIED UP OR THE WIND DIED DOWN.
THEN IT CAME TO ME— I COULD USE...

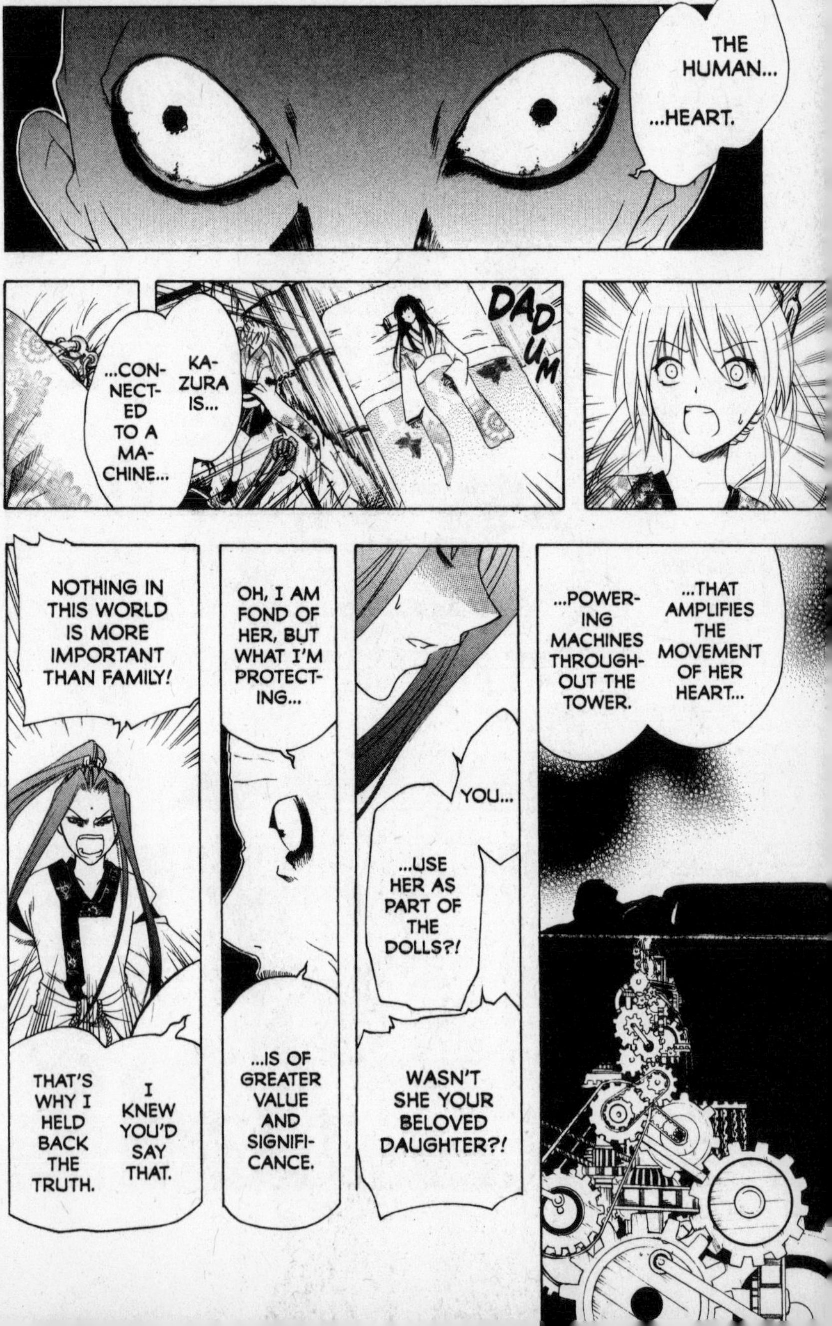
THE HUMAN...
...HEART.
DADUM
KAZURA IS...
...CONNECTED TO A MACHINE...
...THAT AMPLIFIES THE MOVEMENT OF HER HEART...
...POWERING MACHINES THROUGHOUT THE TOWER.
YOU...
...USE HER AS PART OF THE DOLLS?!
WASN'T SHE YOUR BELOVED DAUGHTER?!
OH, I AM FOND OF HER, BUT WHAT I'M PROTECTING...
...IS OF GREATER VALUE AND SIGNIFICANCE.
NOTHING IN THIS WORLD IS MORE IMPORTANT THAN FAMILY!
I KNEW YOU'D SAY THAT.
THAT'S WHY I HELD BACK THE TRUTH.

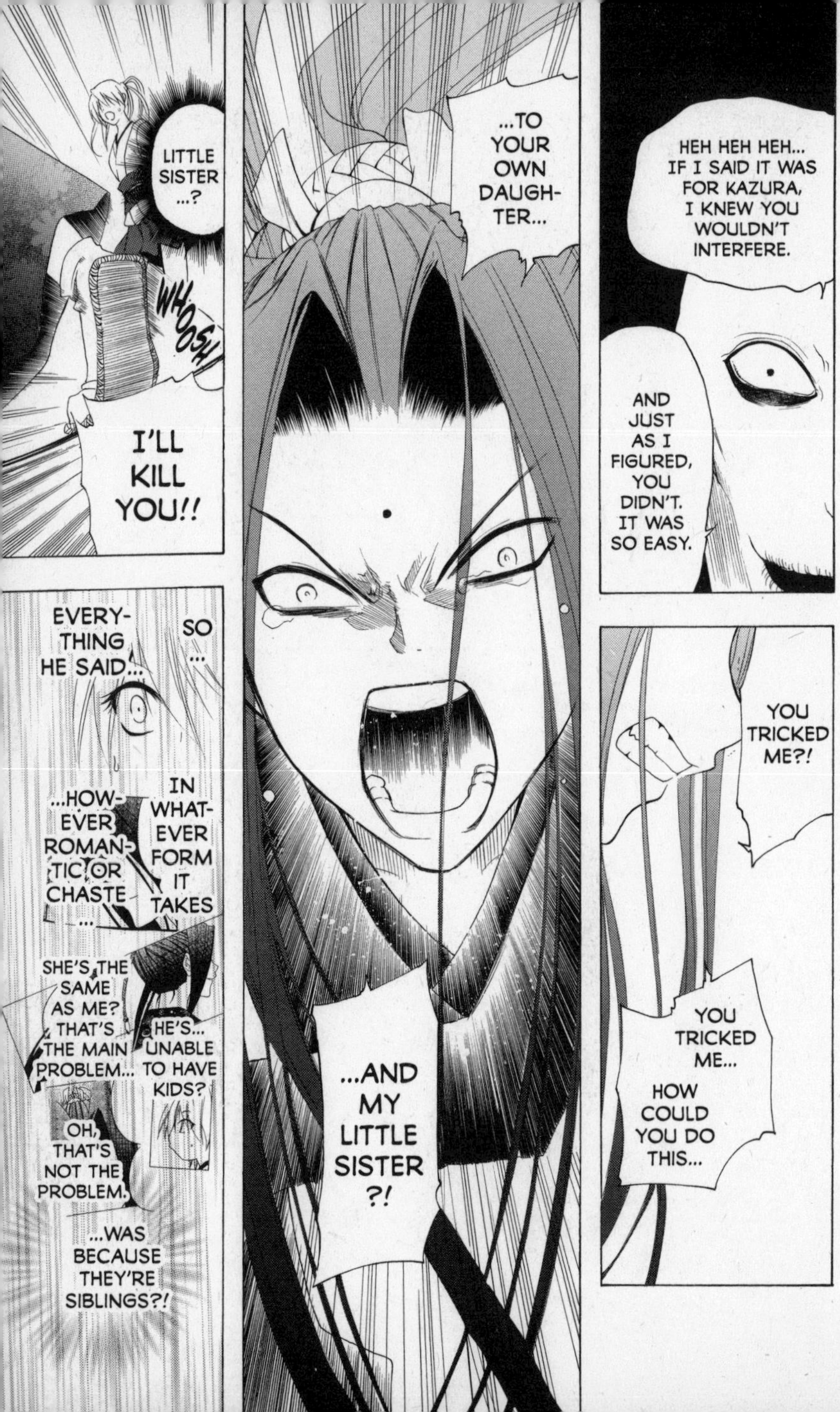
HEH HEH HEH... IF I SAID IT WAS FOR KAZURA, I KNEW YOU WOULDN'T INTERFERE.
AND JUST AS I FIGURED, YOU DIDN'T. IT WAS SO EASY.
YOU TRICKED ME?!
YOU TRICKED ME... HOW COULD YOU DO THIS...
...TO YOUR OWN DAUGHTER...
...AND MY LITTLE SISTER?!
LITTLE SISTER...?
WHOOSH
I'LL KILL YOU!!
SO...
EVERYTHING HE SAID...
IN WHATEVER FORM IT TAKES
...HOWEVER ROMANTIC OR CHASTE...
HE'S... UNABLE TO HAVE KIDS?
SHE'S THE SAME AS ME? THAT'S THE MAIN PROBLEM...
OH, THAT'S NOT THE PROBLEM.
...WAS BECAUSE THEY'RE SIBLINGS?!

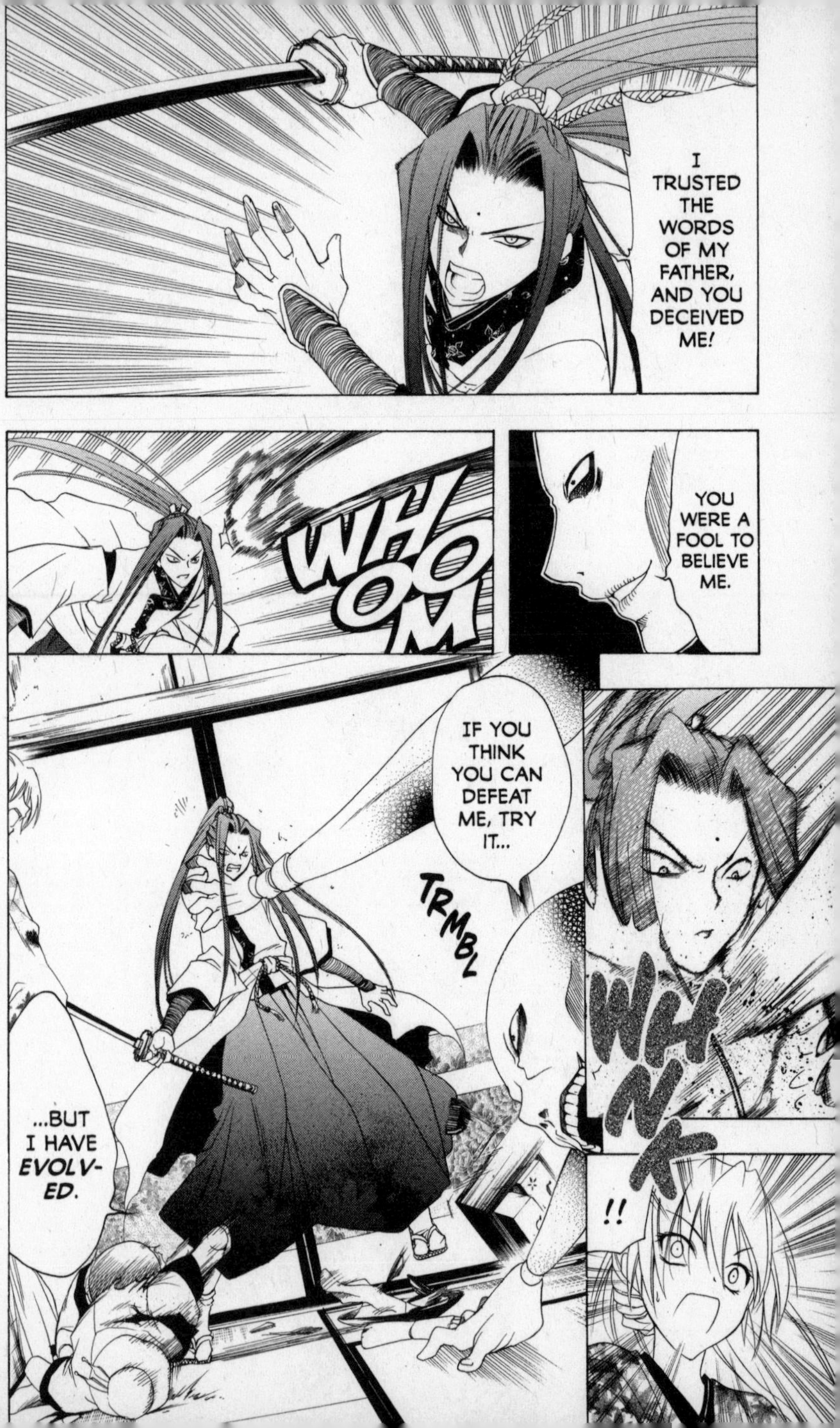
I TRUSTED THE WORDS OF MY FATHER, AND YOU DECEIVED ME!
YOU WERE A FOOL TO BELIEVE ME.
WHOOM
WHNK
!!
IF YOU THINK YOU CAN DEFEAT ME, TRY IT...
TRMBL
...BUT I HAVE EVOLV-ED.

◆ Bonus Manga ◆

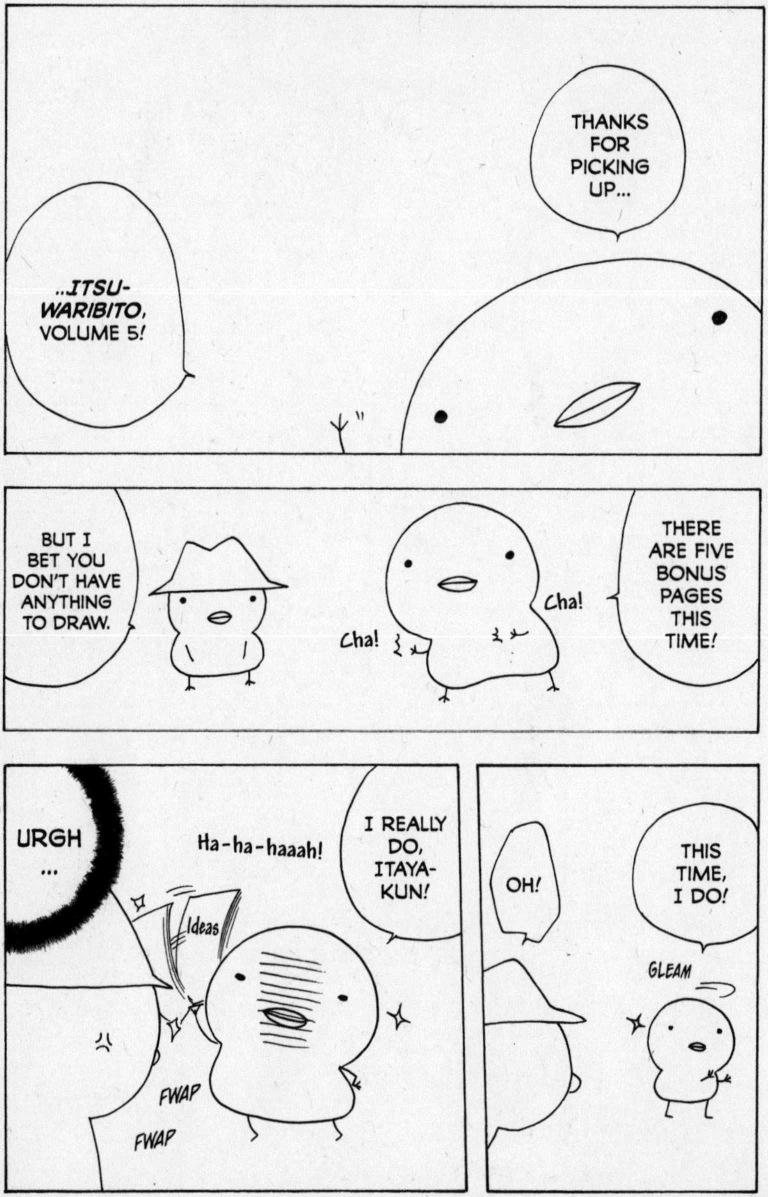
THANKS FOR PICKING UP...
...ITSUWARIBITO, VOLUME 5!
THERE ARE FIVE BONUS PAGES THIS TIME!
Cha!
Cha!
BUT I BET YOU DON'T HAVE ANYTHING TO DRAW.
THIS TIME, I DO!
GLEAM
OH!
I REALLY DO, ITAYA-KUN!
Ha-ha-haaah!
Ideas
URGH ...
FWAP
FWAP

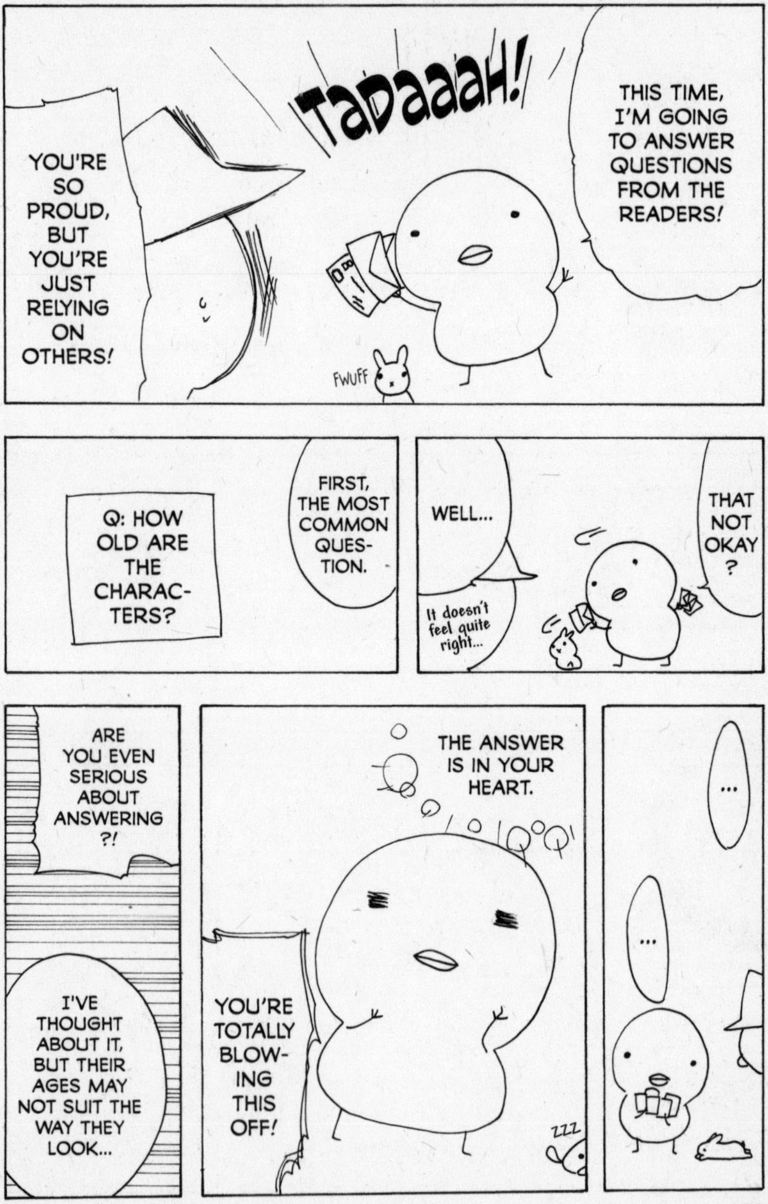
THIS TIME, I'M GOING TO ANSWER QUESTIONS FROM THE READERS!
TADAAAH!
YOU'RE SO PROUD, BUT YOU'RE JUST RELYING ON OTHERS!
FWUFF
THAT NOT OKAY?
WELL...
It doesn't feel quite right...
FIRST, THE MOST COMMON QUES-TION.
Q: HOW OLD ARE THE CHARACTERS?
...
...
THE ANSWER IS IN YOUR HEART.
YOU'RE TOTALLY BLOWING THIS OFF!
ZZZ
ARE YOU EVEN SERIOUS ABOUT ANSWERING?!
I'VE THOUGHT ABOUT IT, BUT THEIR AGES MAY NOT SUIT THE WAY THEY LOOK...

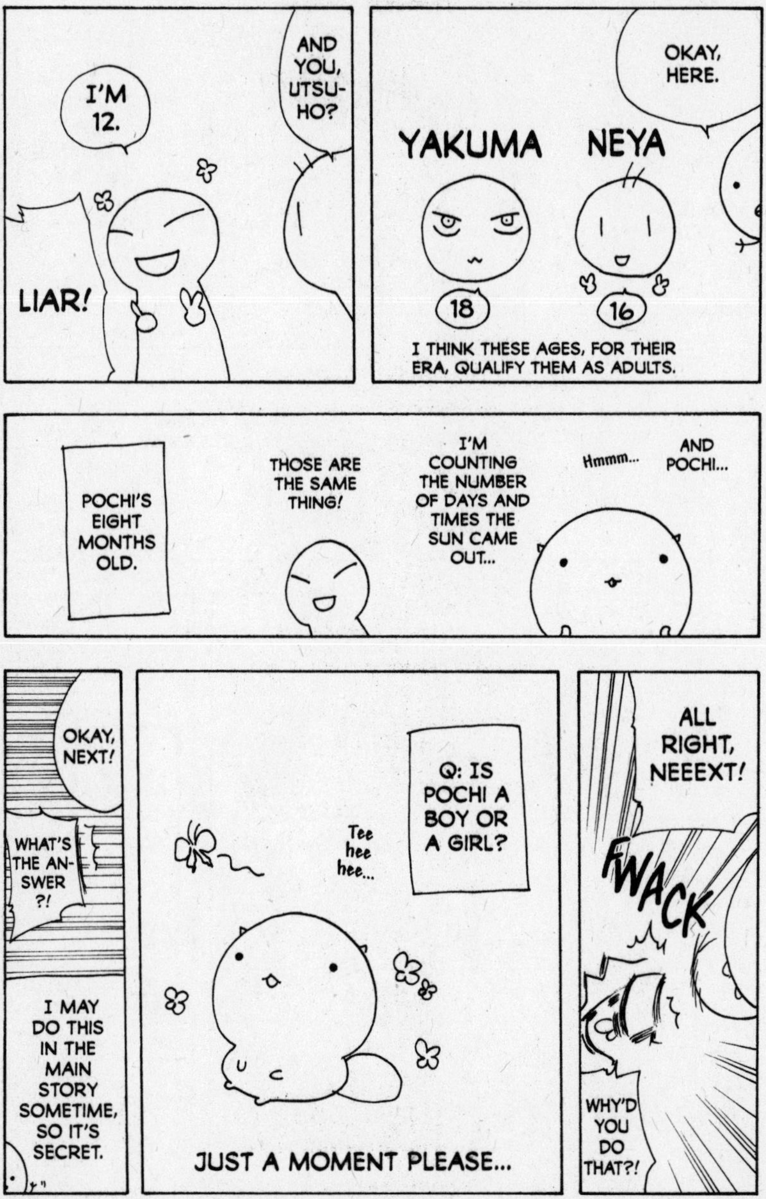
OKAY, HERE.
NEYA
YAKUMA
16
18
I THINK THESE AGES, FOR THEIR ERA, QUALIFY THEM AS ADULTS.
AND YOU, UTSU-HO?
I'M 12.
LIAR!
AND POCHI...
Hmmm...
I'M COUNTING THE NUMBER OF DAYS AND TIMES THE SUN CAME OUT...
THOSE ARE THE SAME THING!
POCHI'S EIGHT MONTHS OLD.
ALL RIGHT, NEEEXT!
FWACK
WHY'D YOU DO THAT?!
Q: IS POCHI A BOY OR A GIRL?
Tee hee hee...
JUST A MOMENT PLEASE...
OKAY, NEXT!
WHAT'S THE AN-SWER ?!
I MAY DO THIS IN THE MAIN STORY SOMETIME, SO IT'S SECRET.

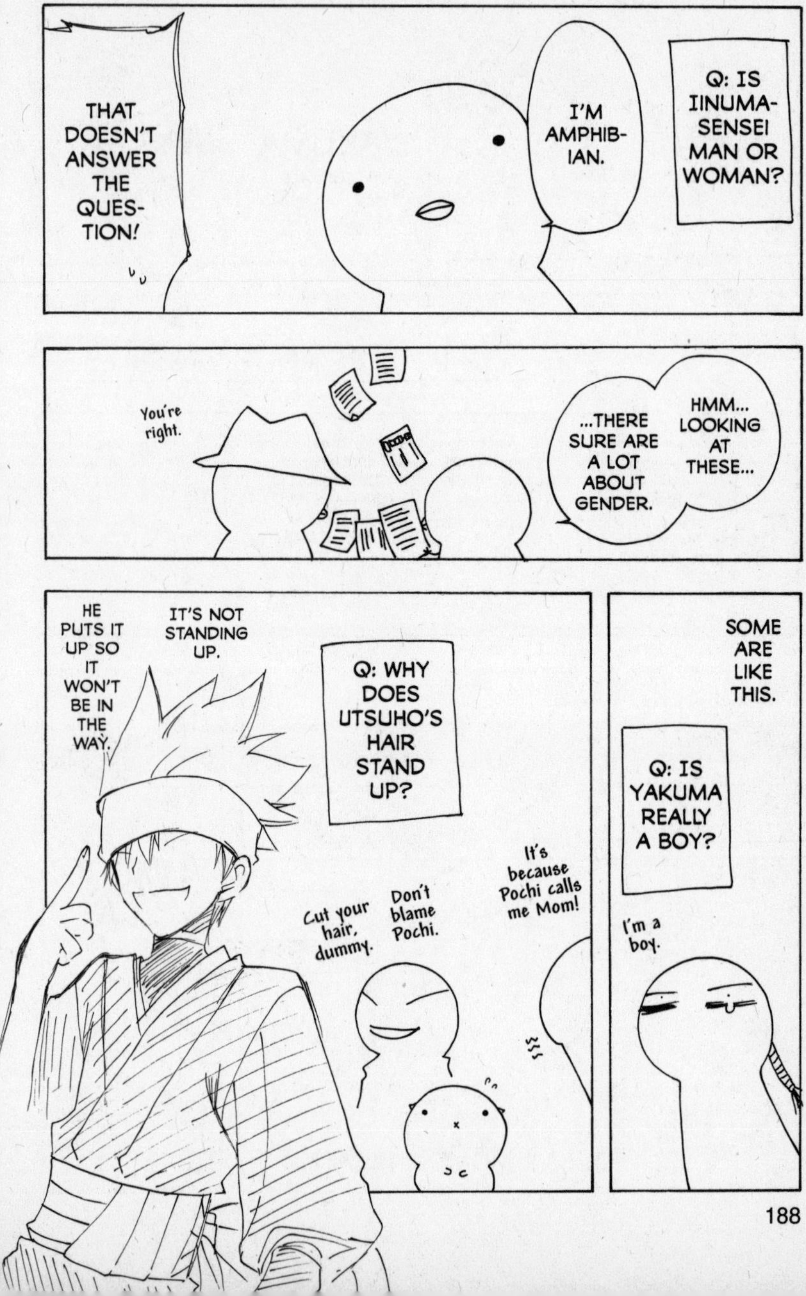
Q: IS IINUMA-SENSEI MAN OR WOMAN?
I'M AMPHIBIAN.
THAT DOESN'T ANSWER THE QUESTION!
HMM... LOOKING AT THESE...
...THERE SURE ARE A LOT ABOUT GENDER.
You're right.
SOME ARE LIKE THIS.
Q: IS YAKUMA REALLY A BOY?
I'm a boy.
Q: WHY DOES UTSUHO'S HAIR STAND UP?
IT'S NOT STANDING UP.
HE PUTS IT UP SO IT WON'T BE IN THE WAY.
It's because Pochi calls me Mom!
Don't blame Pochi.
Cut your hair, dummy.

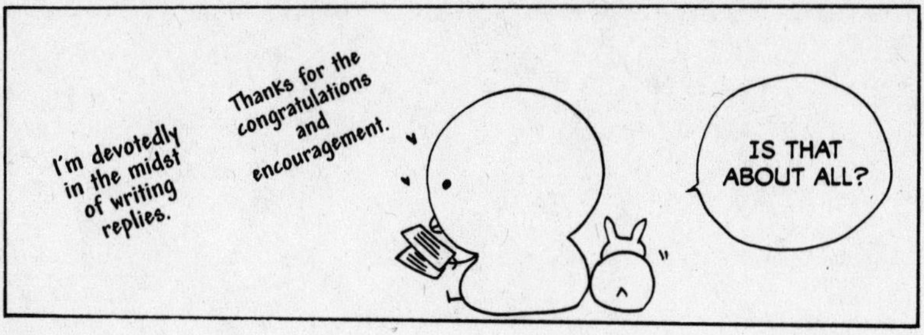
IS THAT ABOUT ALL?
Thanks for the congratulations and encouragement.
I'm devotedly in the midst of writing replies.
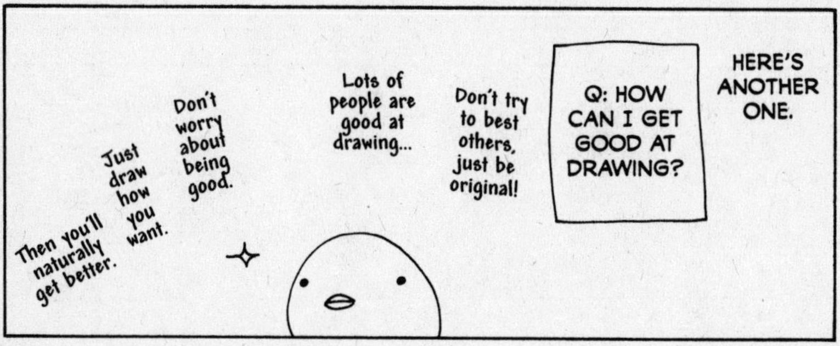
HERE'S ANOTHER ONE.
Q: HOW CAN I GET GOOD AT DRAWING?
Don't try to best others, just be original!
Lots of people are good at drawing...
Don't worry about being good.
Just draw how you want.
Then you'll naturally get better.
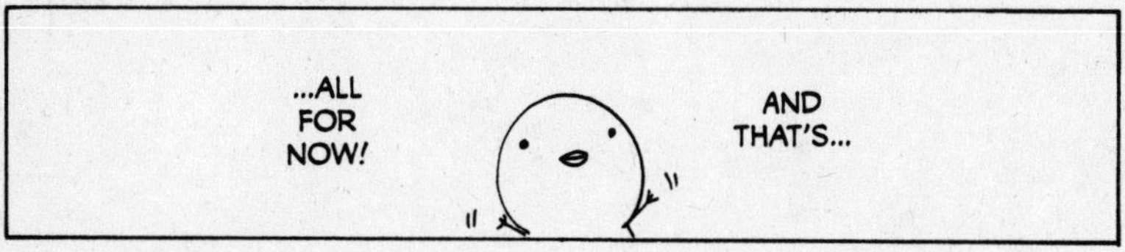
AND THAT'S...
...ALL FOR NOW!
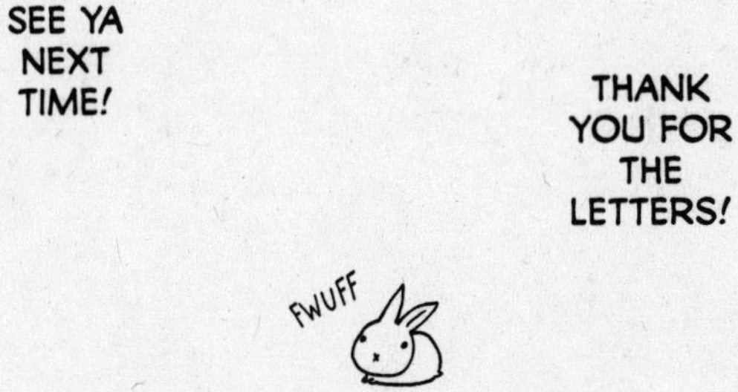
THANK YOU FOR THE LETTERS!
SEE YA NEXT TIME!
FWUFF

ITSUWARIBITO

Volume 5
Shonen Sunday Edition

Story and Art by
YUUKI IINUMA

Original Japanese edition "ITSUWARIBITO UTSUHO"
published by SHOGAKUKAN Inc.

Translation/John Werry
Touch-up Art & Lettering/Susan Daigle-Leach
Design/Matt Hinrichs
Editor/Gary Leach

Printed in the U.S.A.

Published by VIZ Media, LLC
P.O. Box 77010
San Francisco, CA 94107

10 9 8 7 6 5 4 3 2 1
First printing, April 2012

www.viz.com
WWW.SHONENSUNDAY.COM

PARENTAL ADVISORY
ITSUWARIBITO is rated T+ for Older Teen and is recommended for ages 16 and up.
FOR OLDER TEEN
ratings.viz.com

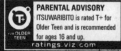

HEY, YAKUMA, CHECK THIS OUT!
IF YOU DRINK THIS...
...YOU WON'T DIE FROM HEART DISEASE.
WHAT?!
TA DA
THAT'S AMAZING!
WHAT'S IT MADE OF?
LICK
DEADLY POISON.
So you won't die from heart disease.
SPLURT

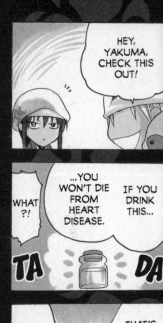

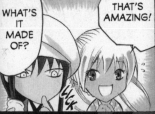

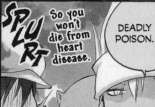